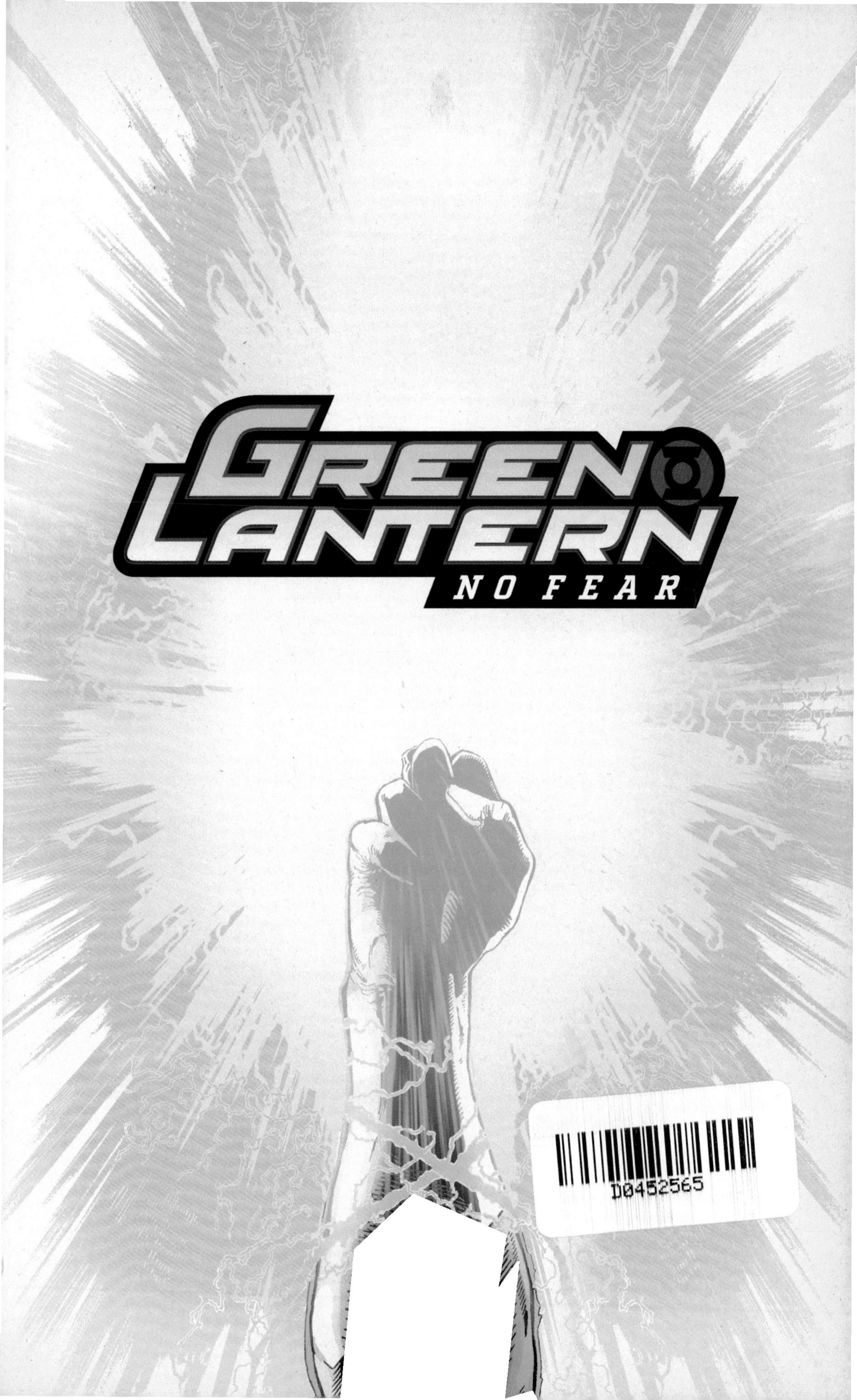
GREEN LANTERN
NO FEAR

GREEN LANTERN
NO FEAR

DC COMICS

Dan DiDio Senior VP-Executive Editor
Peter Tomasi Senior Editor-original series
Michael Siglain Associate Editor-original series
Harvey Richards Assistant Editor-original series
Robert Greenberger Senior Editor-collected edition
Robbin Brosterman Senior Art Director
Paul Levitz President & Publisher
Georg Brewer VP-Design & DC Direct Creative
Richard Bruning Senior VP-Creative Director
Patrick Caldon Executive VP-Finance & Operations
Chris Caramalis VP-Finance
John Cunningham VP-Marketing
Terri Cunningham VP-Managing Editor
Stephanie Fierman Senior VP-Sales & Marketing
Alison Gill VP-Manufacturing
Rich Johnson VP-Book Trade Sales
Hank Kanalz VP-General Manager, WildStorm
Lillian Laserson Senior VP & General Counsel
Jim Lee Editorial Director-WildStorm
Paula Lowitt Senior VP-Business & Legal Affairs
David McKillips VP-Advertising & Custom Publishing
John Nee VP-Business Development
Gregory Noveck Senior VP-Creative Affairs
Cheryl Rubin Senior VP-Brand Management
Jeff Trojan VP-Business Development, DC Direct
Bob Wayne VP-Sales

GREEN LANTERN: NO FEAR
Published by DC Comics.
Cover, introduction, and compilation copyright © 2006 DC Comics.
Originally published in single magazine form as GREEN LANTERN 1-6,
GREEN LANTERN SECRET FILES AND ORIGINS 2005.
Copyright © 2005, 2006 DC Comics. All Rights Reserved.

All characters, the distinctive likenesses thereof and related elements
are trademarks of DC Comics. The stories, characters and incidents
featured in this publication are entirely fictional. DC Comics does not
read or accept unsolicited submissions of ideas, stories, or artwork.

DC Comics
1700 Broadway
New York, NY 10019
A Warner Bros. Entertainment Company
Printed in Canada.
First Printing.

Hardcover ISBN: 1-4012-0466-X
Hardcover ISBN 13: 978-1-4012-0466-2
Softcover ISBN: 1-4012-1058-9
Softcover ISBN 13: 978-1-4012-1058-8

Cover Illustration by Alex Ross.

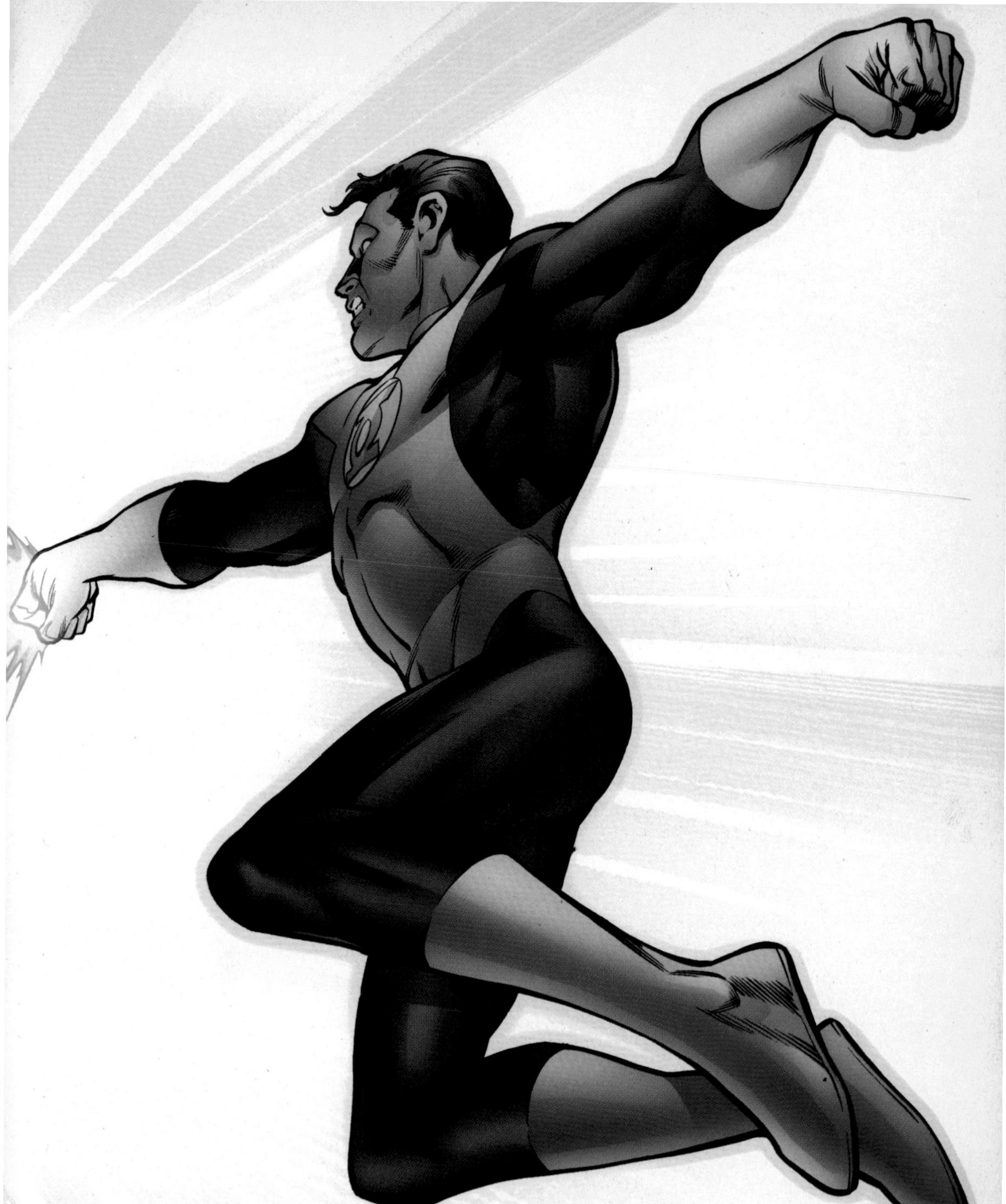

GEOFF JOHNS WRITER

DARWYN COOKE/CARLOS PACHECO
ETHAN VAN SCIVER/SIMONE BIANCHI PENCILLERS

DARWYN COOKE/JESÚS MERINO/ETHAN VAN SCIVER
SIMONE BIANCHI/PRENTIS ROLLINS INKERS

JARED K. FLETCHER/ROB LEIGH LETTERERS

MOOSE BAUMANN/DAVE STEWART/NATHAN EYRING COLORISTS

CARLOS PACHECO & JESÚS MERINO
ALEX ROSS/ETHAN VAN SCIVER ORIGINAL SERIES COVERS

WHAT HAS GONE BEFORE

Evolving from one of the earliest sentient beings in existence, the inhabitants of Maltus achieved an advanced stage of development some five billion years ago. Over the next billion years, several societies rose and fell on Maltus, destroyed by war and plague and restored by philosophy and wisdom. Their society reached an unmatched pinnacle of civilization, with its inhabitants developing unparalleled intellectual and psychic powers.

The Maltusian scientist Krona decided to break his world's greatest taboo by creating a device that would allow him to witness the creation of the universe. Krona activated his time machine, thus observing Creation itself...and unleashed a wave of evil across the universe that spread to more than 50 million worlds.

The Maltusians banished Krona to the farthest reaches of the universe and decided that they would make it their mission to repair the damage he had caused.

They migrated to the known center of the universe, a planet called Oa. There, they began to develop strategies that would enable them to battle the evils Krona had unleashed. They called themselves Oans, and they evolved, over time, into the group of beings who would be known as the Guardians of the Universe.

Their first attempt to stem the tide of evil was to use androids known as Manhunters. Armed with weapons that drew power from a central battery on Oa, the Manhunters did their duty for centuries. Then for unknown reasons, the Manhunters rebelled against their programming and launched a millennia-long battle that culminated with an attack on Oa, where they succeeded in overpowering the Guardians. Ultimately, the Guardians overcame their android constructs, stripping them of their power and banishing them across the universe. A faction of Guardians believed that the Manhunters should have been destroyed outright, but that faction did not prevail.

Undaunted by the failure of the Manhunter androids, the Guardians vowed to once again renew their mission. Using living creatures as their agents — to reduce the likelihood of betrayal — the Guardians selected the most worthy champions from across the galaxies and equipped them, initially, with pistols that were charged by the power battery. In time, these weapons were modified into the power rings, and the warriors were dubbed the Green Lantern Corps. Rori Dag of Rojira was selected by the Guardians to be the first such Green Lantern, and his success led each Guardian to select one species from which a Green Lantern would be chosen.

The women of Oa left the planet after some two and a half billion years, following the teachings of Zamar and journeying to the planet after which she was named. Along the way, they stopped on Korugar, where they took many male lovers. The male Guardians, trying to overcome the emotion of jealousy, left a legacy tying the central power battery's power to the Korugarians. But despite their best intentions, billions of years later, the Guardians' actions would unleash havoc throughout the universe.

In 1066 (by Earth's common calendar), the Manhunters discovered this planet and, sensing that it had "possibilities," they began establishing agents here. Ever since, the Earth has been a focal point for cosmic activity and has remained carefully watched by Sector 2814's resident Green Lantern.

Recent upheavals led all the Guardians — save one named Ganthet — to depart this plane of existence, along with their Zamaron female counterparts. The Corps was destroyed, the main battery was crushed. The line of Green Lanterns dwindled to but a handful, concentrated on Earth.

Then, from the ashes of defeat, the Guardians were reborn, and the power battery was recharged. Their greatest champion, Hal Jordan, was resurrected and this heralded the rebuilding of the Corps itself.

Never has the universe been in such need of these fearless champions.

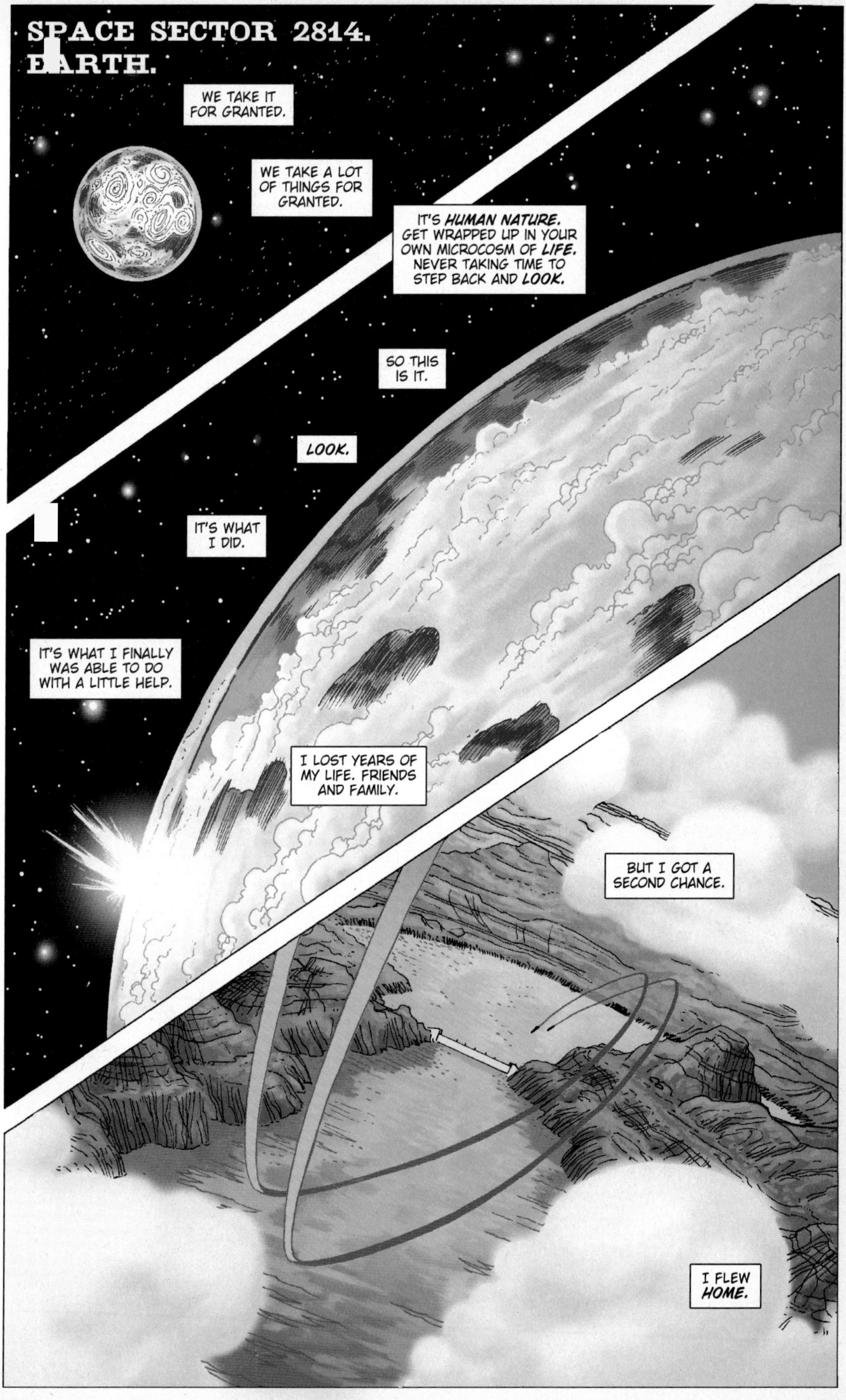
SPACE SECTOR 2814.
EARTH.
WE TAKE IT FOR GRANTED.
WE TAKE A LOT OF THINGS FOR GRANTED.
IT'S *HUMAN NATURE.* GET WRAPPED UP IN YOUR OWN MICROCOSM OF *LIFE.* NEVER TAKING TIME TO STEP BACK AND *LOOK.*
SO THIS IS IT.
LOOK.
IT'S WHAT I DID.
IT'S WHAT I FINALLY WAS ABLE TO DO WITH A LITTLE HELP.
I LOST YEARS OF MY LIFE. FRIENDS AND FAMILY.
BUT I GOT A SECOND CHANCE.
I FLEW *HOME.*

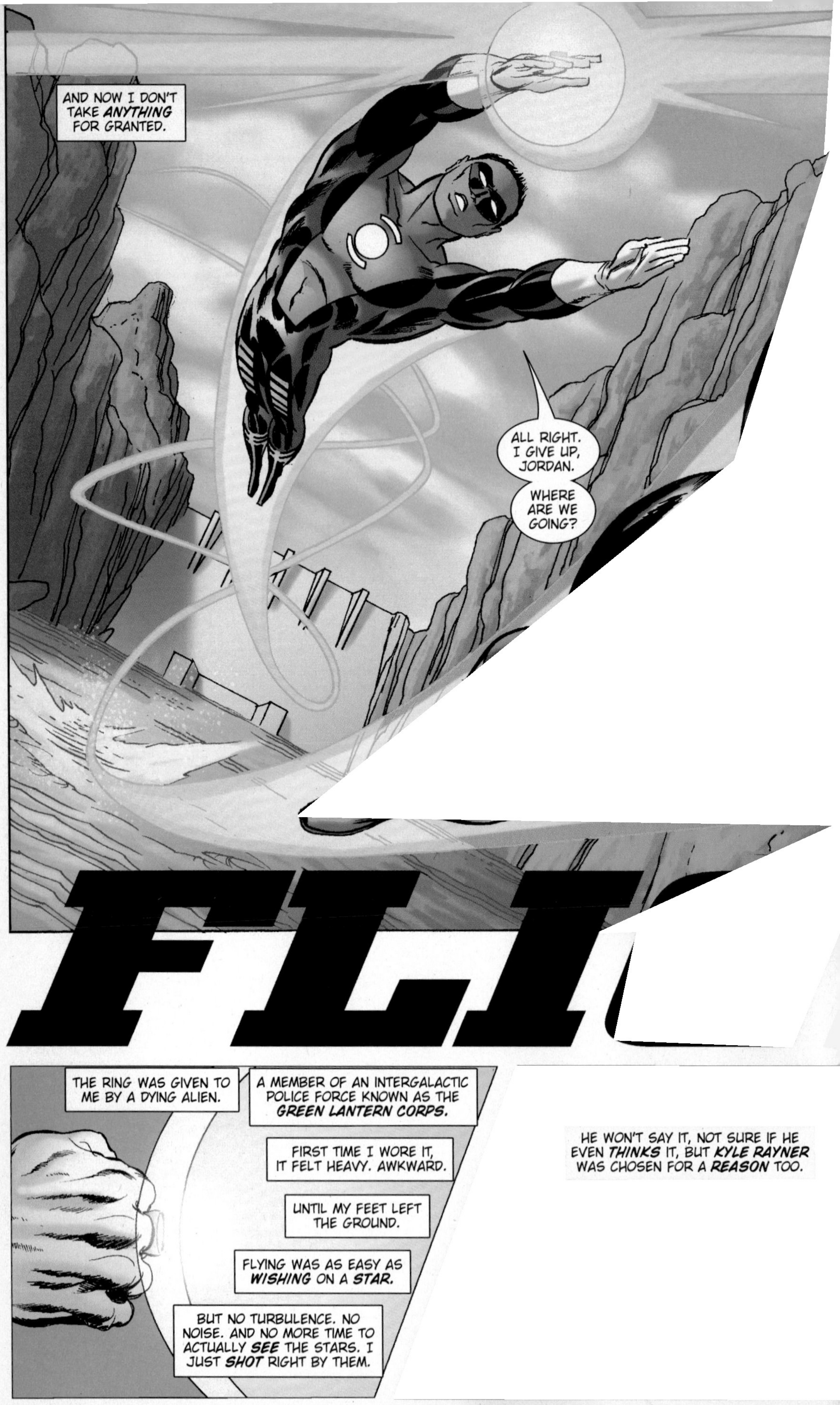
AND NOW I DON'T TAKE ANYTHING FOR GRANTED.
ALL RIGHT. I GIVE UP, JORDAN.
WHERE ARE WE GOING?
FLI
THE RING WAS GIVEN TO ME BY A DYING ALIEN.
A MEMBER OF AN INTERGALACTIC POLICE FORCE KNOWN AS THE GREEN LANTERN CORPS.
FIRST TIME I WORE IT, IT FELT HEAVY. AWKWARD.
UNTIL MY FEET LEFT THE GROUND.
FLYING WAS AS EASY AS WISHING ON A STAR.
BUT NO TURBULENCE. NO NOISE. AND NO MORE TIME TO ACTUALLY SEE THE STARS. I JUST SHOT RIGHT BY THEM.
HE WON'T SAY IT, NOT SURE IF HE EVEN THINKS IT, BUT KYLE RAYNER WAS CHOSEN FOR A REASON TOO.

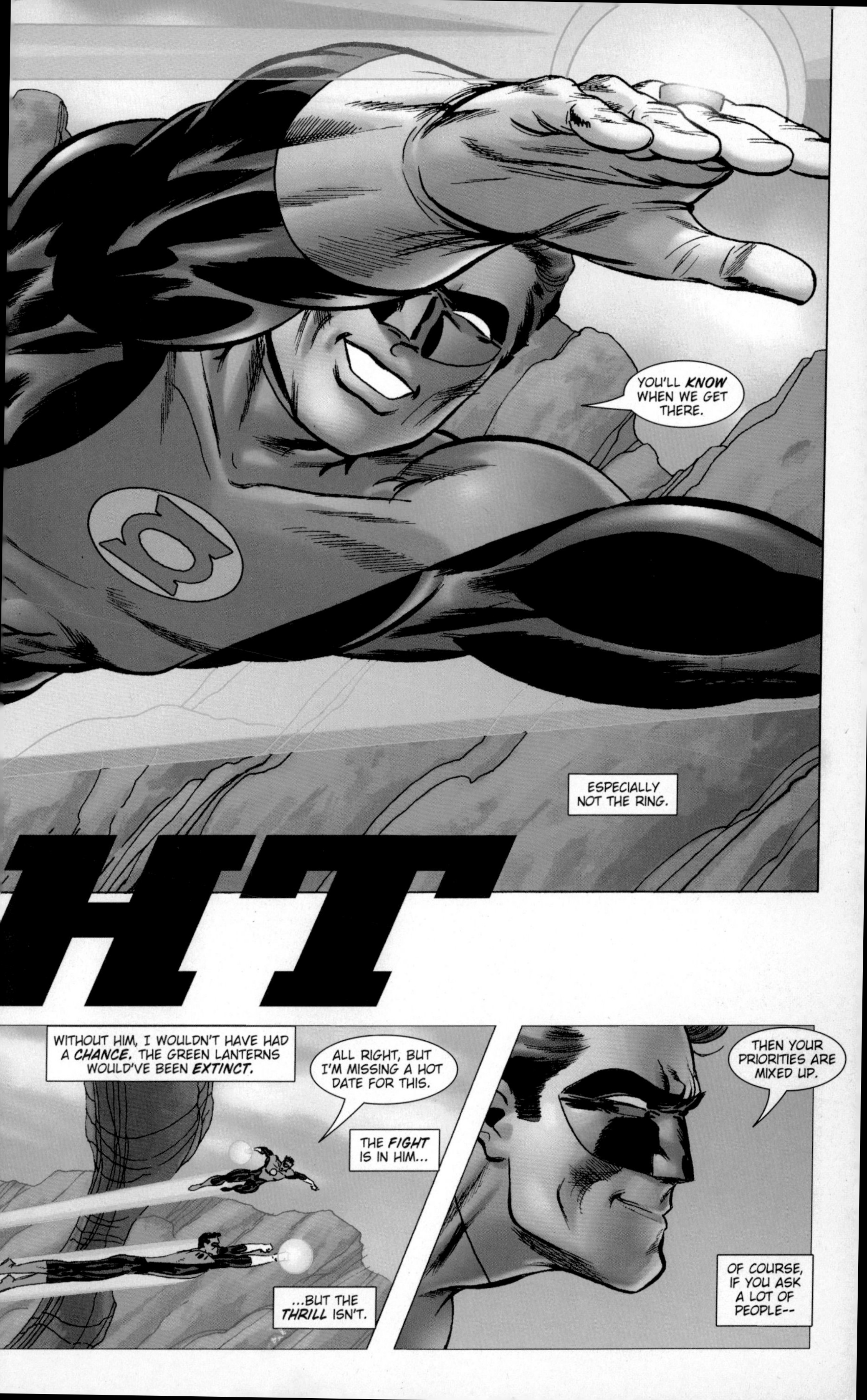

YOU'LL KNOW WHEN WE GET THERE.
ESPECIALLY NOT THE RING.
HT
WITHOUT HIM, I WOULDN'T HAVE HAD A CHANCE. THE GREEN LANTERNS WOULD'VE BEEN EXTINCT.
ALL RIGHT, BUT I'M MISSING A HOT DATE FOR THIS.
THE FIGHT IS IN HIM...
...BUT THE THRILL ISN'T.
THEN YOUR PRIORITIES ARE MIXED UP.
OF COURSE, IF YOU ASK A LOT OF PEOPLE--

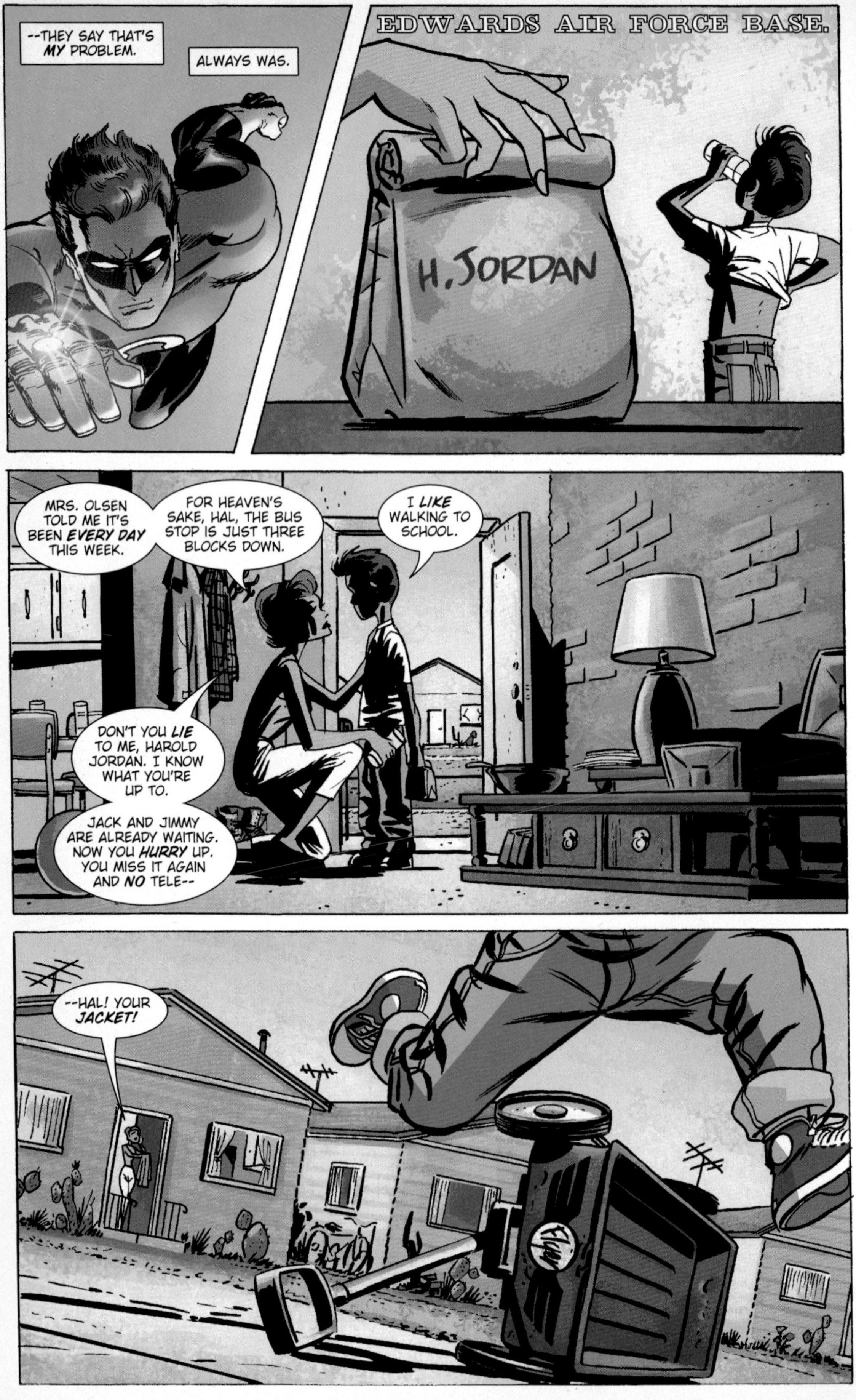
--THEY SAY THAT'S *MY* PROBLEM.
ALWAYS WAS.
EDWARDS AIR FORCE BASE.
H. JORDAN
MRS. OLSEN TOLD ME IT'S BEEN *EVERY DAY* THIS WEEK.
FOR HEAVEN'S SAKE, HAL, THE BUS STOP IS JUST THREE BLOCKS DOWN.
I *LIKE* WALKING TO SCHOOL.
DON'T YOU *LIE* TO ME, HAROLD JORDAN. I KNOW WHAT YOU'RE UP TO.
JACK AND JIMMY ARE ALREADY WAITING. NOW YOU *HURRY* UP. YOU MISS IT AGAIN AND *NO* TELE--
--HAL! YOUR *JACKET!*

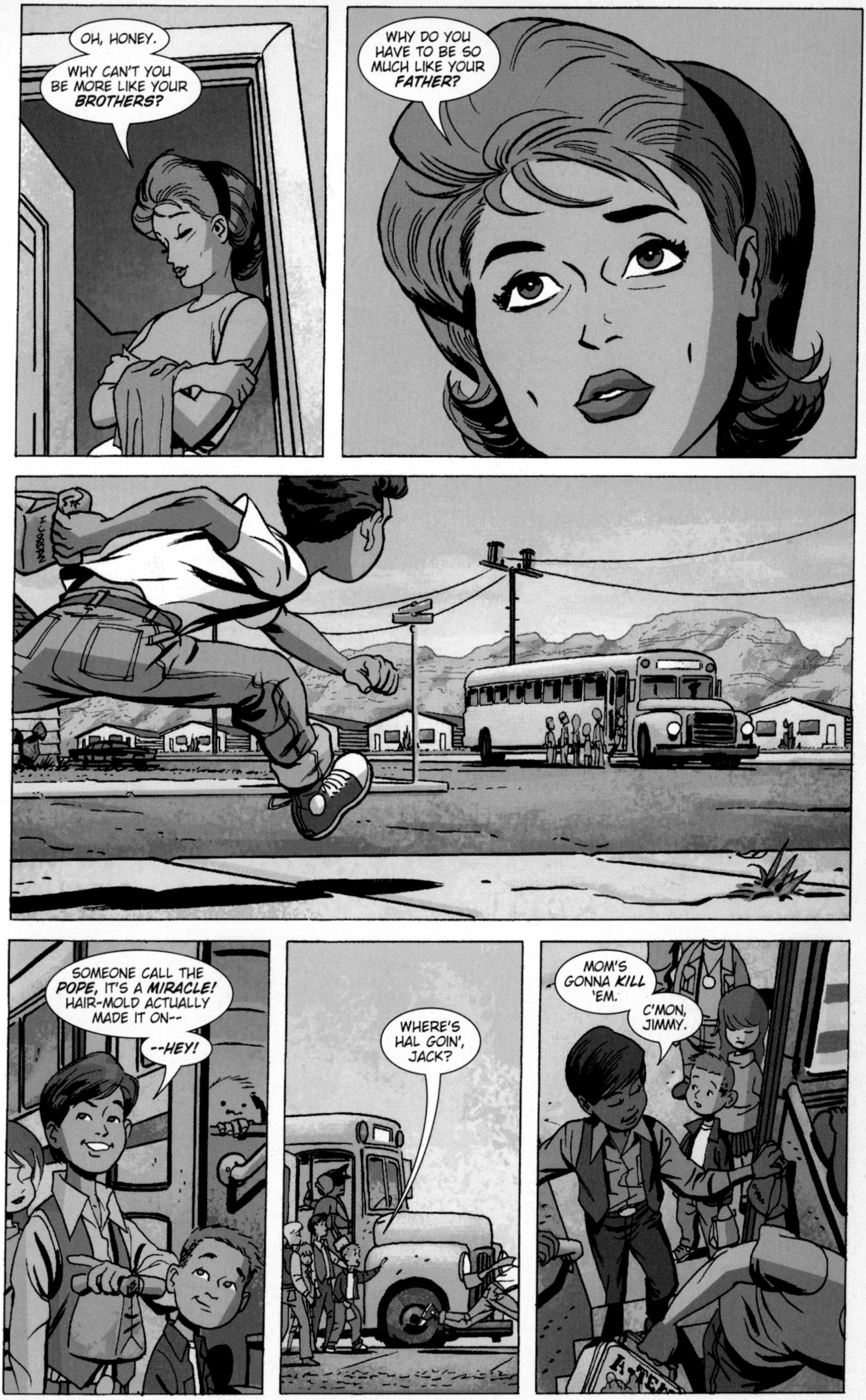
OH, HONEY.
WHY CAN'T YOU BE MORE LIKE YOUR BROTHERS?
WHY DO YOU HAVE TO BE SO MUCH LIKE YOUR FATHER?
SOMEONE CALL THE POPE, IT'S A MIRACLE! HAIR-MOLD ACTUALLY MADE IT ON--
--HEY!
WHERE'S HAL GOIN', JACK?
MOM'S GONNA KILL 'EM.
C'MON, JIMMY.

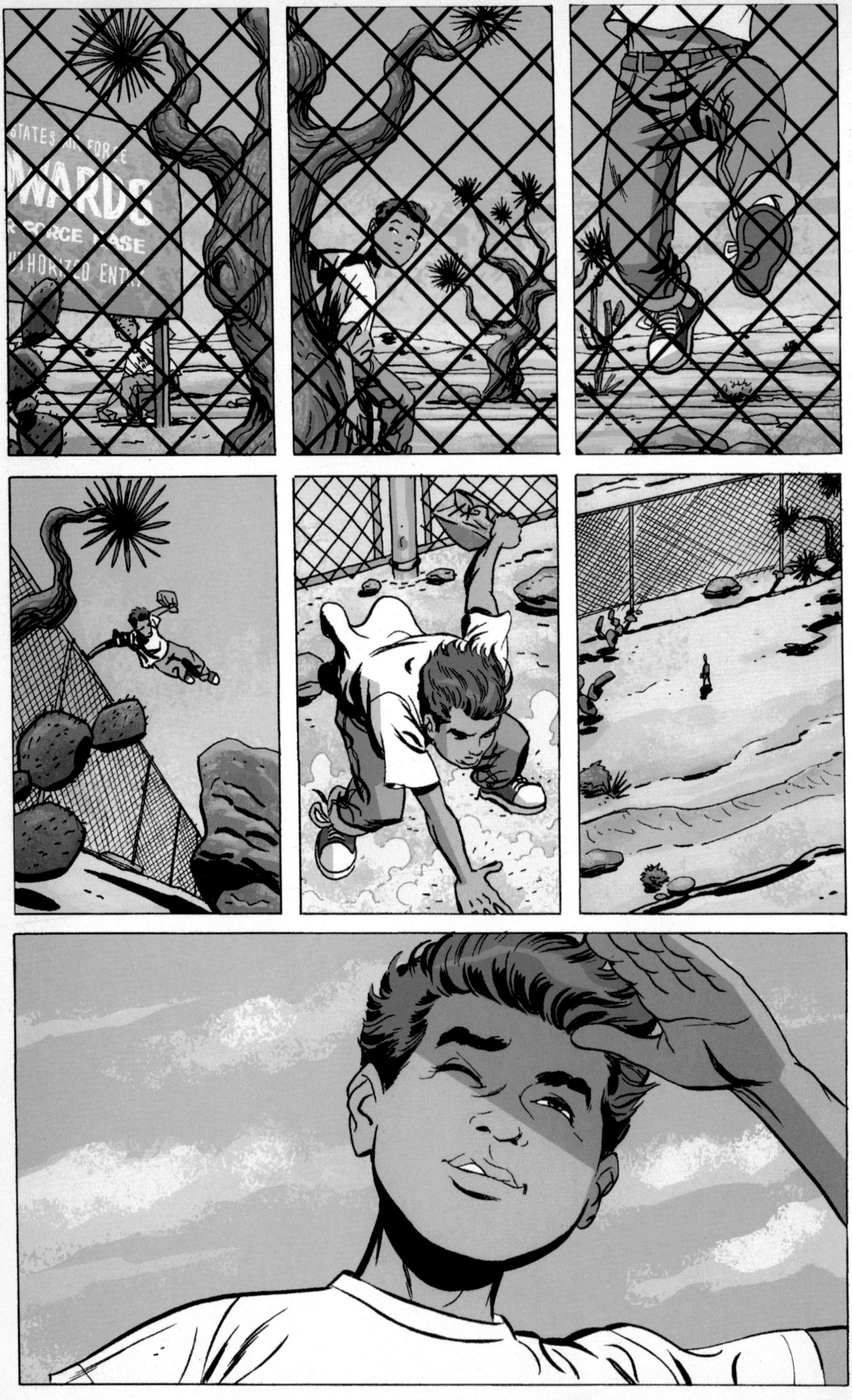

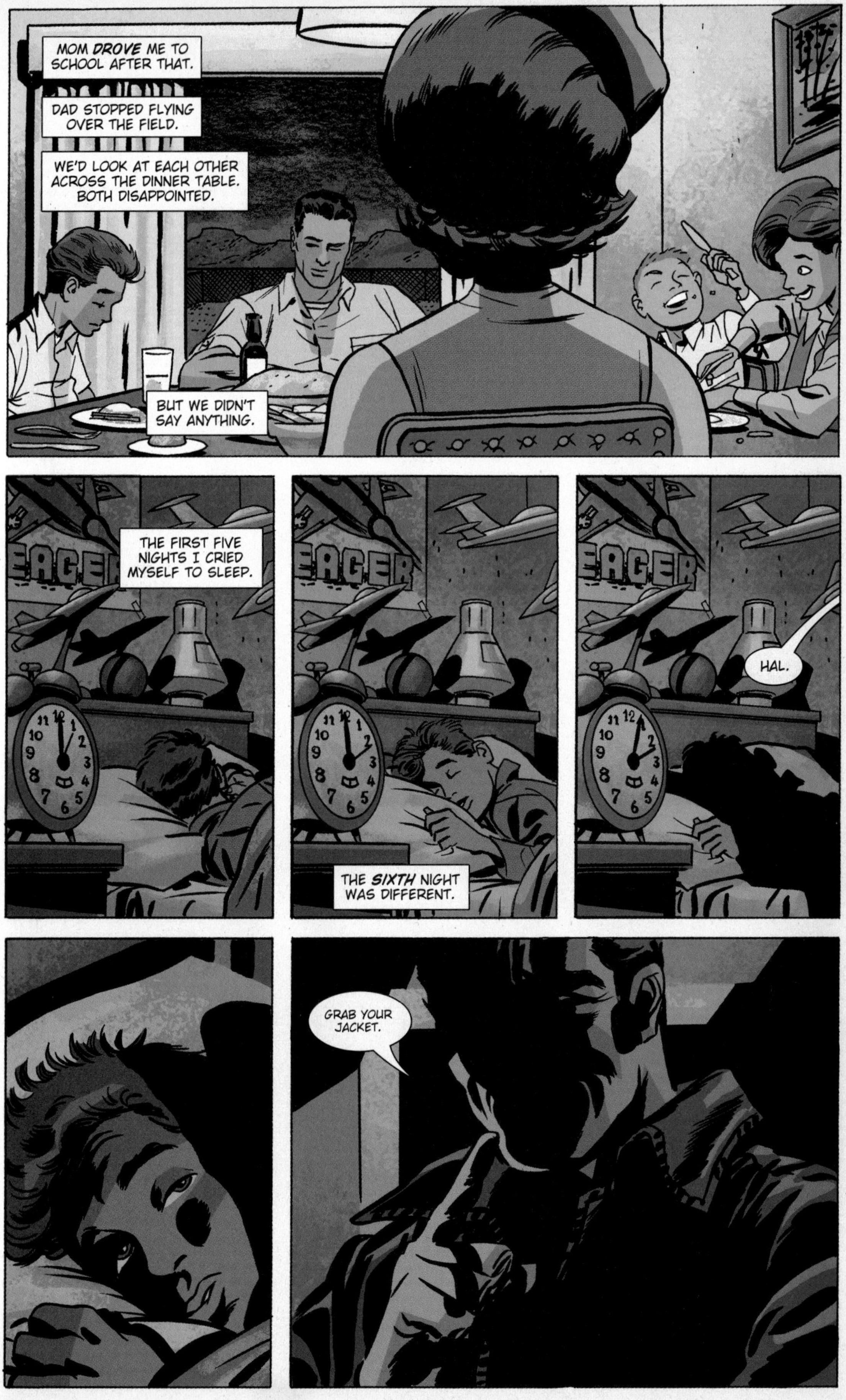
MOM DROVE ME TO SCHOOL AFTER THAT.
DAD STOPPED FLYING OVER THE FIELD.
WE'D LOOK AT EACH OTHER ACROSS THE DINNER TABLE. BOTH DISAPPOINTED.
BUT WE DIDN'T SAY ANYTHING.
THE FIRST FIVE NIGHTS I CRIED MYSELF TO SLEEP.
THE SIXTH NIGHT WAS DIFFERENT.
HAL.
GRAB YOUR JACKET.

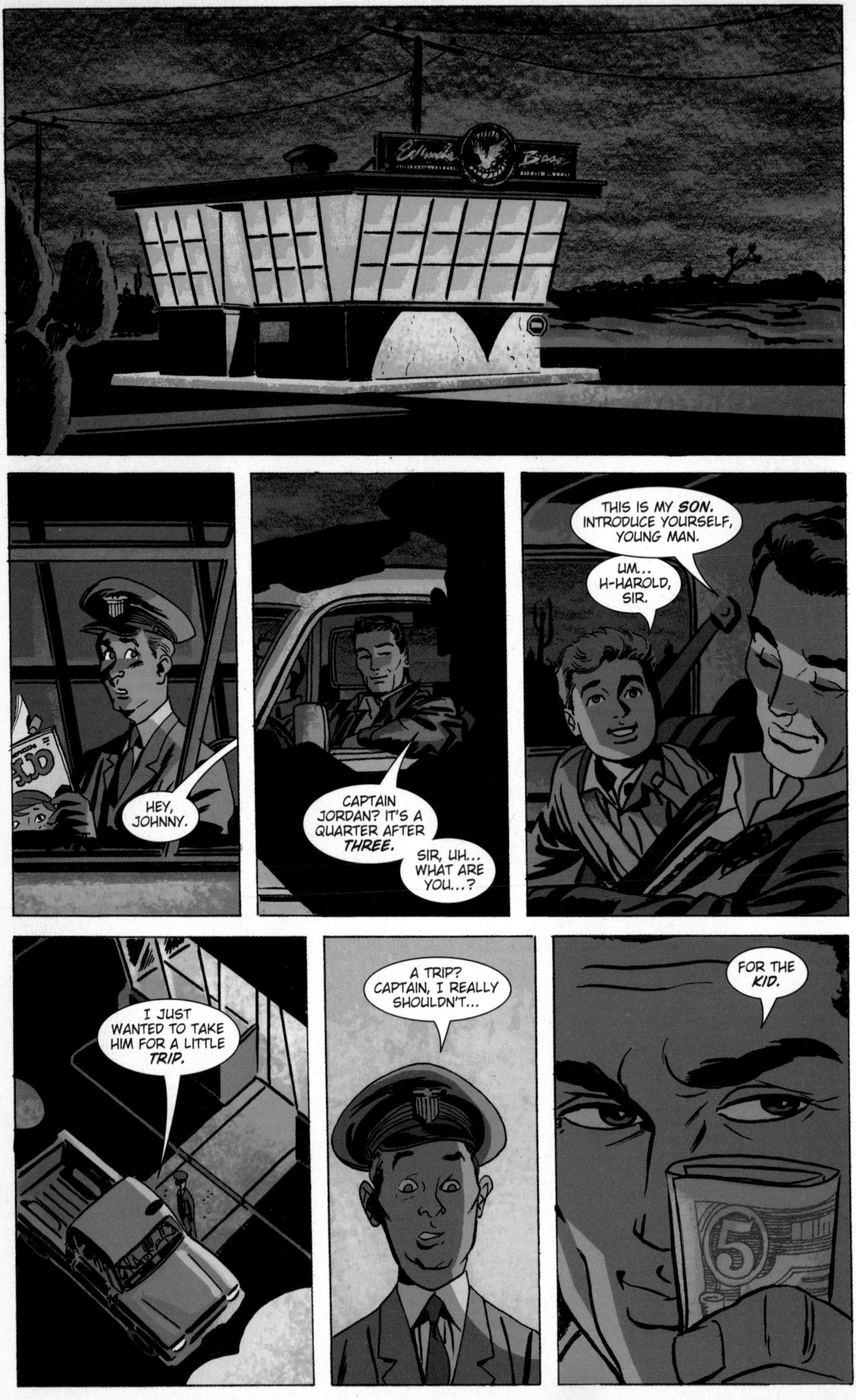
HEY, JOHNNY.
CAPTAIN JORDAN? IT'S A QUARTER AFTER *THREE.*
SIR, UH... WHAT ARE YOU...?
THIS IS MY *SON.* INTRODUCE YOURSELF, YOUNG MAN.
UM... H-HAROLD, SIR.
I JUST WANTED TO TAKE HIM FOR A LITTLE *TRIP.*
A TRIP? CAPTAIN, I REALLY SHOULDN'T...
FOR THE *KID.*

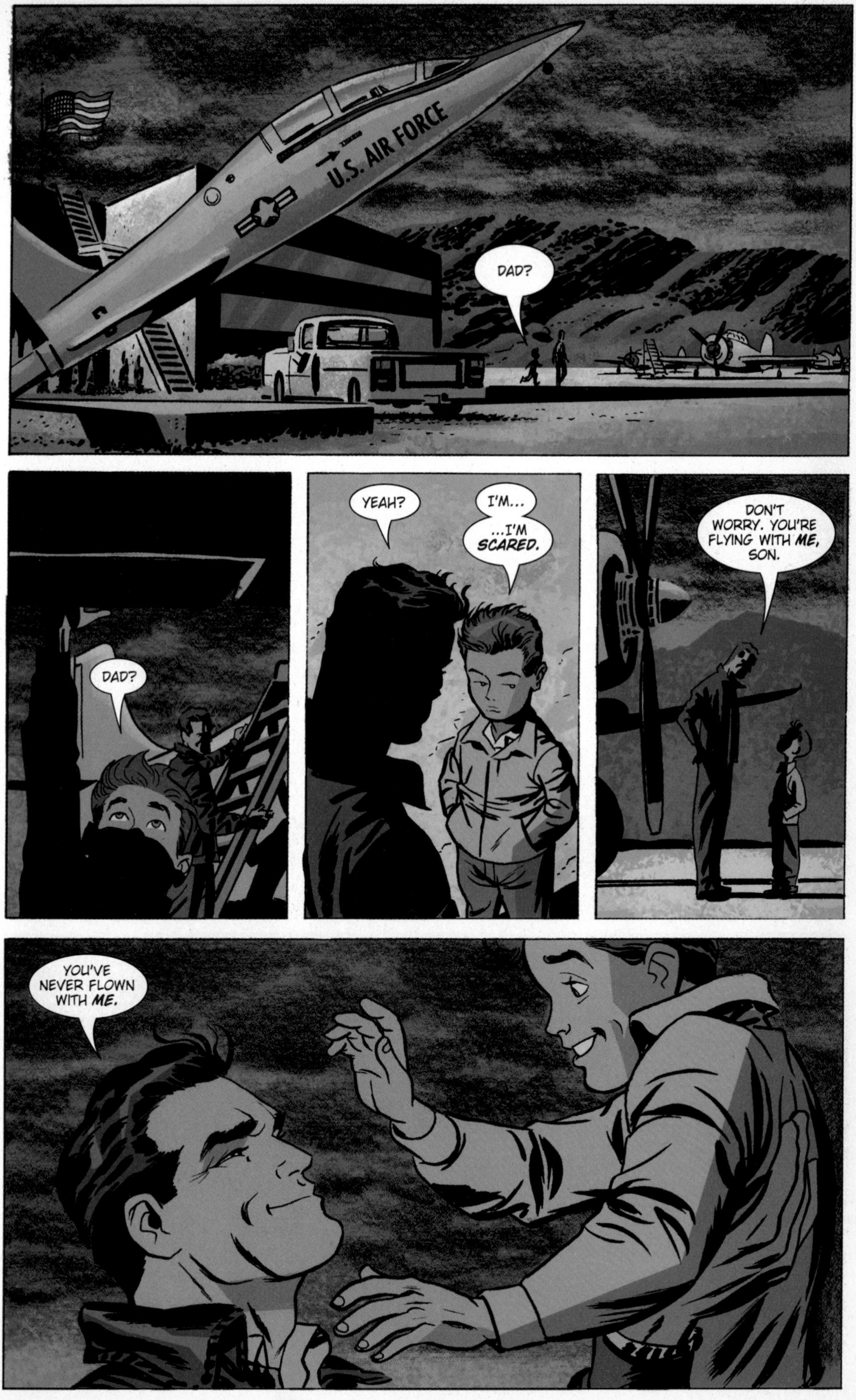
U.S. AIR FORCE
DAD?
DAD?
YEAH?
I'M...
...I'M SCARED.
DON'T WORRY. YOU'RE FLYING WITH ME, SON.
YOU'VE NEVER FLOWN WITH ME.

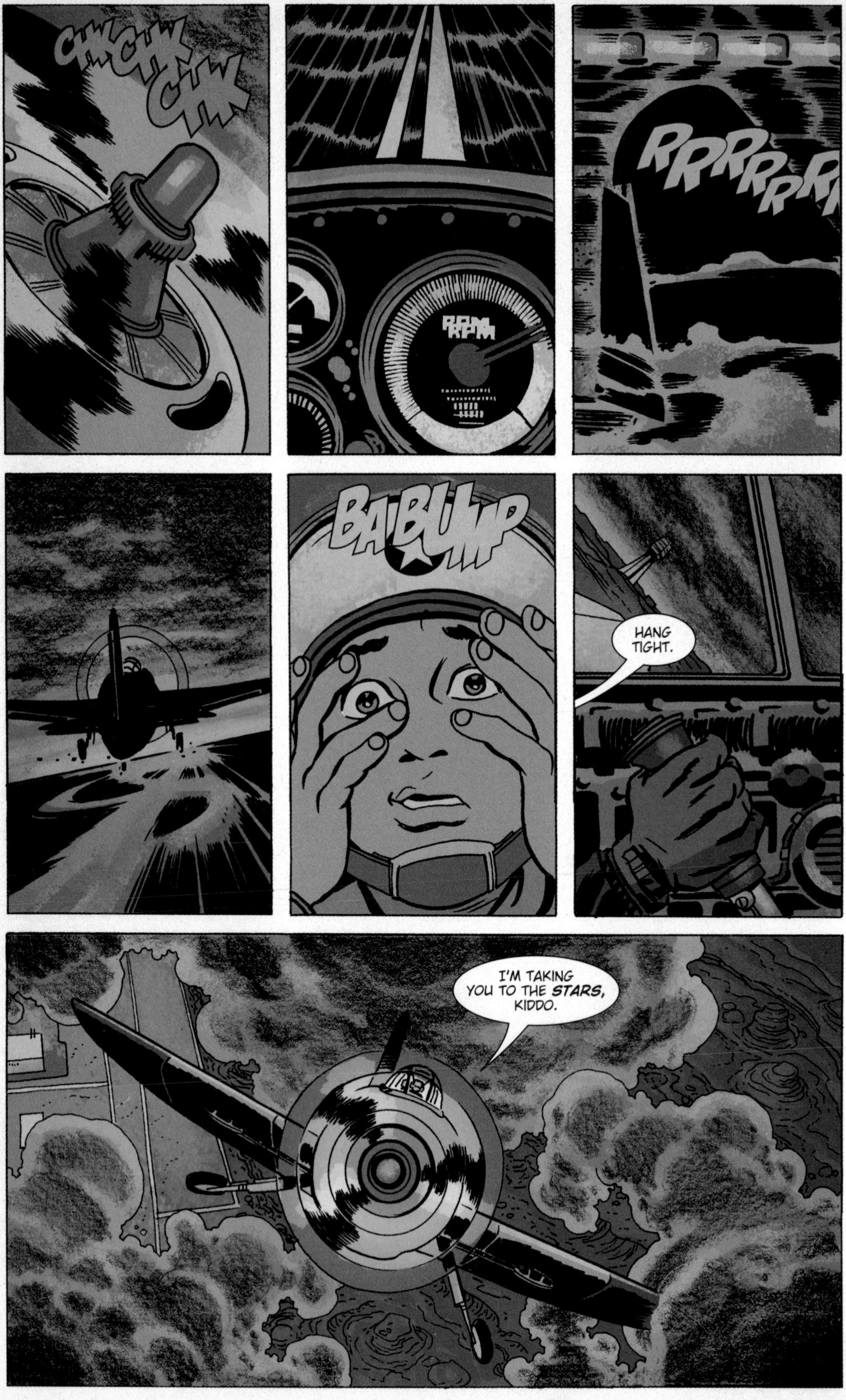
CHK CHK CHK
RPM
RRRRRR
BA-BUMP
HANG TIGHT.
I'M TAKING YOU TO THE STARS, KIDDO.

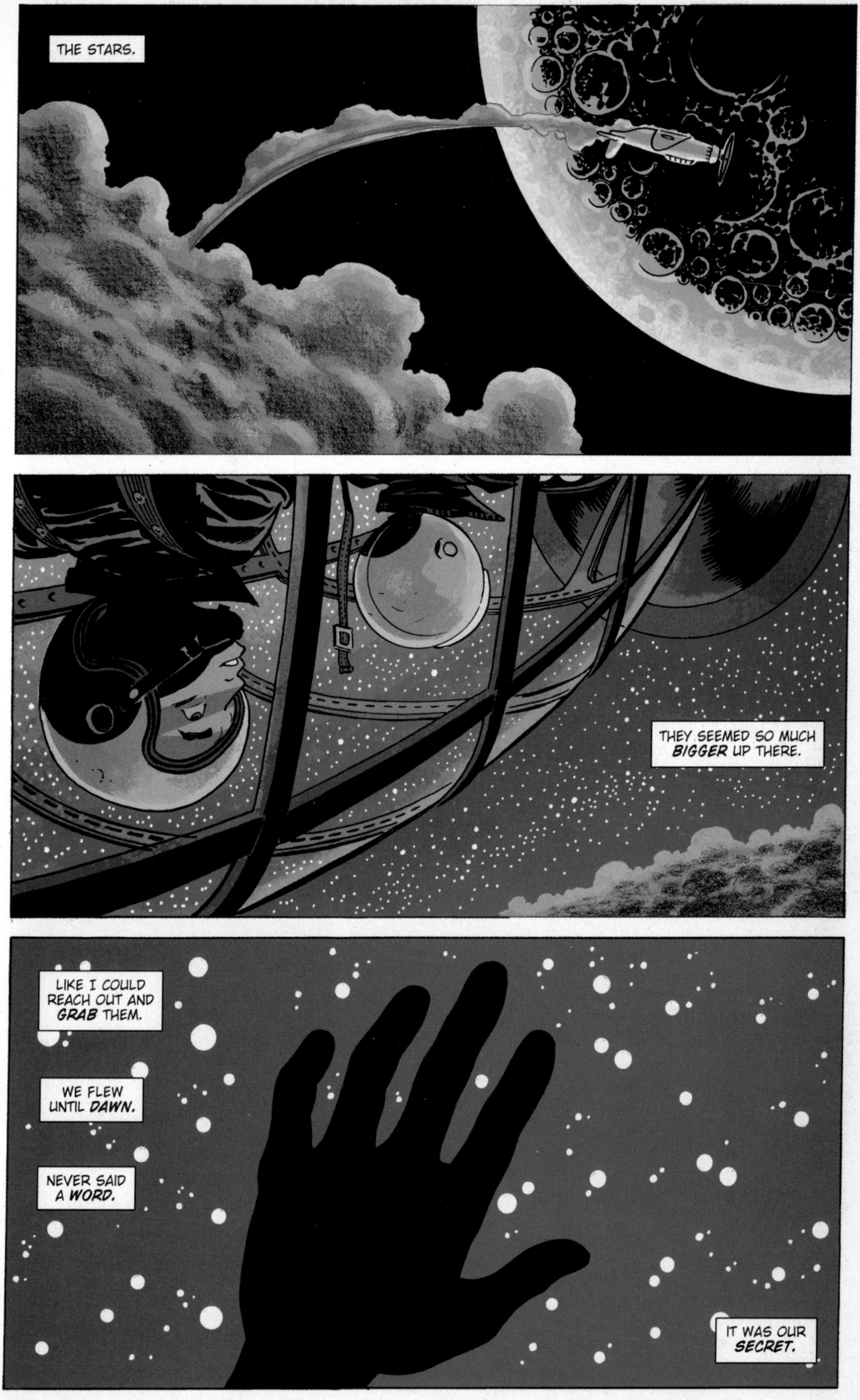
THE STARS.
THEY SEEMED SO MUCH BIGGER UP THERE.
LIKE I COULD REACH OUT AND GRAB THEM.
WE FLEW UNTIL DAWN.
NEVER SAID A WORD.
IT WAS OUR SECRET.

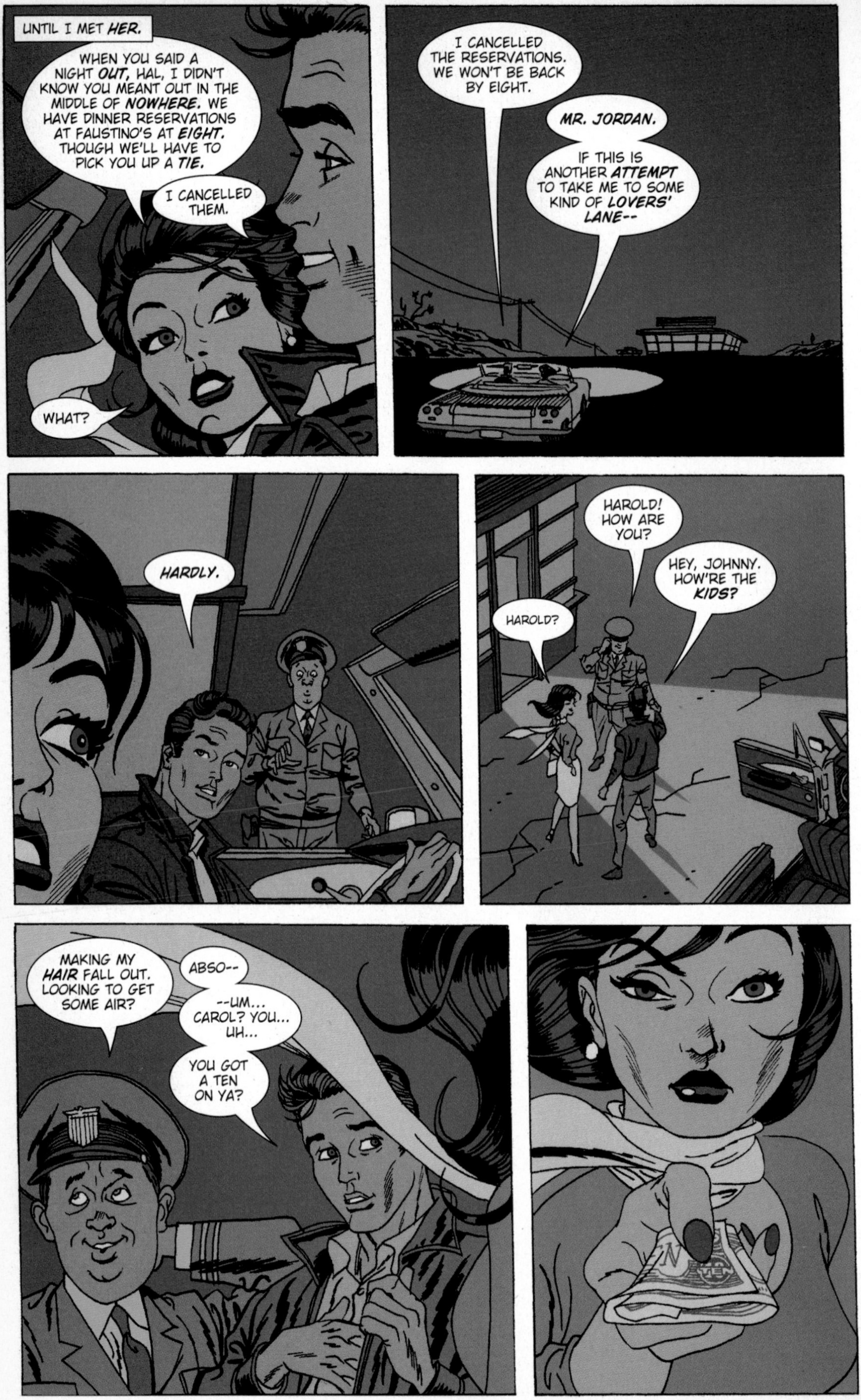
UNTIL I MET HER.
WHEN YOU SAID A NIGHT OUT, HAL, I DIDN'T KNOW YOU MEANT OUT IN THE MIDDLE OF NOWHERE. WE HAVE DINNER RESERVATIONS AT FAUSTINO'S AT EIGHT. THOUGH WE'LL HAVE TO PICK YOU UP A TIE.
I CANCELLED THEM.
WHAT?
I CANCELLED THE RESERVATIONS. WE WON'T BE BACK BY EIGHT.
MR. JORDAN.
IF THIS IS ANOTHER ATTEMPT TO TAKE ME TO SOME KIND OF LOVERS' LANE--
HARDLY.
HAROLD! HOW ARE YOU?
HEY, JOHNNY. HOW'RE THE KIDS?
HAROLD?
MAKING MY HAIR FALL OUT. LOOKING TO GET SOME AIR?
ABSO--
--UM... CAROL? YOU... UH...
YOU GOT A TEN ON YA?

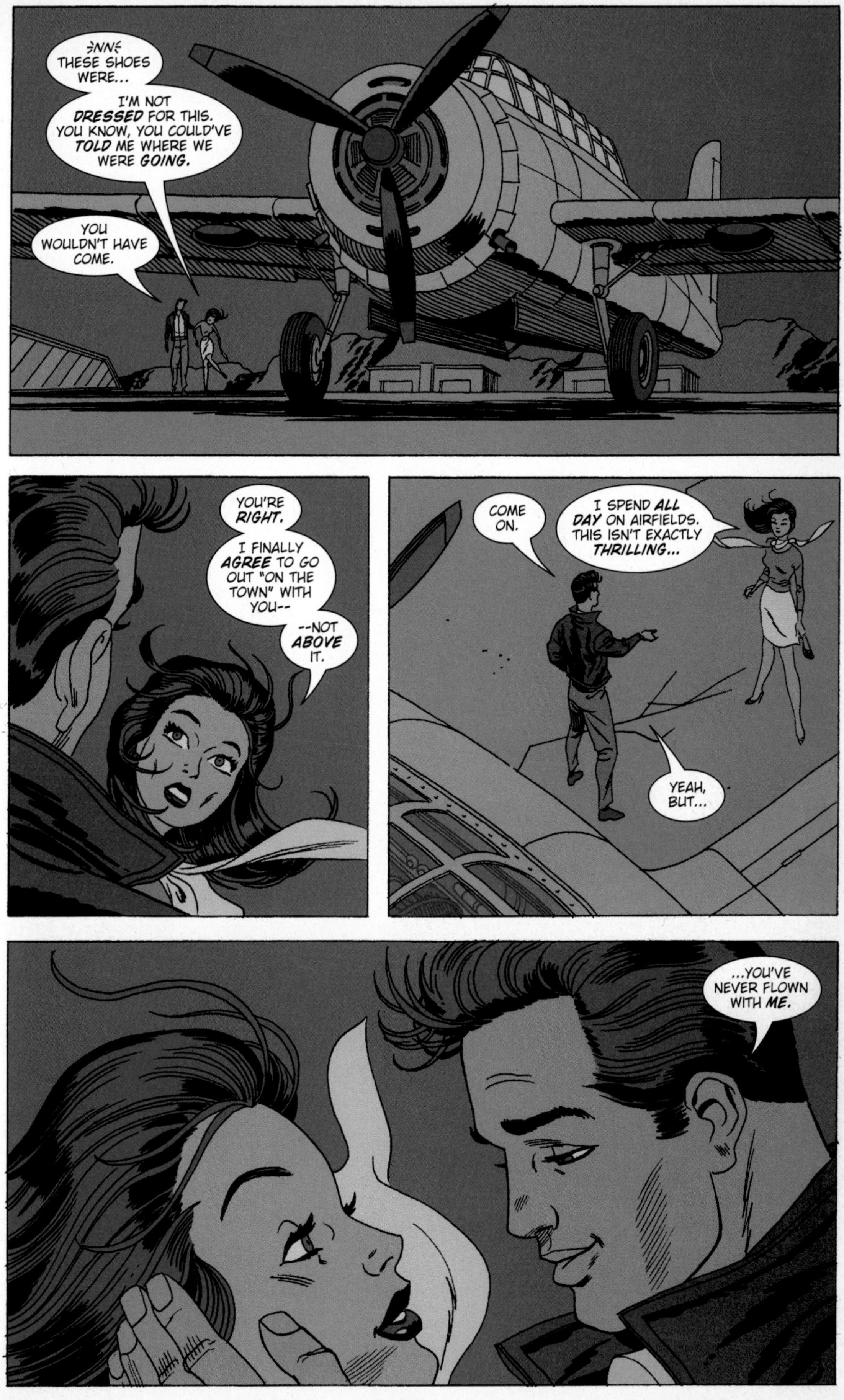

NN
THESE SHOES WERE...
I'M NOT DRESSED FOR THIS. YOU KNOW, YOU COULD'VE TOLD ME WHERE WE WERE GOING.
YOU WOULDN'T HAVE COME.
YOU'RE RIGHT.
I FINALLY AGREE TO GO OUT "ON THE TOWN" WITH YOU--
--NOT ABOVE IT.
COME ON.
I SPEND ALL DAY ON AIRFIELDS. THIS ISN'T EXACTLY THRILLING...
YEAH, BUT...
...YOU'VE NEVER FLOWN WITH ME.

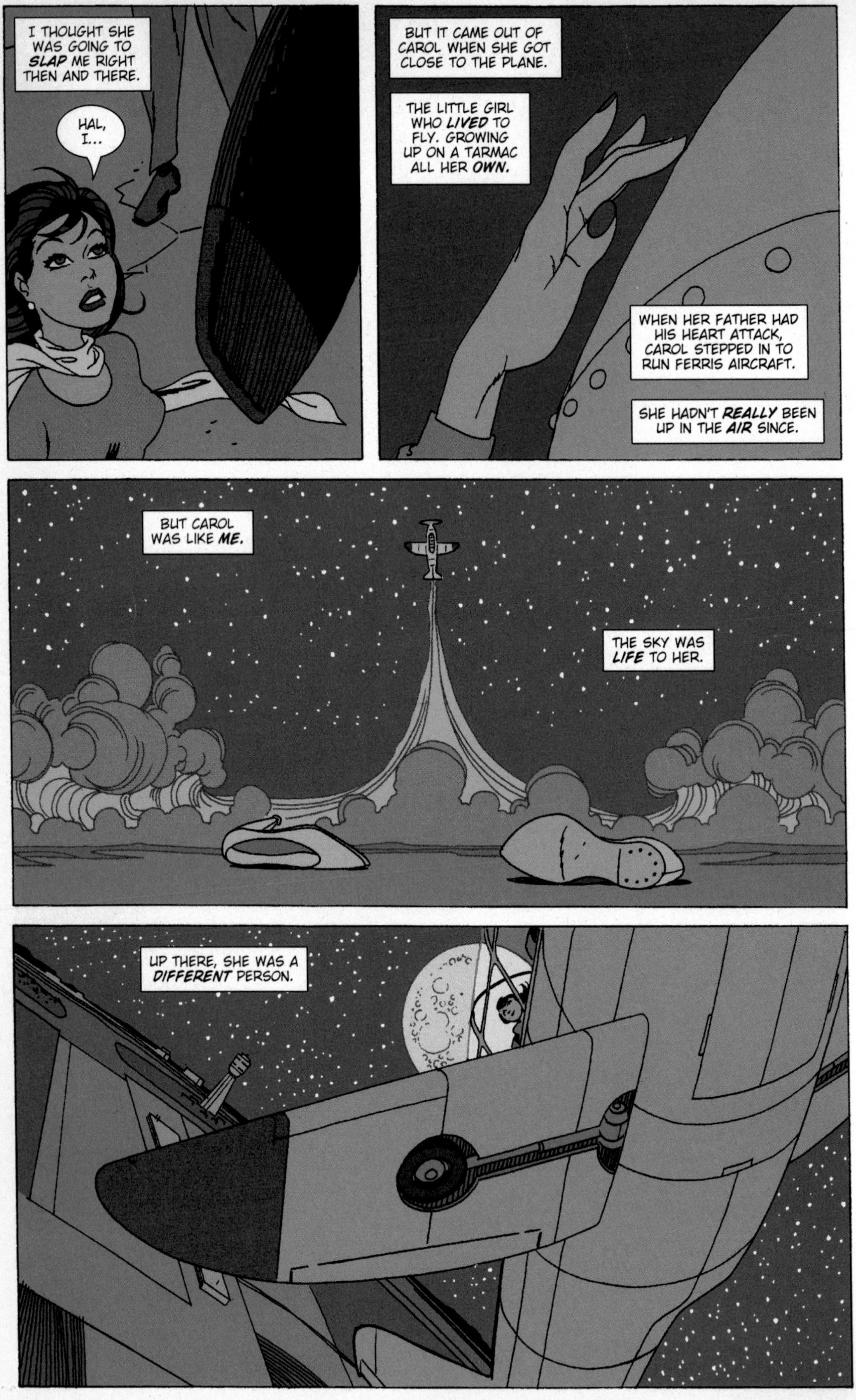
I THOUGHT SHE WAS GOING TO *SLAP* ME RIGHT THEN AND THERE.
HAL, I...
BUT IT CAME OUT OF CAROL WHEN SHE GOT CLOSE TO THE PLANE.
THE LITTLE GIRL WHO *LIVED* TO FLY. GROWING UP ON A TARMAC ALL HER *OWN.*
WHEN HER FATHER HAD HIS HEART ATTACK, CAROL STEPPED IN TO RUN FERRIS AIRCRAFT.
SHE HADN'T *REALLY* BEEN UP IN THE *AIR* SINCE.
BUT CAROL WAS LIKE *ME.*
THE SKY WAS *LIFE* TO HER.
UP THERE, SHE WAS A *DIFFERENT* PERSON.

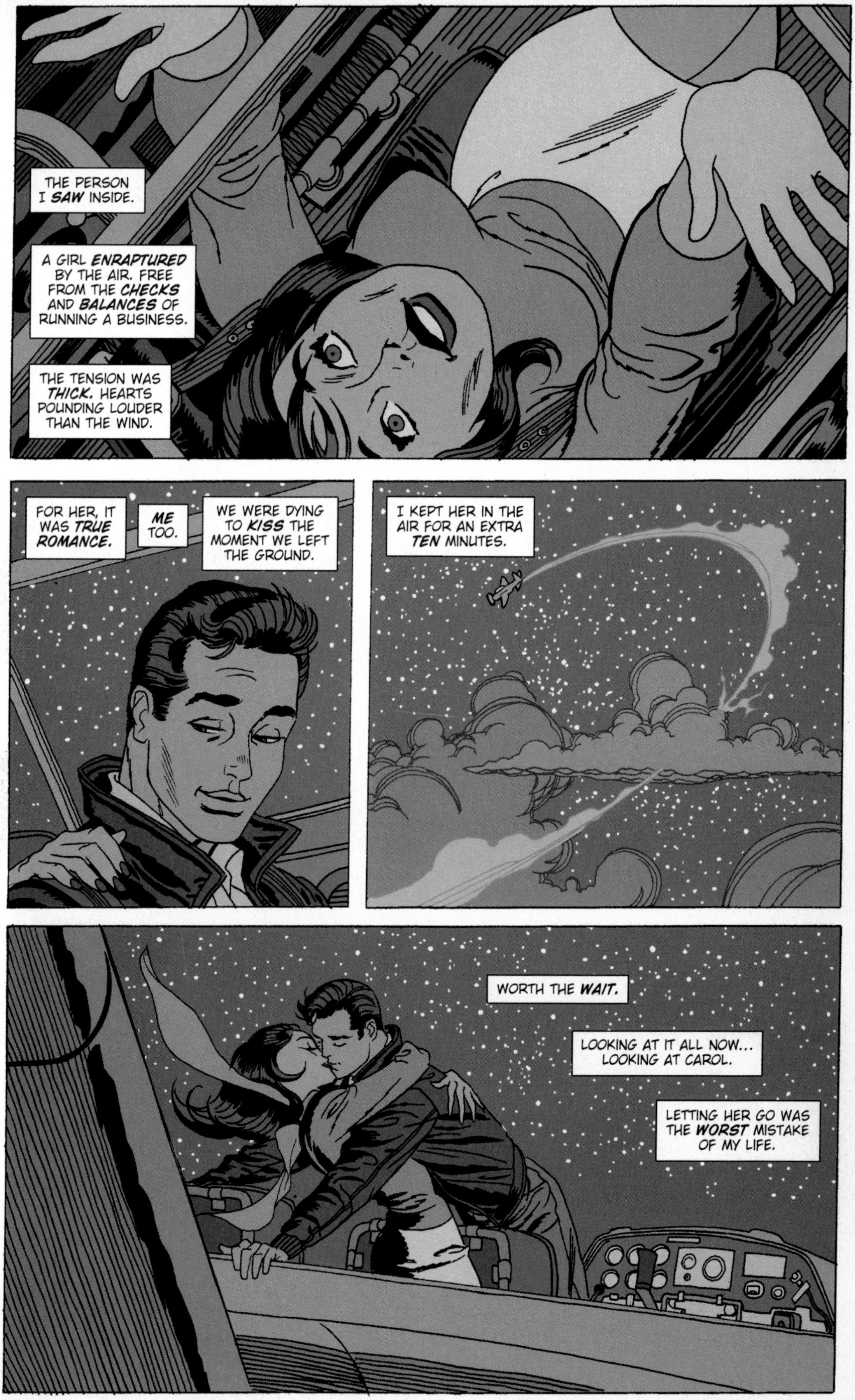
THE PERSON I SAW INSIDE.
A GIRL ENRAPTURED BY THE AIR. FREE FROM THE CHECKS AND BALANCES OF RUNNING A BUSINESS.
THE TENSION WAS THICK. HEARTS POUNDING LOUDER THAN THE WIND.
FOR HER, IT WAS TRUE ROMANCE.
ME TOO.
WE WERE DYING TO KISS THE MOMENT WE LEFT THE GROUND.
I KEPT HER IN THE AIR FOR AN EXTRA TEN MINUTES.
WORTH THE WAIT.
LOOKING AT IT ALL NOW... LOOKING AT CAROL.
LETTING HER GO WAS THE WORST MISTAKE OF MY LIFE.

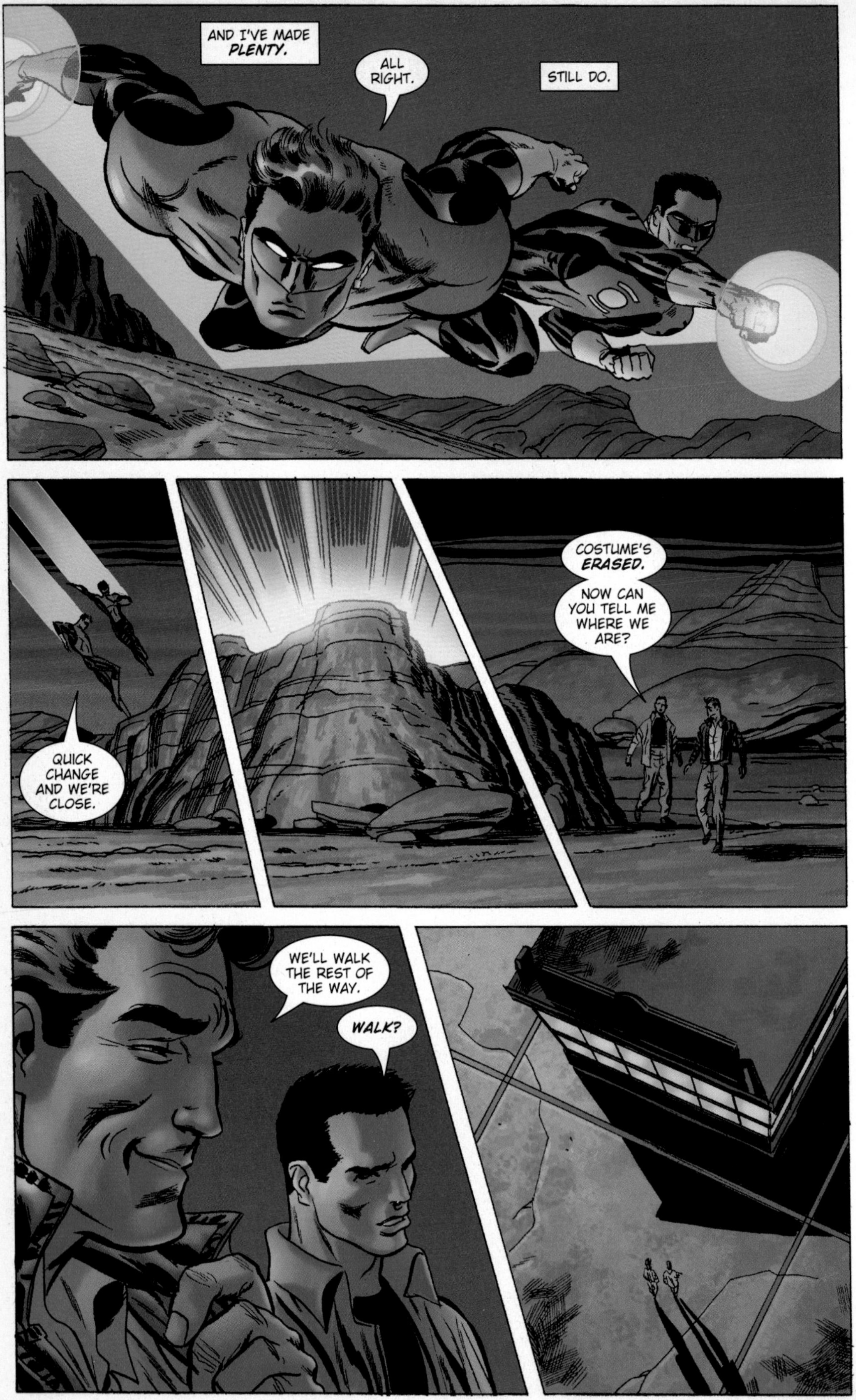
AND I'VE MADE PLENTY.
ALL RIGHT.
STILL DO.
QUICK CHANGE AND WE'RE CLOSE.
COSTUME'S ERASED.
NOW CAN YOU TELL ME WHERE WE ARE?
WE'LL WALK THE REST OF THE WAY.
WALK?

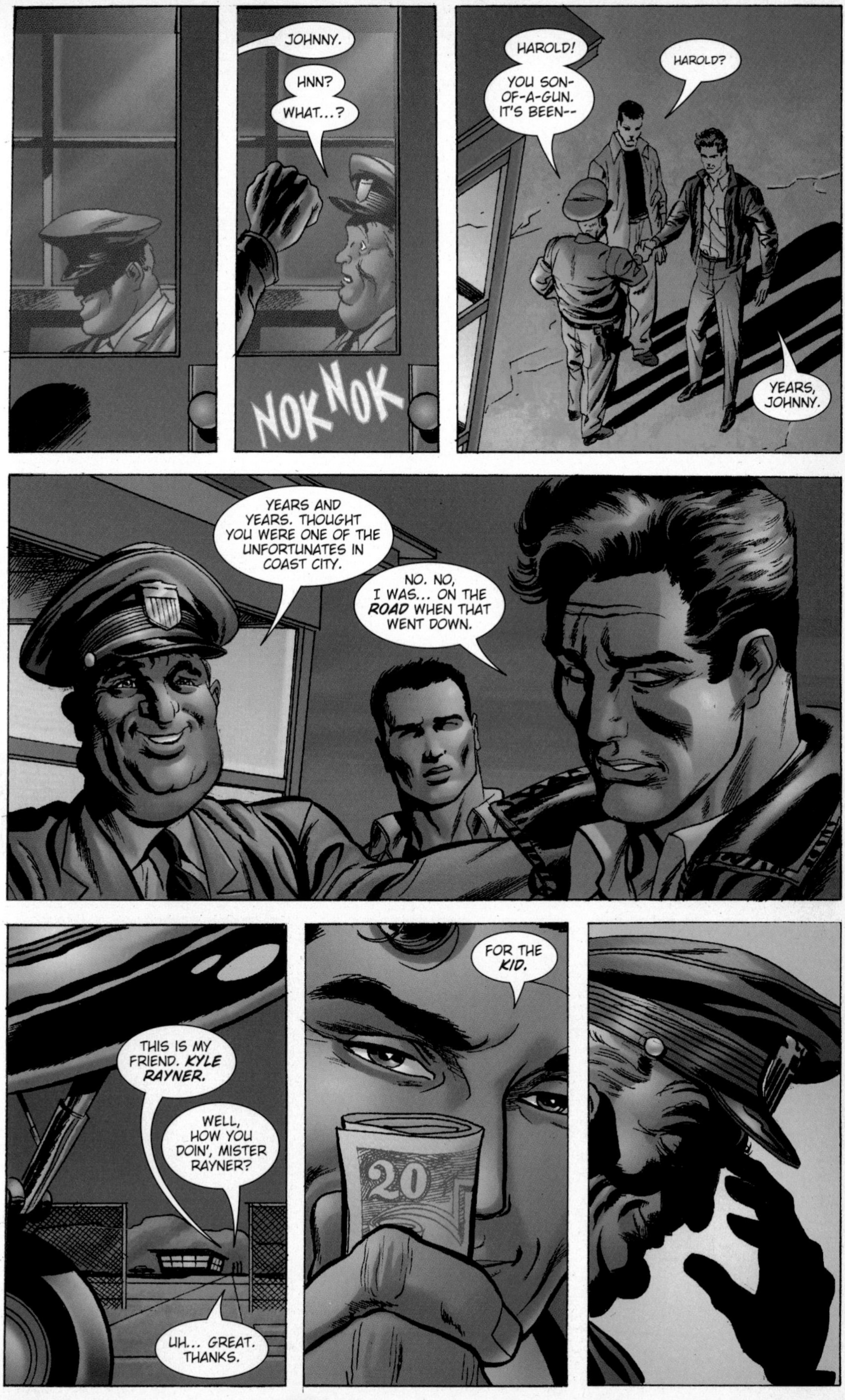
JOHNNY.
HNN?
WHAT...?
NOK NOK
HAROLD!
YOU SON-OF-A-GUN. IT'S BEEN--
HAROLD?
YEARS, JOHNNY.
YEARS AND YEARS. THOUGHT YOU WERE ONE OF THE UNFORTUNATES IN COAST CITY.
NO. NO, I WAS... ON THE ROAD WHEN THAT WENT DOWN.
THIS IS MY FRIEND. KYLE RAYNER.
WELL, HOW YOU DOIN', MISTER RAYNER?
UH... GREAT. THANKS.
FOR THE KID.
20

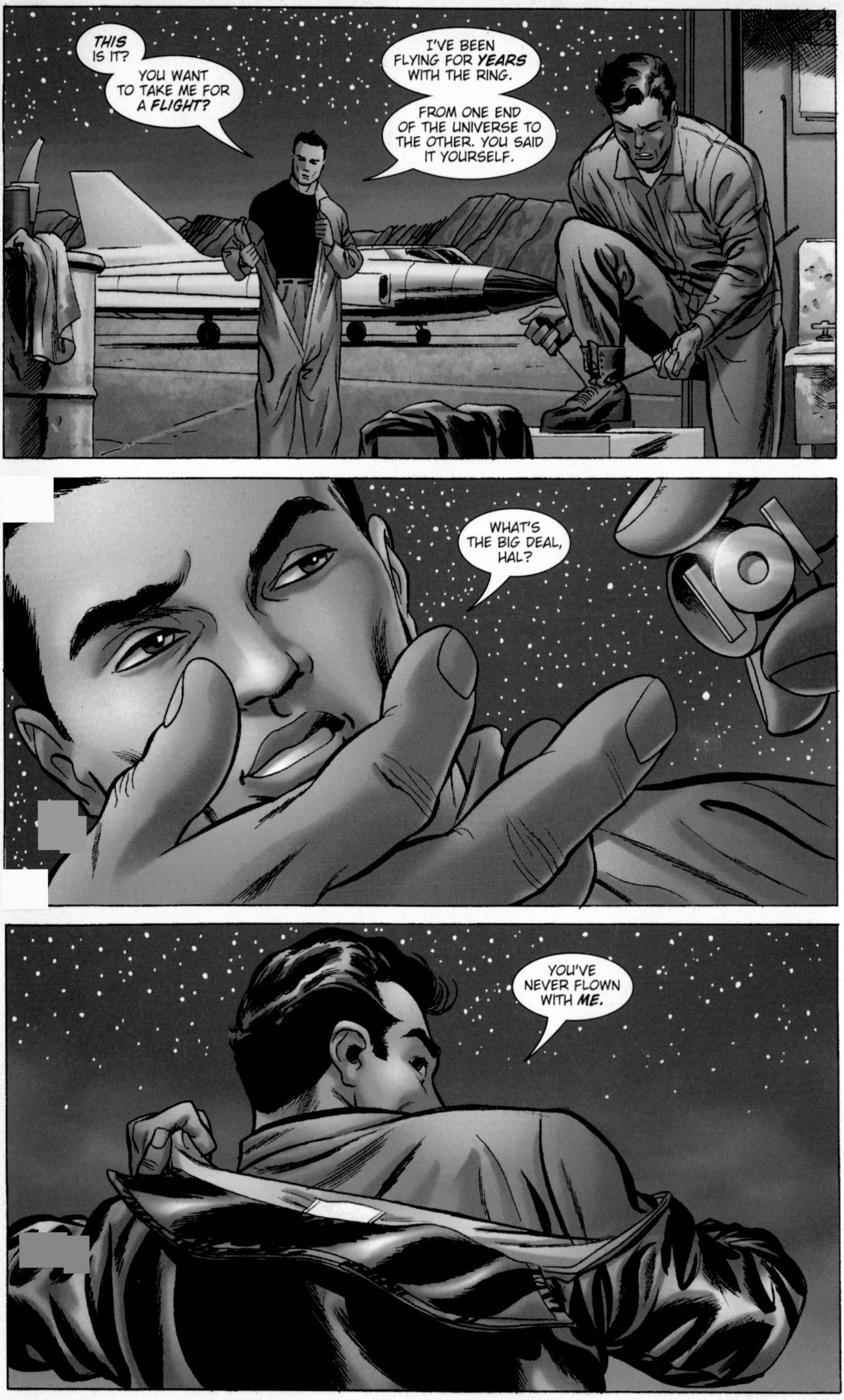
THIS IS IT? YOU WANT TO TAKE ME FOR A FLIGHT?
I'VE BEEN FLYING FOR YEARS WITH THE RING.
FROM ONE END OF THE UNIVERSE TO THE OTHER. YOU SAID IT YOURSELF.
WHAT'S THE BIG DEAL, HAL?
YOU'VE NEVER FLOWN WITH ME.

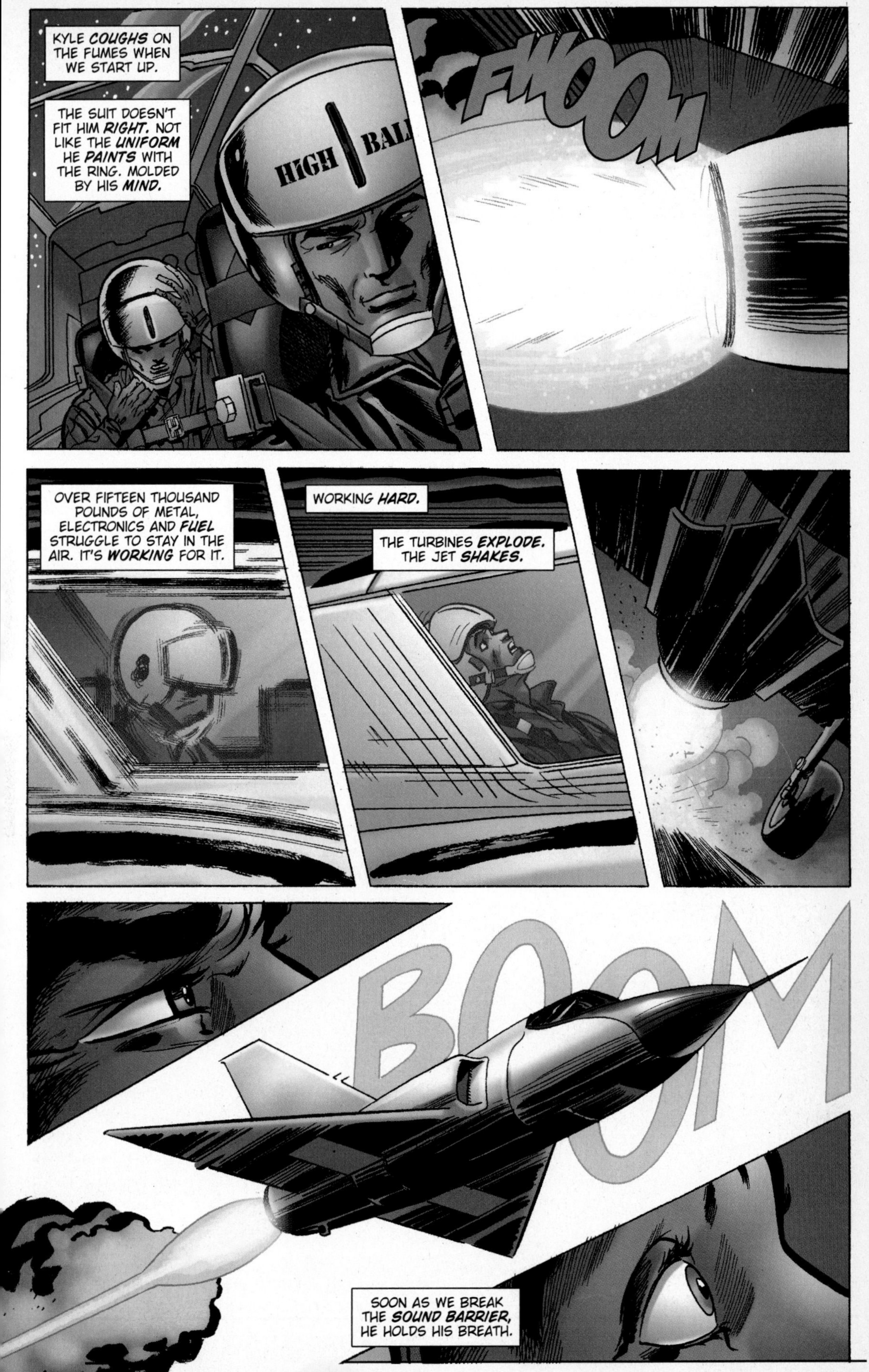
KYLE COUGHS ON THE FUMES WHEN WE START UP.
THE SUIT DOESN'T FIT HIM RIGHT. NOT LIKE THE UNIFORM HE PAINTS WITH THE RING. MOLDED BY HIS MIND.
HIGH BALL
FWOOM
OVER FIFTEEN THOUSAND POUNDS OF METAL, ELECTRONICS AND FUEL STRUGGLE TO STAY IN THE AIR. IT'S WORKING FOR IT.
WORKING HARD.
THE TURBINES EXPLODE. THE JET SHAKES.
BOOM
SOON AS WE BREAK THE SOUND BARRIER, HE HOLDS HIS BREATH.

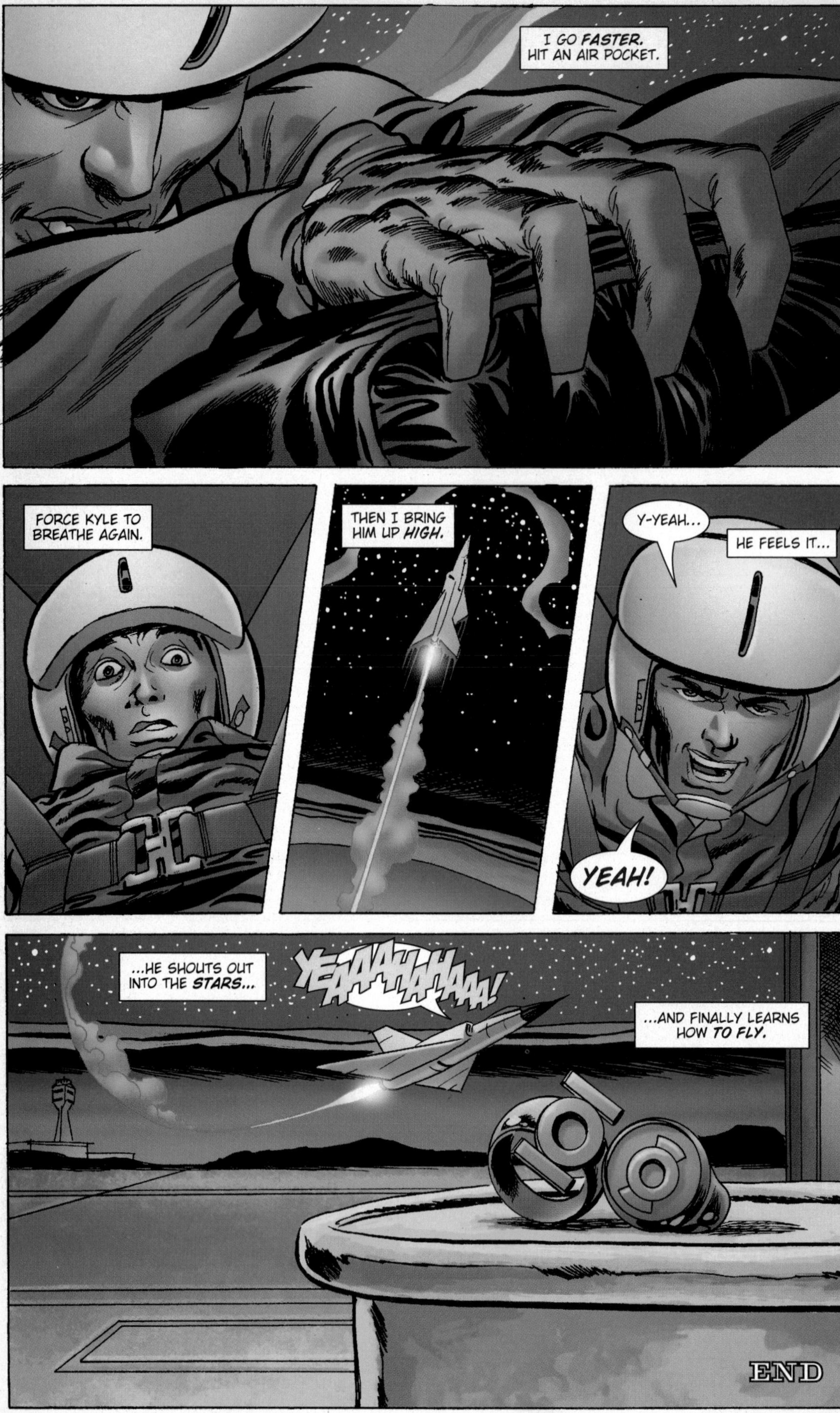
I GO FASTER.
HIT AN AIR POCKET.
FORCE KYLE TO BREATHE AGAIN.
THEN I BRING HIM UP HIGH.
Y-YEAH...
HE FEELS IT...
YEAH!
...HE SHOUTS OUT INTO THE STARS...
YEAAAAHAHAAA!
...AND FINALLY LEARNS HOW TO FLY.
END

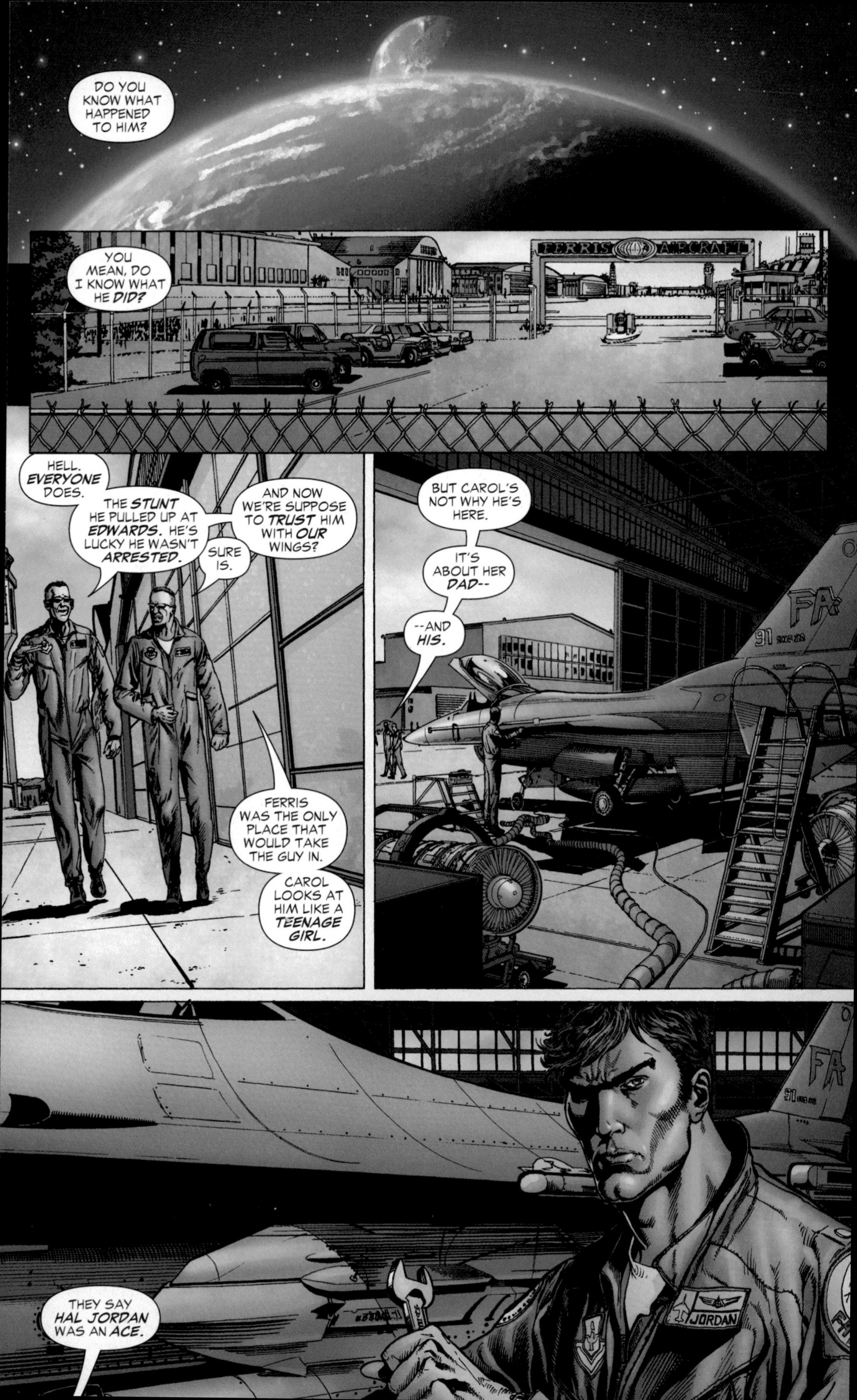
DO YOU KNOW WHAT HAPPENED TO HIM?
YOU MEAN, DO I KNOW WHAT HE DID?
FERRIS AIRCRAFT
HELL. EVERYONE DOES.
THE STUNT HE PULLED UP AT EDWARDS. HE'S LUCKY HE WASN'T ARRESTED.
SURE IS.
AND NOW WE'RE SUPPOSE TO TRUST HIM WITH OUR WINGS?
FERRIS WAS THE ONLY PLACE THAT WOULD TAKE THE GUY IN.
CAROL LOOKS AT HIM LIKE A TEENAGE GIRL.
BUT CAROL'S NOT WHY HE'S HERE.
IT'S ABOUT HER DAD--
--AND HIS.
THEY SAY HAL JORDAN WAS AN ACE.
JORDAN

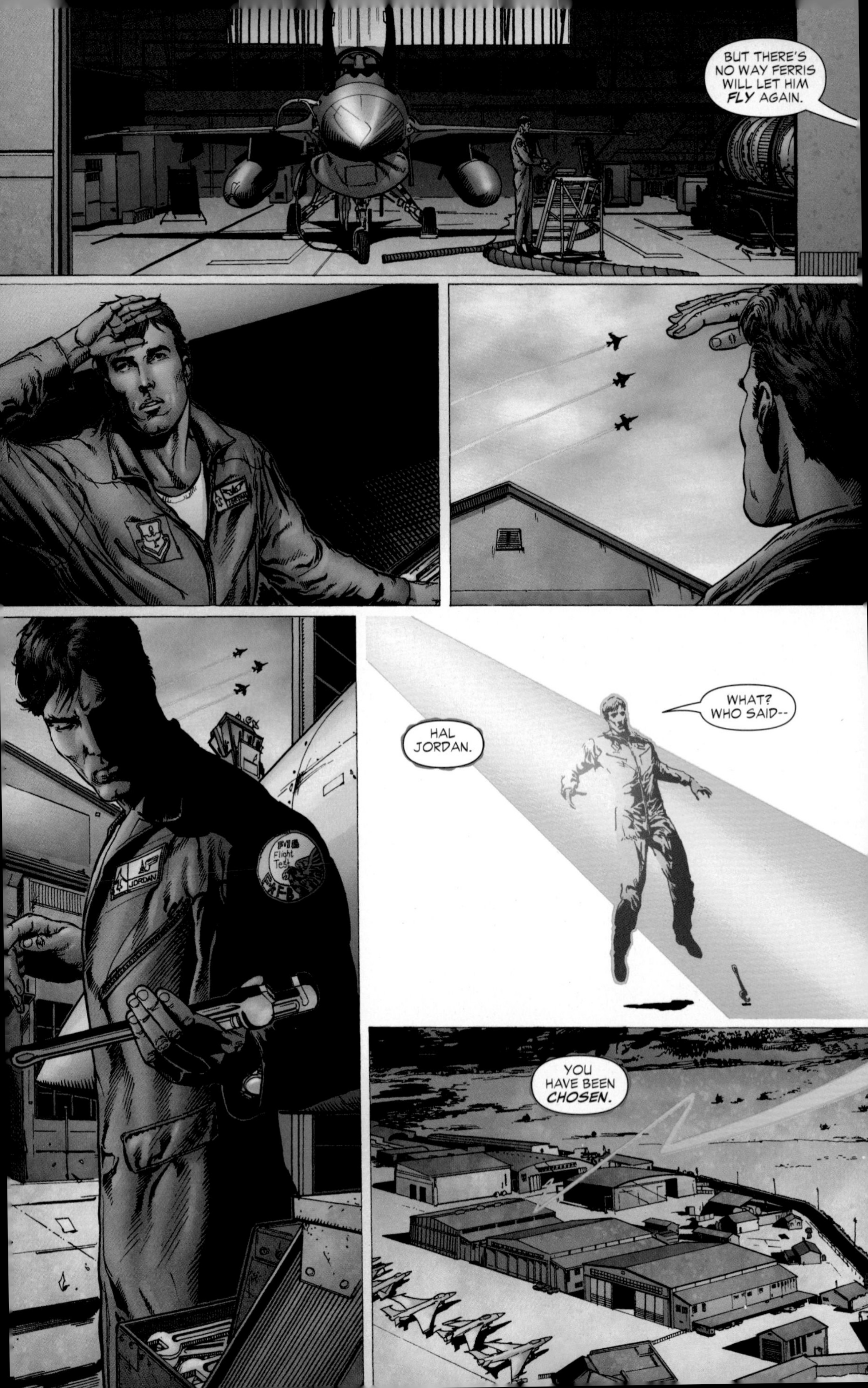
BUT THERE'S NO WAY FERRIS WILL LET HIM FLY AGAIN.
JORDAN
Flight Test
WHAT? WHO SAID--
HAL JORDAN.
YOU HAVE BEEN CHOSEN.

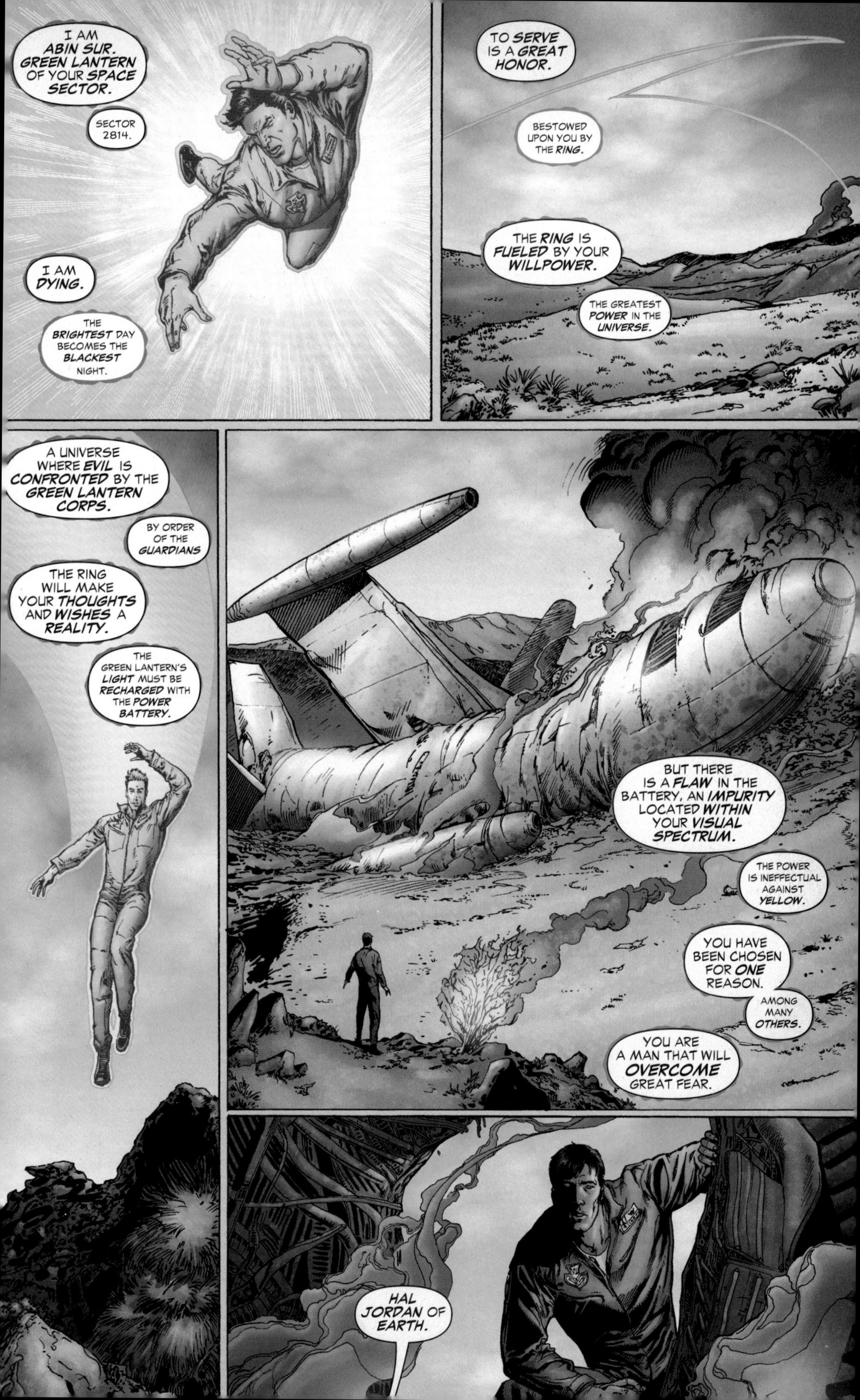
I AM ABIN SUR. GREEN LANTERN OF YOUR SPACE SECTOR.
SECTOR 2814.
I AM DYING.
THE BRIGHTEST DAY BECOMES THE BLACKEST NIGHT.
TO SERVE IS A GREAT HONOR.
BESTOWED UPON YOU BY THE RING.
THE RING IS FUELED BY YOUR WILLPOWER.
THE GREATEST POWER IN THE UNIVERSE.
A UNIVERSE WHERE EVIL IS CONFRONTED BY THE GREEN LANTERN CORPS.
BY ORDER OF THE GUARDIANS
THE RING WILL MAKE YOUR THOUGHTS AND WISHES A REALITY.
THE GREEN LANTERN'S LIGHT MUST BE RECHARGED WITH THE POWER BATTERY.
BUT THERE IS A FLAW IN THE BATTERY, AN IMPURITY LOCATED WITHIN YOUR VISUAL SPECTRUM.
THE POWER IS INEFFECTUAL AGAINST YELLOW.
YOU HAVE BEEN CHOSEN FOR ONE REASON.
AMONG MANY OTHERS.
YOU ARE A MAN THAT WILL OVERCOME GREAT FEAR.
HAL JORDAN OF EARTH.

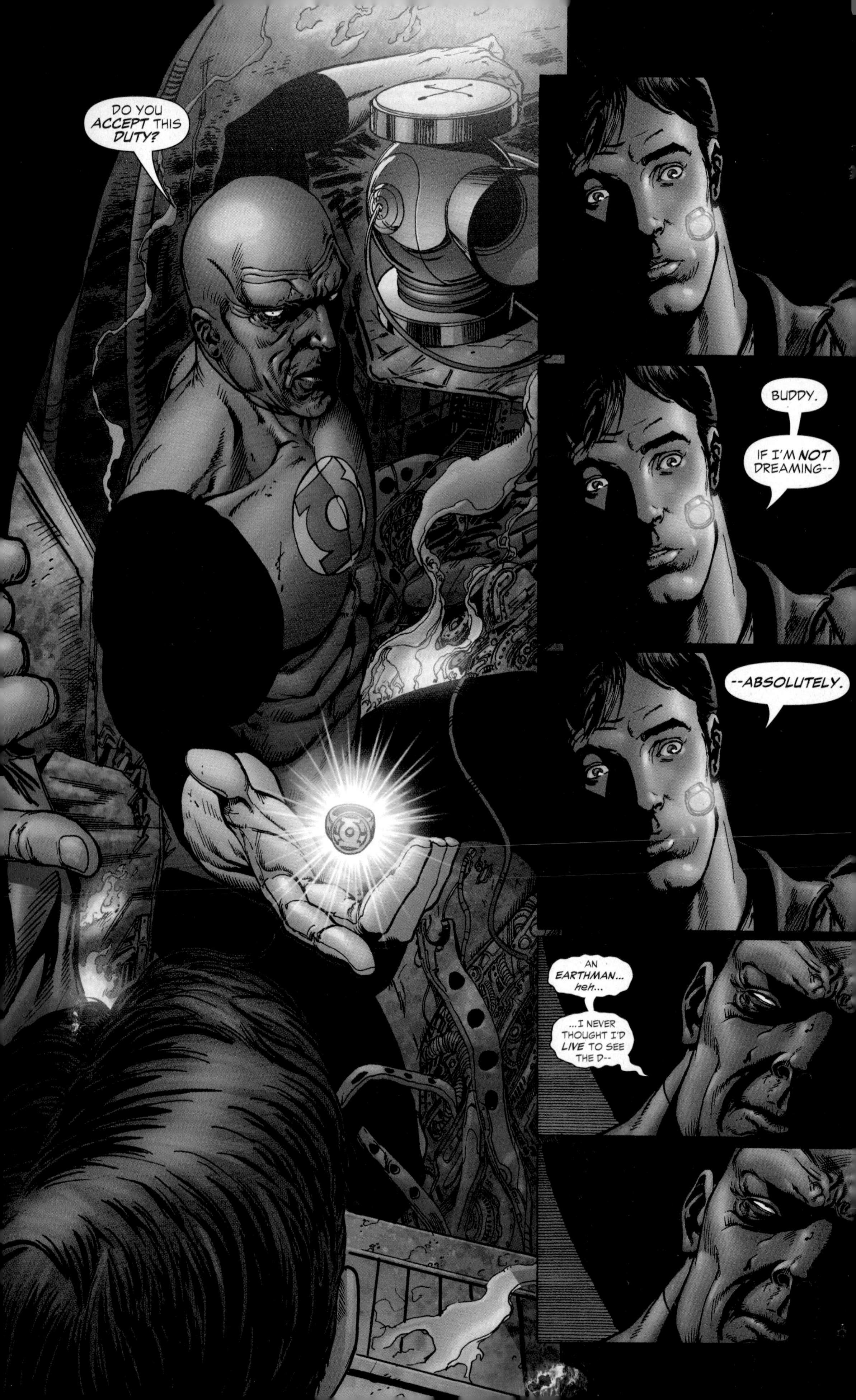

DO YOU ACCEPT THIS DUTY?
BUDDY.
IF I'M NOT DREAMING--
--ABSOLUTELY.
AN EARTHMAN... heh...
...I NEVER THOUGHT I'D LIVE TO SEE THE D--

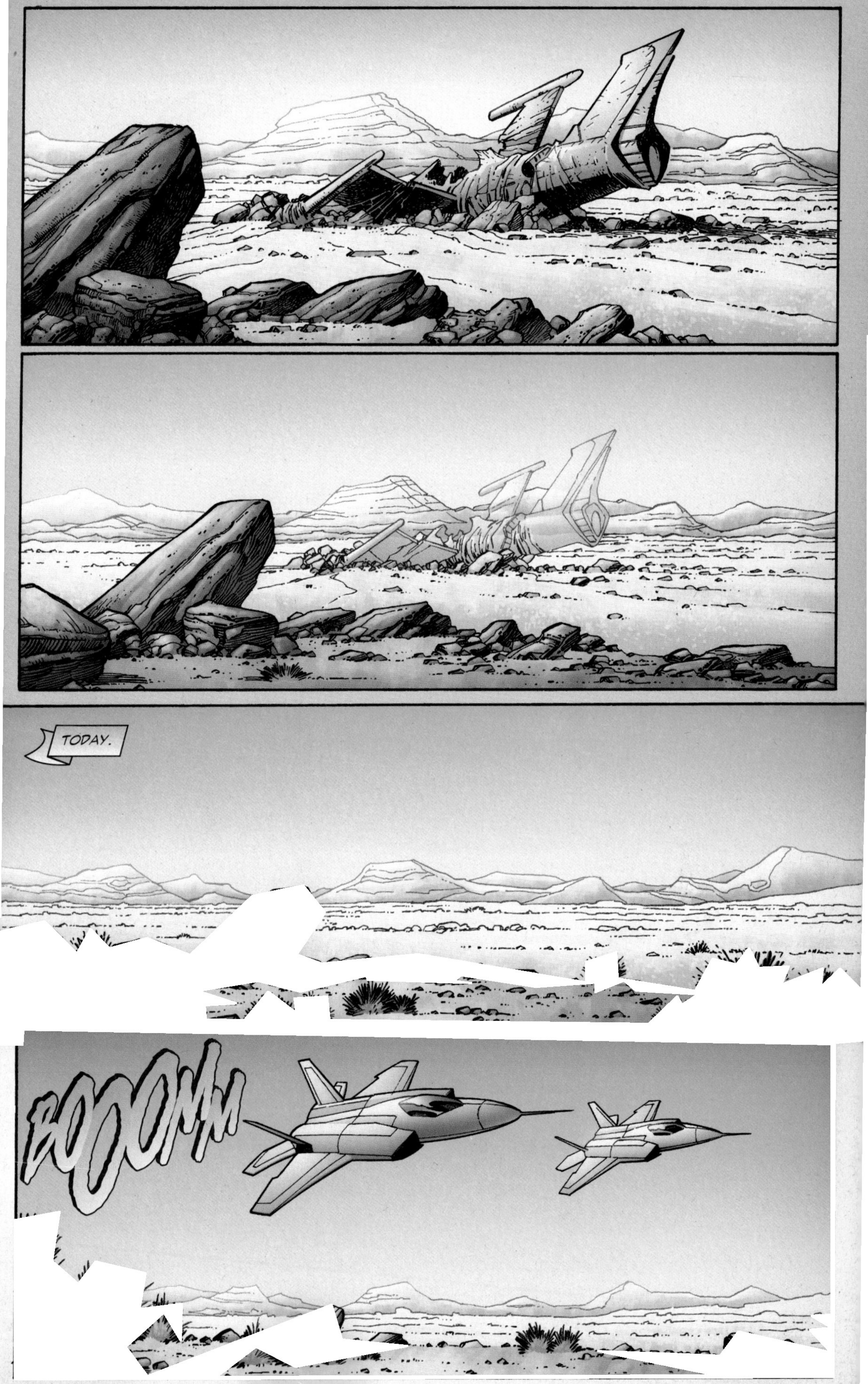
TODAY.
BOOOMM

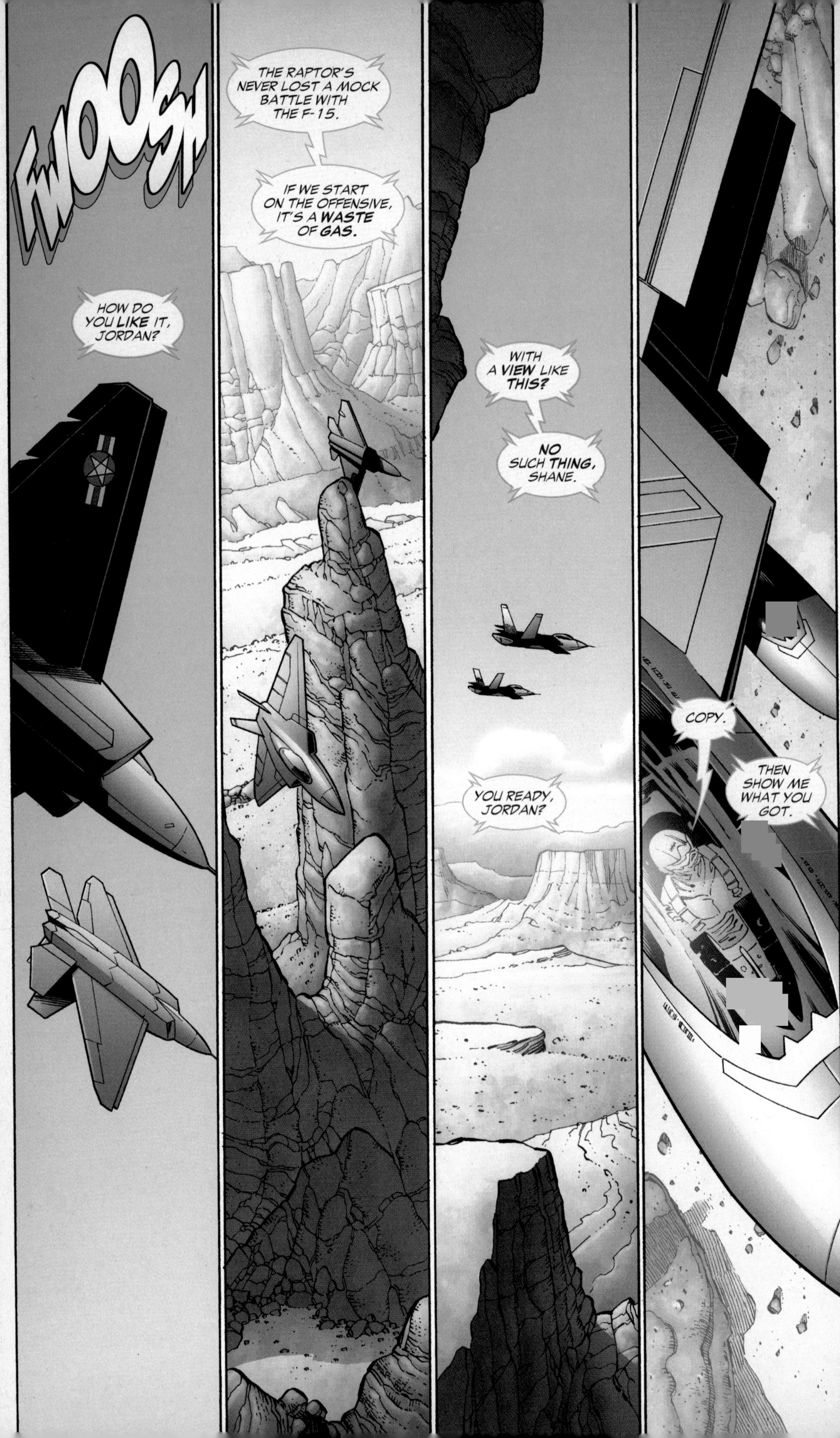
FWOOSH
HOW DO YOU LIKE IT, JORDAN?
THE RAPTOR'S NEVER LOST A MOCK BATTLE WITH THE F-15.
IF WE START ON THE OFFENSIVE, IT'S A WASTE OF GAS.
WITH A VIEW LIKE THIS?
NO SUCH THING, SHANE.
YOU READY, JORDAN?
COPY.
THEN SHOW ME WHAT YOU GOT.

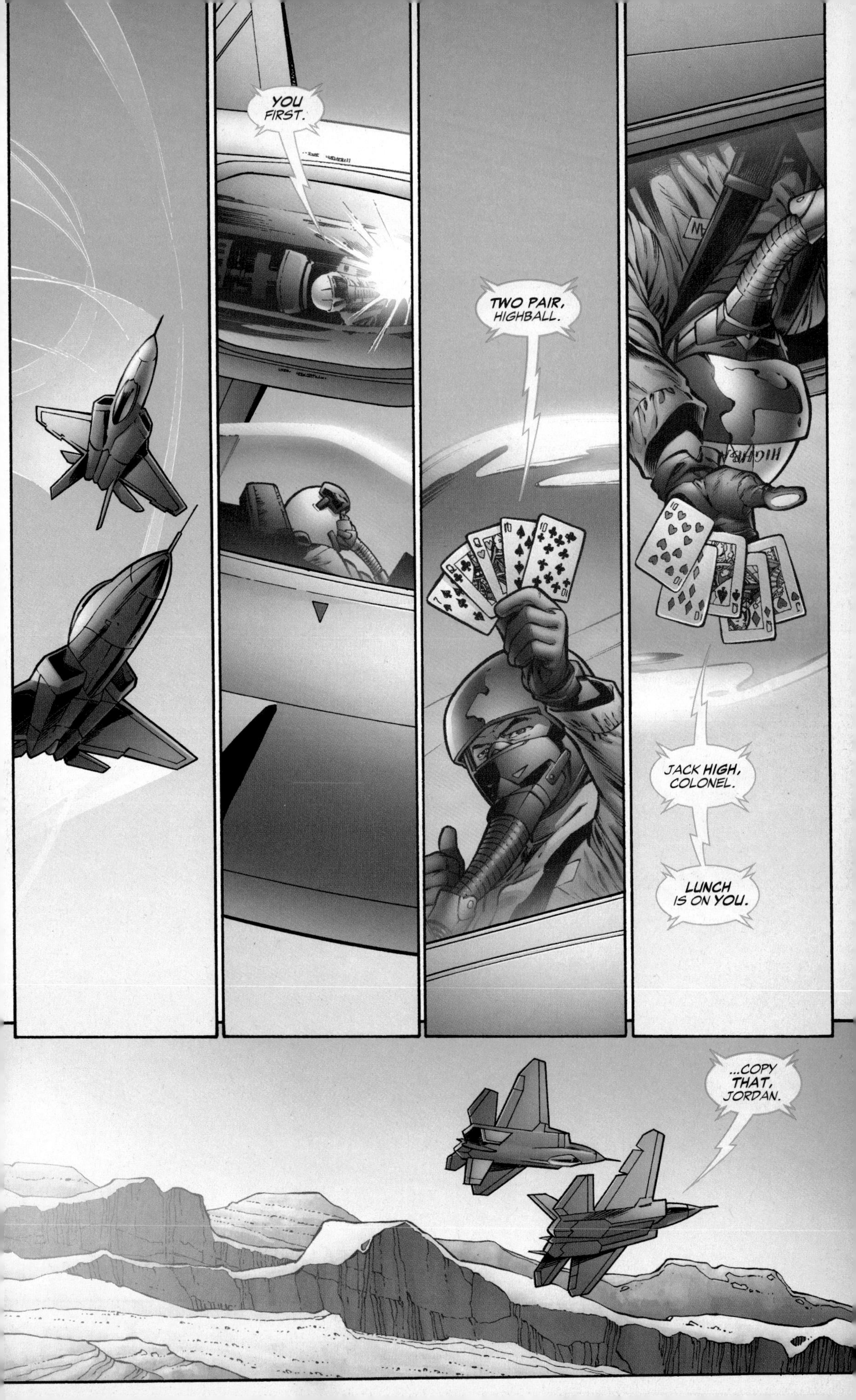
YOU FIRST.
TWO PAIR, HIGHBALL.
JACK HIGH, COLONEL.
LUNCH IS ON YOU.
...COPY THAT, JORDAN.

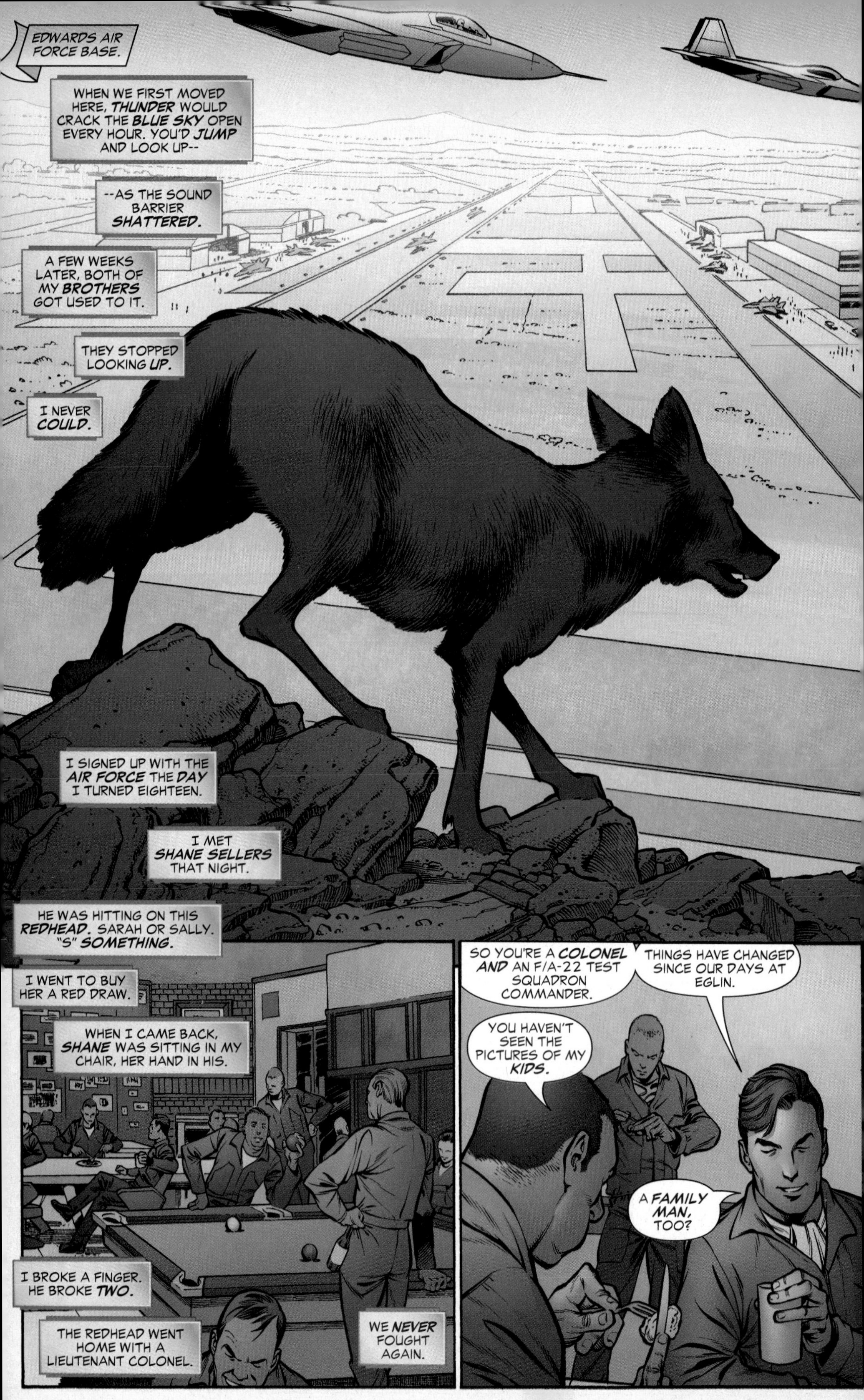
EDWARDS AIR FORCE BASE.
WHEN WE FIRST MOVED HERE, THUNDER WOULD CRACK THE BLUE SKY OPEN EVERY HOUR. YOU'D JUMP AND LOOK UP--
--AS THE SOUND BARRIER SHATTERED.
A FEW WEEKS LATER, BOTH OF MY BROTHERS GOT USED TO IT.
THEY STOPPED LOOKING UP.
I NEVER COULD.
I SIGNED UP WITH THE AIR FORCE THE DAY I TURNED EIGHTEEN.
I MET SHANE SELLERS THAT NIGHT.
HE WAS HITTING ON THIS REDHEAD. SARAH OR SALLY. "S" SOMETHING.
I WENT TO BUY HER A RED DRAW.
WHEN I CAME BACK, SHANE WAS SITTING IN MY CHAIR, HER HAND IN HIS.
I BROKE A FINGER. HE BROKE TWO.
THE REDHEAD WENT HOME WITH A LIEUTENANT COLONEL.
WE NEVER FOUGHT AGAIN.
SO YOU'RE A COLONEL AND AN F/A-22 TEST SQUADRON COMMANDER.
THINGS HAVE CHANGED SINCE OUR DAYS AT EGLIN.
YOU HAVEN'T SEEN THE PICTURES OF MY KIDS.
A FAMILY MAN, TOO?

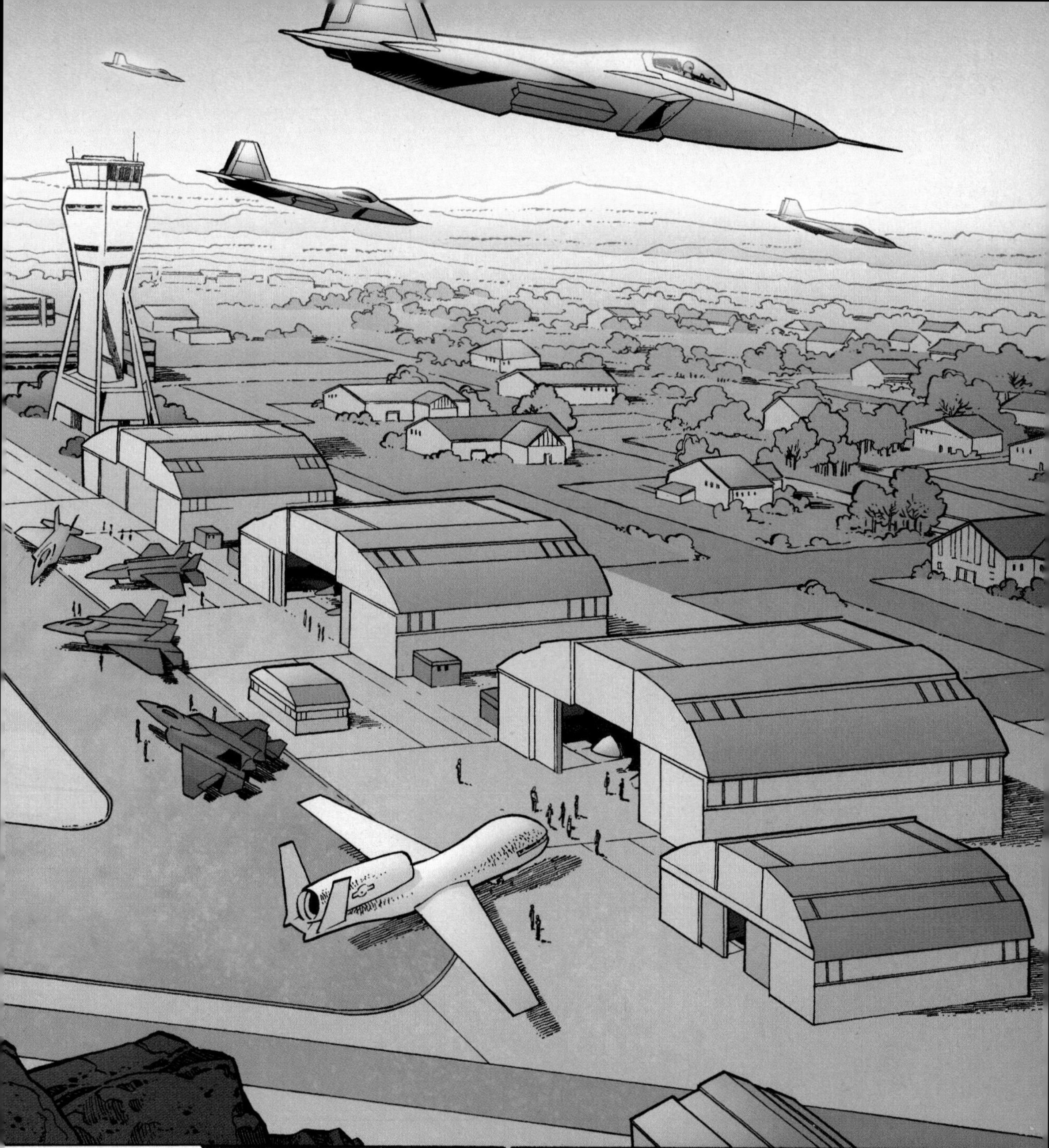

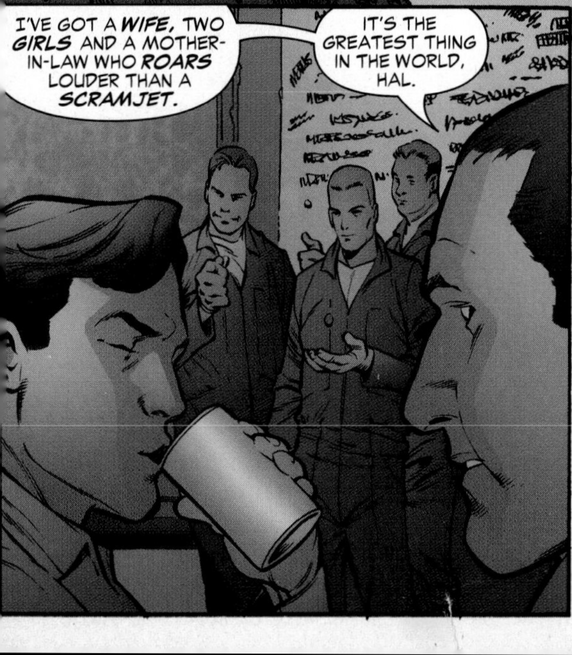
I'VE GOT A WIFE, TWO GIRLS AND A MOTHER-IN-LAW WHO ROARS LOUDER THAN A SCRAMJET.
IT'S THE GREATEST THING IN THE WORLD, HAL.

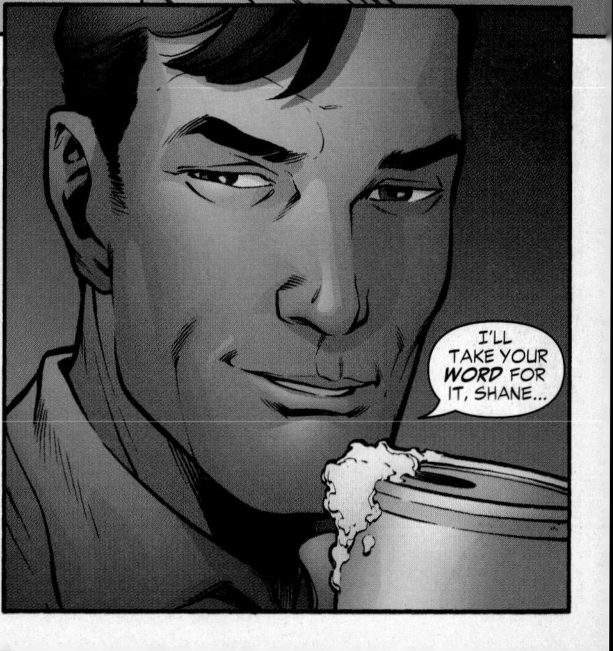
I'LL TAKE YOUR WORD FOR IT, SHANE...

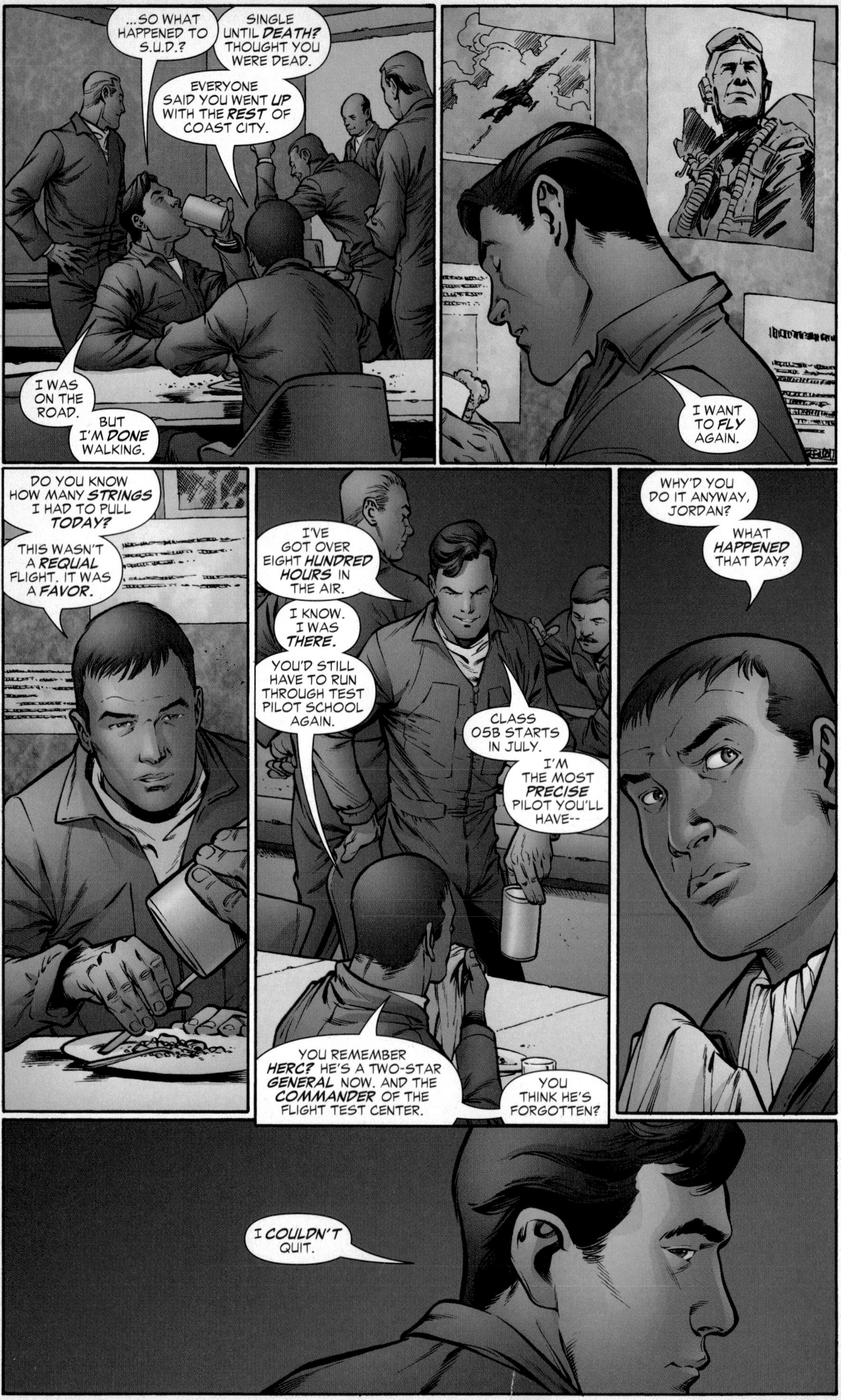
...SO WHAT HAPPENED TO S.U.D.?
SINGLE UNTIL DEATH? THOUGHT YOU WERE DEAD.
EVERYONE SAID YOU WENT UP WITH THE REST OF COAST CITY.
I WAS ON THE ROAD.
BUT I'M DONE WALKING.
I WANT TO FLY AGAIN.
DO YOU KNOW HOW MANY STRINGS I HAD TO PULL TODAY?
THIS WASN'T A REQUAL FLIGHT. IT WAS A FAVOR.
I'VE GOT OVER EIGHT HUNDRED HOURS IN THE AIR.
I KNOW. I WAS THERE.
YOU'D STILL HAVE TO RUN THROUGH TEST PILOT SCHOOL AGAIN.
CLASS 05B STARTS IN JULY.
I'M THE MOST PRECISE PILOT YOU'LL HAVE--
YOU REMEMBER HERC? HE'S A TWO-STAR GENERAL NOW. AND THE COMMANDER OF THE FLIGHT TEST CENTER.
YOU THINK HE'S FORGOTTEN?
WHY'D YOU DO IT ANYWAY, JORDAN?
WHAT HAPPENED THAT DAY?
I COULDN'T QUIT.

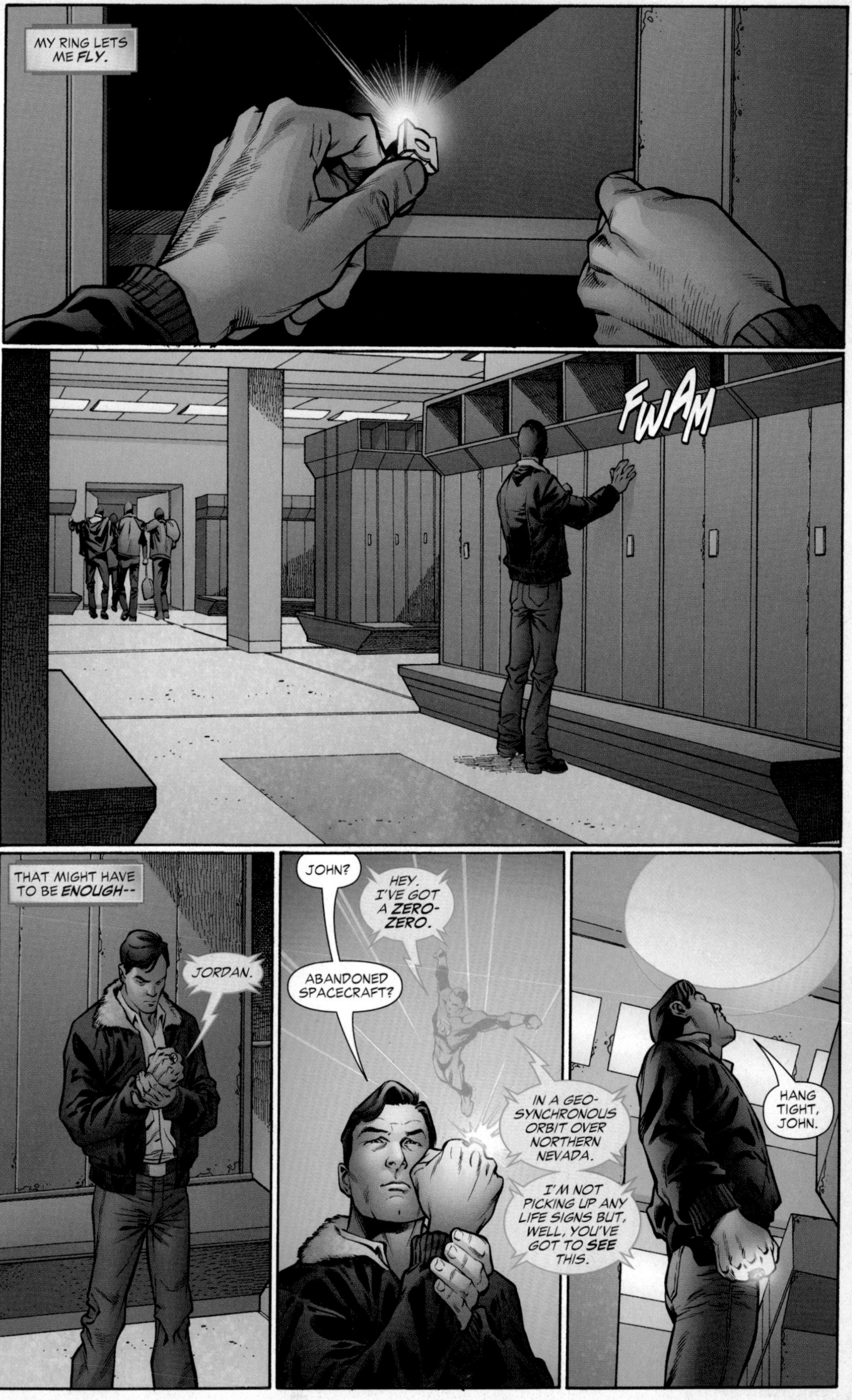
MY RING LETS ME FLY.
FWAM
THAT MIGHT HAVE TO BE ENOUGH--
JORDAN.
JOHN?
HEY. I'VE GOT A ZERO-ZERO.
ABANDONED SPACECRAFT?
IN A GEO-SYNCHRONOUS ORBIT OVER NORTHERN NEVADA.
I'M NOT PICKING UP ANY LIFE SIGNS BUT, WELL, YOU'VE GOT TO SEE THIS.
HANG TIGHT, JOHN.

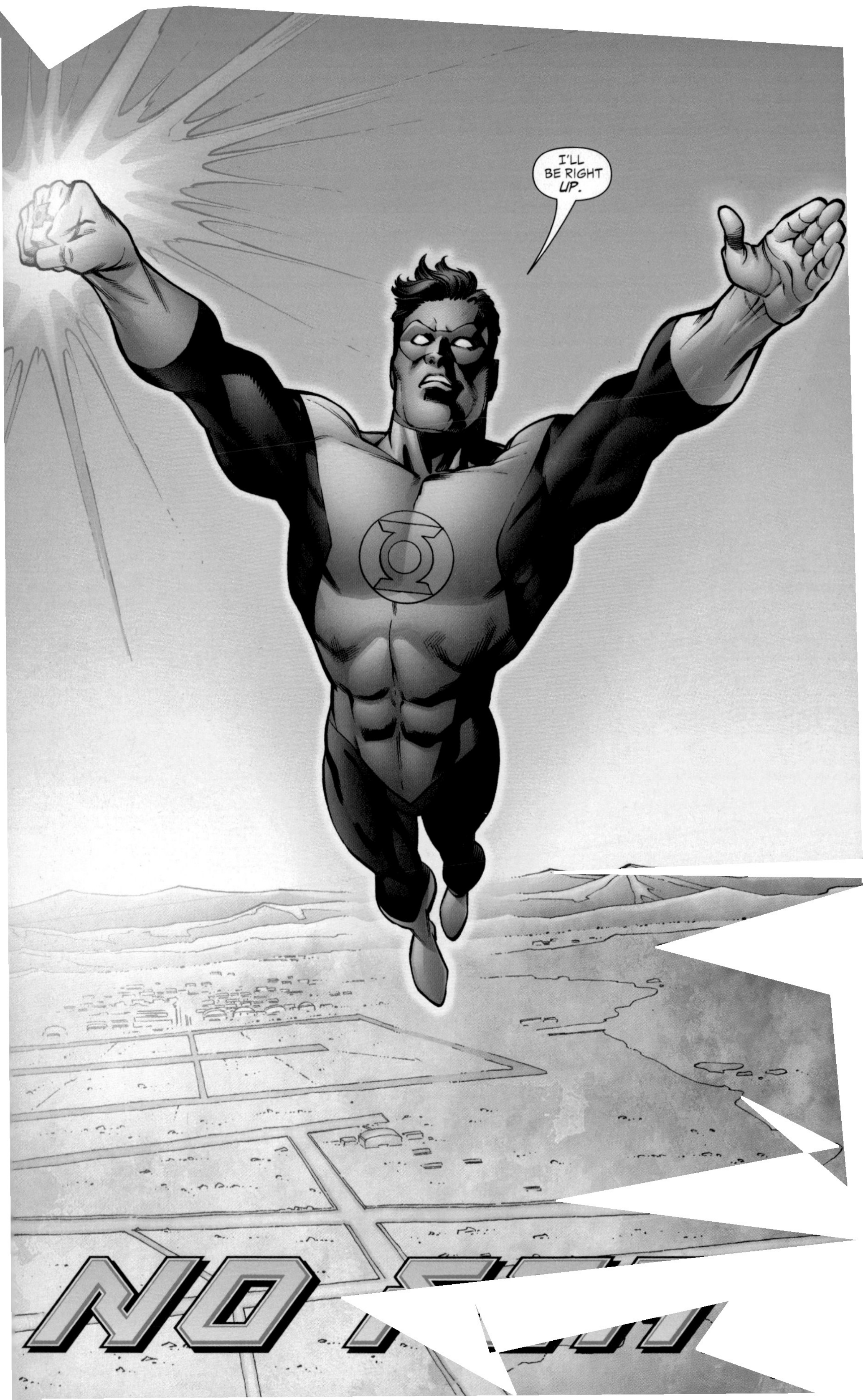
I'LL BE RIGHT UP.
NO

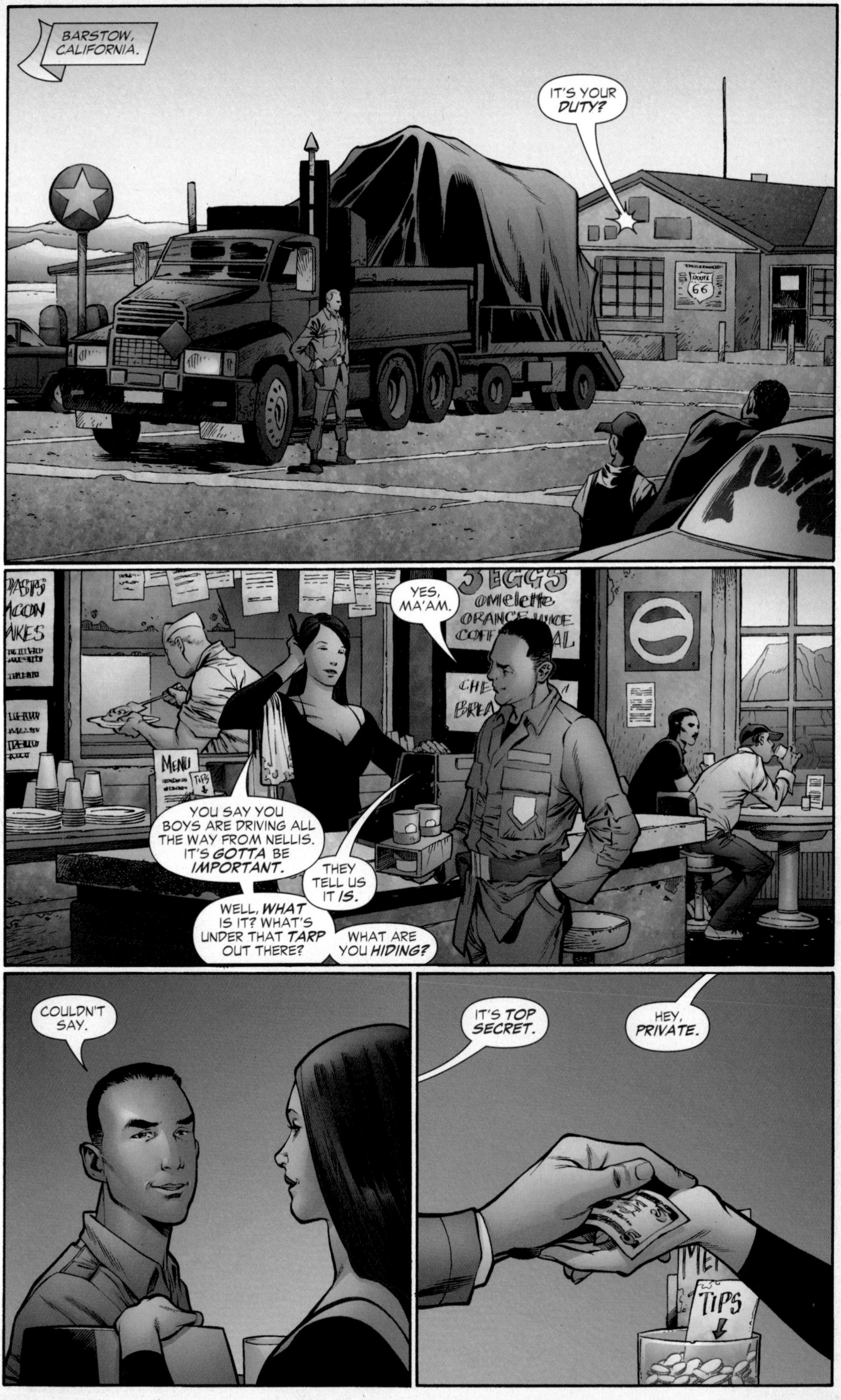
BARSTOW, CALIFORNIA.
IT'S YOUR *DUTY?*
ROUTE 66
YES, MA'AM.
YOU SAY YOU BOYS ARE DRIVING ALL THE WAY FROM NELLIS. IT'S *GOTTA* BE *IMPORTANT.*
THEY TELL US IT *IS.*
WELL, *WHAT* IS IT? WHAT'S UNDER THAT *TARP* OUT THERE?
WHAT ARE YOU *HIDING?*
COULDN'T SAY.
IT'S *TOP SECRET.*
HEY, *PRIVATE.*
TIPS

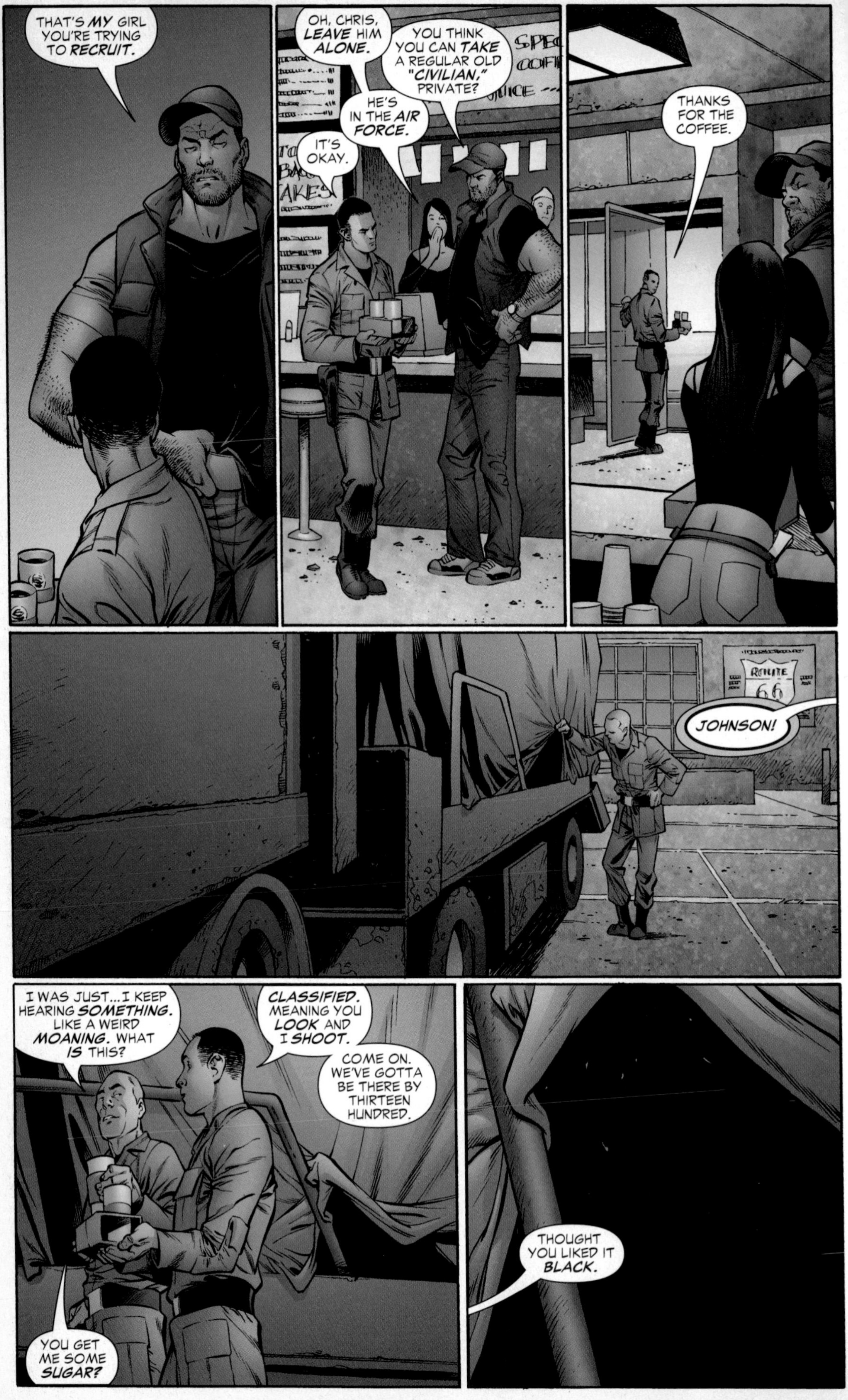
THAT'S MY GIRL YOU'RE TRYING TO RECRUIT.
OH, CHRIS, LEAVE HIM ALONE.
HE'S IN THE AIR FORCE.
IT'S OKAY.
YOU THINK YOU CAN TAKE A REGULAR OLD "CIVILIAN," PRIVATE?
THANKS FOR THE COFFEE.
ROUTE 66
JOHNSON!
I WAS JUST... I KEEP HEARING SOMETHING. LIKE A WEIRD MOANING. WHAT IS THIS?
CLASSIFIED. MEANING YOU LOOK AND I SHOOT.
COME ON. WE'VE GOTTA BE THERE BY THIRTEEN HUNDRED.
YOU GET ME SOME SUGAR?
THOUGHT YOU LIKED IT BLACK.

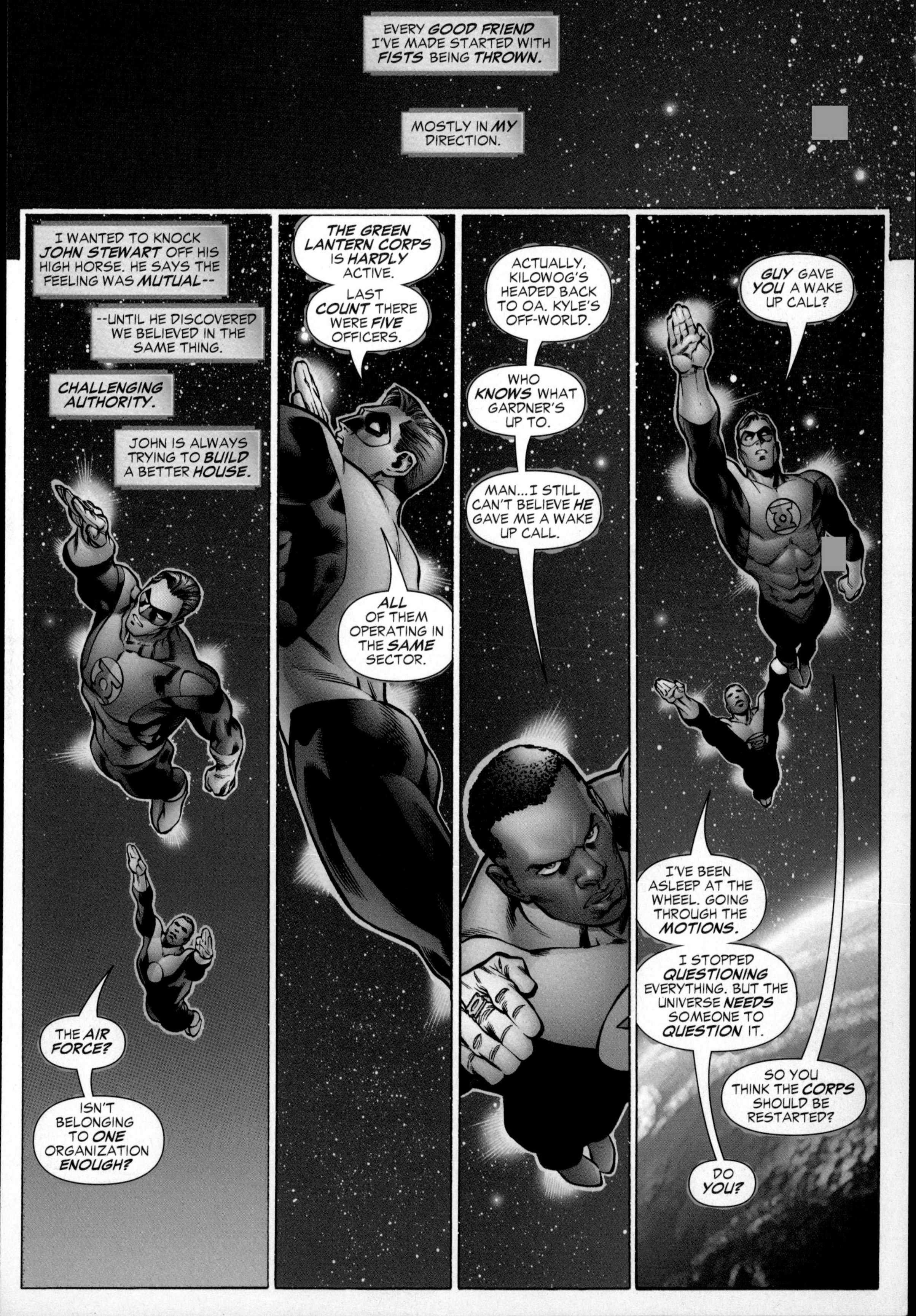

EVERY GOOD FRIEND I'VE MADE STARTED WITH FISTS BEING THROWN.
MOSTLY IN MY DIRECTION.
I WANTED TO KNOCK JOHN STEWART OFF HIS HIGH HORSE. HE SAYS THE FEELING WAS MUTUAL--
--UNTIL HE DISCOVERED WE BELIEVED IN THE SAME THING.
CHALLENGING AUTHORITY.
JOHN IS ALWAYS TRYING TO BUILD A BETTER HOUSE.
THE AIR FORCE?
ISN'T BELONGING TO ONE ORGANIZATION ENOUGH?
THE GREEN LANTERN CORPS IS HARDLY ACTIVE.
LAST COUNT THERE WERE FIVE OFFICERS.
ALL OF THEM OPERATING IN THE SAME SECTOR.
ACTUALLY, KILOWOG'S HEADED BACK TO OA. KYLE'S OFF-WORLD.
WHO KNOWS WHAT GARDNER'S UP TO.
MAN...I STILL CAN'T BELIEVE HE GAVE ME A WAKE UP CALL.
GUY GAVE YOU A WAKE UP CALL?
I'VE BEEN ASLEEP AT THE WHEEL. GOING THROUGH THE MOTIONS.
I STOPPED QUESTIONING EVERYTHING. BUT THE UNIVERSE NEEDS SOMEONE TO QUESTION IT.
SO YOU THINK THE CORPS SHOULD BE RESTARTED?
DO YOU?

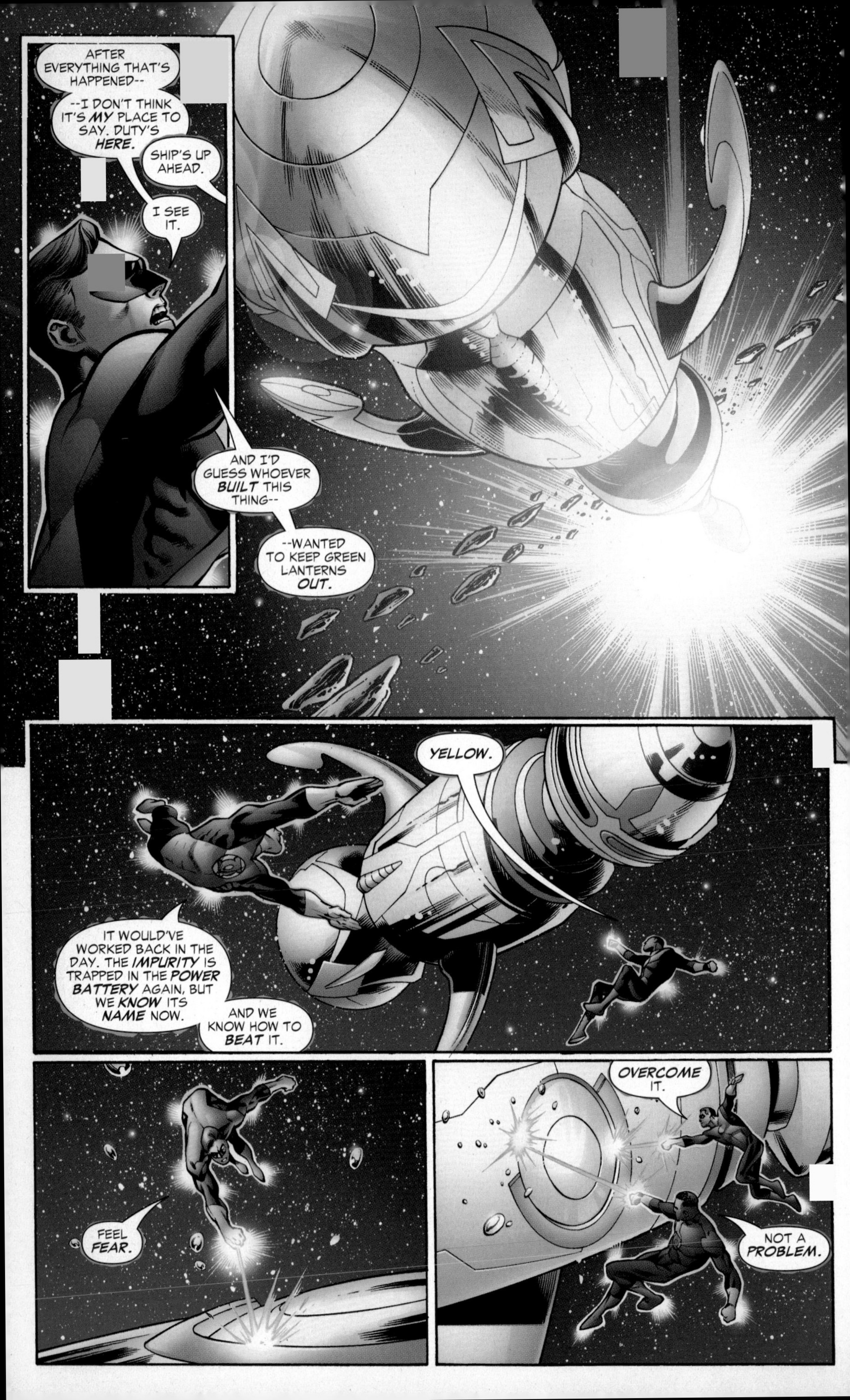
AFTER EVERYTHING THAT'S HAPPENED--
--I DON'T THINK IT'S MY PLACE TO SAY. DUTY'S HERE.
SHIP'S UP AHEAD.
I SEE IT.
AND I'D GUESS WHOEVER BUILT THIS THING--
--WANTED TO KEEP GREEN LANTERNS OUT.
YELLOW.
IT WOULD'VE WORKED BACK IN THE DAY. THE IMPURITY IS TRAPPED IN THE POWER BATTERY AGAIN, BUT WE KNOW ITS NAME NOW.
AND WE KNOW HOW TO BEAT IT.
FEEL FEAR.
OVERCOME IT.
NOT A PROBLEM.

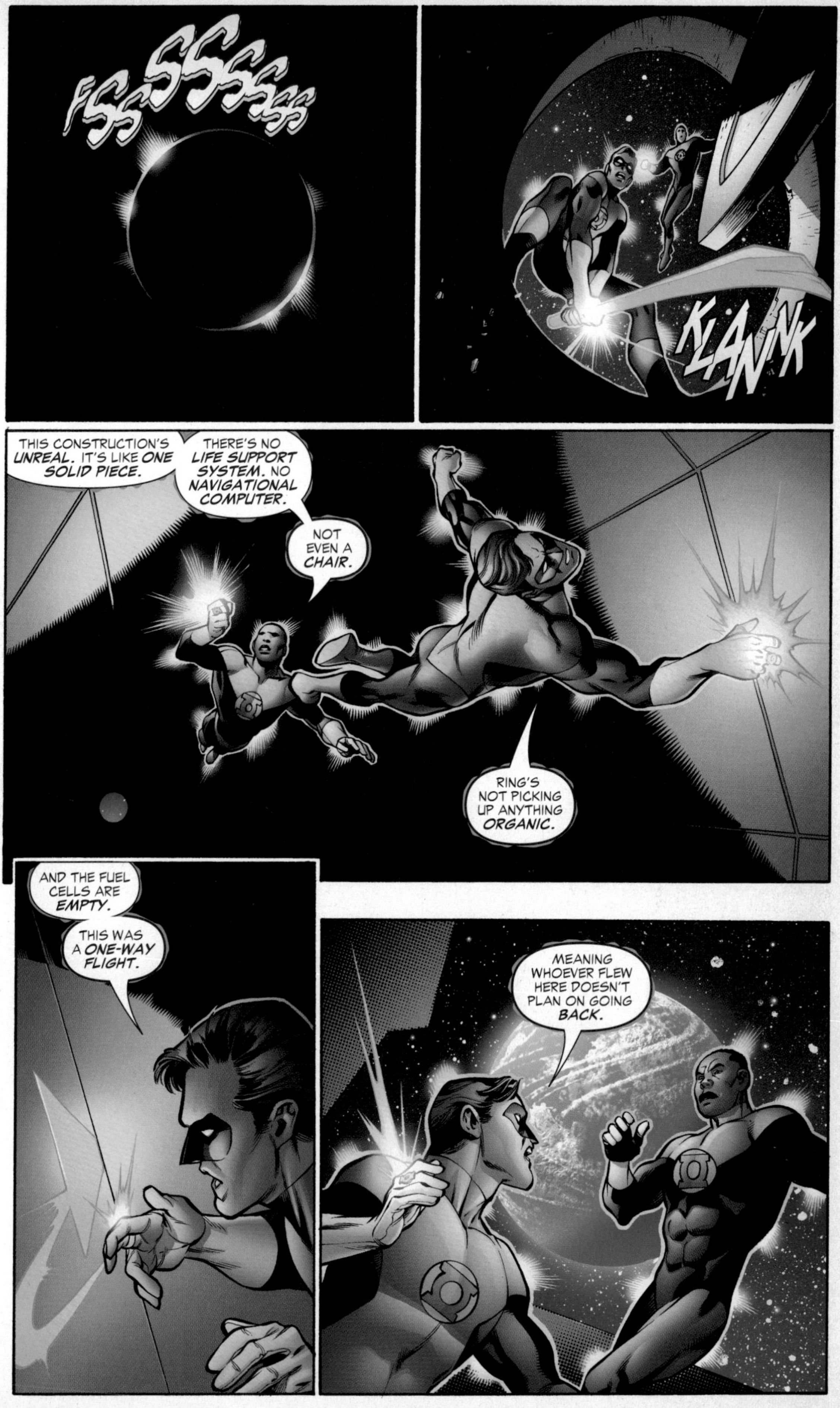
FSSSSSSSSS
KLANNK
THIS CONSTRUCTION'S UNREAL. IT'S LIKE ONE SOLID PIECE.
THERE'S NO LIFE SUPPORT SYSTEM. NO NAVIGATIONAL COMPUTER.
NOT EVEN A CHAIR.
RING'S NOT PICKING UP ANYTHING ORGANIC.
AND THE FUEL CELLS ARE EMPTY.
THIS WAS A ONE-WAY FLIGHT.
MEANING WHOEVER FLEW HERE DOESN'T PLAN ON GOING BACK.

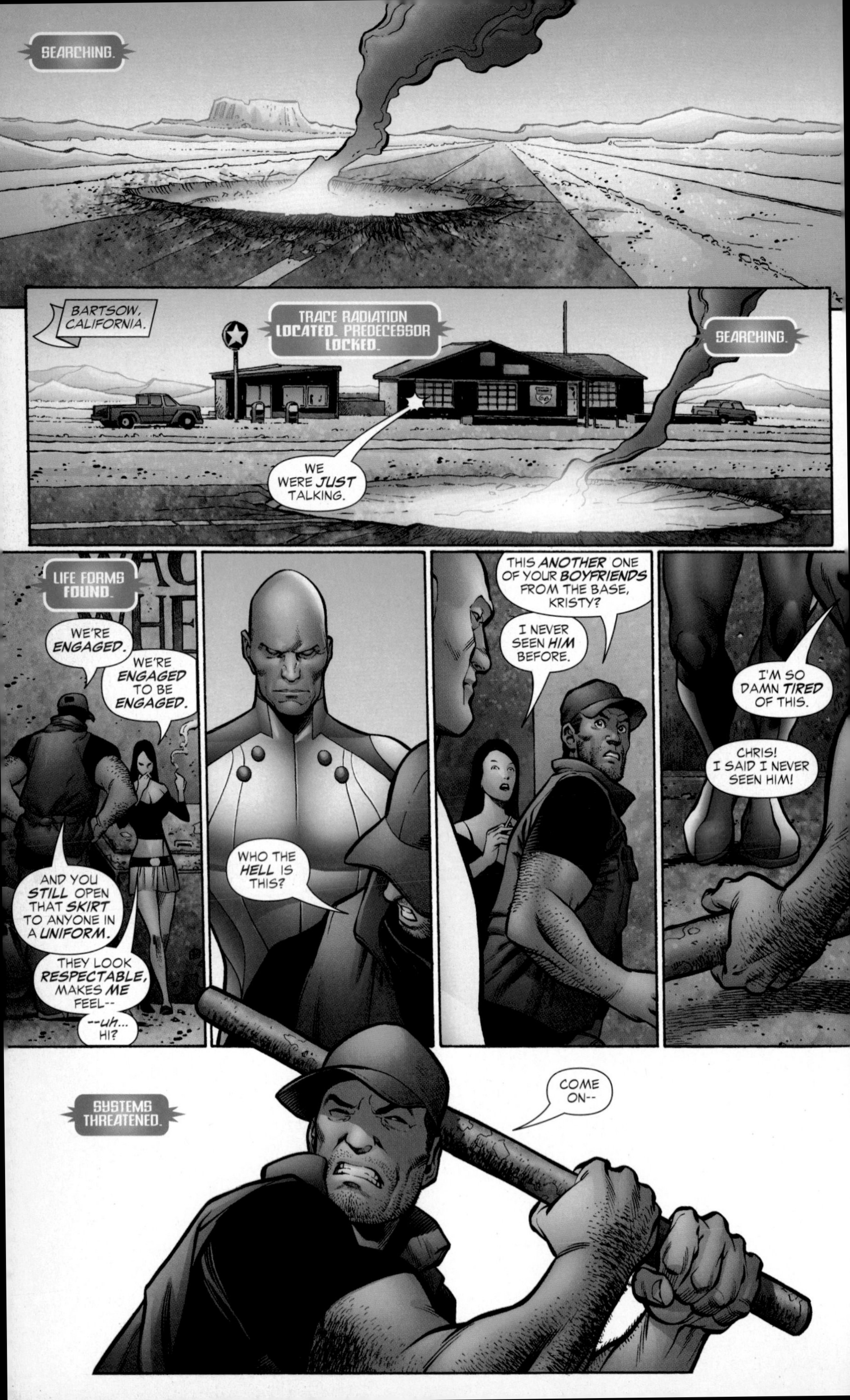
SEARCHING.
BARTSOW, CALIFORNIA.
TRACE RADIATION LOCATED. PREDECESSOR LOCKED.
SEARCHING.
WE WERE JUST TALKING.
LIFE FORMS FOUND.
WE'RE ENGAGED.
WE'RE ENGAGED TO BE ENGAGED.
AND YOU STILL OPEN THAT SKIRT TO ANYONE IN A UNIFORM.
THEY LOOK RESPECTABLE, MAKES ME FEEL--
--uh... HI?
WHO THE HELL IS THIS?
THIS ANOTHER ONE OF YOUR BOYFRIENDS FROM THE BASE, KRISTY?
I NEVER SEEN HIM BEFORE.
I'M SO DAMN TIRED OF THIS.
CHRIS! I SAID I NEVER SEEN HIM!
SYSTEMS THREATENED.
COME ON--

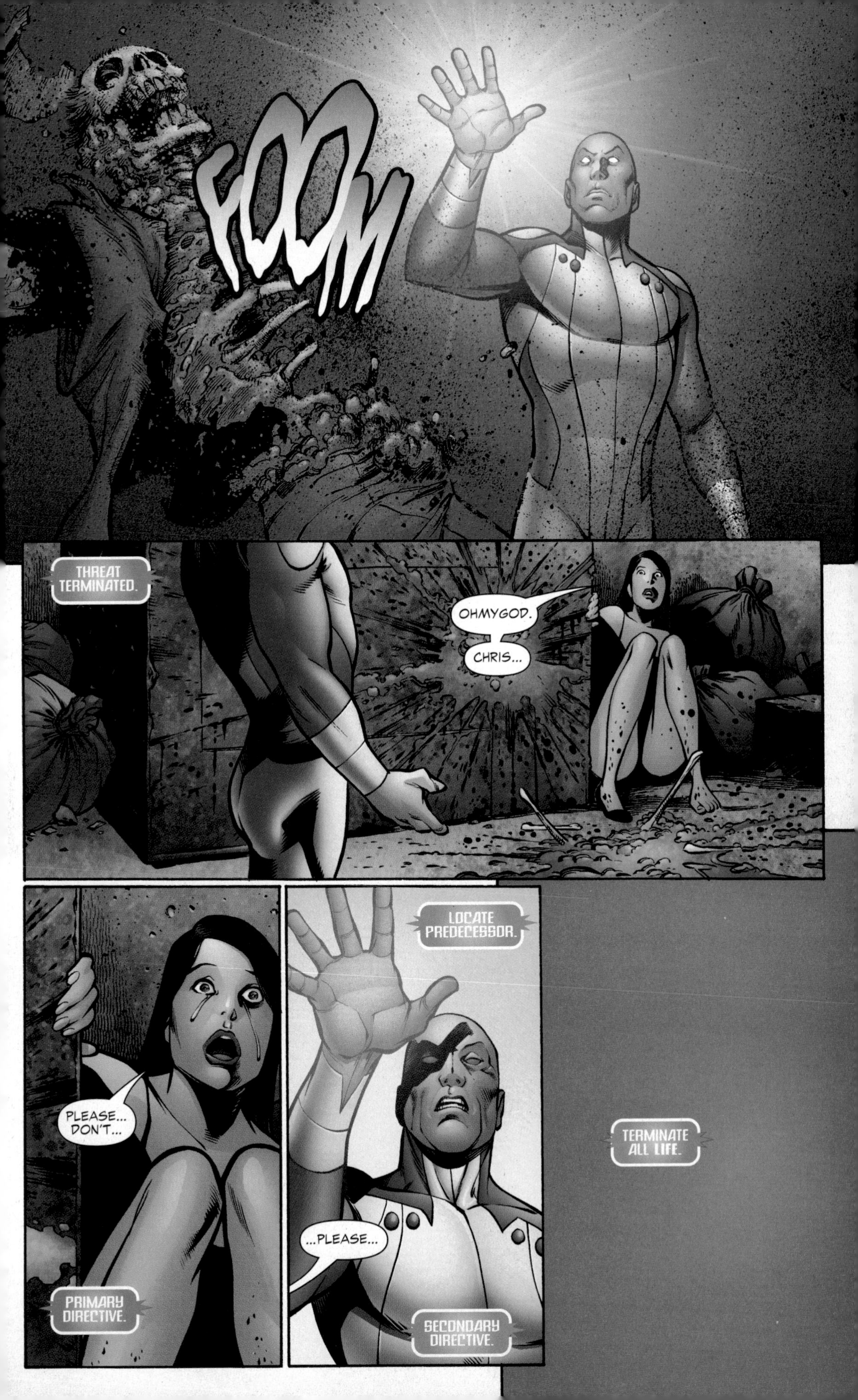
FOOM
THREAT TERMINATED.
OHMYGOD.
CHRIS...
PLEASE... DON'T...
PRIMARY DIRECTIVE.
LOCATE PREDECESSOR.
...PLEASE...
SECONDARY DIRECTIVE.
TERMINATE ALL LIFE.

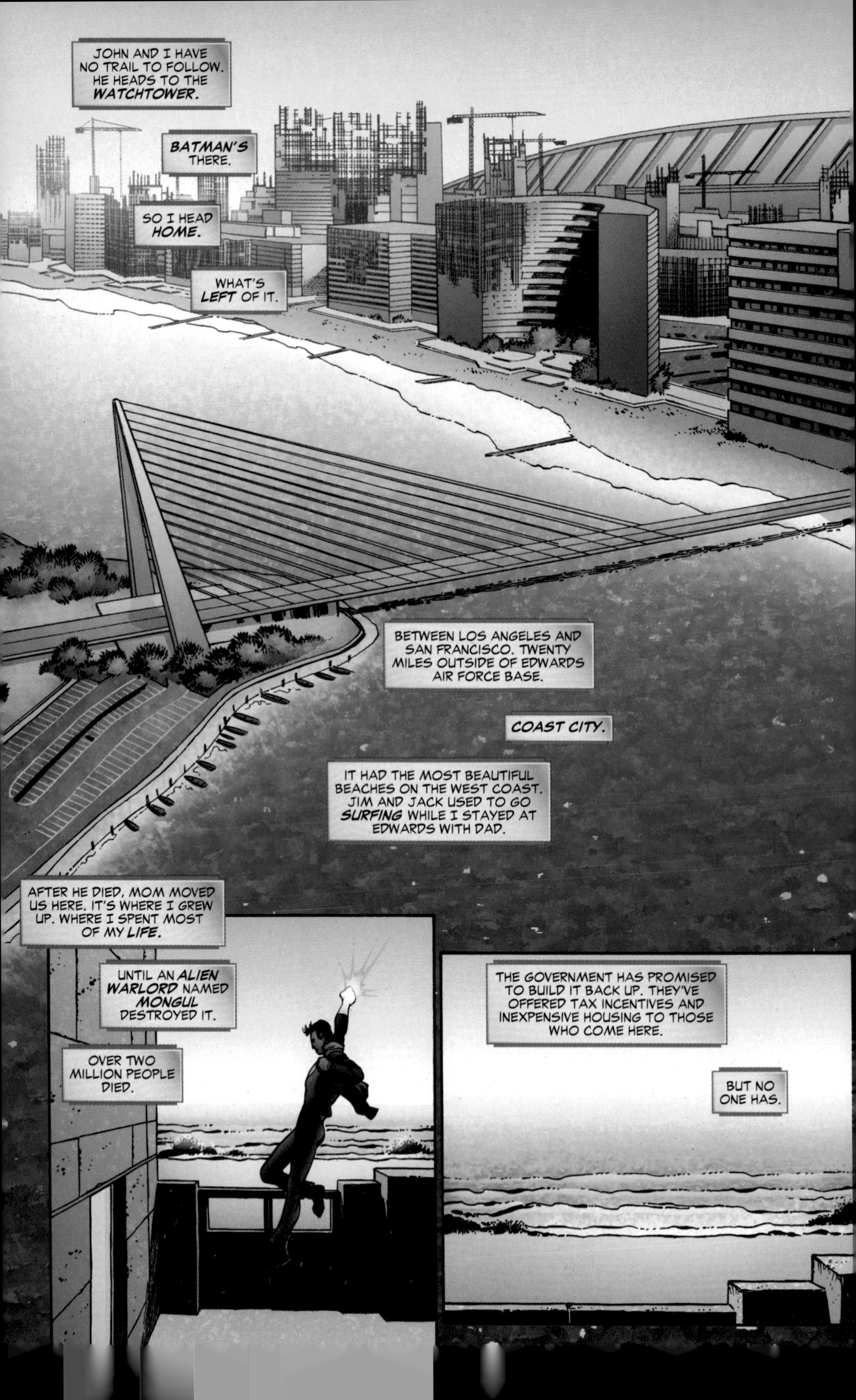
JOHN AND I HAVE NO TRAIL TO FOLLOW. HE HEADS TO THE WATCHTOWER.
BATMAN'S THERE.
SO I HEAD HOME.
WHAT'S LEFT OF IT.
BETWEEN LOS ANGELES AND SAN FRANCISCO. TWENTY MILES OUTSIDE OF EDWARDS AIR FORCE BASE.
COAST CITY.
IT HAD THE MOST BEAUTIFUL BEACHES ON THE WEST COAST. JIM AND JACK USED TO GO SURFING WHILE I STAYED AT EDWARDS WITH DAD.
AFTER HE DIED, MOM MOVED US HERE. IT'S WHERE I GREW UP. WHERE I SPENT MOST OF MY LIFE.
UNTIL AN ALIEN WARLORD NAMED MONGUL DESTROYED IT.
OVER TWO MILLION PEOPLE DIED.
THE GOVERNMENT HAS PROMISED TO BUILD IT BACK UP. THEY'VE OFFERED TAX INCENTIVES AND INEXPENSIVE HOUSING TO THOSE WHO COME HERE.
BUT NO ONE HAS.

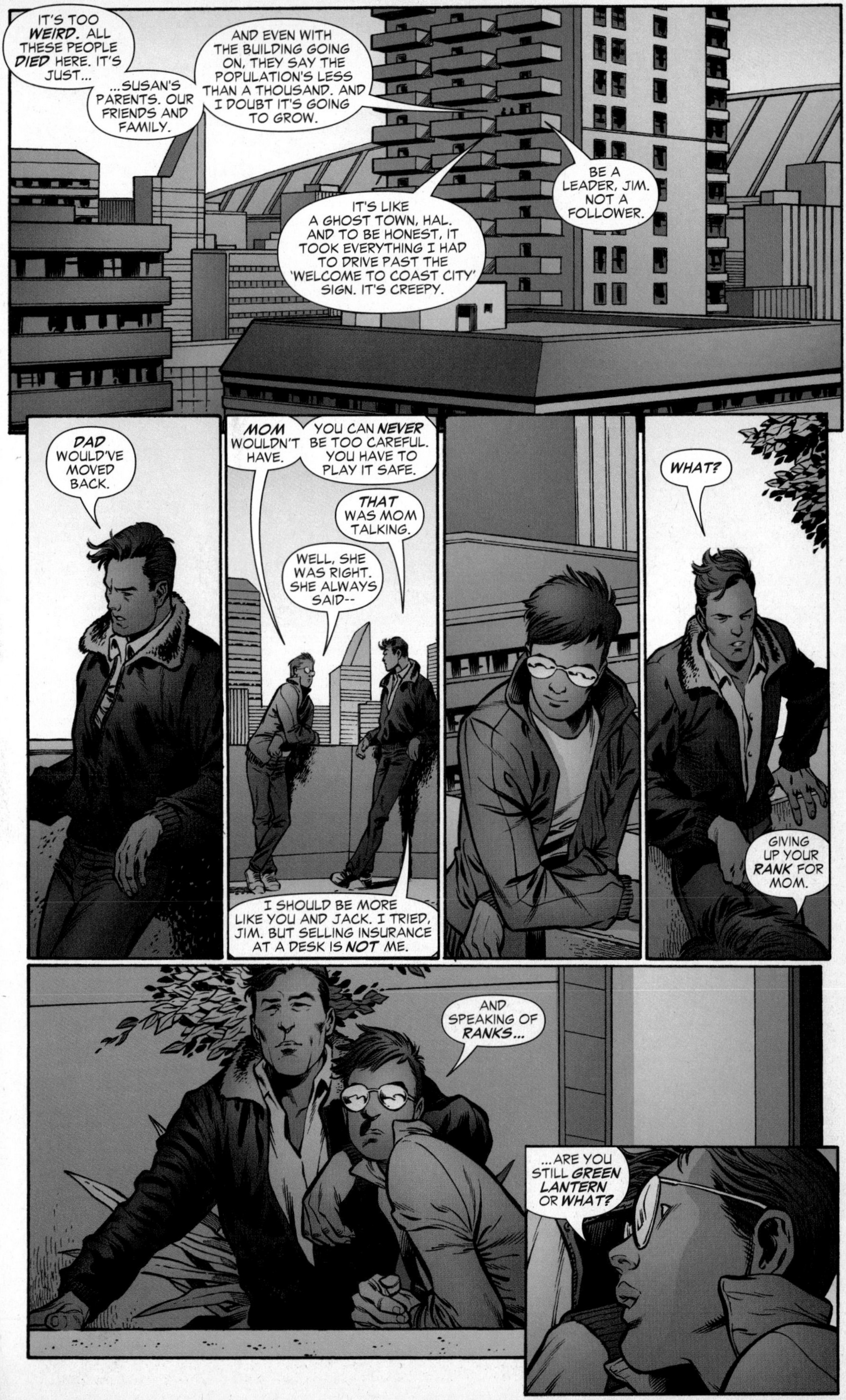
IT'S TOO WEIRD. ALL THESE PEOPLE DIED HERE. IT'S JUST...
...SUSAN'S PARENTS. OUR FRIENDS AND FAMILY.
AND EVEN WITH THE BUILDING GOING ON, THEY SAY THE POPULATION'S LESS THAN A THOUSAND. AND I DOUBT IT'S GOING TO GROW.
IT'S LIKE A GHOST TOWN, HAL. AND TO BE HONEST, IT TOOK EVERYTHING I HAD TO DRIVE PAST THE 'WELCOME TO COAST CITY' SIGN. IT'S CREEPY.
BE A LEADER, JIM. NOT A FOLLOWER.
DAD WOULD'VE MOVED BACK.
MOM WOULDN'T HAVE.
YOU CAN NEVER BE TOO CAREFUL. YOU HAVE TO PLAY IT SAFE.
THAT WAS MOM TALKING.
WELL, SHE WAS RIGHT. SHE ALWAYS SAID--
I SHOULD BE MORE LIKE YOU AND JACK. I TRIED, JIM. BUT SELLING INSURANCE AT A DESK IS NOT ME.
WHAT?
GIVING UP YOUR RANK FOR MOM.
AND SPEAKING OF RANKS...
...ARE YOU STILL GREEN LANTERN OR WHAT?

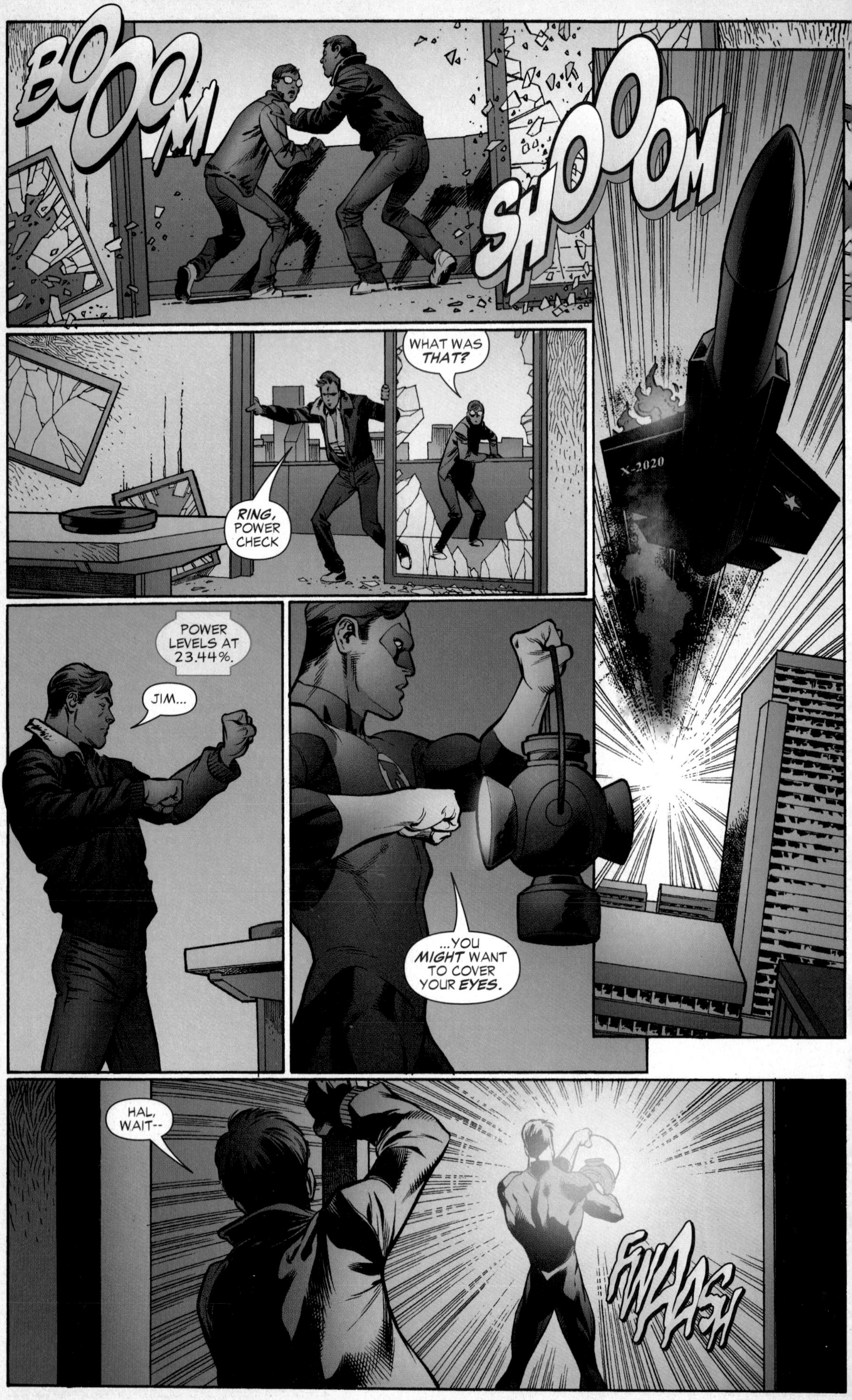
BOOOOM
SHOOOOM
X-2020
WHAT WAS THAT?
RING, POWER CHECK
POWER LEVELS AT 23.44%.
JIM...
...YOU MIGHT WANT TO COVER YOUR EYES.
HAL, WAIT--
FWAASH

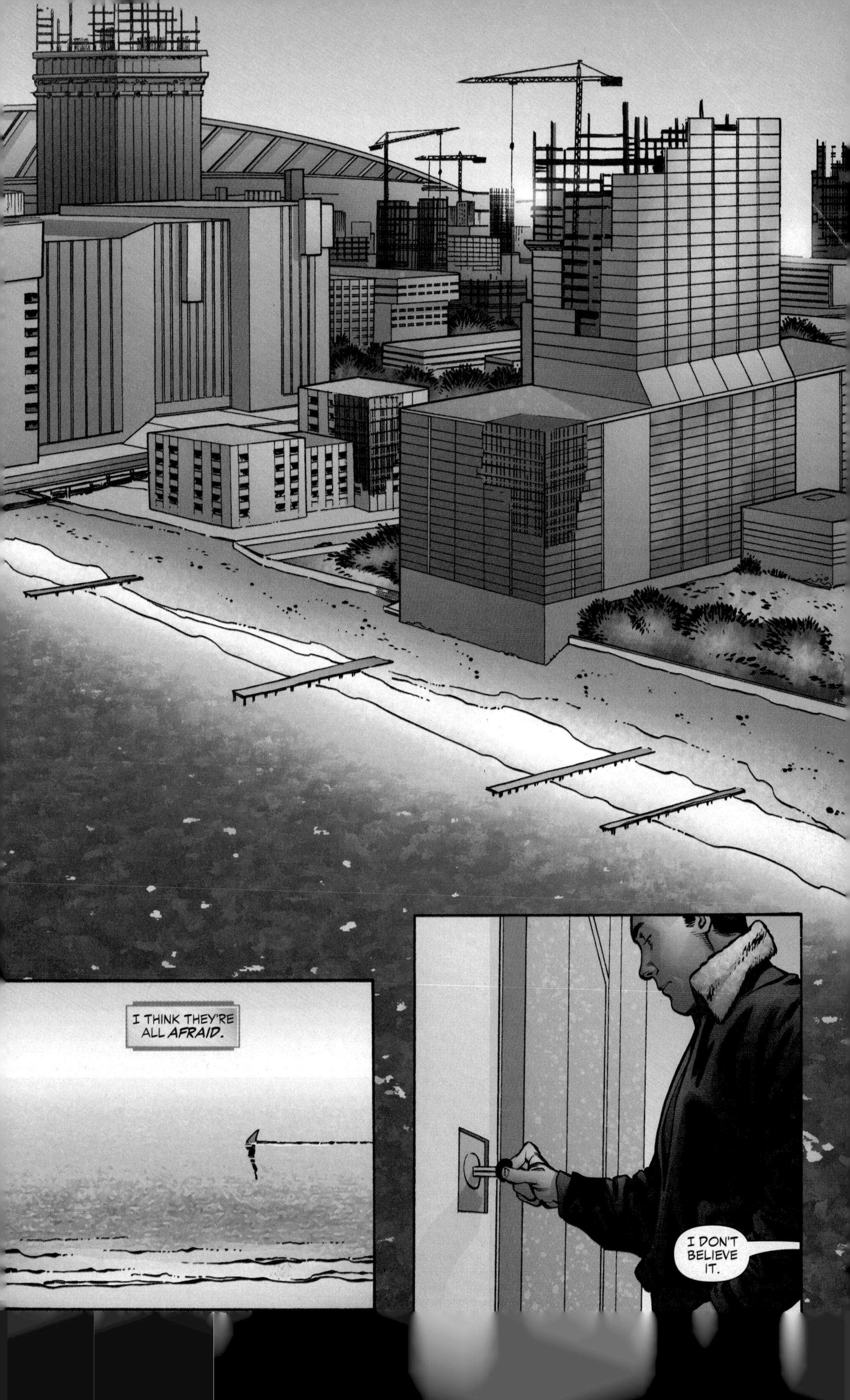
I THINK THEY'RE ALL *AFRAID*.
I DON'T BELIEVE IT.

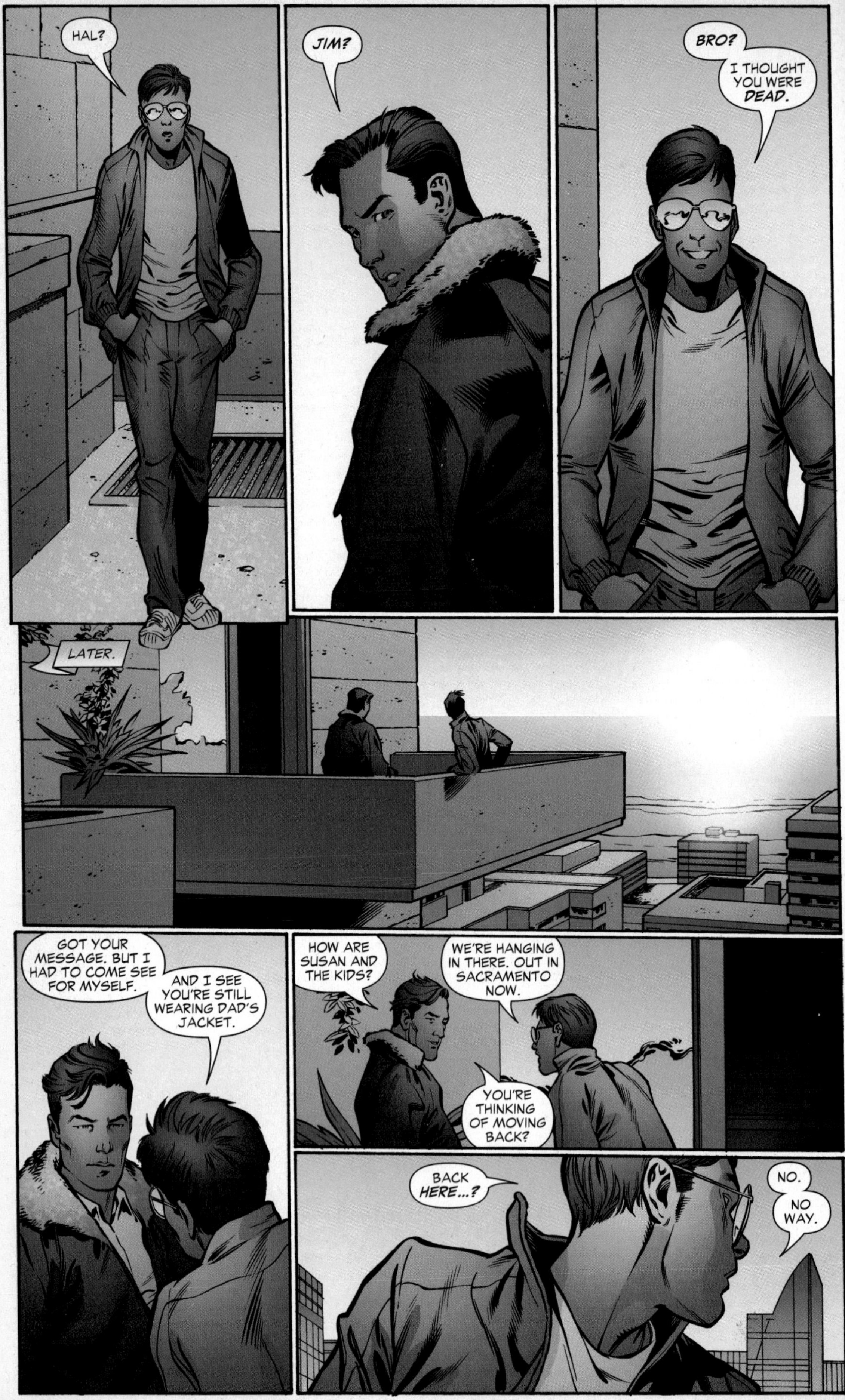

HAL?
JIM?
BRO?
I THOUGHT YOU WERE DEAD.
LATER.
GOT YOUR MESSAGE. BUT I HAD TO COME SEE FOR MYSELF.
AND I SEE YOU'RE STILL WEARING DAD'S JACKET.
HOW ARE SUSAN AND THE KIDS?
WE'RE HANGING IN THERE. OUT IN SACRAMENTO NOW.
YOU'RE THINKING OF MOVING BACK?
BACK HERE...?
NO.
NO WAY.

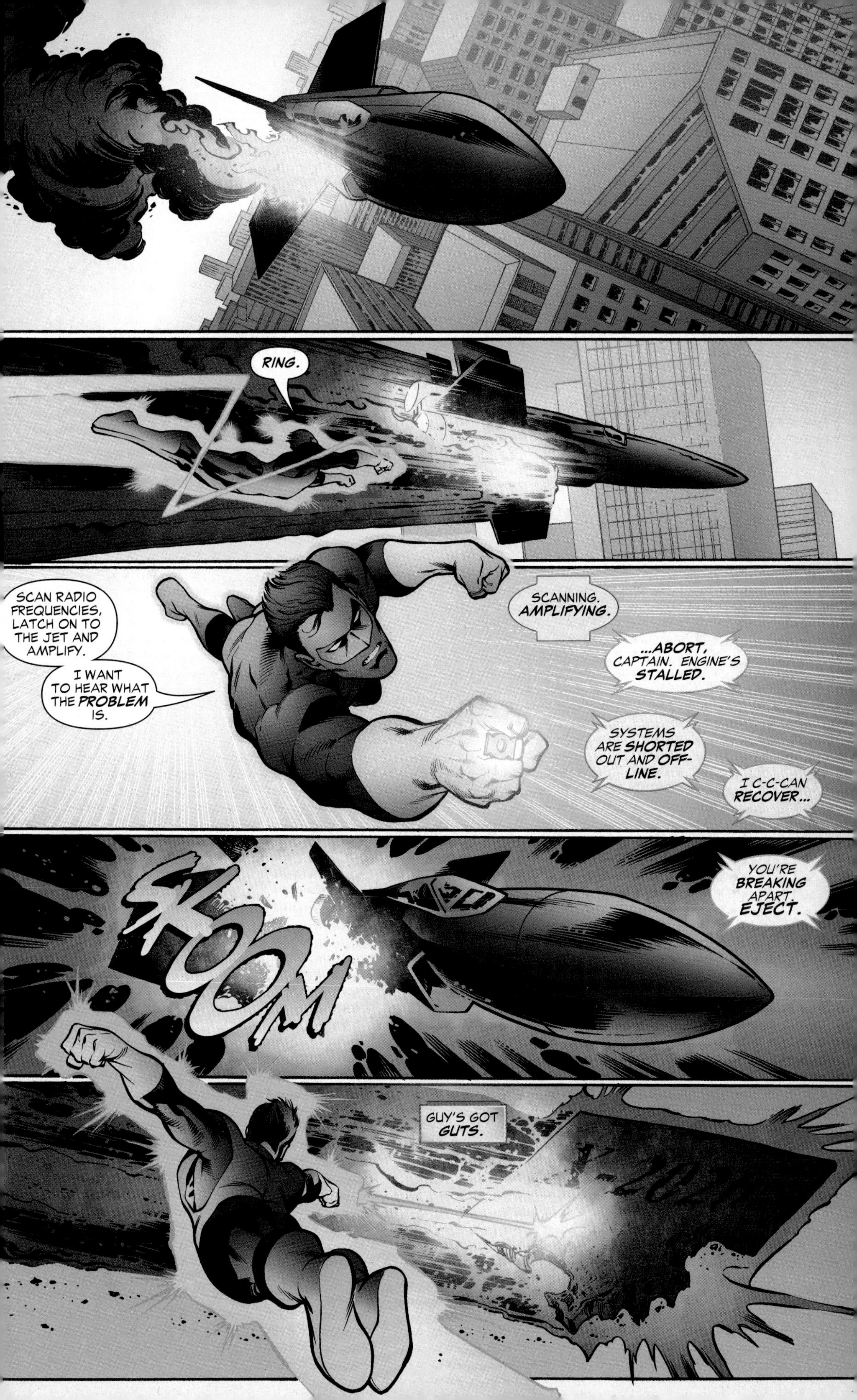

RING.
SCAN RADIO FREQUENCIES, LATCH ON TO THE JET AND AMPLIFY.
I WANT TO HEAR WHAT THE PROBLEM IS.
SCANNING. AMPLIFYING.
...ABORT, CAPTAIN. ENGINE'S STALLED.
SYSTEMS ARE SHORTED OUT AND OFF-LINE.
I C-C-CAN RECOVER...
SKOOM
YOU'RE BREAKING APART. EJECT.
GUY'S GOT GUTS.

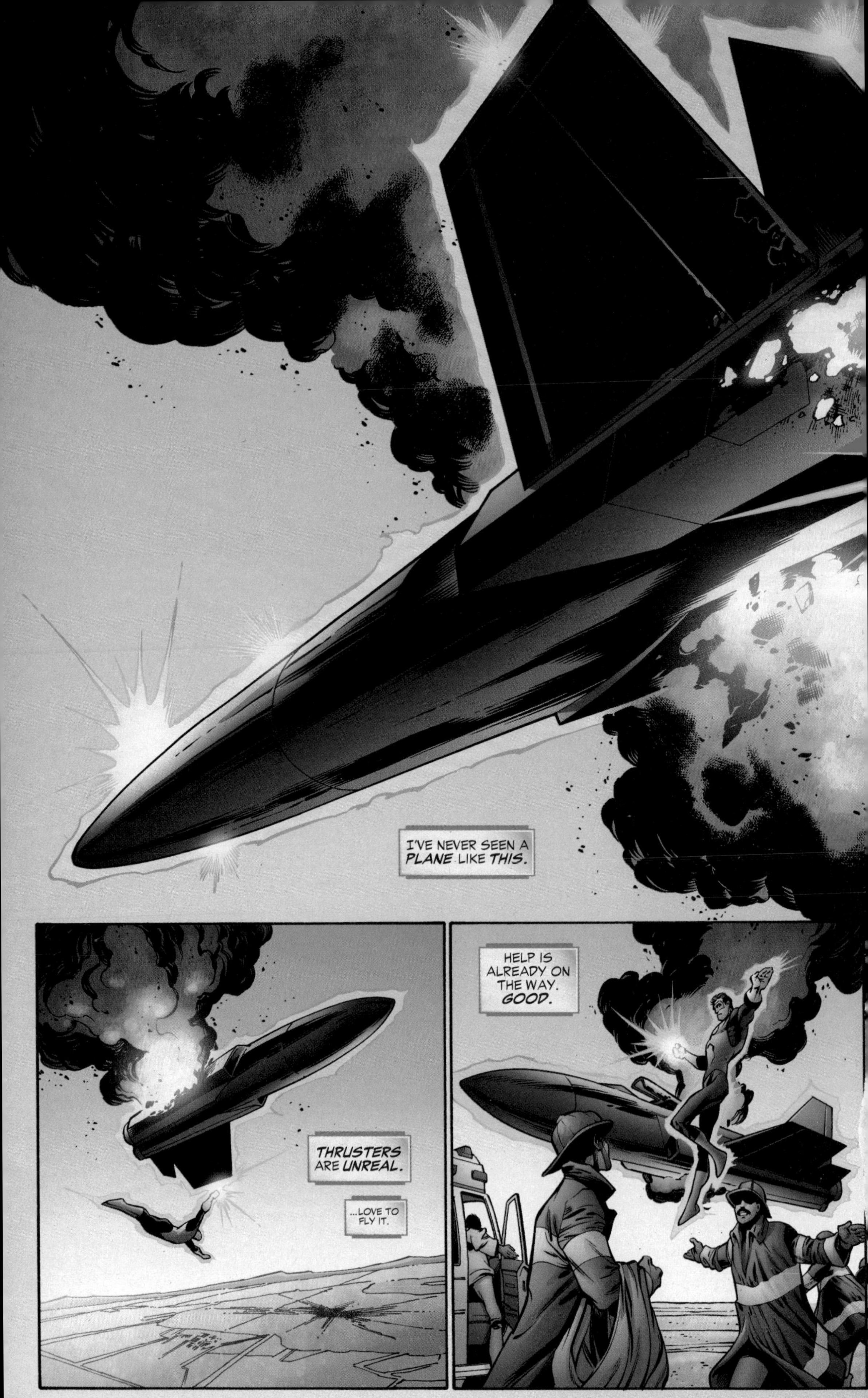
I'VE NEVER SEEN A PLANE LIKE THIS.
THRUSTERS ARE UNREAL.
...LOVE TO FLY IT.
HELP IS ALREADY ON THE WAY. GOOD.

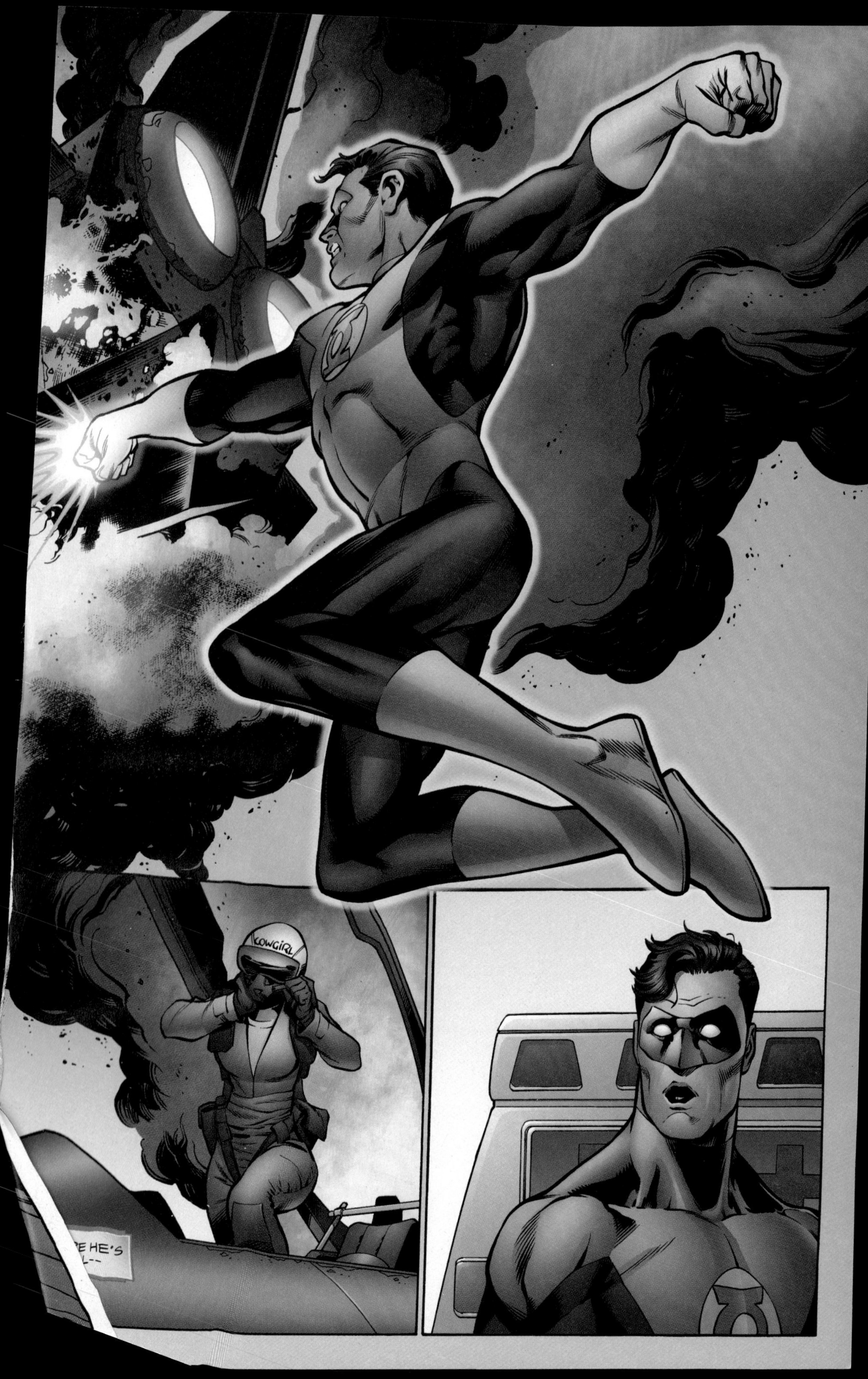
COWGIRL
HE'S

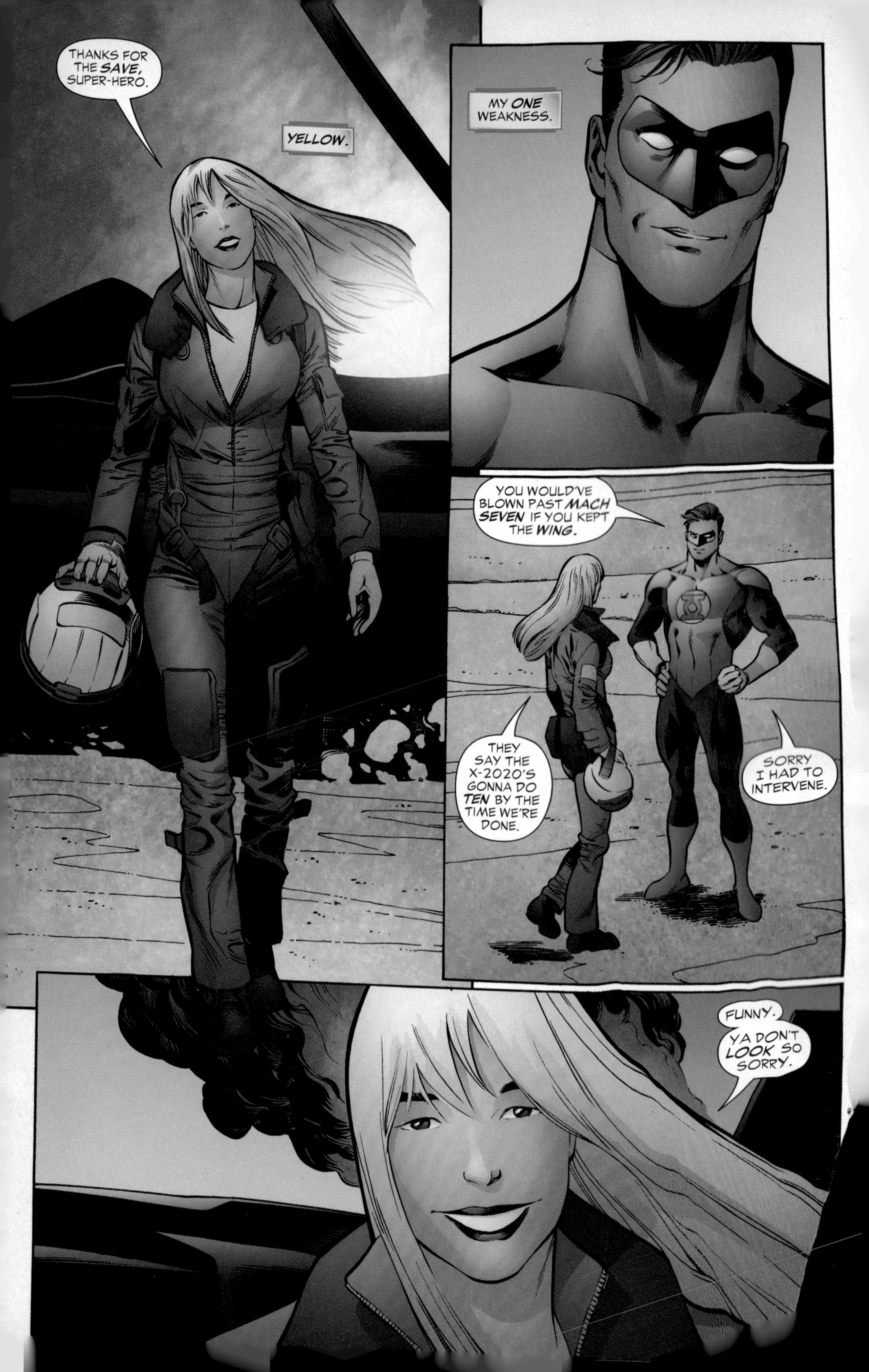
THANKS FOR THE SAVE, SUPER-HERO.
YELLOW.
MY ONE WEAKNESS.
YOU WOULD'VE BLOWN PAST MACH SEVEN IF YOU KEPT THE WING.
THEY SAY THE X-2020'S GONNA DO TEN BY THE TIME WE'RE DONE.
SORRY I HAD TO INTERVENE.
FUNNY.
YA DON'T LOOK SO SORRY.

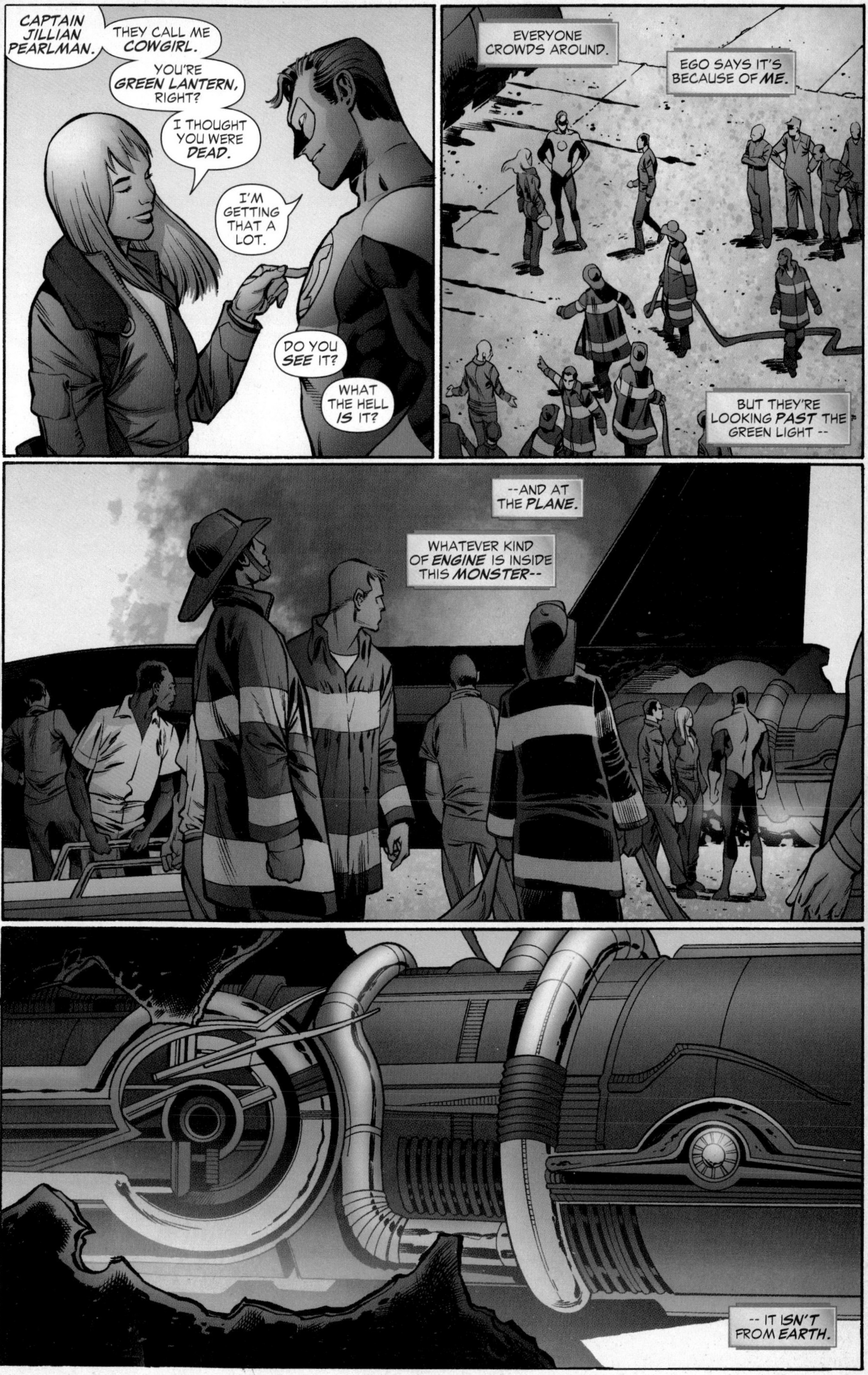
CAPTAIN JILLIAN PEARLMAN.
THEY CALL ME COWGIRL.
YOU'RE GREEN LANTERN, RIGHT?
I THOUGHT YOU WERE DEAD.
I'M GETTING THAT A LOT.
DO YOU SEE IT?
WHAT THE HELL IS IT?
EVERYONE CROWDS AROUND.
EGO SAYS IT'S BECAUSE OF ME.
BUT THEY'RE LOOKING PAST THE GREEN LIGHT --
--AND AT THE PLANE.
WHATEVER KIND OF ENGINE IS INSIDE THIS MONSTER--
-- IT ISN'T FROM EARTH.

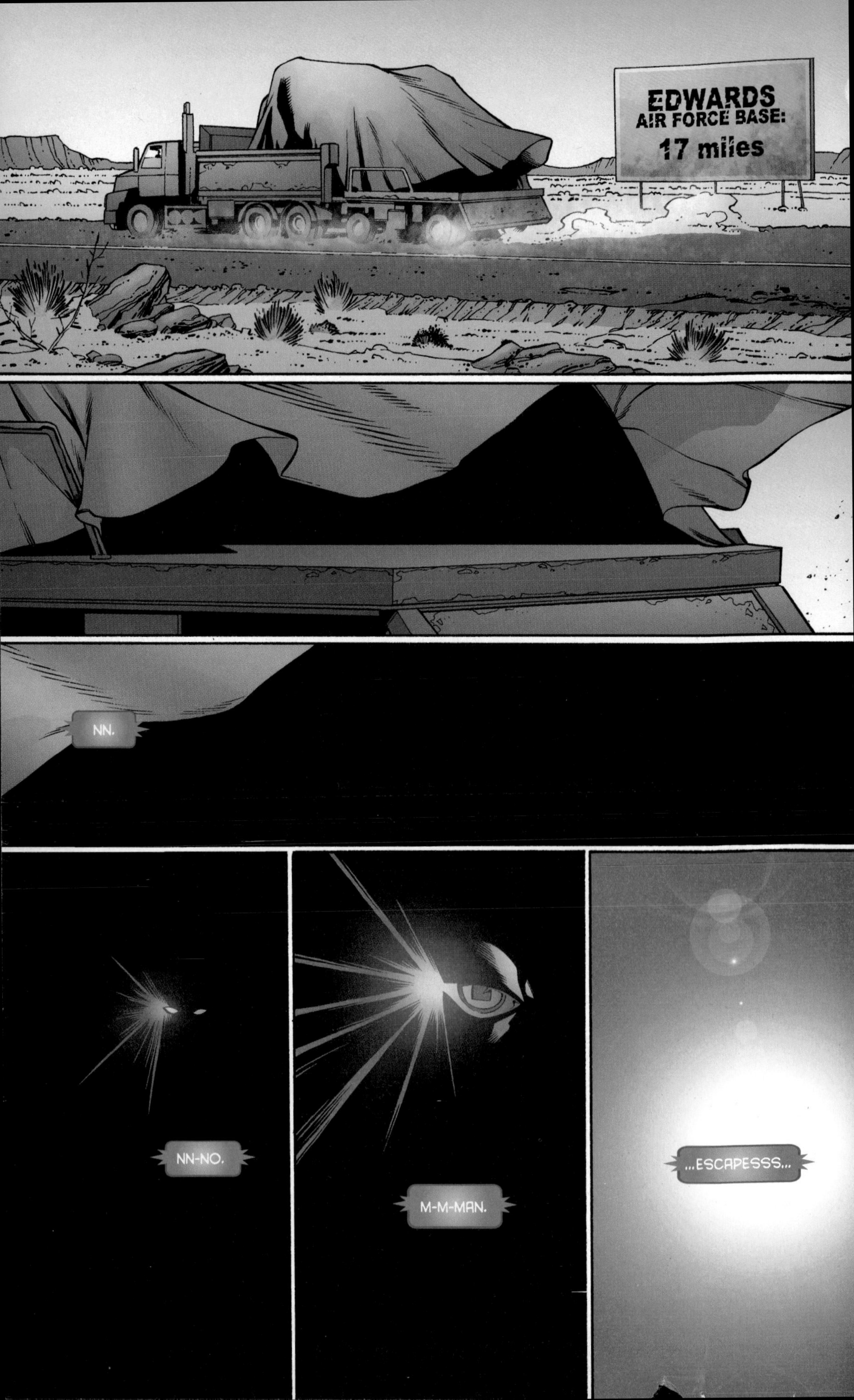

EDWARDS AIR FORCE BASE: 17 miles
NN.
NN-NO.
M-M-MAN.
...ESCAPESSS...

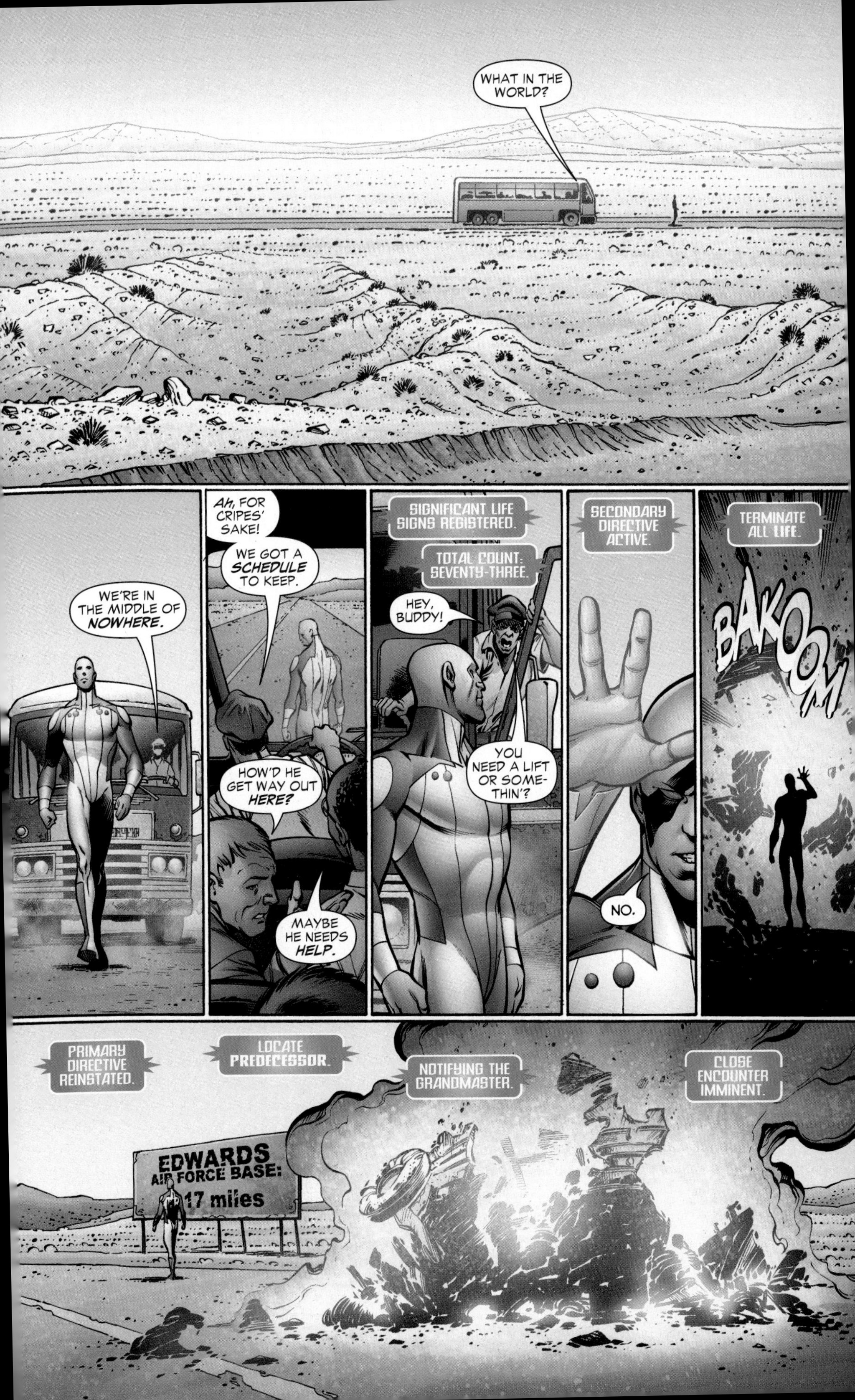

WHAT IN THE WORLD?
WE'RE IN THE MIDDLE OF NOWHERE.
Ah, FOR CRIPES' SAKE!
WE GOT A SCHEDULE TO KEEP.
HOW'D HE GET WAY OUT HERE?
MAYBE HE NEEDS HELP.
SIGNIFICANT LIFE SIGNS REGISTERED.
TOTAL COUNT: SEVENTY-THREE.
HEY, BUDDY!
YOU NEED A LIFT OR SOME-THIN'?
SECONDARY DIRECTIVE ACTIVE.
NO.
TERMINATE ALL LIFE.
BAKOOM
PRIMARY DIRECTIVE REINSTATED.
LOCATE PREDECESSOR.
NOTIFYING THE GRANDMASTER.
CLOSE ENCOUNTER IMMINENT.
EDWARDS AIR FORCE BASE: 17 miles

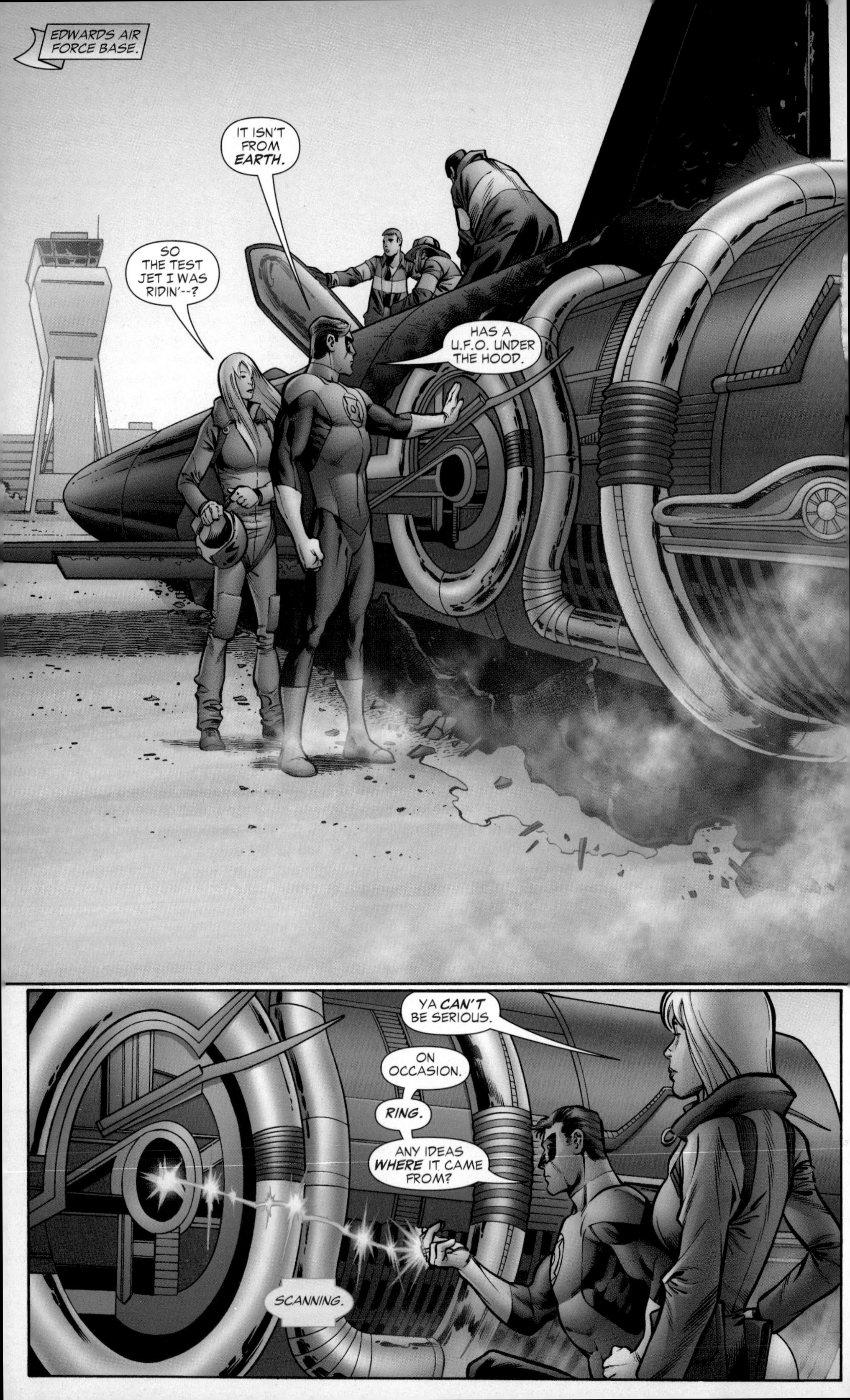
EDWARDS AIR FORCE BASE.
IT ISN'T FROM EARTH.
SO THE TEST JET I WAS RIDIN'--?
HAS A U.F.O. UNDER THE HOOD.
YA CAN'T BE SERIOUS.
ON OCCASION.
RING.
ANY IDEAS WHERE IT CAME FROM?
SCANNING.

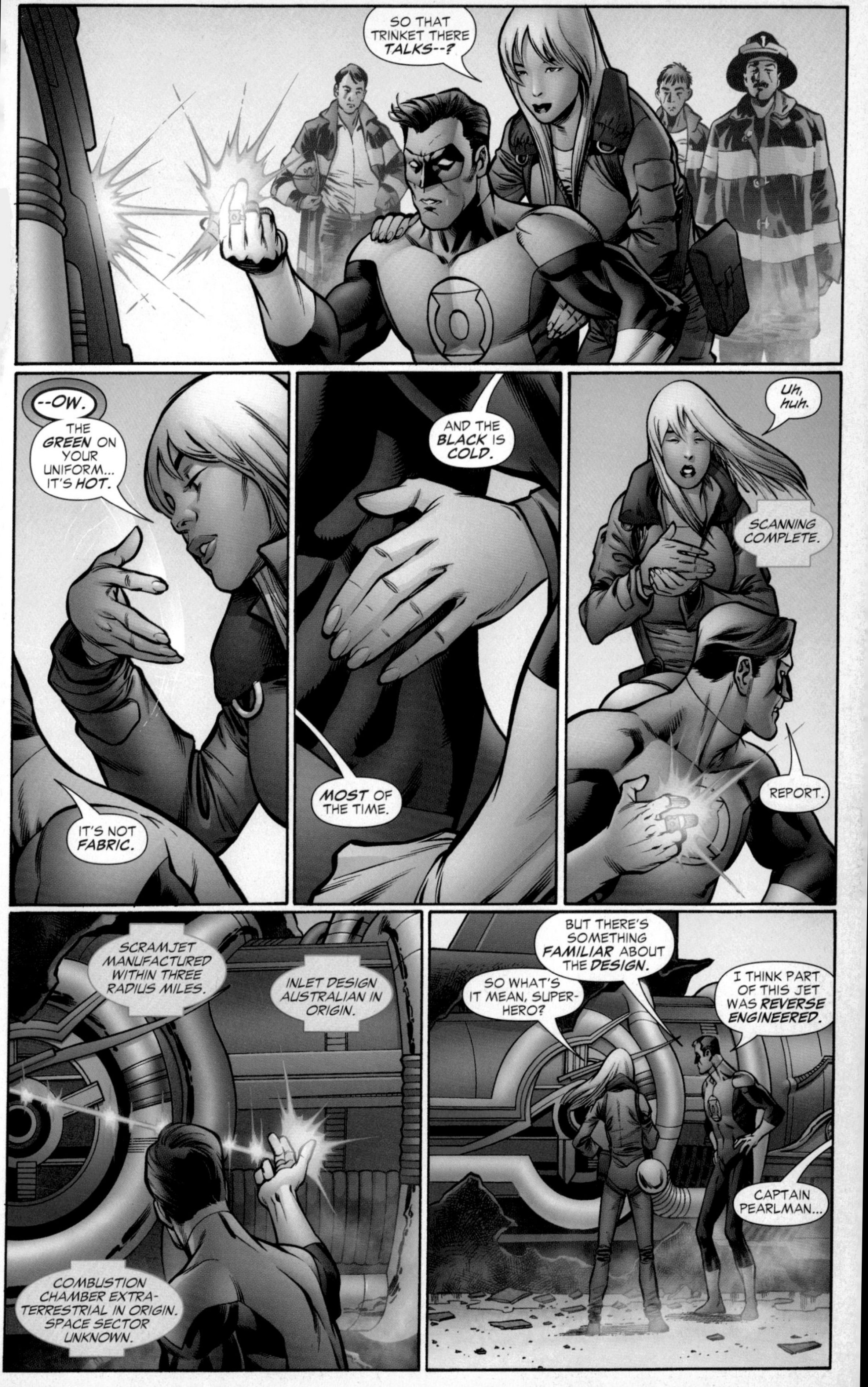

SO THAT TRINKET THERE TALKS--?
--OW.
THE GREEN ON YOUR UNIFORM... IT'S HOT.
IT'S NOT FABRIC.
AND THE BLACK IS COLD.
MOST OF THE TIME.
Uh, huh.
SCANNING COMPLETE.
REPORT.
SCRAMJET MANUFACTURED WITHIN THREE RADIUS MILES.
INLET DESIGN AUSTRALIAN IN ORIGIN.
COMBUSTION CHAMBER EXTRA-TERRESTRIAL IN ORIGIN. SPACE SECTOR UNKNOWN.
BUT THERE'S SOMETHING FAMILIAR ABOUT THE DESIGN.
SO WHAT'S IT MEAN, SUPER-HERO?
I THINK PART OF THIS JET WAS REVERSE ENGINEERED.
CAPTAIN PEARLMAN...

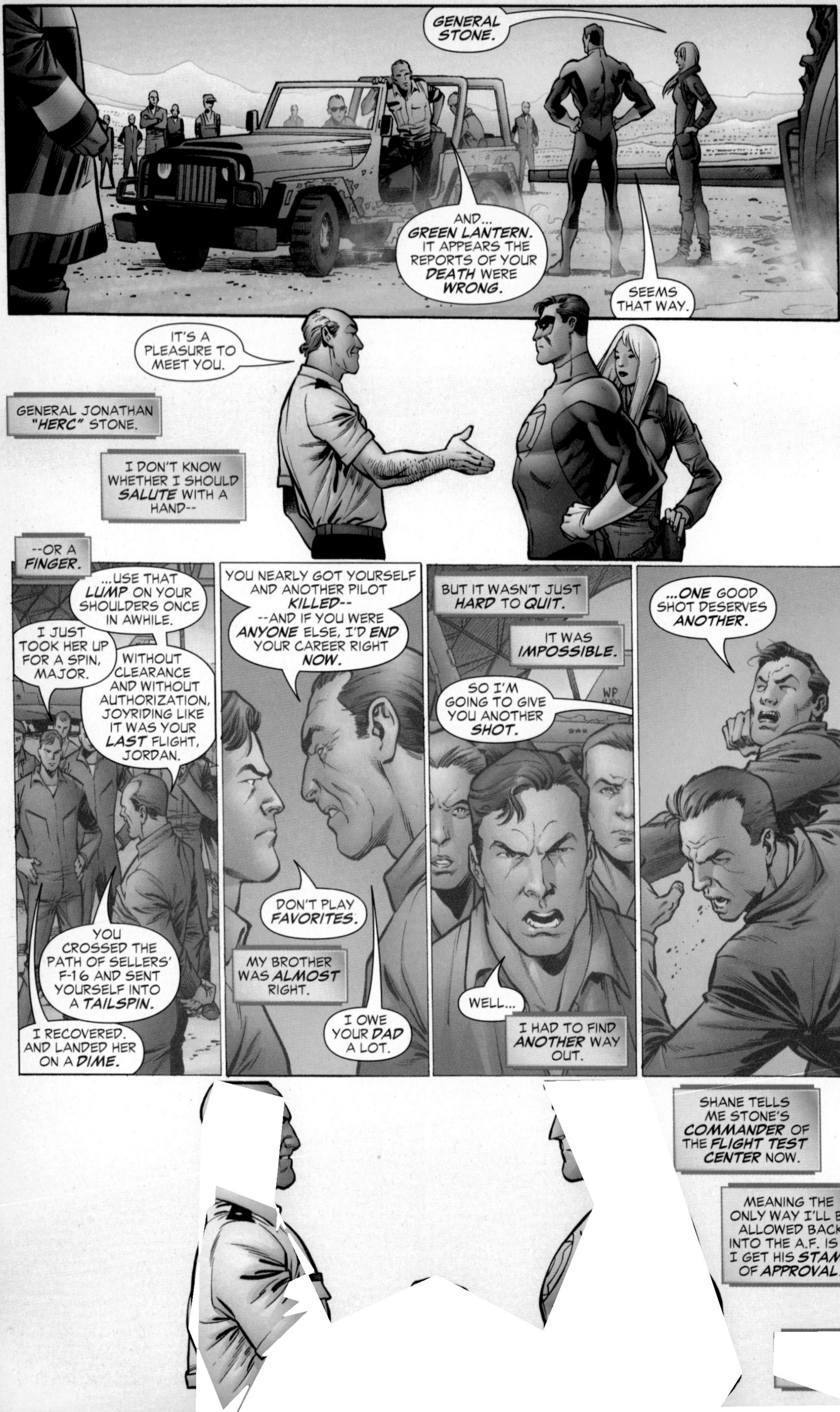
GENERAL STONE.
AND... GREEN LANTERN. IT APPEARS THE REPORTS OF YOUR DEATH WERE WRONG.
SEEMS THAT WAY.
IT'S A PLEASURE TO MEET YOU.
GENERAL JONATHAN "HERC" STONE.
I DON'T KNOW WHETHER I SHOULD SALUTE WITH A HAND--
--OR A FINGER.
I JUST TOOK HER UP FOR A SPIN, MAJOR.
WITHOUT CLEARANCE AND WITHOUT AUTHORIZATION, JOYRIDING LIKE IT WAS YOUR LAST FLIGHT, JORDAN.
YOU CROSSED THE PATH OF SELLERS' F-16 AND SENT YOURSELF INTO A TAILSPIN.
I RECOVERED. AND LANDED HER ON A DIME.
...USE THAT LUMP ON YOUR SHOULDERS ONCE IN AWHILE.
YOU NEARLY GOT YOURSELF AND ANOTHER PILOT KILLED--
--AND IF YOU WERE ANYONE ELSE, I'D END YOUR CAREER RIGHT NOW.
DON'T PLAY FAVORITES.
MY BROTHER WAS ALMOST RIGHT.
I OWE YOUR DAD A LOT.
BUT IT WASN'T JUST HARD TO QUIT.
IT WAS IMPOSSIBLE.
SO I'M GOING TO GIVE YOU ANOTHER SHOT.
WELL...
I HAD TO FIND ANOTHER WAY OUT.
...ONE GOOD SHOT DESERVES ANOTHER.
SHANE TELLS ME STONE'S COMMANDER OF THE FLIGHT TEST CENTER NOW.
MEANING THE ONLY WAY I'LL BE ALLOWED BACK INTO THE A.F. IS IF I GET HIS STAMP OF APPROVAL.

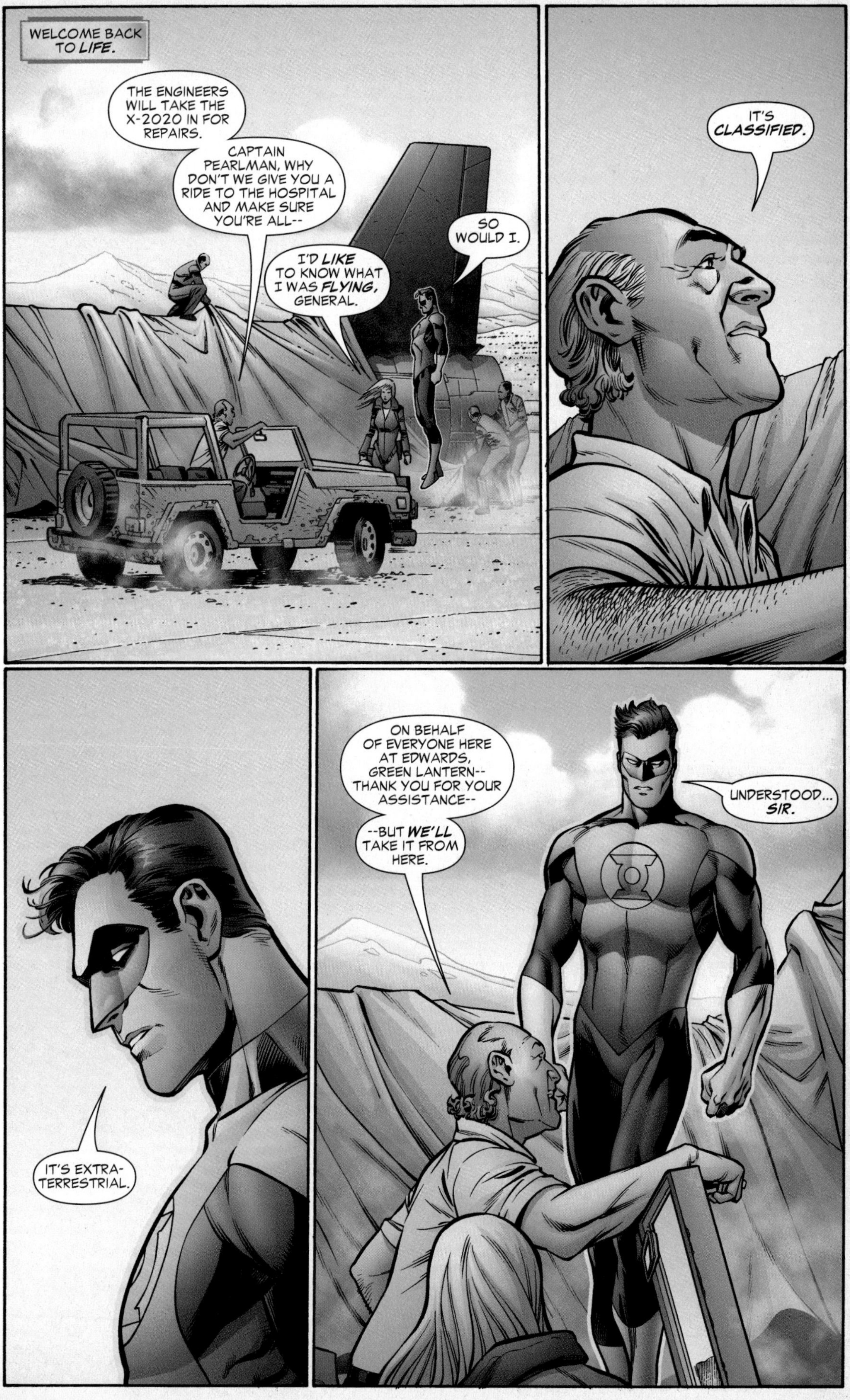
WELCOME BACK TO *LIFE.*
THE ENGINEERS WILL TAKE THE X-2020 IN FOR REPAIRS.
CAPTAIN PEARLMAN, WHY DON'T WE GIVE YOU A RIDE TO THE HOSPITAL AND MAKE SURE YOU'RE ALL--
I'D *LIKE* TO KNOW WHAT I WAS *FLYING,* GENERAL.
SO WOULD I.
IT'S *CLASSIFIED.*
IT'S EXTRA-TERRESTRIAL.
ON BEHALF OF EVERYONE HERE AT EDWARDS, GREEN LANTERN-- THANK YOU FOR YOUR ASSISTANCE--
--BUT *WE'LL* TAKE IT FROM HERE.
UNDERSTOOD... *SIR.*

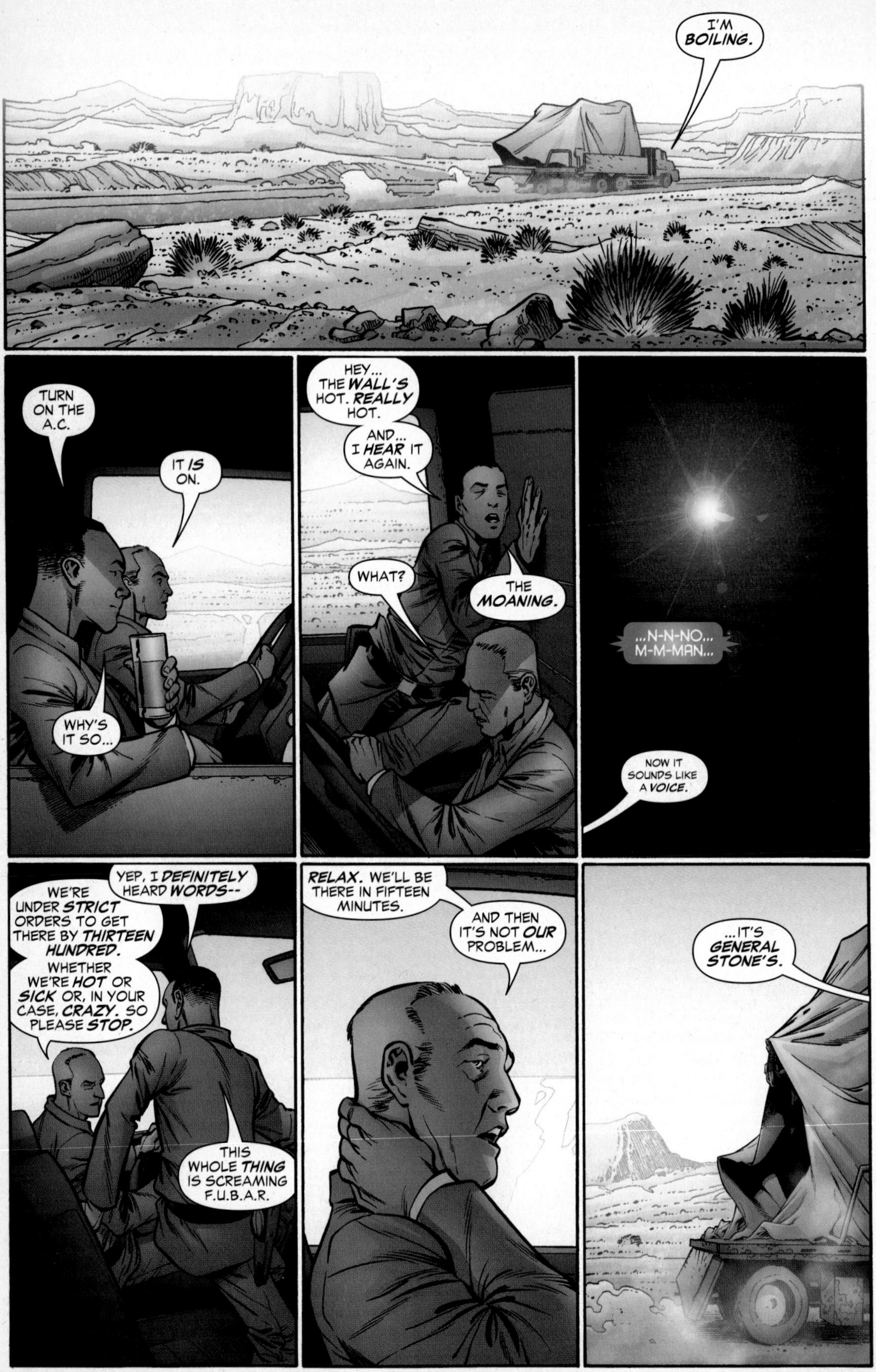
I'M BOILING.
TURN ON THE A.C.
IT IS ON.
WHY'S IT SO...
HEY... THE WALL'S HOT. REALLY HOT.
AND... I HEAR IT AGAIN.
WHAT?
THE MOANING.
...N-N-NO... M-M-MAN...
NOW IT SOUNDS LIKE A VOICE.
YEP, I DEFINITELY HEARD WORDS--
WE'RE UNDER STRICT ORDERS TO GET THERE BY THIRTEEN HUNDRED. WHETHER WE'RE HOT OR SICK OR, IN YOUR CASE, CRAZY. SO PLEASE STOP.
THIS WHOLE THING IS SCREAMING F.U.B.A.R.
RELAX. WE'LL BE THERE IN FIFTEEN MINUTES.
AND THEN IT'S NOT OUR PROBLEM...
...IT'S GENERAL STONE'S.

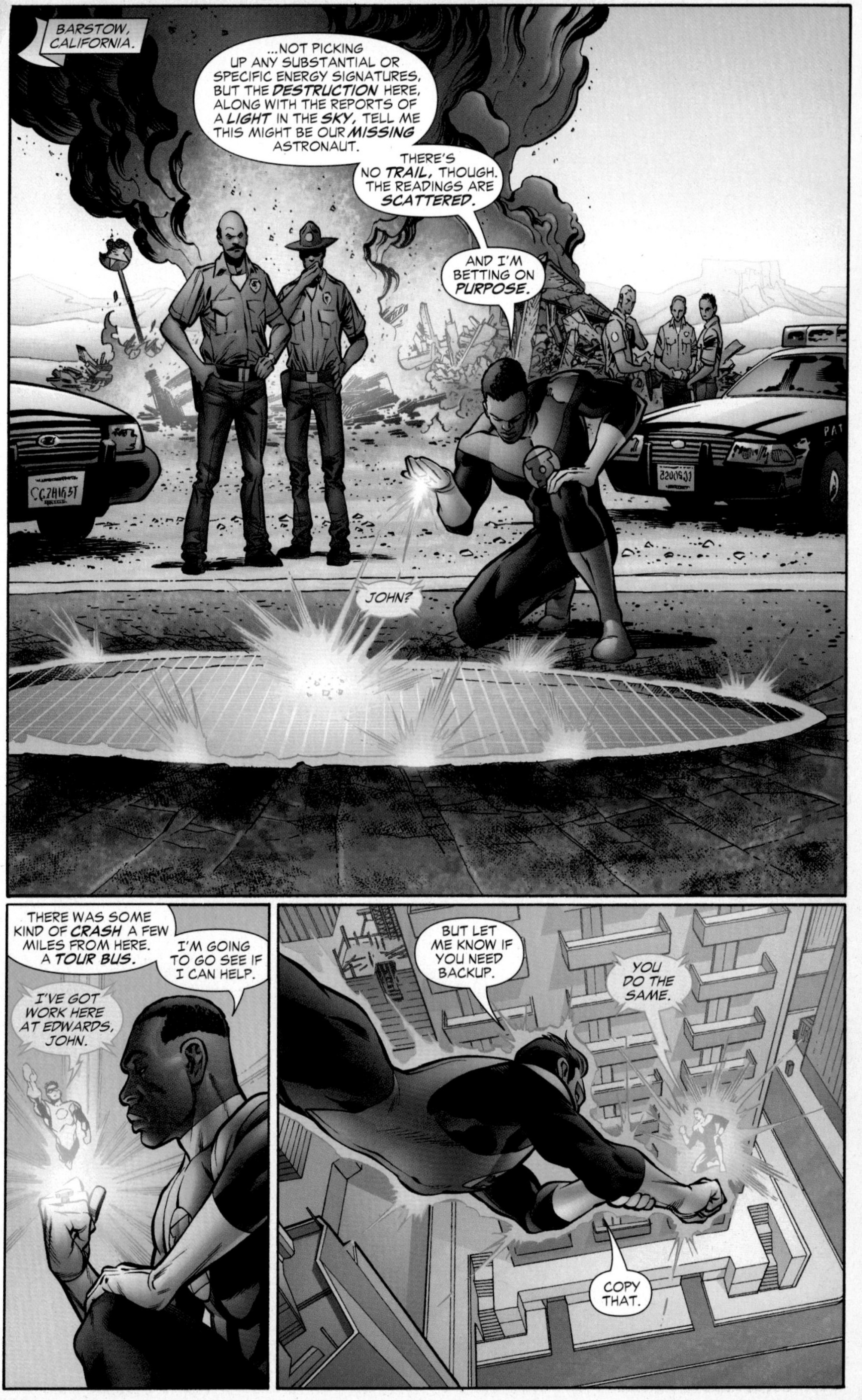
BARSTOW, CALIFORNIA.
...NOT PICKING UP ANY SUBSTANTIAL OR SPECIFIC ENERGY SIGNATURES, BUT THE DESTRUCTION HERE, ALONG WITH THE REPORTS OF A LIGHT IN THE SKY, TELL ME THIS MIGHT BE OUR MISSING ASTRONAUT.
THERE'S NO TRAIL, THOUGH. THE READINGS ARE SCATTERED.
AND I'M BETTING ON PURPOSE.
JOHN?
THERE WAS SOME KIND OF CRASH A FEW MILES FROM HERE. A TOUR BUS.
I'M GOING TO GO SEE IF I CAN HELP.
I'VE GOT WORK HERE AT EDWARDS, JOHN.
BUT LET ME KNOW IF YOU NEED BACKUP.
YOU DO THE SAME.
COPY THAT.

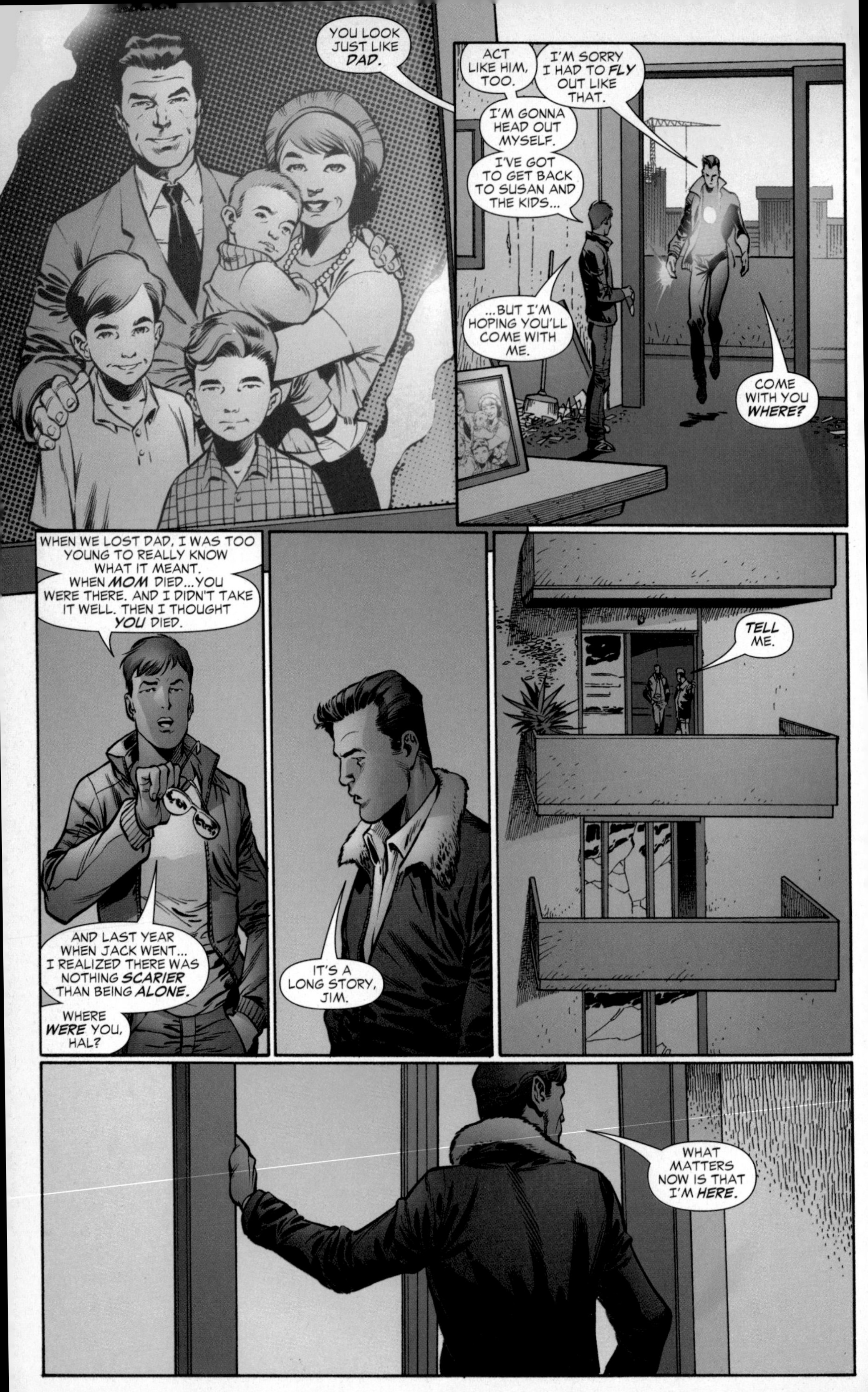

YOU LOOK JUST LIKE DAD.
ACT LIKE HIM, TOO.
I'M SORRY I HAD TO FLY OUT LIKE THAT.
I'M GONNA HEAD OUT MYSELF.
I'VE GOT TO GET BACK TO SUSAN AND THE KIDS...
...BUT I'M HOPING YOU'LL COME WITH ME.
COME WITH YOU WHERE?
WHEN WE LOST DAD, I WAS TOO YOUNG TO REALLY KNOW WHAT IT MEANT. WHEN MOM DIED...YOU WERE THERE. AND I DIDN'T TAKE IT WELL. THEN I THOUGHT YOU DIED.
AND LAST YEAR WHEN JACK WENT... I REALIZED THERE WAS NOTHING SCARIER THAN BEING ALONE.
WHERE WERE YOU, HAL?
IT'S A LONG STORY, JIM.
TELL ME.
WHAT MATTERS NOW IS THAT I'M HERE.

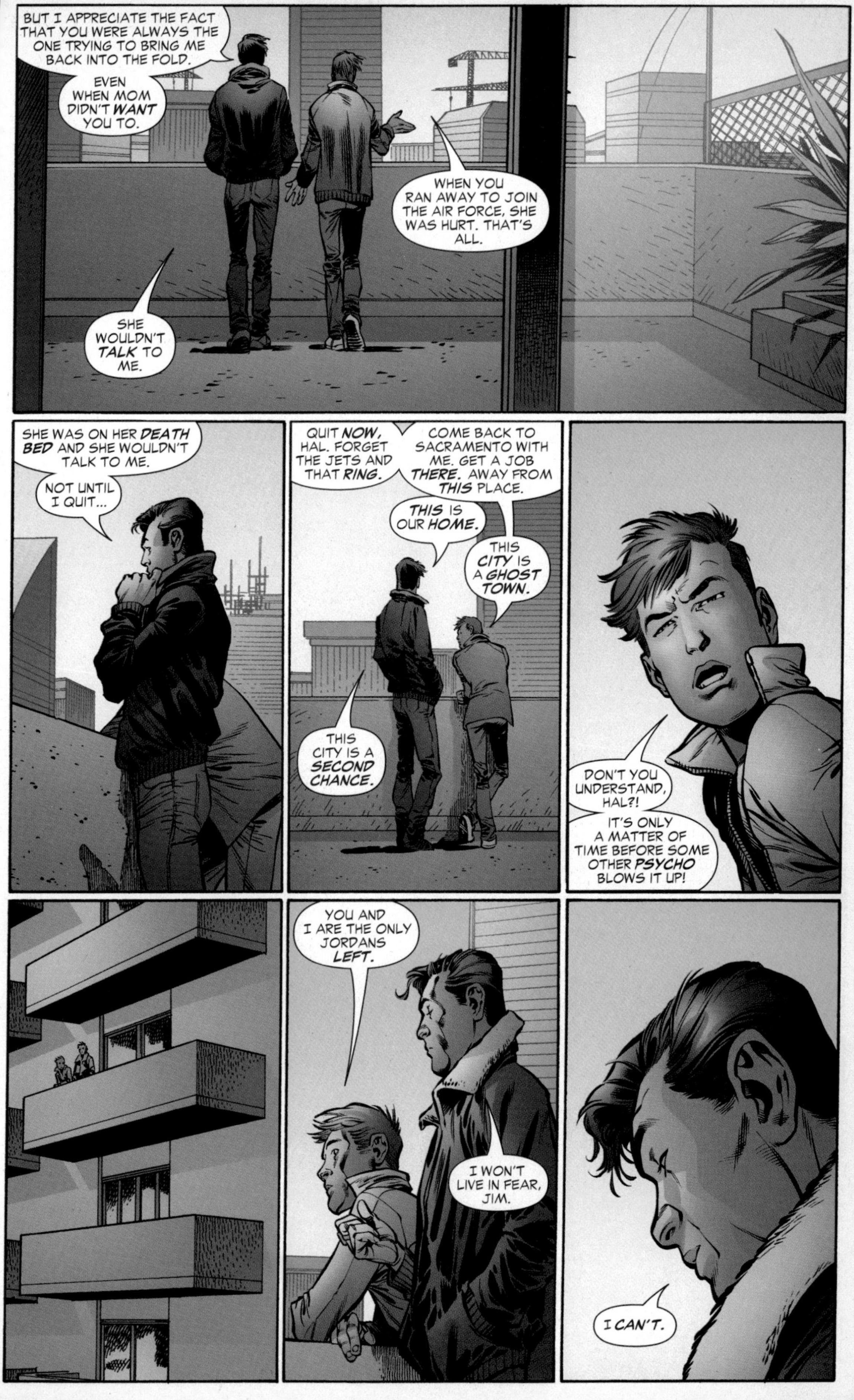

BUT I APPRECIATE THE FACT THAT YOU WERE ALWAYS THE ONE TRYING TO BRING ME BACK INTO THE FOLD.
EVEN WHEN MOM DIDN'T WANT YOU TO.
WHEN YOU RAN AWAY TO JOIN THE AIR FORCE, SHE WAS HURT. THAT'S ALL.
SHE WOULDN'T TALK TO ME.
SHE WAS ON HER DEATH BED AND SHE WOULDN'T TALK TO ME.
NOT UNTIL I QUIT...
QUIT NOW, HAL. FORGET THE JETS AND THAT RING.
COME BACK TO SACRAMENTO WITH ME. GET A JOB THERE. AWAY FROM THIS PLACE.
THIS IS OUR HOME.
THIS CITY IS A GHOST TOWN.
THIS CITY IS A SECOND CHANCE.
DON'T YOU UNDERSTAND, HAL?!
IT'S ONLY A MATTER OF TIME BEFORE SOME OTHER PSYCHO BLOWS IT UP!
YOU AND I ARE THE ONLY JORDANS LEFT.
I WON'T LIVE IN FEAR, JIM.
I CAN'T.

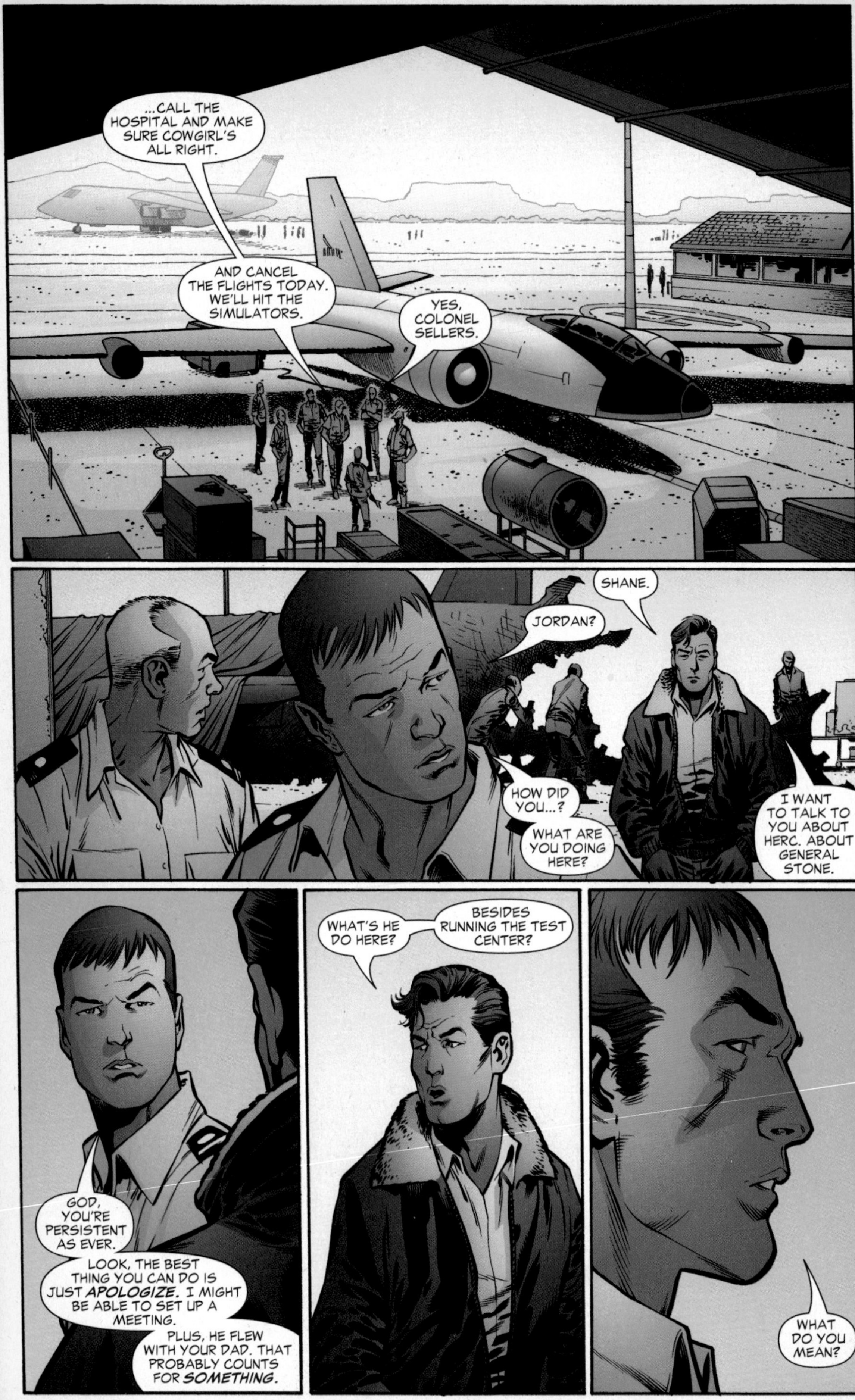
...CALL THE HOSPITAL AND MAKE SURE COWGIRL'S ALL RIGHT.
AND CANCEL THE FLIGHTS TODAY. WE'LL HIT THE SIMULATORS.
YES, COLONEL SELLERS.
SHANE.
JORDAN?
HOW DID YOU...?
WHAT ARE YOU DOING HERE?
I WANT TO TALK TO YOU ABOUT HERC. ABOUT GENERAL STONE.
GOD, YOU'RE PERSISTENT AS EVER.
LOOK, THE BEST THING YOU CAN DO IS JUST APOLOGIZE. I MIGHT BE ABLE TO SET UP A MEETING.
PLUS, HE FLEW WITH YOUR DAD. THAT PROBABLY COUNTS FOR SOMETHING.
WHAT'S HE DO HERE?
BESIDES RUNNING THE TEST CENTER?
WHAT DO YOU MEAN?

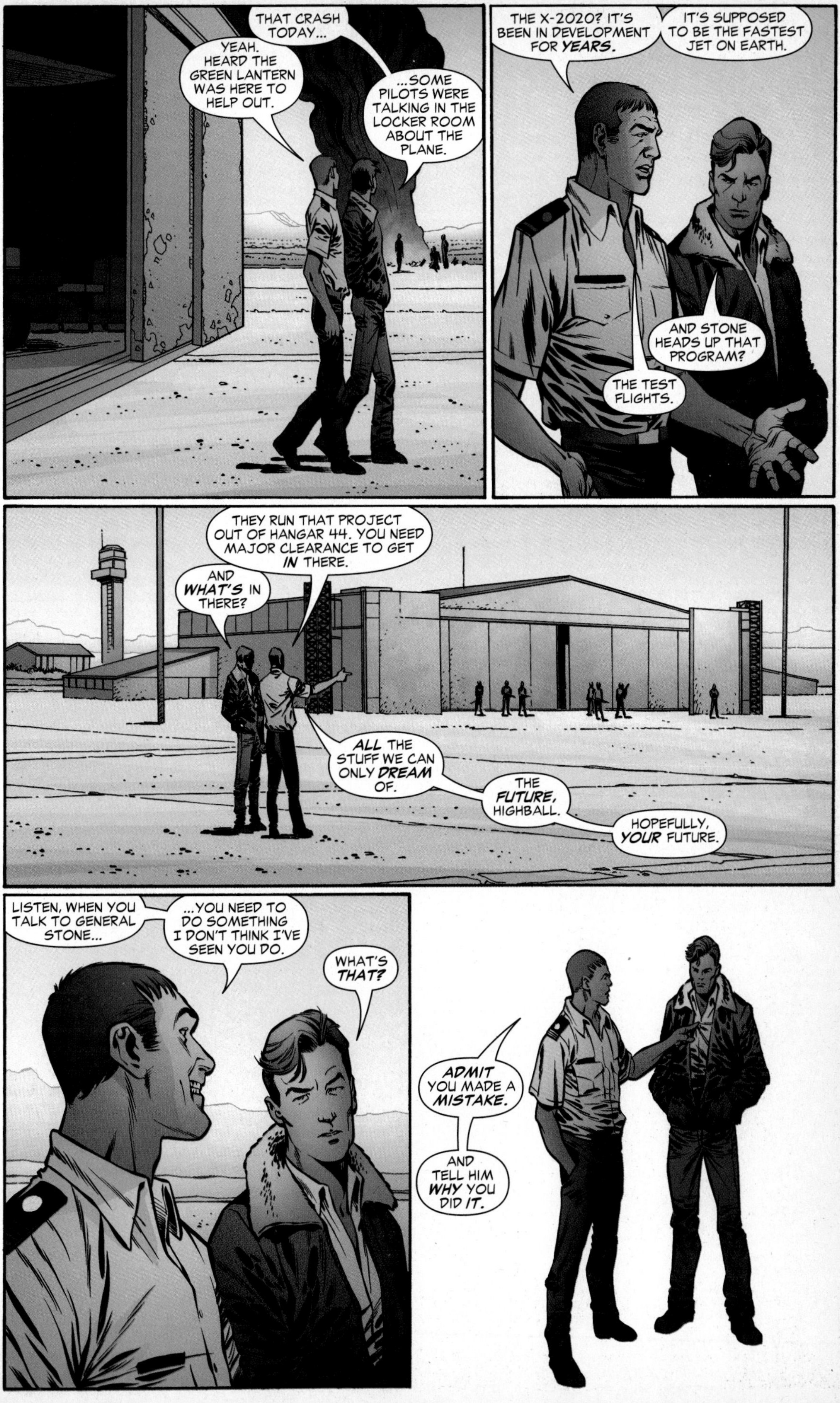
THAT CRASH TODAY...
YEAH. HEARD THE GREEN LANTERN WAS HERE TO HELP OUT.
...SOME PILOTS WERE TALKING IN THE LOCKER ROOM ABOUT THE PLANE.
THE X-2020? IT'S BEEN IN DEVELOPMENT FOR YEARS.
IT'S SUPPOSED TO BE THE FASTEST JET ON EARTH.
AND STONE HEADS UP THAT PROGRAM?
THE TEST FLIGHTS.
THEY RUN THAT PROJECT OUT OF HANGAR 44. YOU NEED MAJOR CLEARANCE TO GET IN THERE.
AND WHAT'S IN THERE?
ALL THE STUFF WE CAN ONLY DREAM OF.
THE FUTURE, HIGHBALL.
HOPEFULLY, YOUR FUTURE.
LISTEN, WHEN YOU TALK TO GENERAL STONE...
...YOU NEED TO DO SOMETHING I DON'T THINK I'VE SEEN YOU DO.
WHAT'S THAT?
ADMIT YOU MADE A MISTAKE.
AND TELL HIM WHY YOU DID IT.

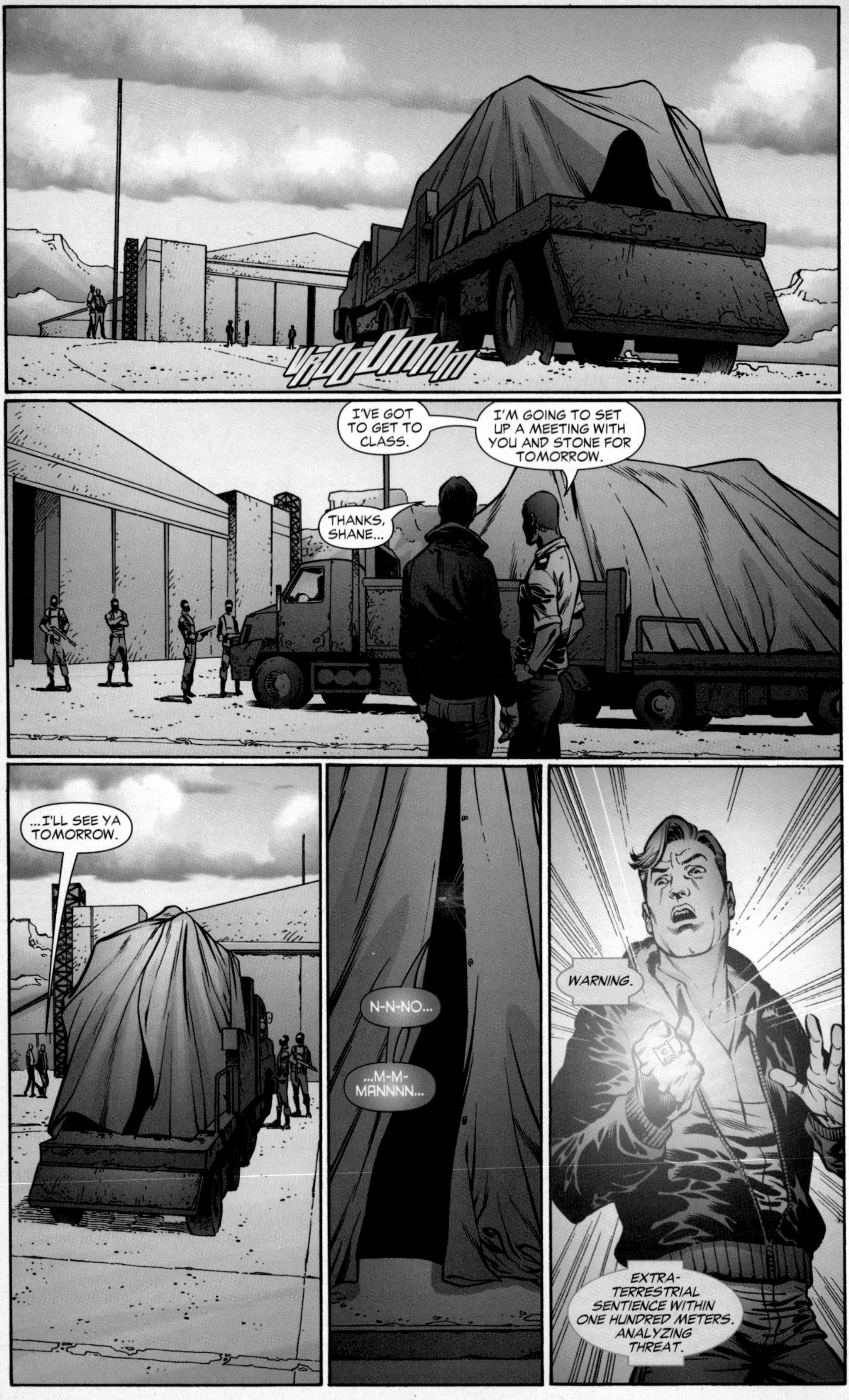
VROOOMMM
I'VE GOT TO GET TO CLASS.
I'M GOING TO SET UP A MEETING WITH YOU AND STONE FOR TOMORROW.
THANKS, SHANE...
...I'LL SEE YA TOMORROW.
N-N-NO...
...M-M-MANNNN...
WARNING.
EXTRA-TERRESTRIAL SENTIENCE WITHIN ONE HUNDRED METERS. ANALYZING THREAT.

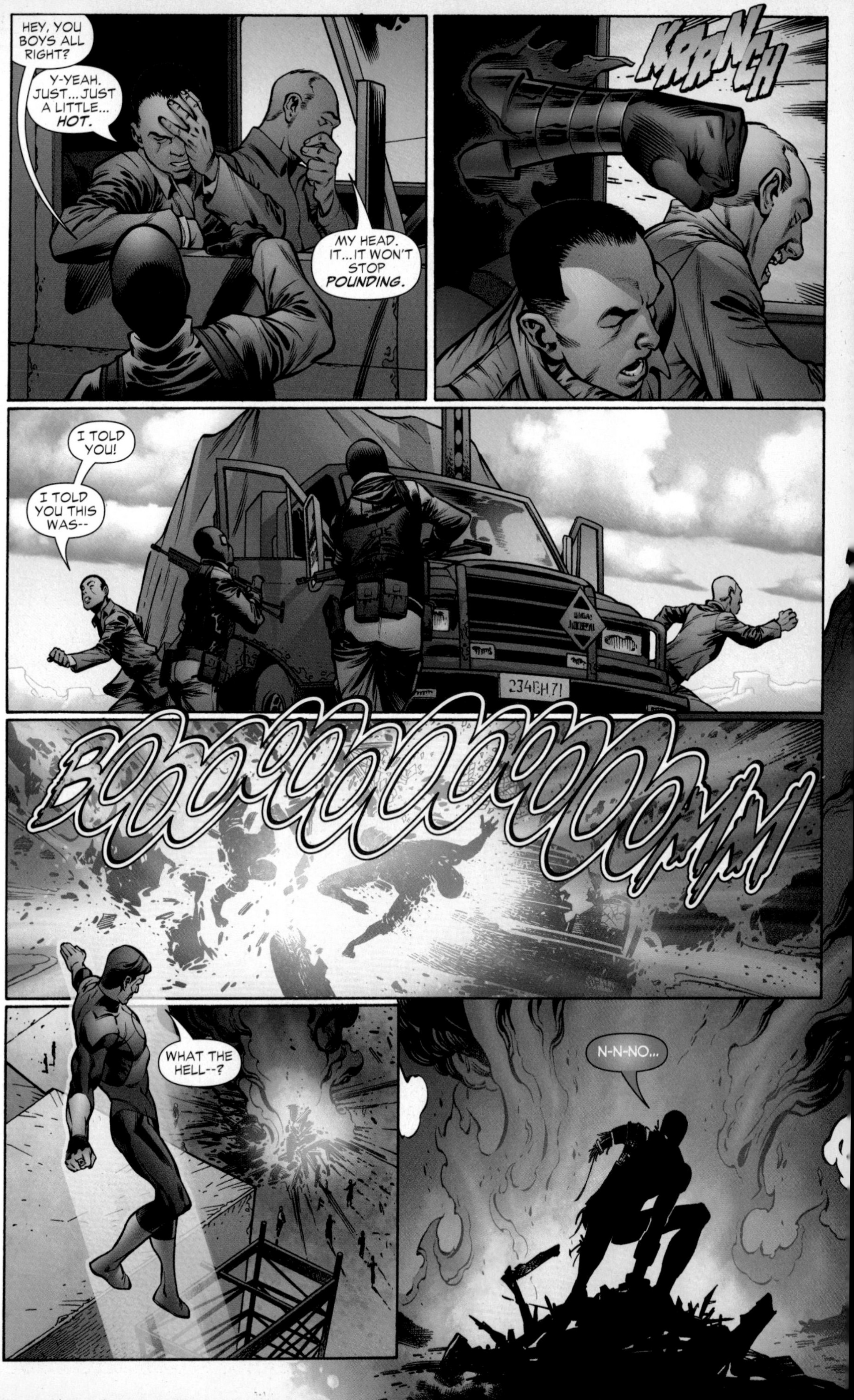
HEY, YOU BOYS ALL RIGHT?
Y-YEAH. JUST...JUST A LITTLE... HOT.
MY HEAD. IT...IT WON'T STOP POUNDING.
KRRNCH
I TOLD YOU!
I TOLD YOU THIS WAS--
234GH71
BOOOOOOOOOOOOOM
WHAT THE HELL--?
N-N-NO...

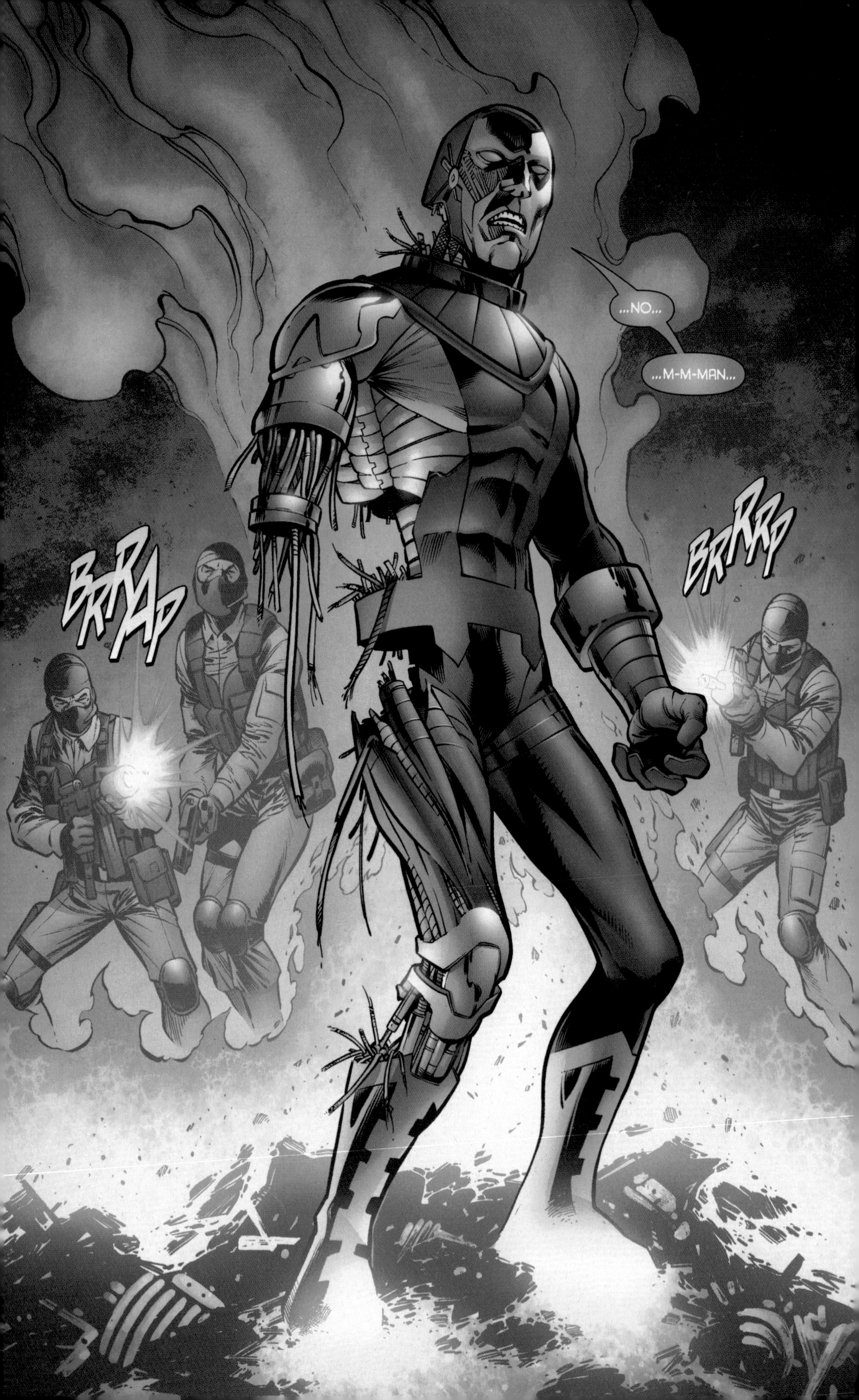
...NO...
...M-M-MAN...
BRRAP
BRRRP

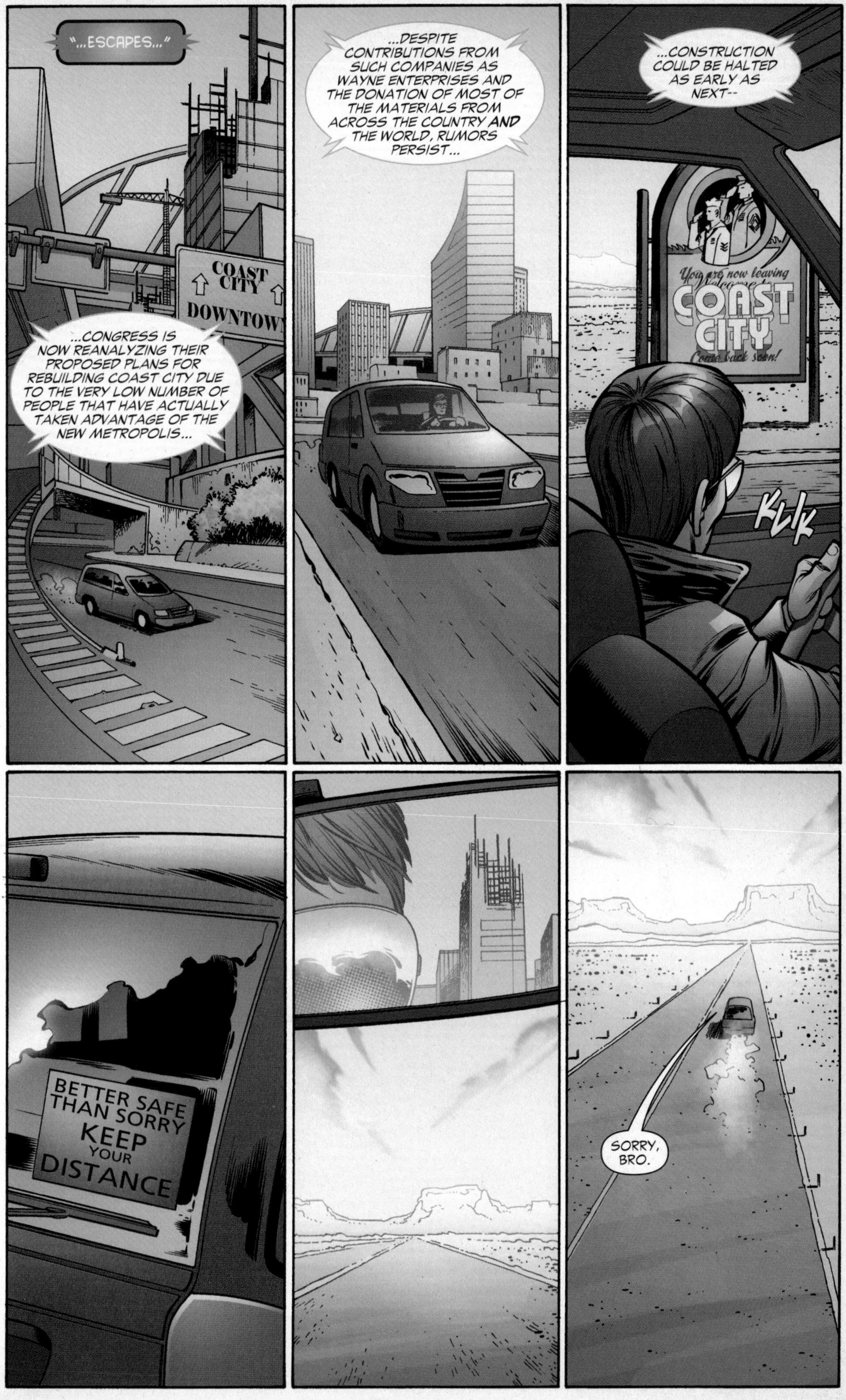
"...ESCAPES..."
COAST CITY
DOWNTOWN
...CONGRESS IS NOW REANALYZING THEIR PROPOSED PLANS FOR REBUILDING COAST CITY DUE TO THE VERY LOW NUMBER OF PEOPLE THAT HAVE ACTUALLY TAKEN ADVANTAGE OF THE NEW METROPOLIS...
...DESPITE CONTRIBUTIONS FROM SUCH COMPANIES AS WAYNE ENTERPRISES AND THE DONATION OF MOST OF THE MATERIALS FROM ACROSS THE COUNTRY AND THE WORLD, RUMORS PERSIST...
...CONSTRUCTION COULD BE HALTED AS EARLY AS NEXT--
You are now leaving
COAST CITY
Come back soon!
KLIK
BETTER SAFE THAN SORRY
KEEP YOUR DISTANCE
SORRY, BRO.

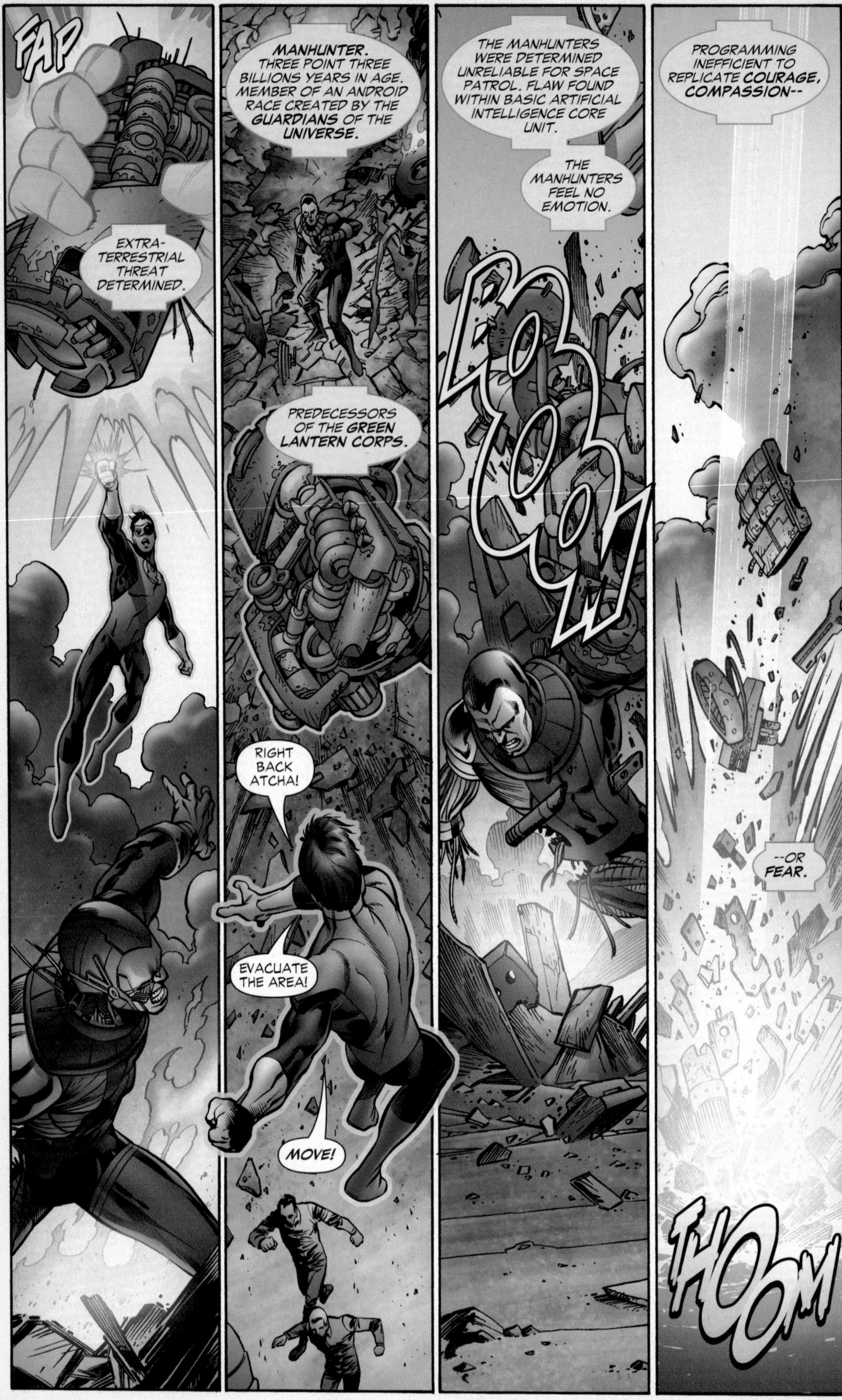
FAP
EXTRA-TERRESTRIAL THREAT DETERMINED.
MANHUNTER. THREE POINT THREE BILLIONS YEARS IN AGE. MEMBER OF AN ANDROID RACE CREATED BY THE GUARDIANS OF THE UNIVERSE.
PREDECESSORS OF THE GREEN LANTERN CORPS.
RIGHT BACK ATCHA!
EVACUATE THE AREA!
MOVE!
THE MANHUNTERS WERE DETERMINED UNRELIABLE FOR SPACE PATROL. FLAW FOUND WITHIN BASIC ARTIFICIAL INTELLIGENCE CORE UNIT.
THE MANHUNTERS FEEL NO EMOTION.
BOOOM
PROGRAMMING INEFFICIENT TO REPLICATE COURAGE, COMPASSION--
--OR FEAR.
THOOM

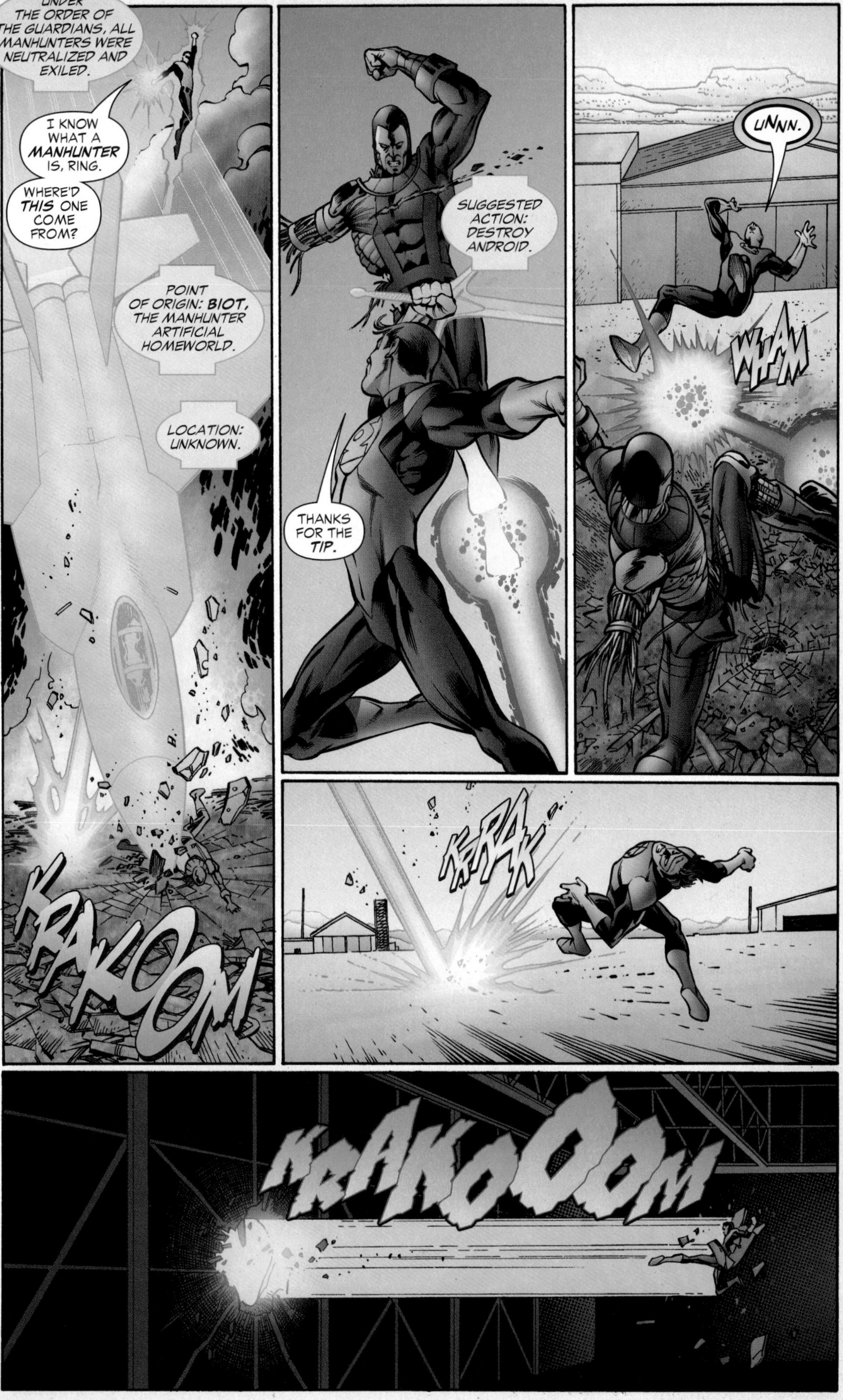
UNDER THE ORDER OF THE GUARDIANS, ALL MANHUNTERS WERE NEUTRALIZED AND EXILED.
I KNOW WHAT A MANHUNTER IS, RING.
WHERE'D THIS ONE COME FROM?
POINT OF ORIGIN: BIOT, THE MANHUNTER ARTIFICIAL HOMEWORLD.
LOCATION: UNKNOWN.
KRAKOOM
SUGGESTED ACTION: DESTROY ANDROID.
THANKS FOR THE TIP.
UNNN.
WHAM
KRRAK
KRAKOOOM

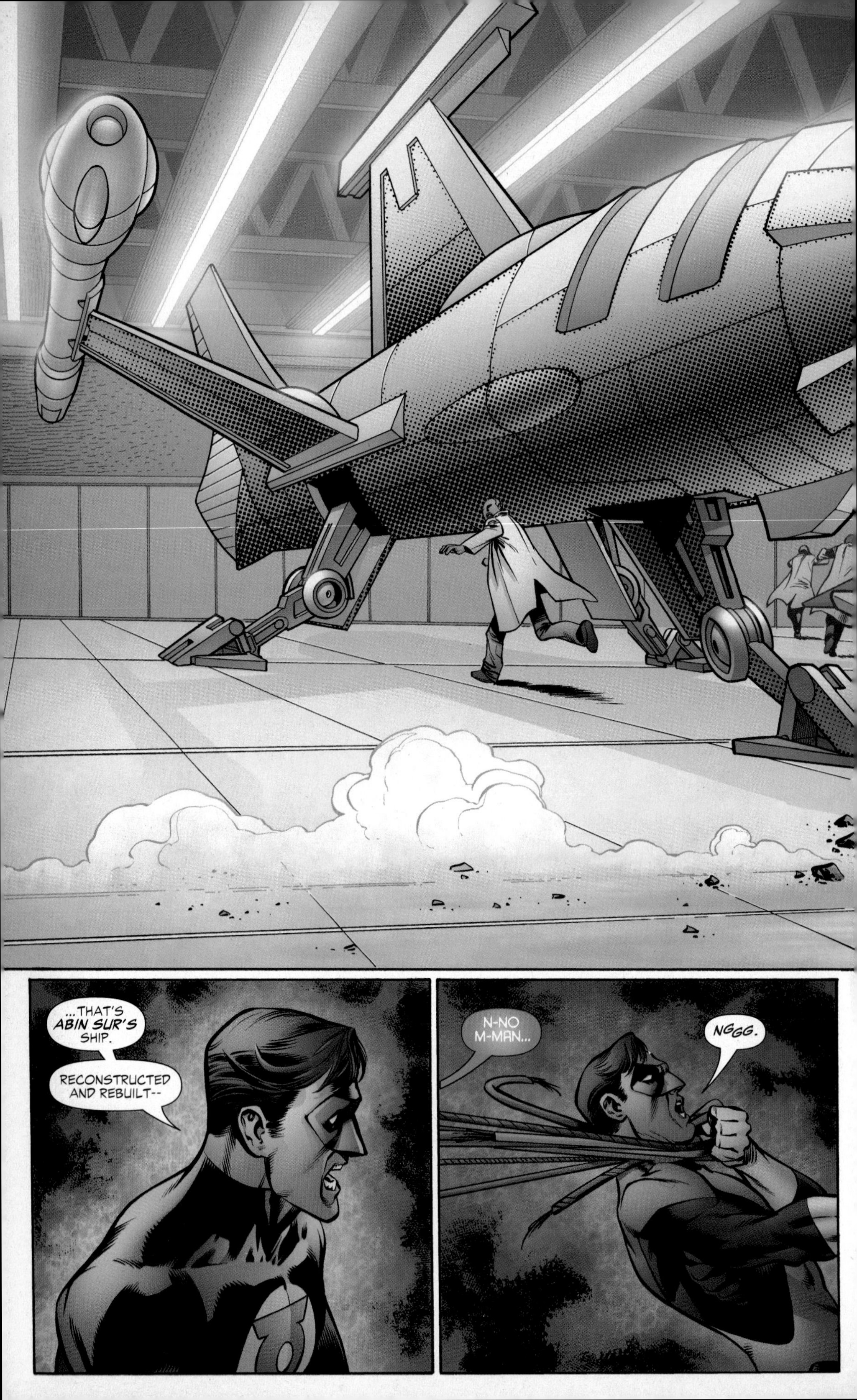
...THAT'S ABIN SUR'S SHIP.
RECONSTRUCTED AND REBUILT--
N-NO M-MAN...
NGGG.

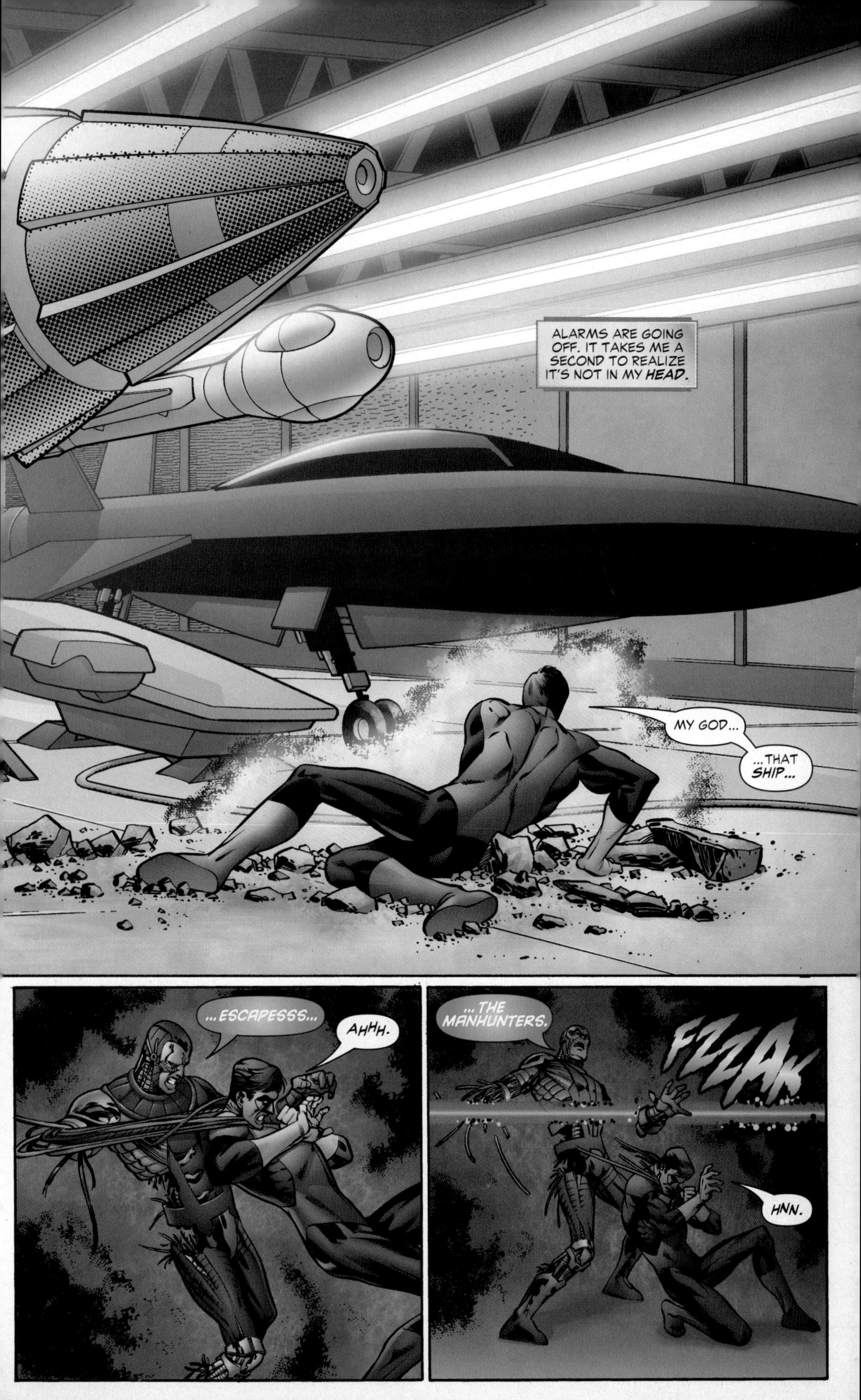
ALARMS ARE GOING OFF. IT TAKES ME A SECOND TO REALIZE IT'S NOT IN MY HEAD.
MY GOD...
...THAT SHIP...
...ESCAPESSS...
AHHH.
...THE MANHUNTERS.
FZZAK
HNN.

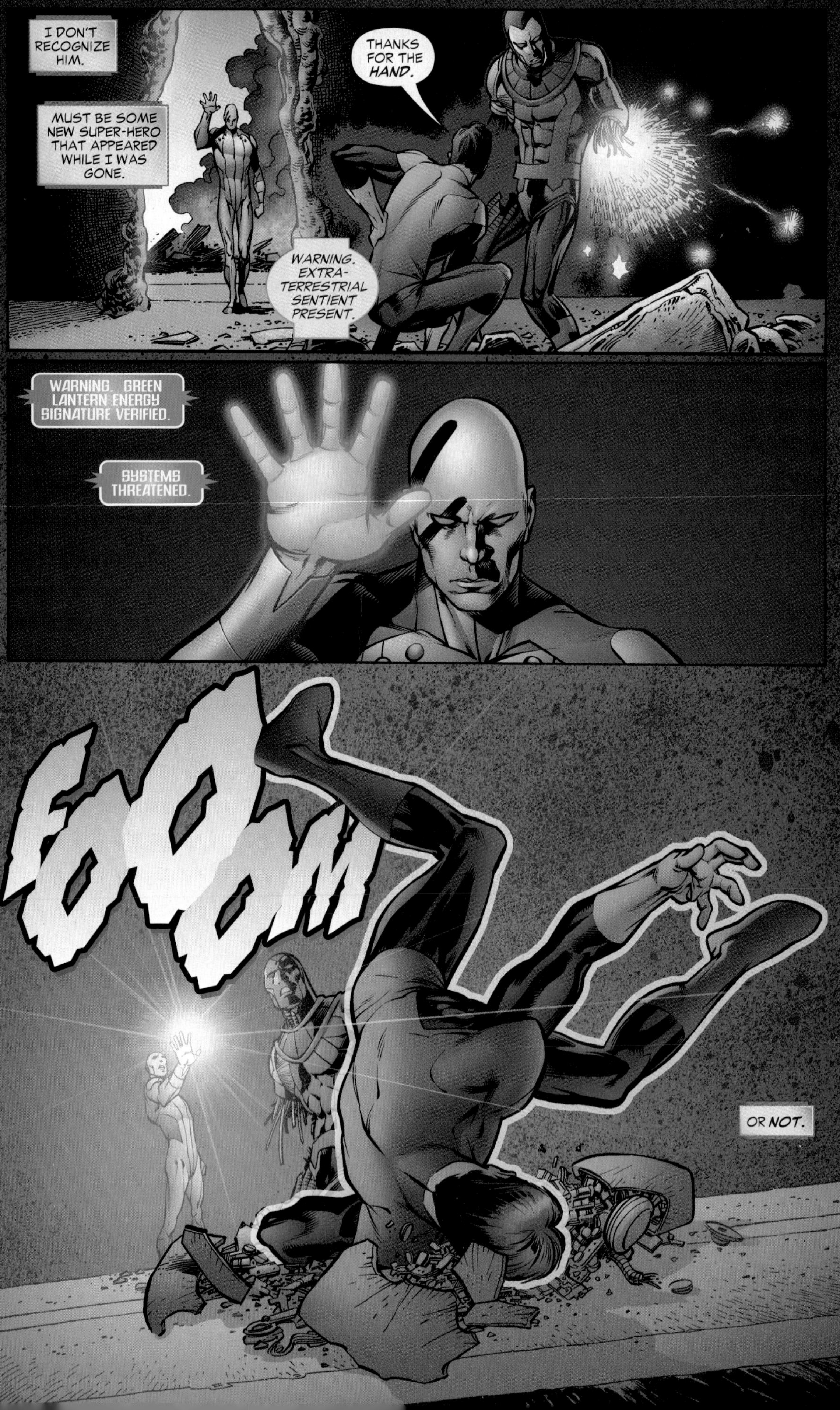
I DON'T RECOGNIZE HIM.
MUST BE SOME NEW SUPER-HERO THAT APPEARED WHILE I WAS GONE.
THANKS FOR THE *HAND*.
WARNING. EXTRA-TERRESTRIAL SENTIENT PRESENT.
WARNING. GREEN LANTERN ENERGY SIGNATURE VERIFIED.
SYSTEMS THREATENED.
OR *NOT*.

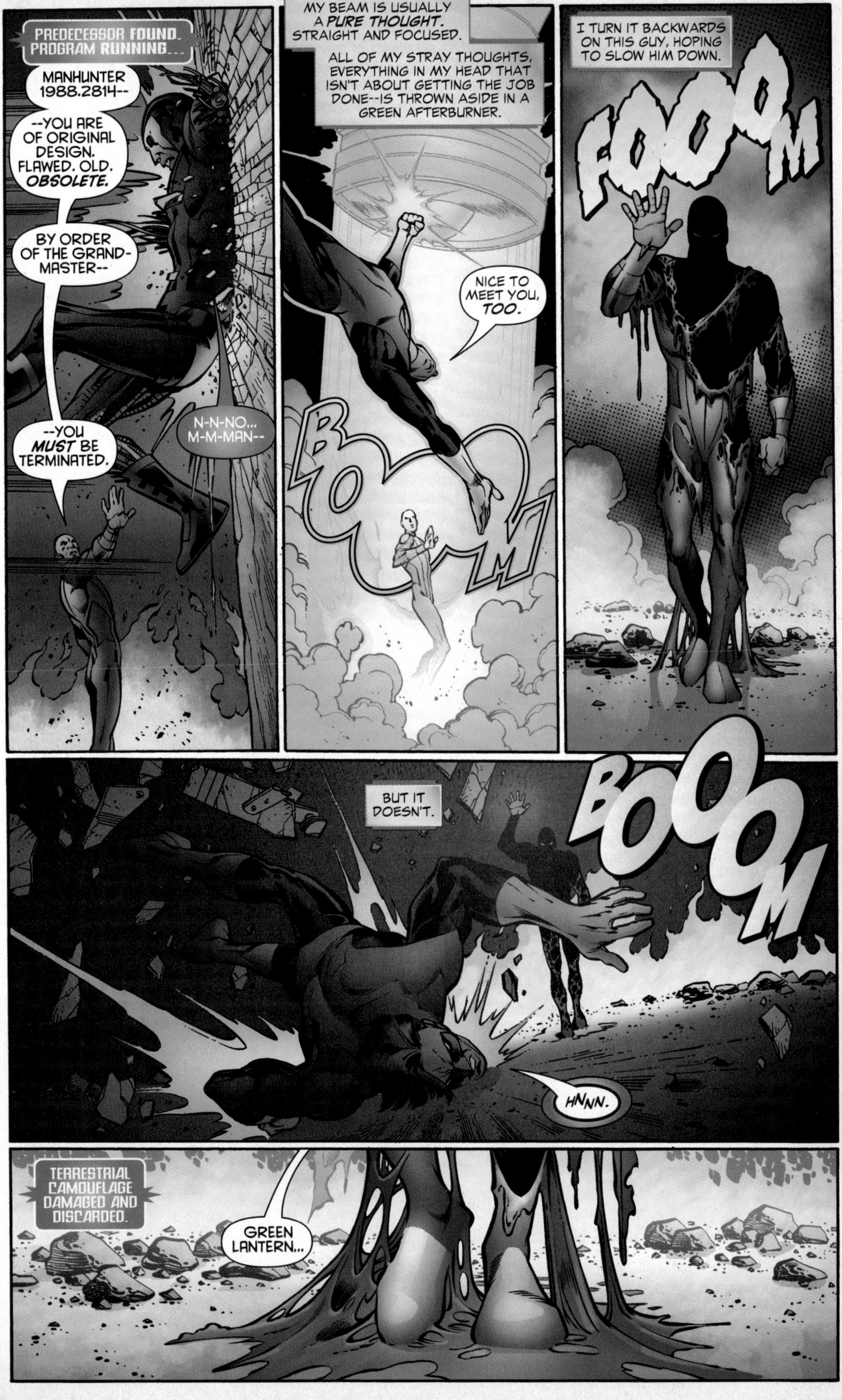
PREDECESSOR FOUND. PROGRAM RUNNING...
MANHUNTER 1988.2814--
--YOU ARE OF ORIGINAL DESIGN. FLAWED. OLD. OBSOLETE.
BY ORDER OF THE GRAND-MASTER--
--YOU MUST BE TERMINATED.
N-N-NO... M-M-MAN--
MY BEAM IS USUALLY A PURE THOUGHT. STRAIGHT AND FOCUSED.
ALL OF MY STRAY THOUGHTS, EVERYTHING IN MY HEAD THAT ISN'T ABOUT GETTING THE JOB DONE--IS THROWN ASIDE IN A GREEN AFTERBURNER.
NICE TO MEET YOU, TOO.
BOOM
I TURN IT BACKWARDS ON THIS GUY, HOPING TO SLOW HIM DOWN.
FOOOM
BUT IT DOESN'T.
BOOOM
HNNN.
TERRESTRIAL CAMOUFLAGE DAMAGED AND DISCARDED.
GREEN LANTERN...

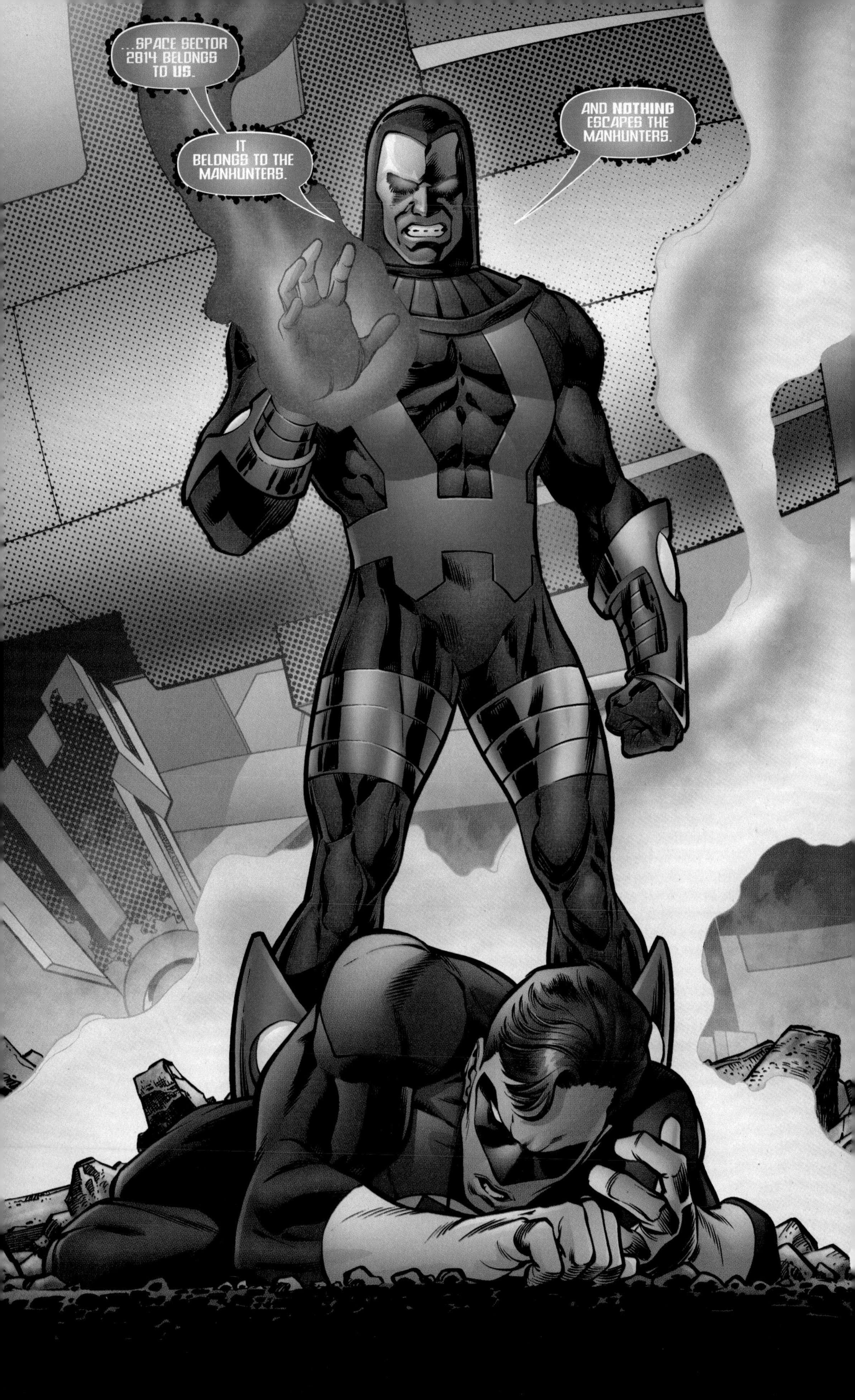
...SPACE SECTOR 2814 BELONGS TO US.
IT BELONGS TO THE MANHUNTERS.
AND NOTHING ESCAPES THE MANHUNTERS.

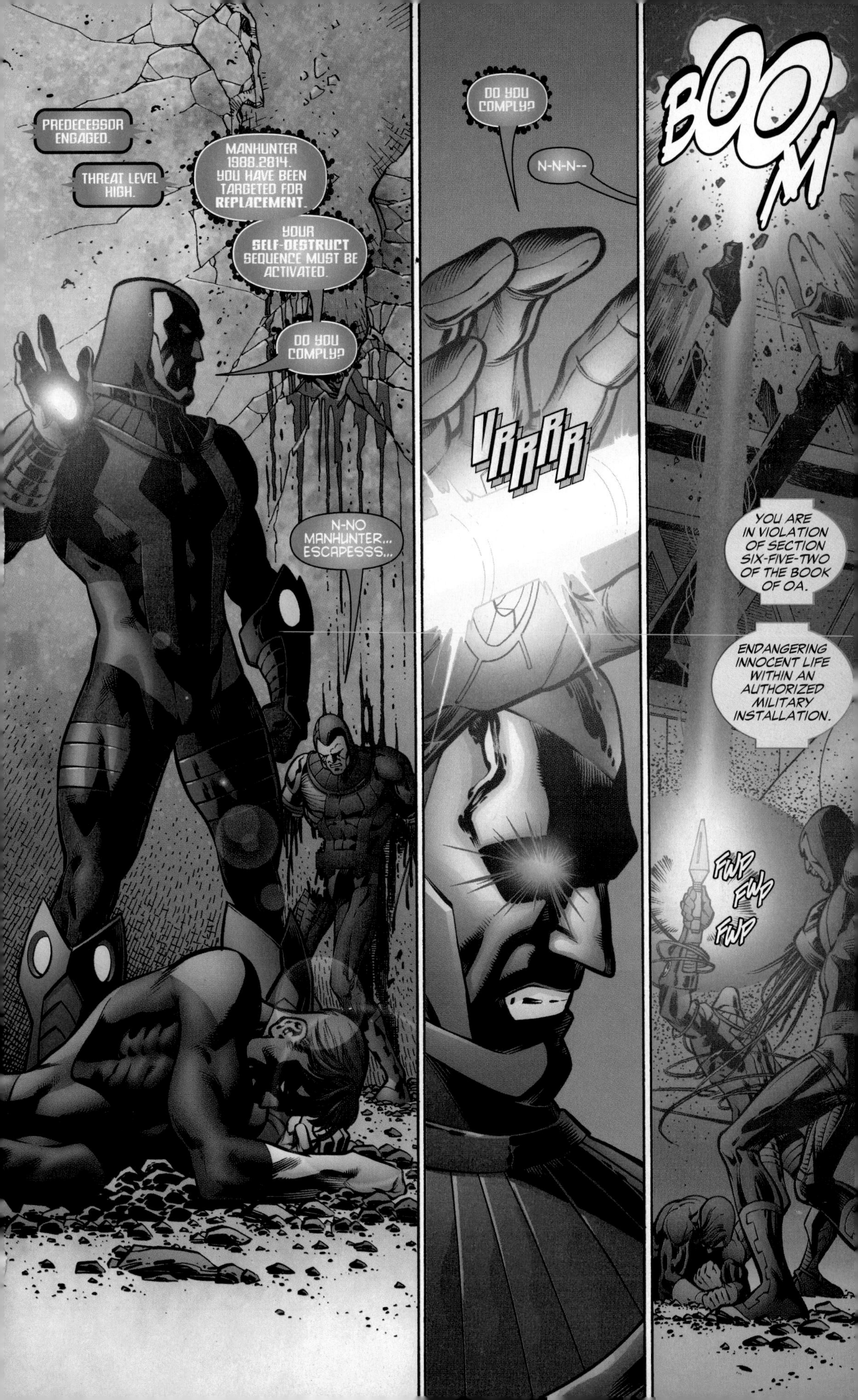
PREDECESSOR ENGAGED.
THREAT LEVEL HIGH.
MANHUNTER 1988.2814. YOU HAVE BEEN TARGETED FOR REPLACEMENT.
YOUR SELF-DESTRUCT SEQUENCE MUST BE ACTIVATED.
DO YOU COMPLY?
N-NO MANHUNTER... ESCAPESSS...
DO YOU COMPLY?
N-N-N--
VRRRR
BOOM
YOU ARE IN VIOLATION OF SECTION SIX-FIVE-TWO OF THE BOOK OF OA.
ENDANGERING INNOCENT LIFE WITHIN AN AUTHORIZED MILITARY INSTALLATION.
FWP FWP FWP

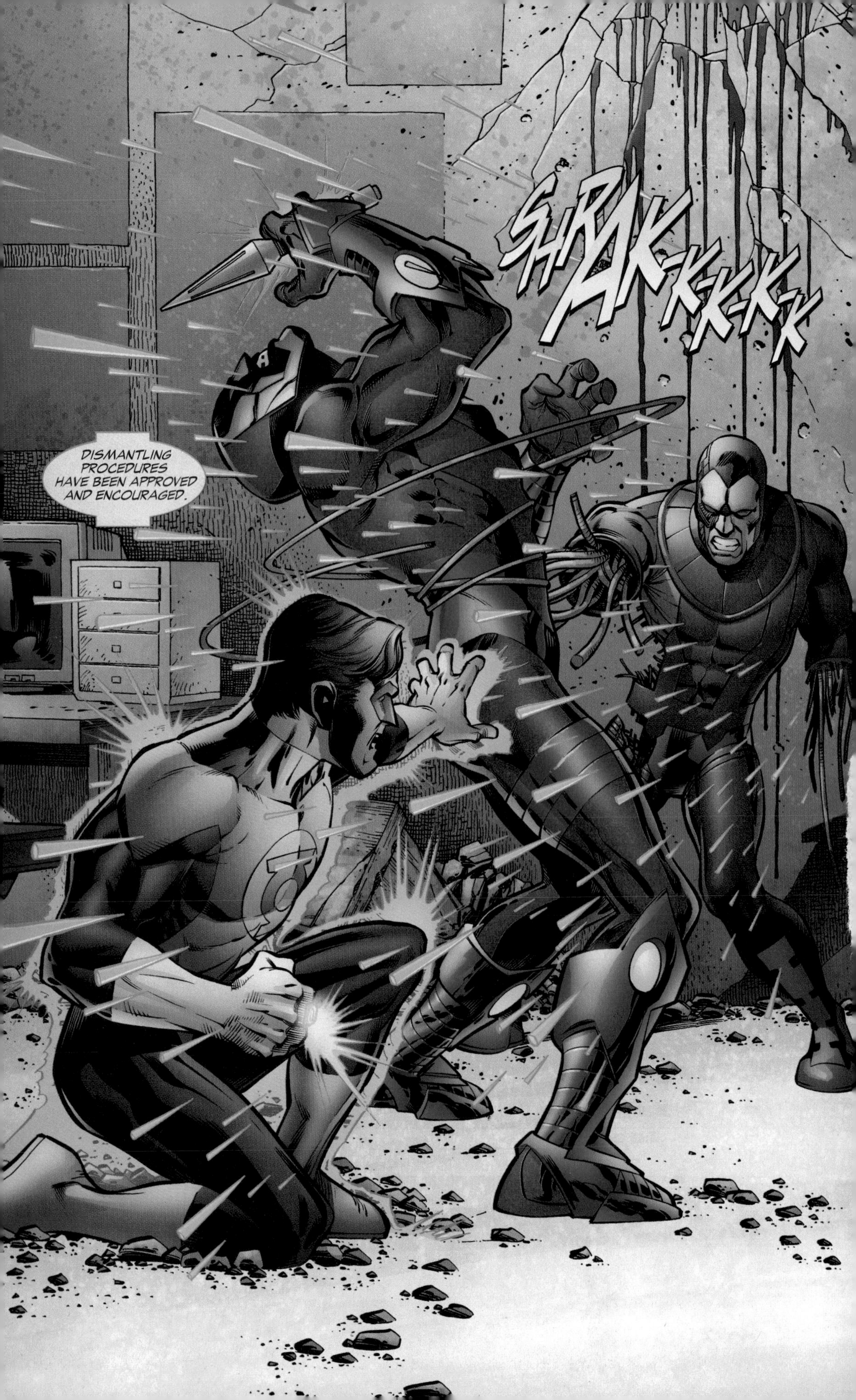
SHRAK-K-K-K-K
DISMANTLING PROCEDURES HAVE BEEN APPROVED AND ENCOURAGED.

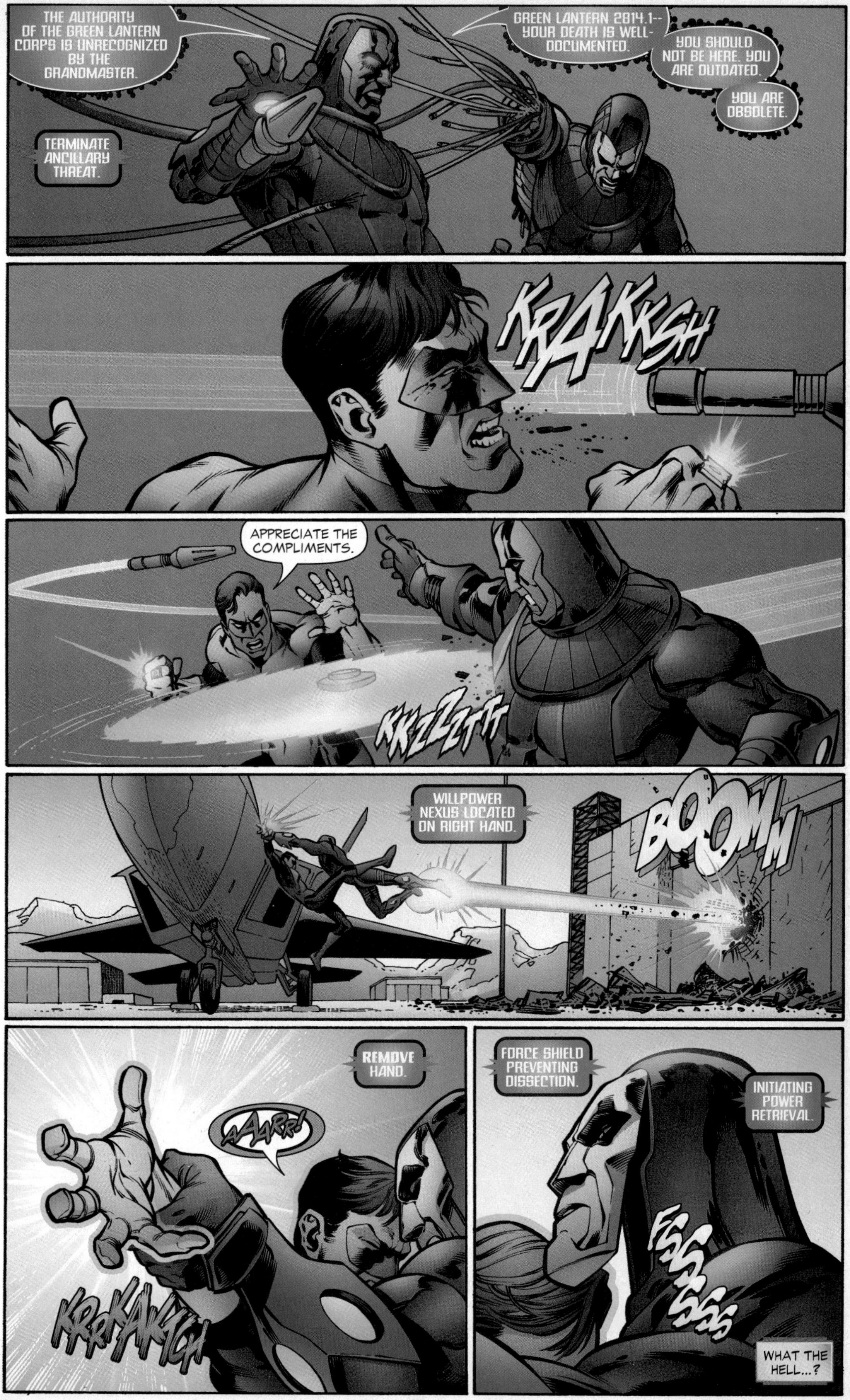

THE AUTHORITY OF THE GREEN LANTERN CORPS IS UNRECOGNIZED BY THE GRANDMASTER.
GREEN LANTERN 2814.1-- YOUR DEATH IS WELL-DOCUMENTED.
YOU SHOULD NOT BE HERE. YOU ARE OUTDATED.
YOU ARE OBSOLETE.
TERMINATE ANCILLARY THREAT.
KRAKKSH
APPRECIATE THE COMPLIMENTS.
KKZZZZTTT
WILLPOWER NEXUS LOCATED ON RIGHT HAND.
BOOMM
REMOVE HAND.
AAARR!
KRRKAKKTCH
FORCE SHIELD PREVENTING DISSECTION.
INITIATING POWER RETRIEVAL.
FSSSSSS
WHAT THE HELL...?

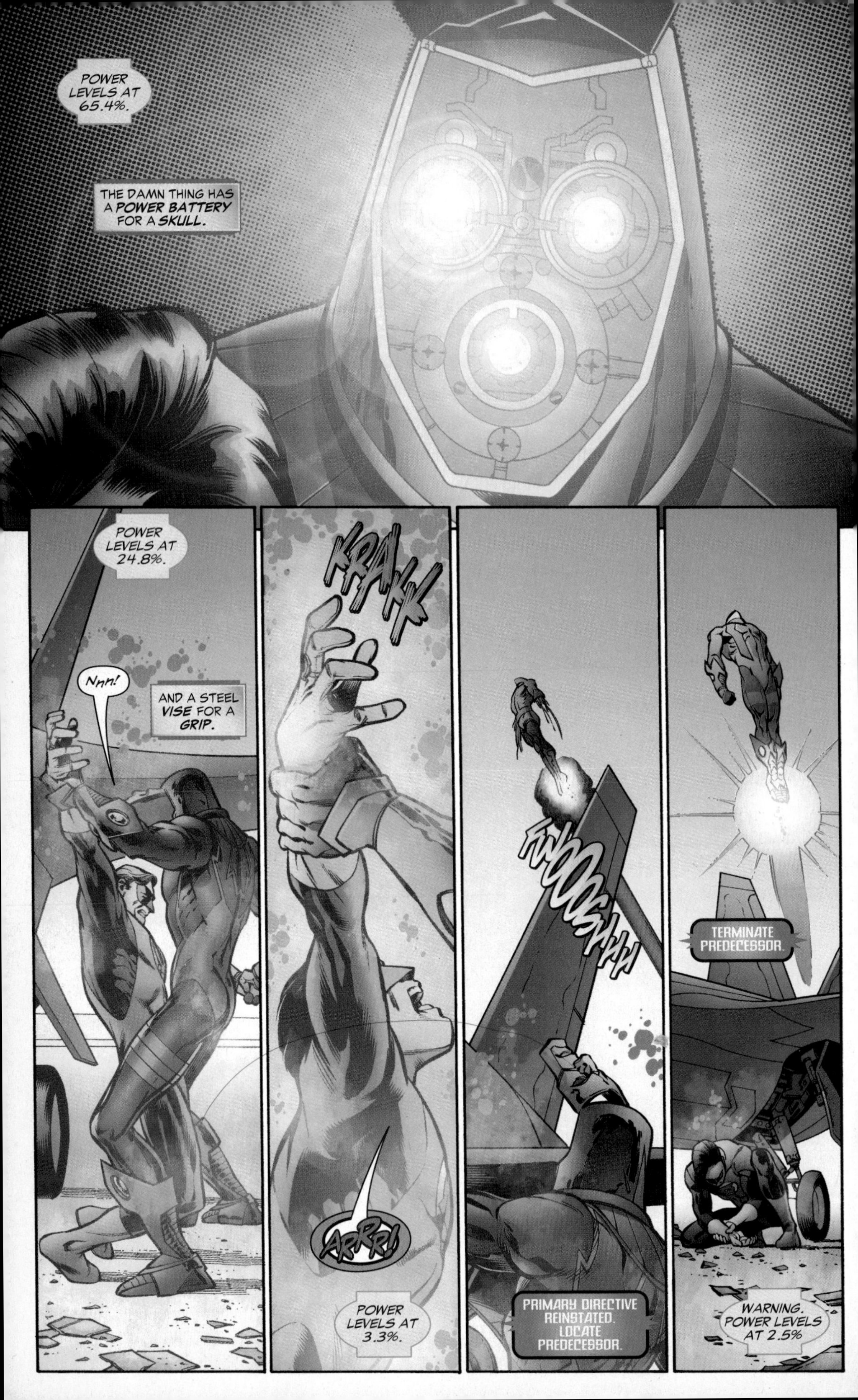
POWER LEVELS AT 65.4%.
THE DAMN THING HAS A POWER BATTERY FOR A SKULL.
POWER LEVELS AT 24.8%.
Nnn!
AND A STEEL VISE FOR A GRIP.
KRAKK
ARRR!
POWER LEVELS AT 3.3%.
FWOOOSHHH
PRIMARY DIRECTIVE REINSTATED. LOCATE PREDECESSOR.
TERMINATE PREDECESSOR.
WARNING. POWER LEVELS AT 2.5%

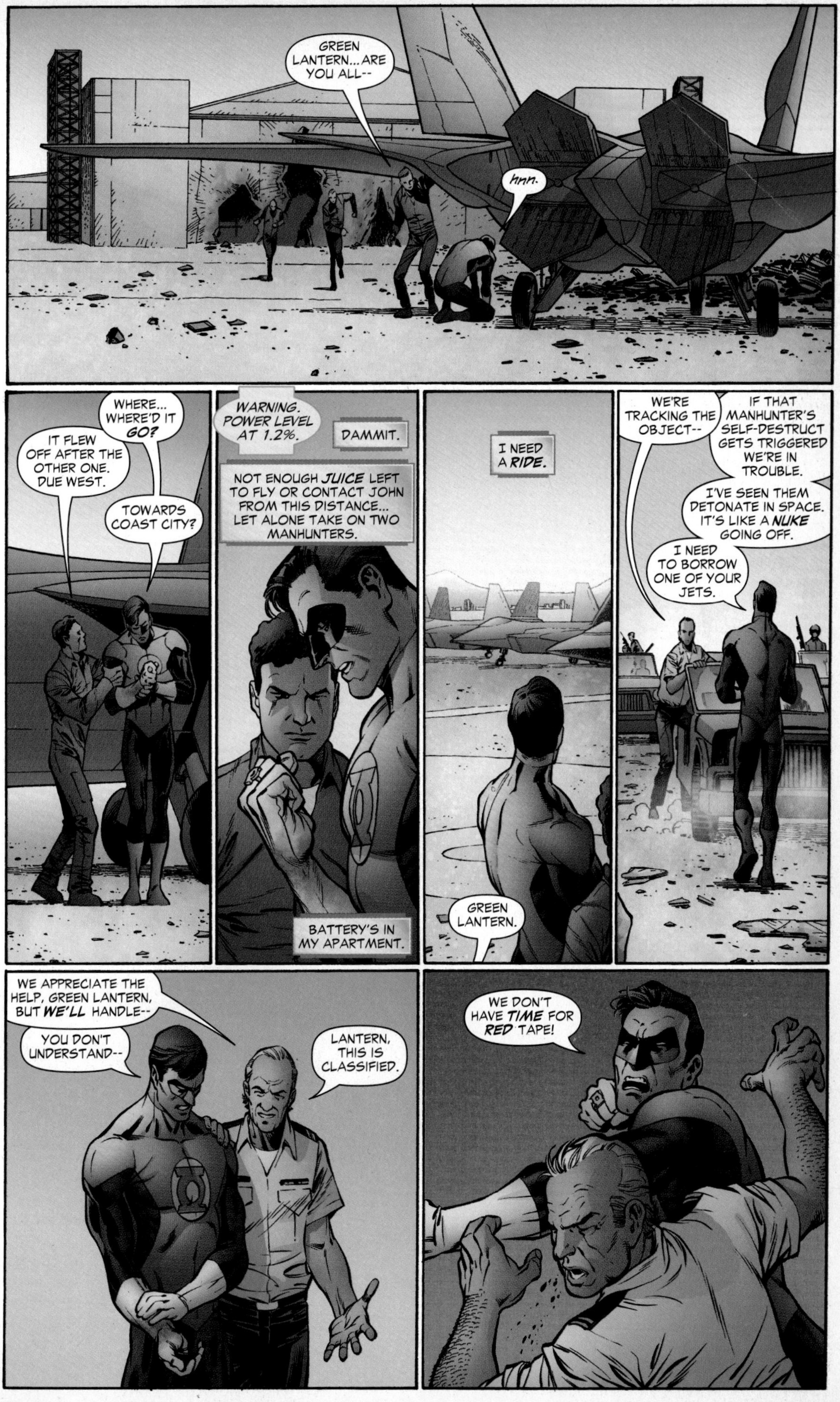
GREEN LANTERN... ARE YOU ALL--
hnn.
WHERE... WHERE'D IT GO?
IT FLEW OFF AFTER THE OTHER ONE. DUE WEST.
TOWARDS COAST CITY?
WARNING. POWER LEVEL AT 1.2%.
DAMMIT.
NOT ENOUGH JUICE LEFT TO FLY OR CONTACT JOHN FROM THIS DISTANCE... LET ALONE TAKE ON TWO MANHUNTERS.
BATTERY'S IN MY APARTMENT.
I NEED A RIDE.
GREEN LANTERN.
WE'RE TRACKING THE OBJECT--
IF THAT MANHUNTER'S SELF-DESTRUCT GETS TRIGGERED WE'RE IN TROUBLE.
I'VE SEEN THEM DETONATE IN SPACE. IT'S LIKE A NUKE GOING OFF.
I NEED TO BORROW ONE OF YOUR JETS.
WE APPRECIATE THE HELP, GREEN LANTERN, BUT WE'LL HANDLE--
YOU DON'T UNDERSTAND--
LANTERN, THIS IS CLASSIFIED.
WE DON'T HAVE TIME FOR RED TAPE!

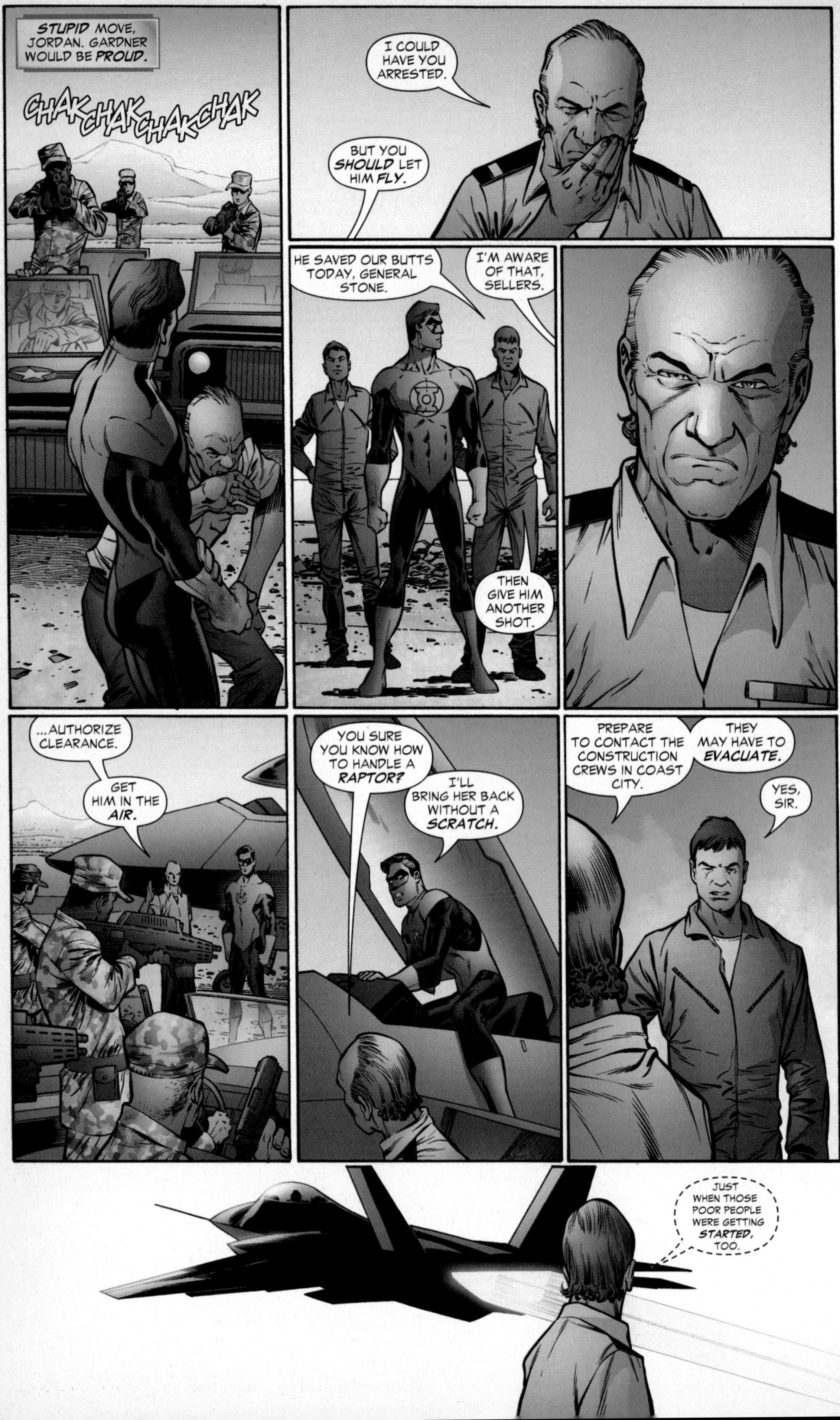
STUPID MOVE, JORDAN. GARDNER WOULD BE PROUD.
CHAKCHAKCHAKCHAK
I COULD HAVE YOU ARRESTED.
BUT YOU SHOULD LET HIM FLY.
HE SAVED OUR BUTTS TODAY, GENERAL STONE.
I'M AWARE OF THAT, SELLERS.
THEN GIVE HIM ANOTHER SHOT.
...AUTHORIZE CLEARANCE.
GET HIM IN THE AIR.
YOU SURE YOU KNOW HOW TO HANDLE A RAPTOR?
I'LL BRING HER BACK WITHOUT A SCRATCH.
PREPARE TO CONTACT THE CONSTRUCTION CREWS IN COAST CITY.
THEY MAY HAVE TO EVACUATE.
YES, SIR.
JUST WHEN THOSE POOR PEOPLE WERE GETTING STARTED, TOO.

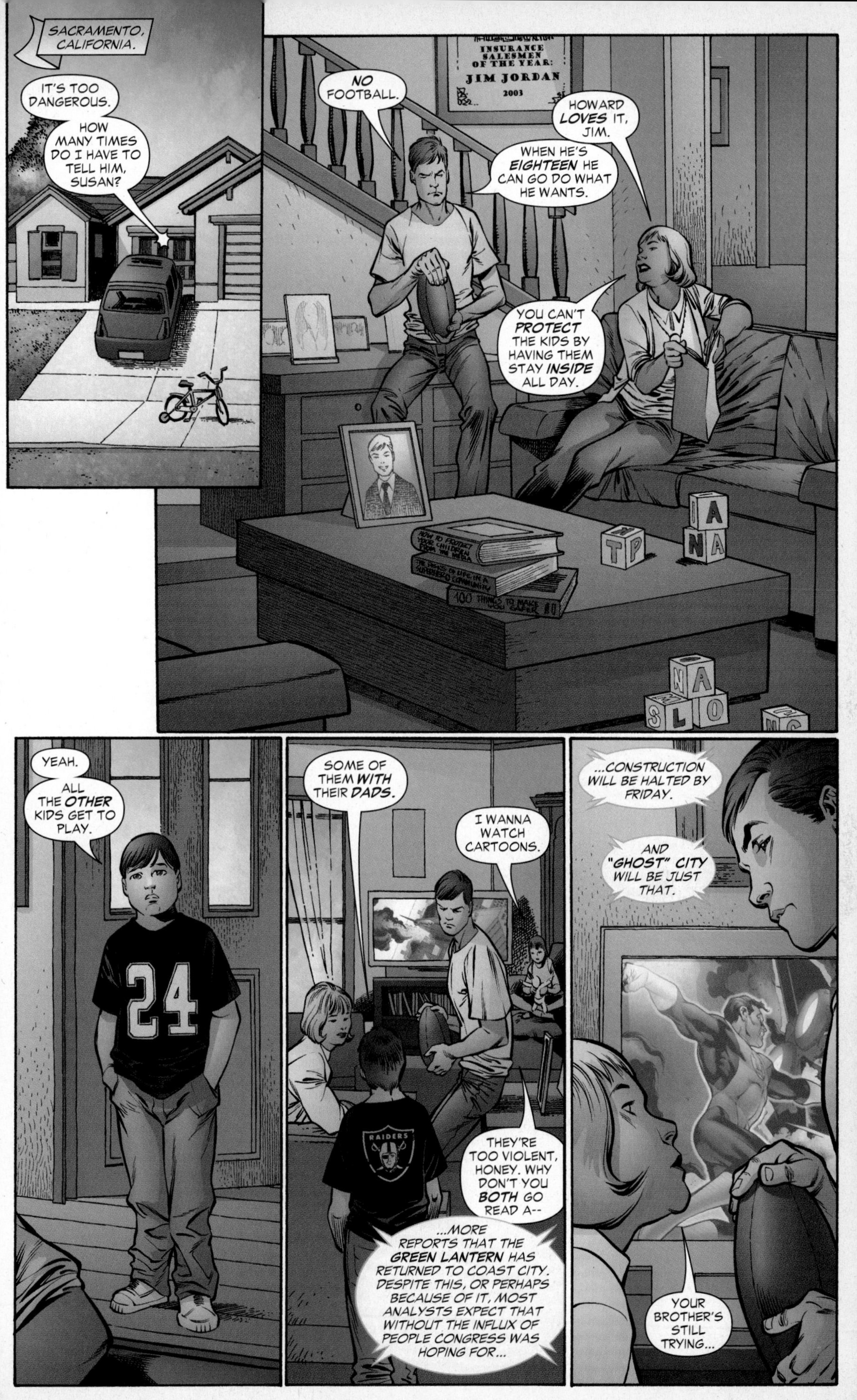
SACRAMENTO, CALIFORNIA.
IT'S TOO DANGEROUS.
HOW MANY TIMES DO I HAVE TO TELL HIM, SUSAN?
INSURANCE SALESMEN OF THE YEAR: JIM JORDAN 2003
NO FOOTBALL.
HOWARD LOVES IT, JIM.
WHEN HE'S EIGHTEEN HE CAN GO DO WHAT HE WANTS.
YOU CAN'T PROTECT THE KIDS BY HAVING THEM STAY INSIDE ALL DAY.
HOW TO PROTECT YOUR CHILDREN FROM THE MEDIA
100 THINGS TO MAKE YOU SAFER
YEAH.
ALL THE OTHER KIDS GET TO PLAY.
24
SOME OF THEM WITH THEIR DADS.
I WANNA WATCH CARTOONS.
THEY'RE TOO VIOLENT, HONEY. WHY DON'T YOU BOTH GO READ A--
RAIDERS
...MORE REPORTS THAT THE GREEN LANTERN HAS RETURNED TO COAST CITY. DESPITE THIS, OR PERHAPS BECAUSE OF IT, MOST ANALYSTS EXPECT THAT WITHOUT THE INFLUX OF PEOPLE CONGRESS WAS HOPING FOR...
...CONSTRUCTION WILL BE HALTED BY FRIDAY.
AND "GHOST" CITY WILL BE JUST THAT.
YOUR BROTHER'S STILL TRYING...

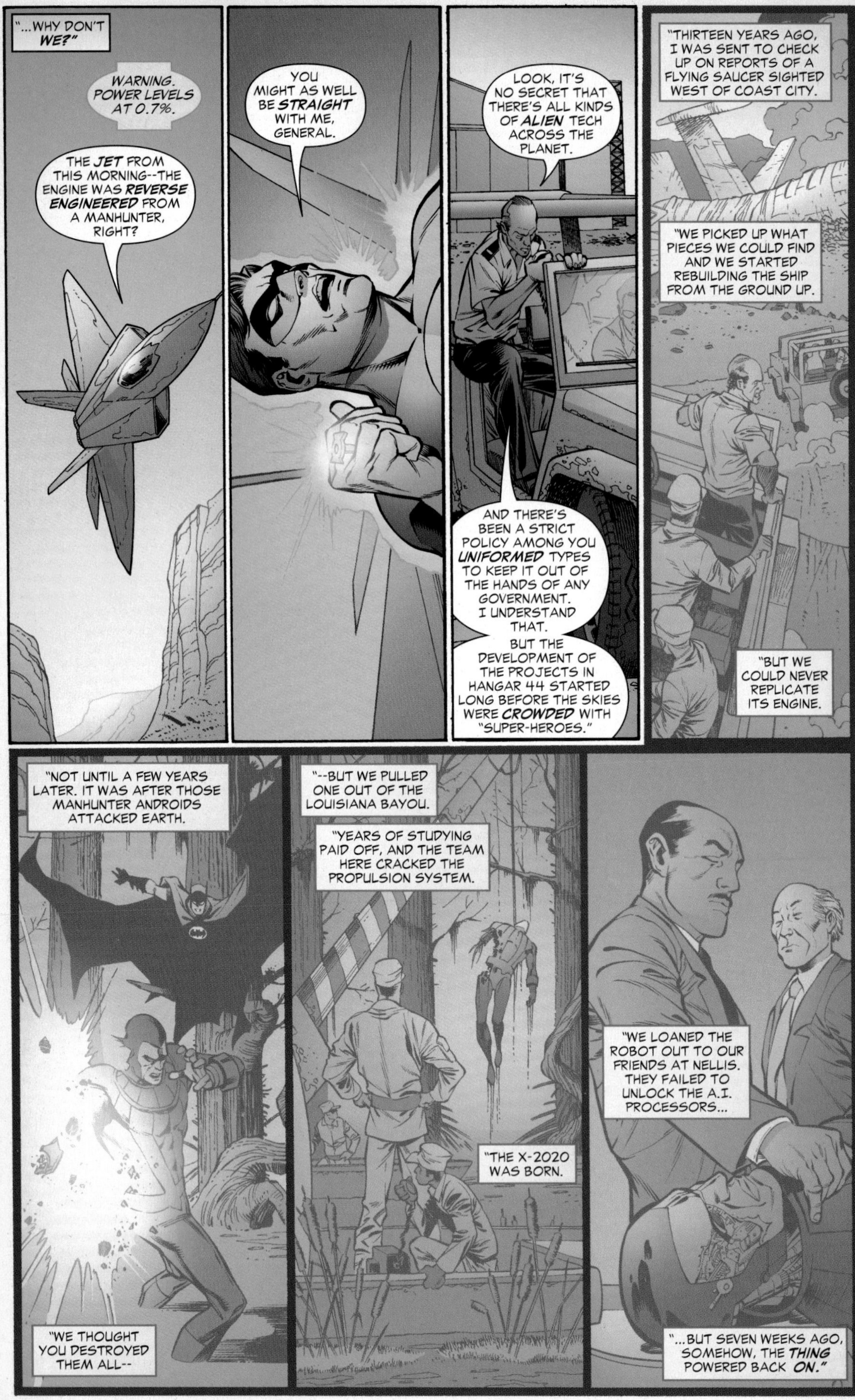
"...WHY DON'T WE?"
WARNING. POWER LEVELS AT 0.7%.
THE JET FROM THIS MORNING--THE ENGINE WAS REVERSE ENGINEERED FROM A MANHUNTER, RIGHT?
YOU MIGHT AS WELL BE STRAIGHT WITH ME, GENERAL.
LOOK, IT'S NO SECRET THAT THERE'S ALL KINDS OF ALIEN TECH ACROSS THE PLANET.
AND THERE'S BEEN A STRICT POLICY AMONG YOU UNIFORMED TYPES TO KEEP IT OUT OF THE HANDS OF ANY GOVERNMENT. I UNDERSTAND THAT.
BUT THE DEVELOPMENT OF THE PROJECTS IN HANGAR 44 STARTED LONG BEFORE THE SKIES WERE CROWDED WITH "SUPER-HEROES."
"THIRTEEN YEARS AGO, I WAS SENT TO CHECK UP ON REPORTS OF A FLYING SAUCER SIGHTED WEST OF COAST CITY.
"WE PICKED UP WHAT PIECES WE COULD FIND AND WE STARTED REBUILDING THE SHIP FROM THE GROUND UP.
"BUT WE COULD NEVER REPLICATE ITS ENGINE.
"NOT UNTIL A FEW YEARS LATER. IT WAS AFTER THOSE MANHUNTER ANDROIDS ATTACKED EARTH.
"WE THOUGHT YOU DESTROYED THEM ALL--
"--BUT WE PULLED ONE OUT OF THE LOUISIANA BAYOU.
"YEARS OF STUDYING PAID OFF, AND THE TEAM HERE CRACKED THE PROPULSION SYSTEM.
"THE X-2020 WAS BORN.
"WE LOANED THE ROBOT OUT TO OUR FRIENDS AT NELLIS. THEY FAILED TO UNLOCK THE A.I. PROCESSORS...
"...BUT SEVEN WEEKS AGO, SOMEHOW, THE THING POWERED BACK ON."

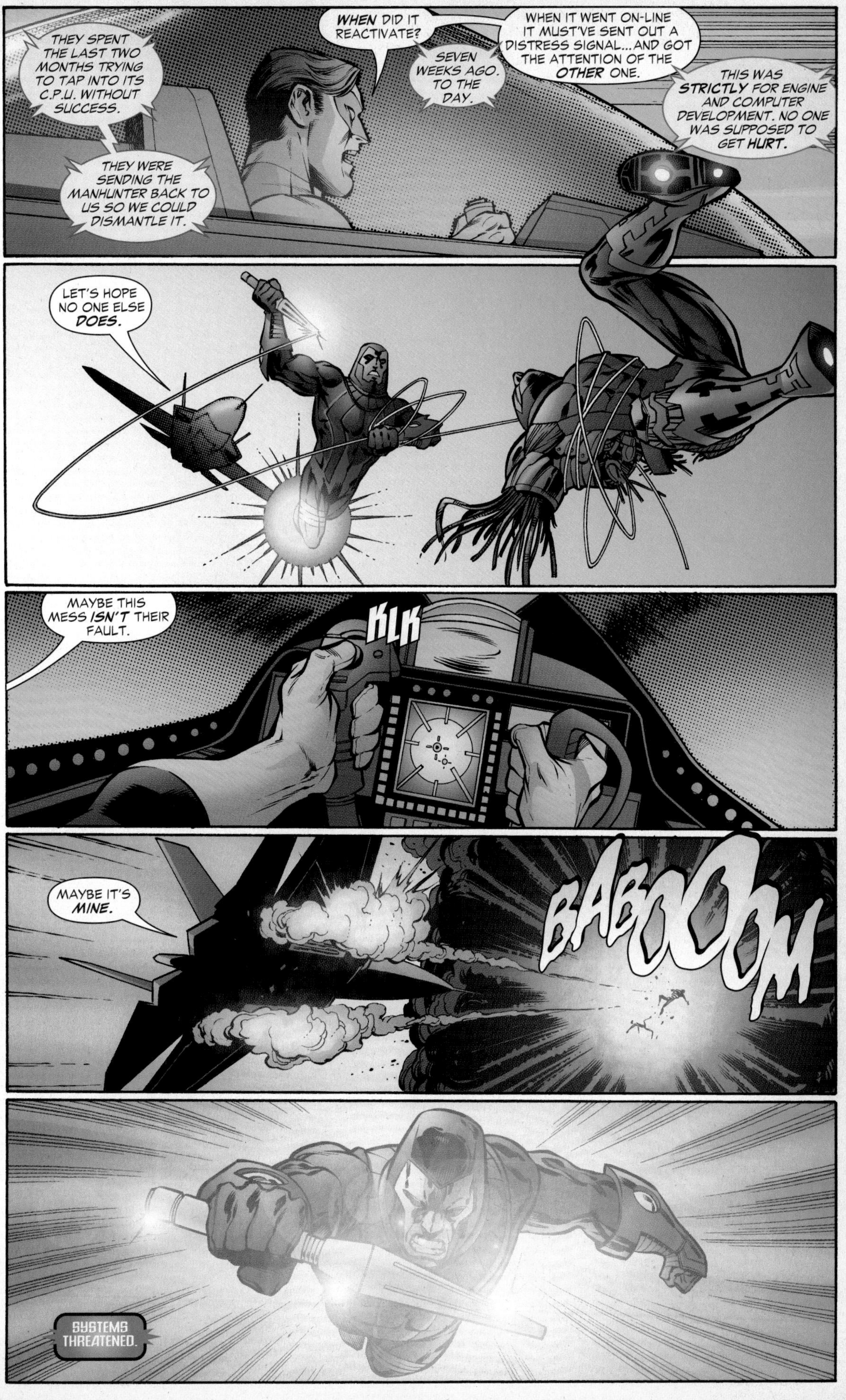
THEY SPENT THE LAST TWO MONTHS TRYING TO TAP INTO ITS C.P.U. WITHOUT SUCCESS.
THEY WERE SENDING THE MANHUNTER BACK TO US SO WE COULD DISMANTLE IT.
WHEN DID IT REACTIVATE?
SEVEN WEEKS AGO. TO THE DAY.
WHEN IT WENT ON-LINE IT MUST'VE SENT OUT A DISTRESS SIGNAL... AND GOT THE ATTENTION OF THE OTHER ONE.
THIS WAS STRICTLY FOR ENGINE AND COMPUTER DEVELOPMENT. NO ONE WAS SUPPOSED TO GET HURT.
LET'S HOPE NO ONE ELSE DOES.
MAYBE THIS MESS ISN'T THEIR FAULT.
KLK
MAYBE IT'S MINE.
BABOOOM
SYSTEMS THREATENED.

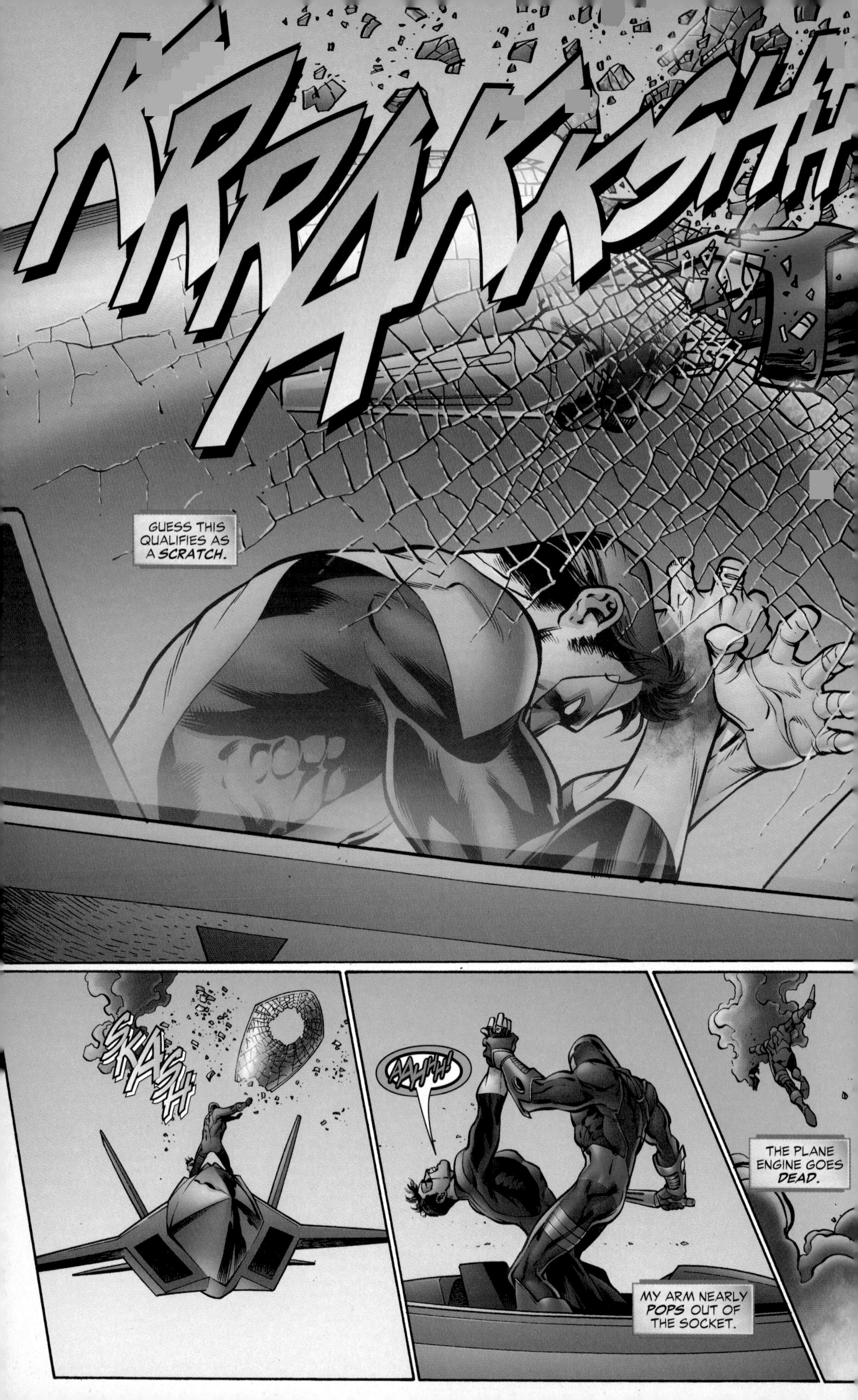
KRRAKKSHH
GUESS THIS QUALIFIES AS A SCRATCH.
SKASH
AAHHH!
MY ARM NEARLY POPS OUT OF THE SOCKET.
THE PLANE ENGINE GOES DEAD.

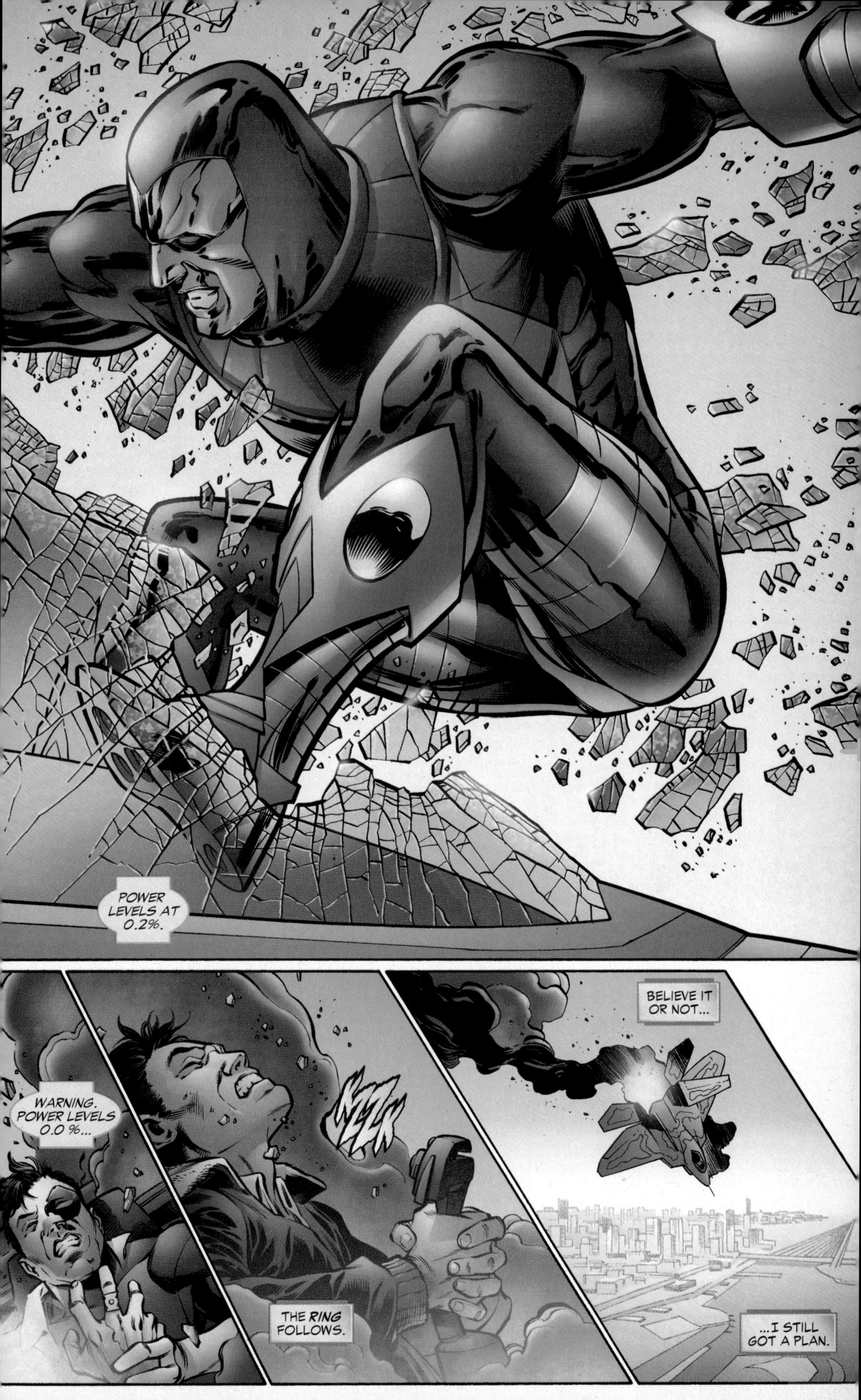
POWER LEVELS AT 0.2%.
WARNING. POWER LEVELS 0.0 %...
KZZK
THE RING FOLLOWS.
BELIEVE IT OR NOT...
...I STILL GOT A PLAN.

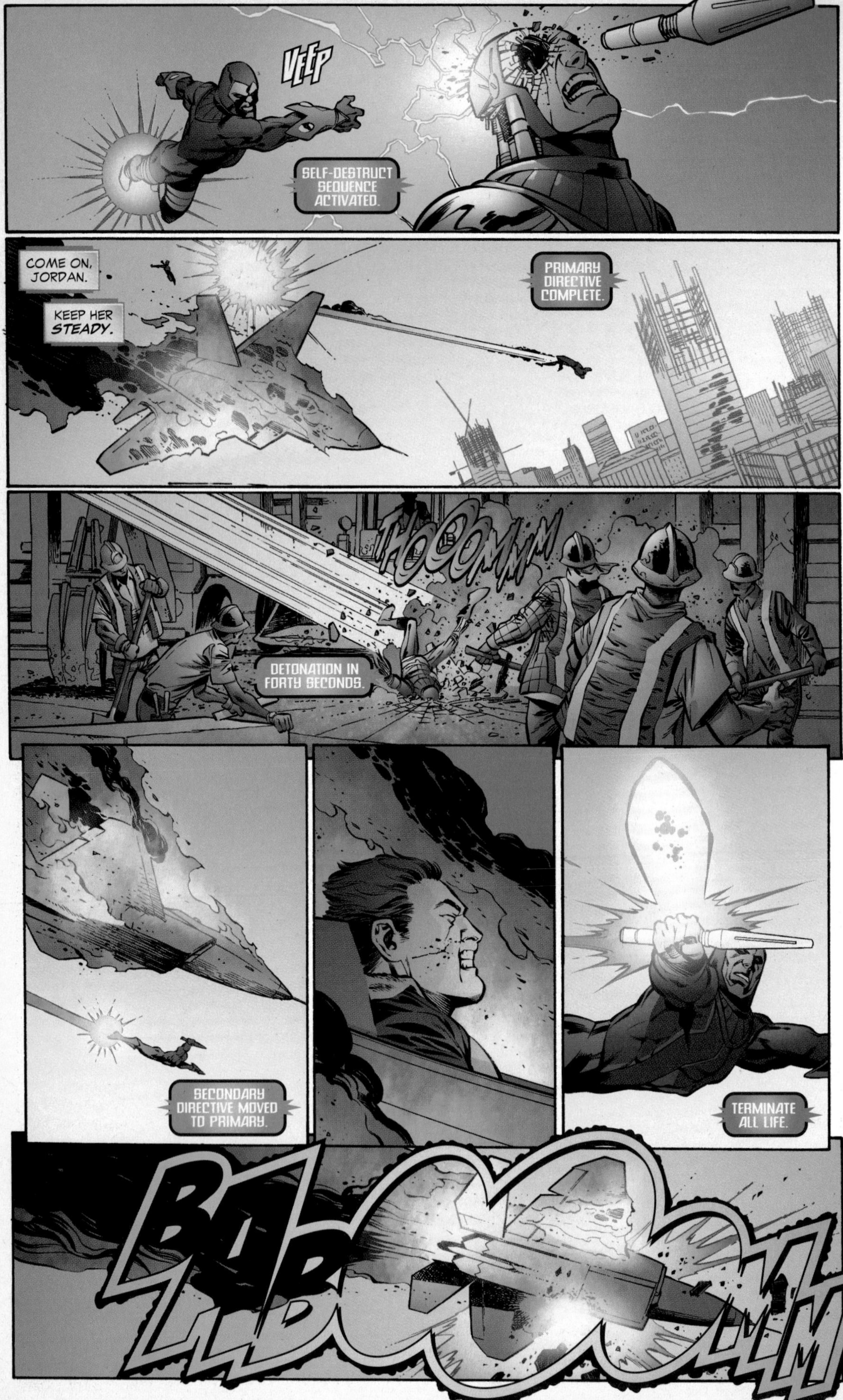
VEEP
SELF-DESTRUCT SEQUENCE ACTIVATED.
COME ON, JORDAN.
KEEP HER STEADY.
PRIMARY DIRECTIVE COMPLETE.
THOOOMMM
DETONATION IN FORTY SECONDS.
SECONDARY DIRECTIVE MOVED TO PRIMARY.
TERMINATE ALL LIFE.
BABOOOOMM

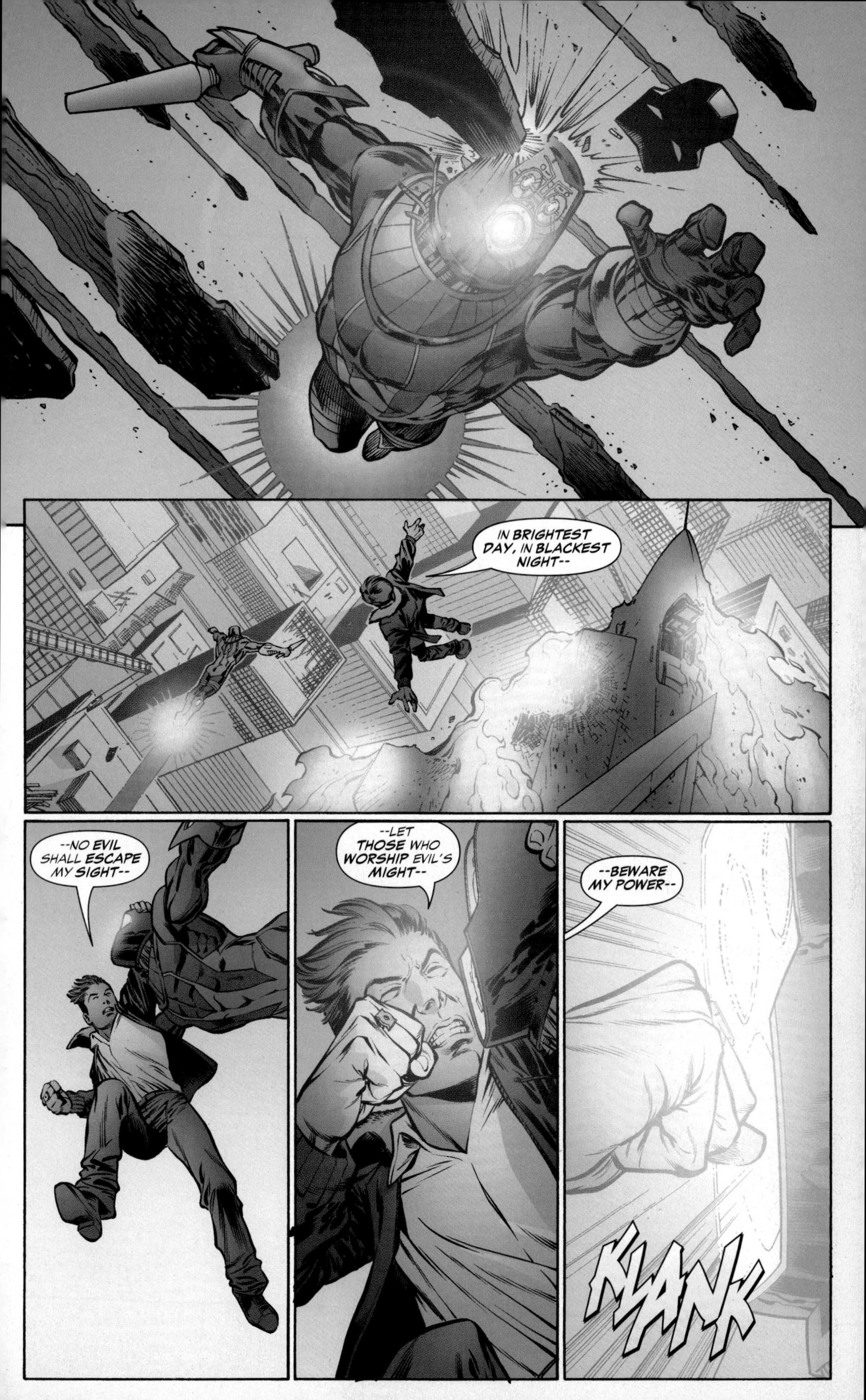
IN BRIGHTEST DAY, IN BLACKEST NIGHT--
--NO EVIL SHALL ESCAPE MY SIGHT--
--LET THOSE WHO WORSHIP EVIL'S MIGHT--
--BEWARE MY POWER--
KLANK

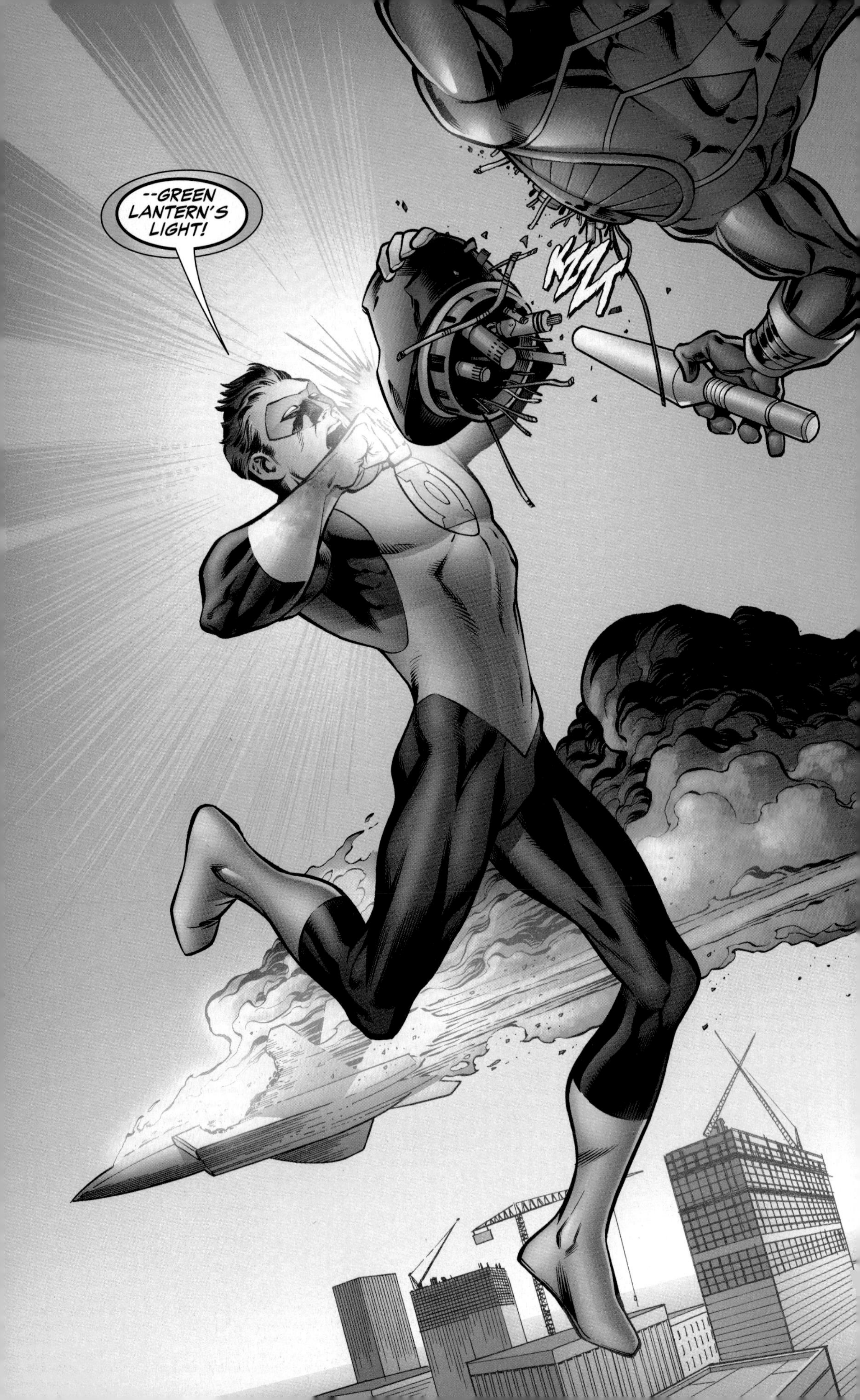
--GREEN LANTERN'S LIGHT!
KZZT

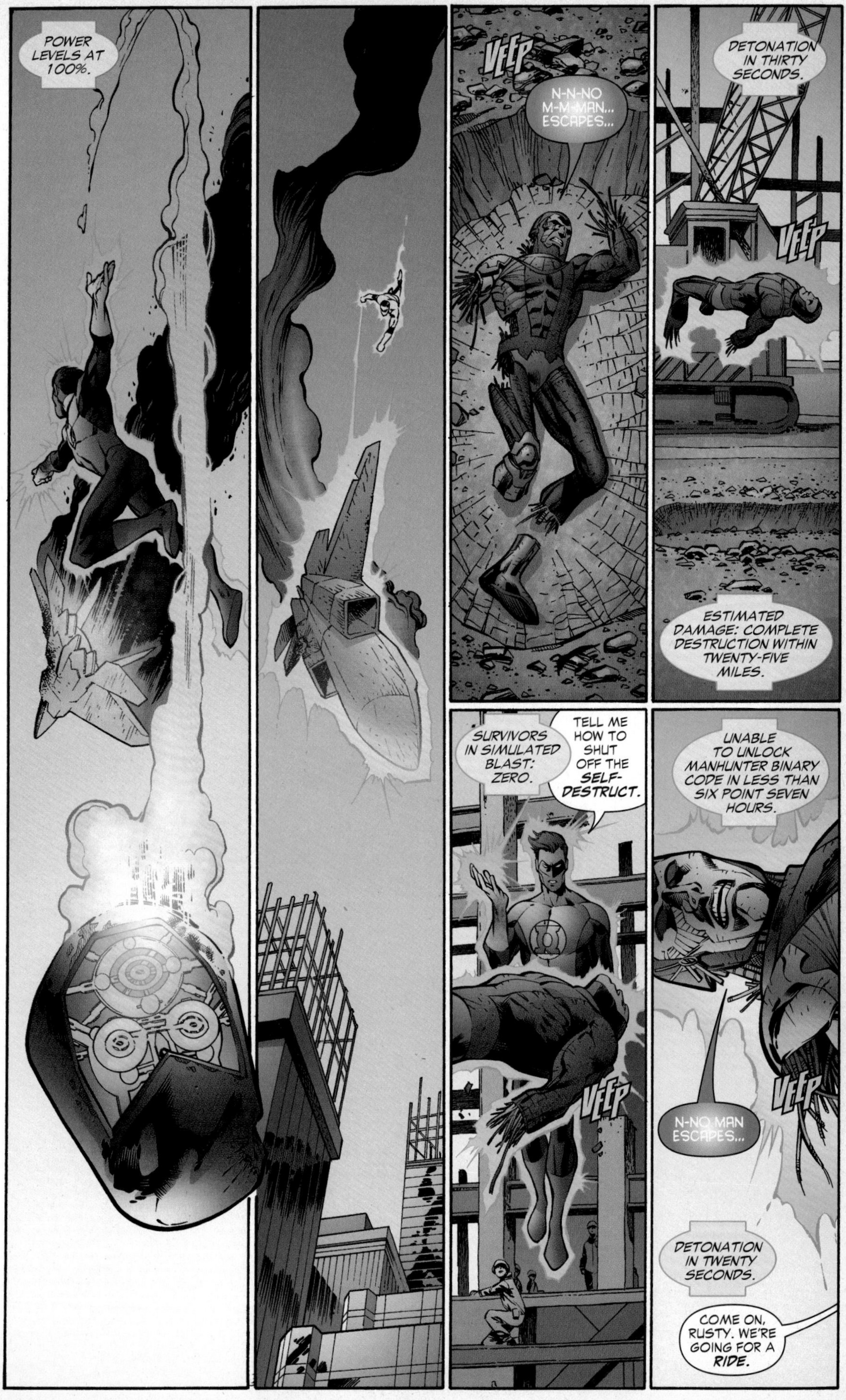
POWER LEVELS AT 100%.
VEEP
N-N-NO M-M-MAN... ESCAPES...
DETONATION IN THIRTY SECONDS.
VEEP
ESTIMATED DAMAGE: COMPLETE DESTRUCTION WITHIN TWENTY-FIVE MILES.
SURVIVORS IN SIMULATED BLAST: ZERO.
TELL ME HOW TO SHUT OFF THE SELF-DESTRUCT.
VEEP
UNABLE TO UNLOCK MANHUNTER BINARY CODE IN LESS THAN SIX POINT SEVEN HOURS.
VEEP
N-NO MAN ESCAPES...
DETONATION IN TWENTY SECONDS.
COME ON, RUSTY. WE'RE GOING FOR A RIDE.

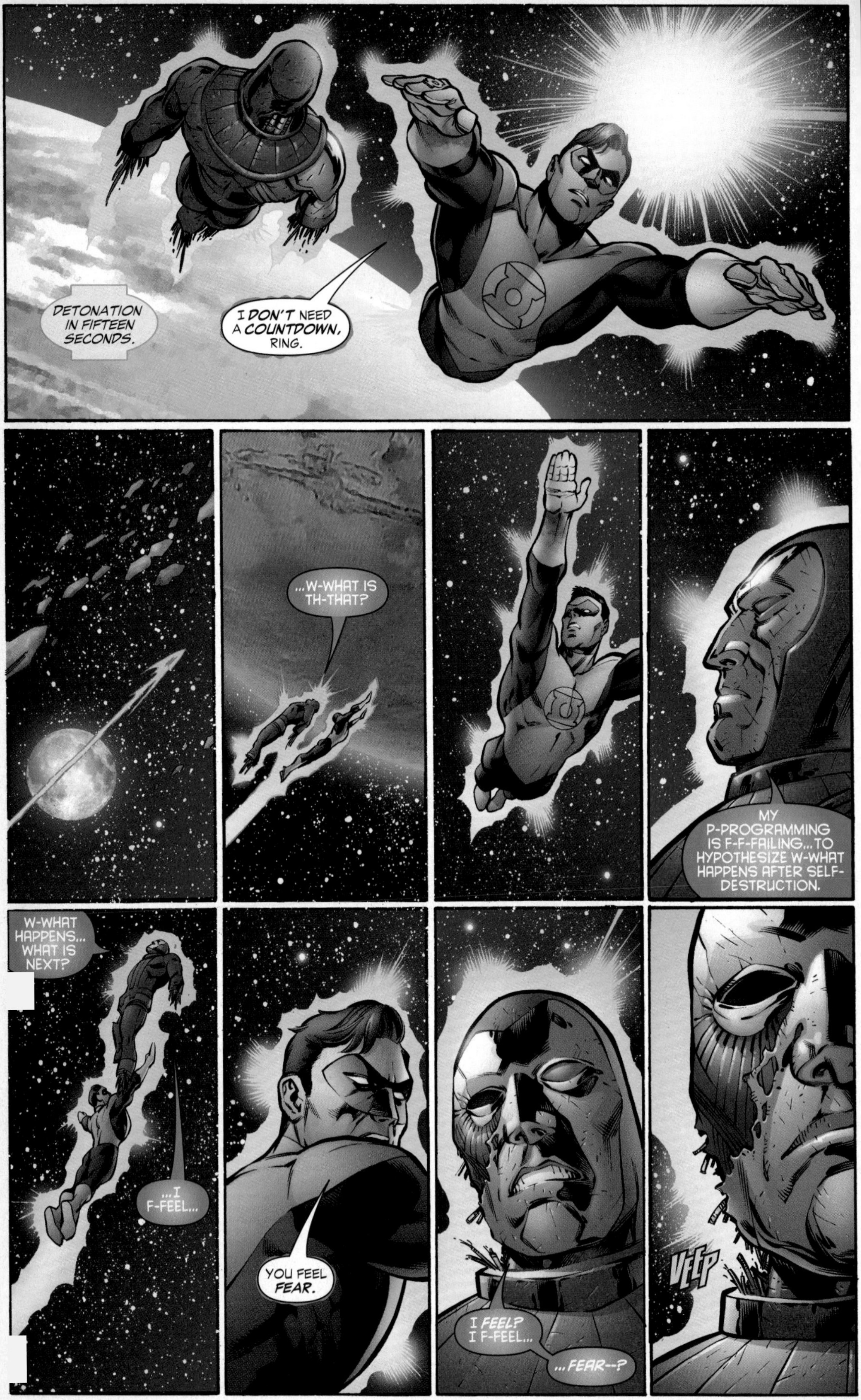
DETONATION IN FIFTEEN SECONDS.
I DON'T NEED A COUNTDOWN, RING.
...W-WHAT IS TH-THAT?
MY P-PROGRAMMING IS F-F-FAILING...TO HYPOTHESIZE W-WHAT HAPPENS AFTER SELF-DESTRUCTION.
W-WHAT HAPPENS... WHAT IS NEXT?
...I F-FEEL...
YOU FEEL FEAR.
I FEEL? I F-FEEL...
...FEAR--?
VEEP

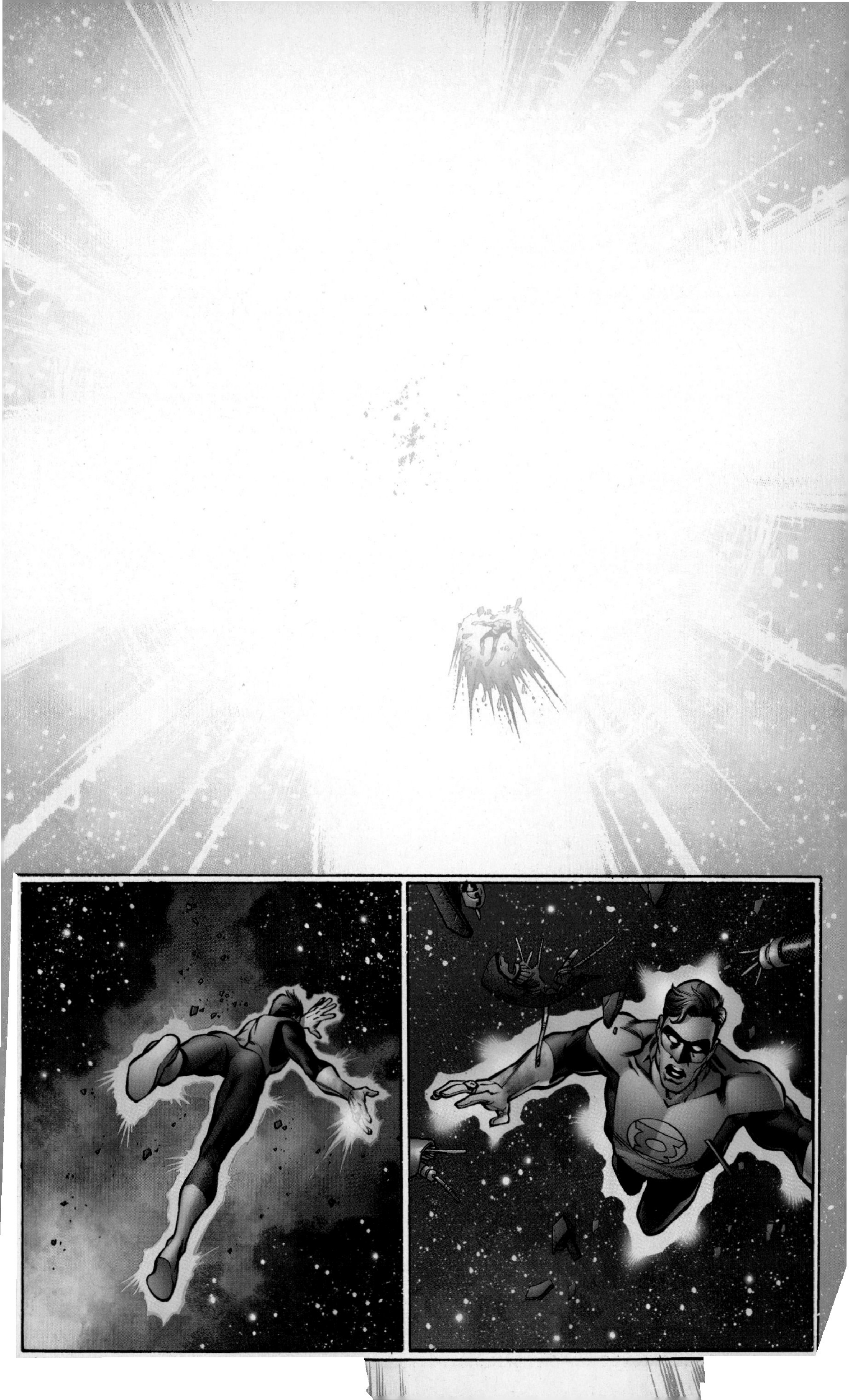

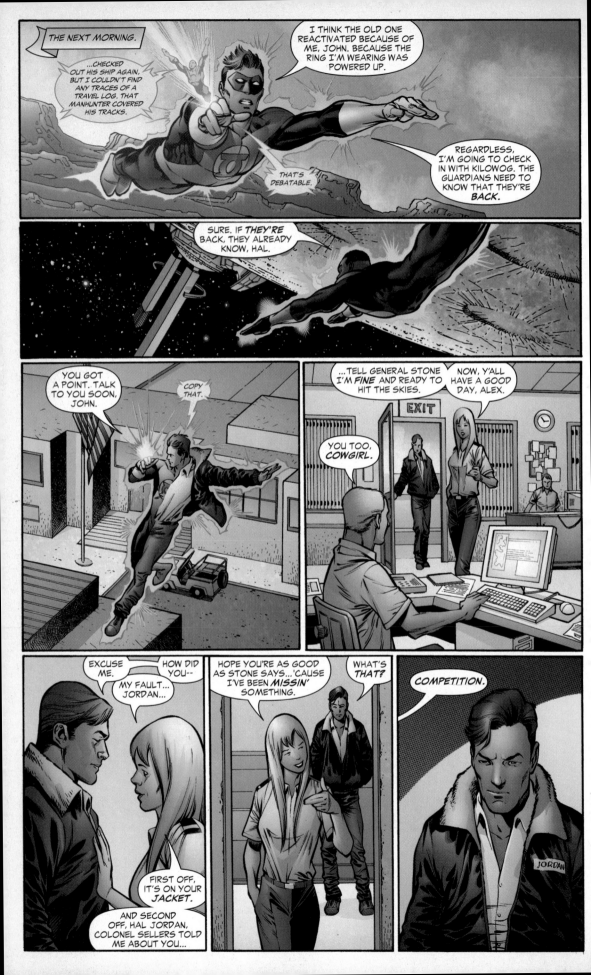

THE NEXT MORNING.

...CHECKED OUT HIS SHIP AGAIN, BUT I COULDN'T FIND ANY TRACES OF A TRAVEL LOG. THAT MANHUNTER COVERED HIS TRACKS.

I THINK THE OLD ONE REACTIVATED BECAUSE OF ME, JOHN. BECAUSE THE RING I'M WEARING WAS POWERED UP.

THAT'S DEBATABLE.

REGARDLESS, I'M GOING TO CHECK IN WITH KILOWOG. THE GUARDIANS NEED TO KNOW THAT THEY'RE BACK.

SURE. IF THEY'RE BACK, THEY ALREADY KNOW, HAL.

YOU GOT A POINT. TALK TO YOU SOON, JOHN.

COPY THAT.

...TELL GENERAL STONE I'M FINE AND READY TO HIT THE SKIES.

NOW, Y'ALL HAVE A GOOD DAY, ALEX.

YOU TOO, COWGIRL.

EXIT

EXCUSE ME.

HOW DID YOU--

MY FAULT... JORDAN...

HOPE YOU'RE AS GOOD AS STONE SAYS...'CAUSE I'VE BEEN MISSIN' SOMETHING.

WHAT'S THAT?

COMPETITION.

FIRST OFF, IT'S ON YOUR JACKET.

AND SECOND OFF, HAL JORDAN, COLONEL SELLERS TOLD ME ABOUT YOU...

JORDAN

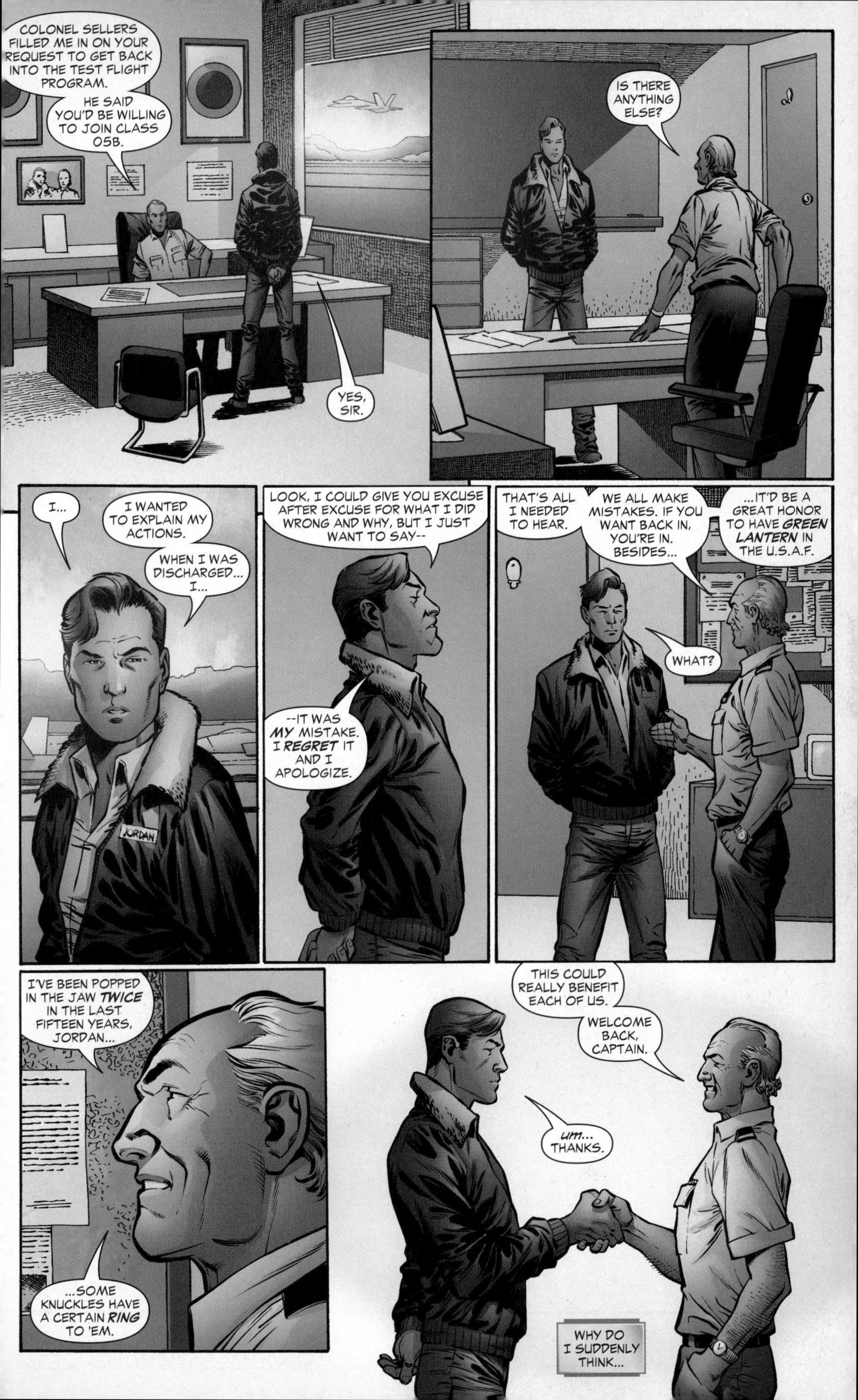
COLONEL SELLERS FILLED ME IN ON YOUR REQUEST TO GET BACK INTO THE TEST FLIGHT PROGRAM.
HE SAID YOU'D BE WILLING TO JOIN CLASS 05B.
YES, SIR.
IS THERE ANYTHING ELSE?
I...
I WANTED TO EXPLAIN MY ACTIONS.
WHEN I WAS DISCHARGED... I...
LOOK, I COULD GIVE YOU EXCUSE AFTER EXCUSE FOR WHAT I DID WRONG AND WHY, BUT I JUST WANT TO SAY--
--IT WAS MY MISTAKE. I REGRET IT AND I APOLOGIZE.
THAT'S ALL I NEEDED TO HEAR.
WE ALL MAKE MISTAKES. IF YOU WANT BACK IN, YOU'RE IN. BESIDES...
...IT'D BE A GREAT HONOR TO HAVE GREEN LANTERN IN THE U.S.A.F.
WHAT?
I'VE BEEN POPPED IN THE JAW TWICE IN THE LAST FIFTEEN YEARS, JORDAN...
...SOME KNUCKLES HAVE A CERTAIN RING TO 'EM.
THIS COULD REALLY BENEFIT EACH OF US.
WELCOME BACK, CAPTAIN.
UM... THANKS.
WHY DO I SUDDENLY THINK...

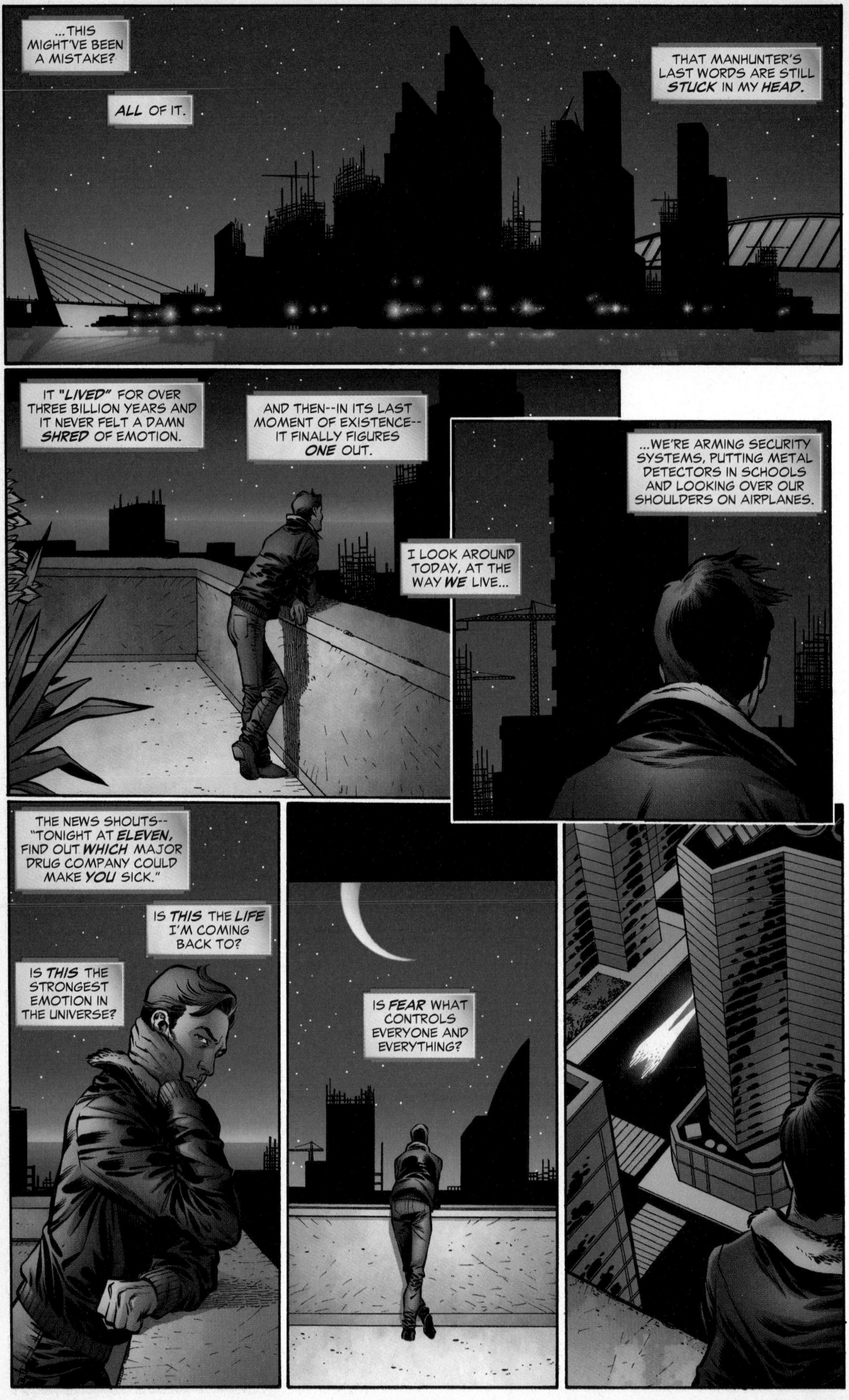
...THIS MIGHT'VE BEEN A MISTAKE?
ALL OF IT.
THAT MANHUNTER'S LAST WORDS ARE STILL STUCK IN MY HEAD.
IT "LIVED" FOR OVER THREE BILLION YEARS AND IT NEVER FELT A DAMN SHRED OF EMOTION.
AND THEN--IN ITS LAST MOMENT OF EXISTENCE--IT FINALLY FIGURES ONE OUT.
I LOOK AROUND TODAY, AT THE WAY WE LIVE...
...WE'RE ARMING SECURITY SYSTEMS, PUTTING METAL DETECTORS IN SCHOOLS AND LOOKING OVER OUR SHOULDERS ON AIRPLANES.
THE NEWS SHOUTS--"TONIGHT AT ELEVEN, FIND OUT WHICH MAJOR DRUG COMPANY COULD MAKE YOU SICK."
IS THIS THE LIFE I'M COMING BACK TO?
IS THIS THE STRONGEST EMOTION IN THE UNIVERSE?
IS FEAR WHAT CONTROLS EVERYONE AND EVERYTHING?

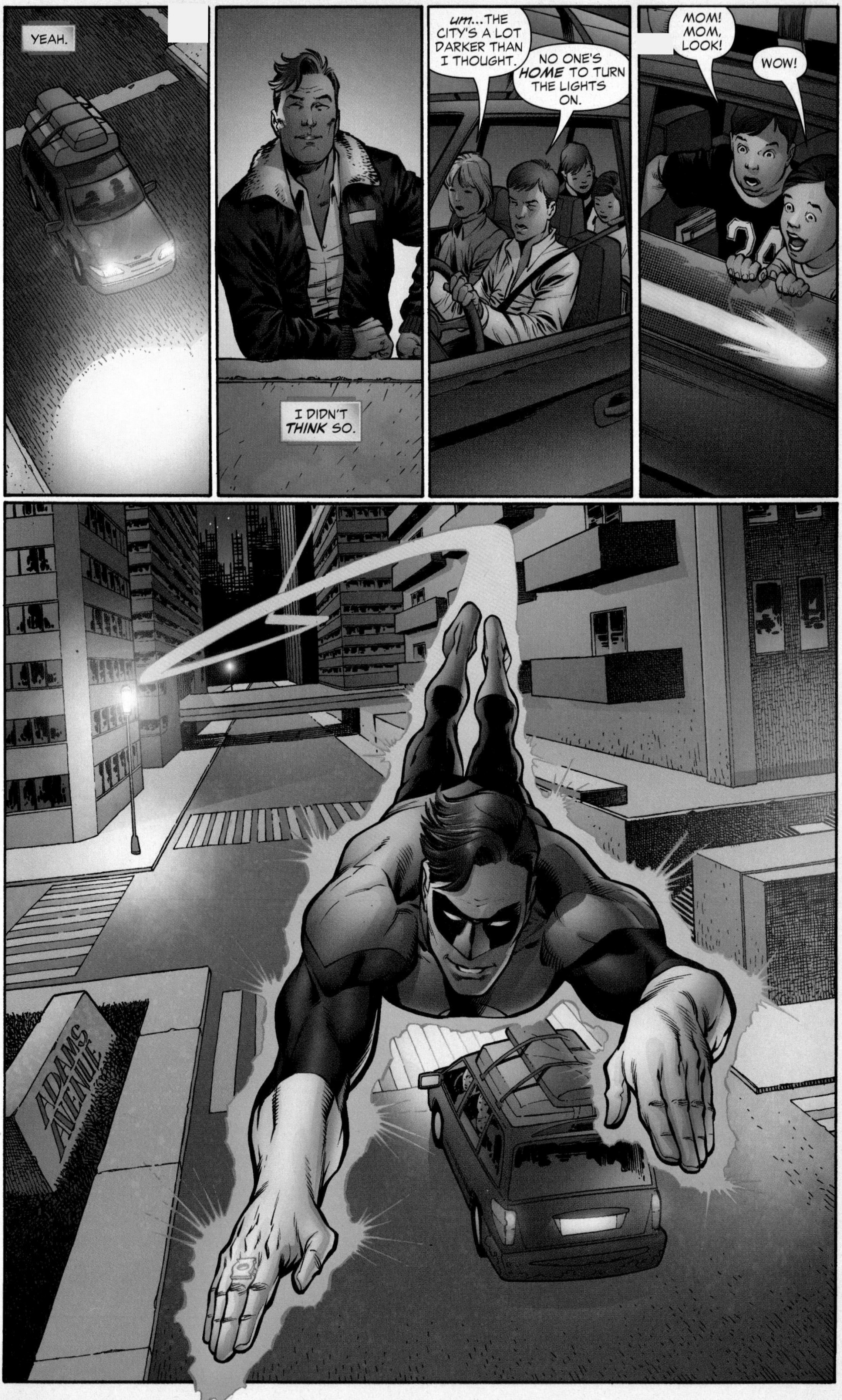
YEAH.
I DIDN'T THINK SO.
um... THE CITY'S A LOT DARKER THAN I THOUGHT.
NO ONE'S HOME TO TURN THE LIGHTS ON.
MOM! MOM, LOOK!
WOW!
ADAMS AVENUE

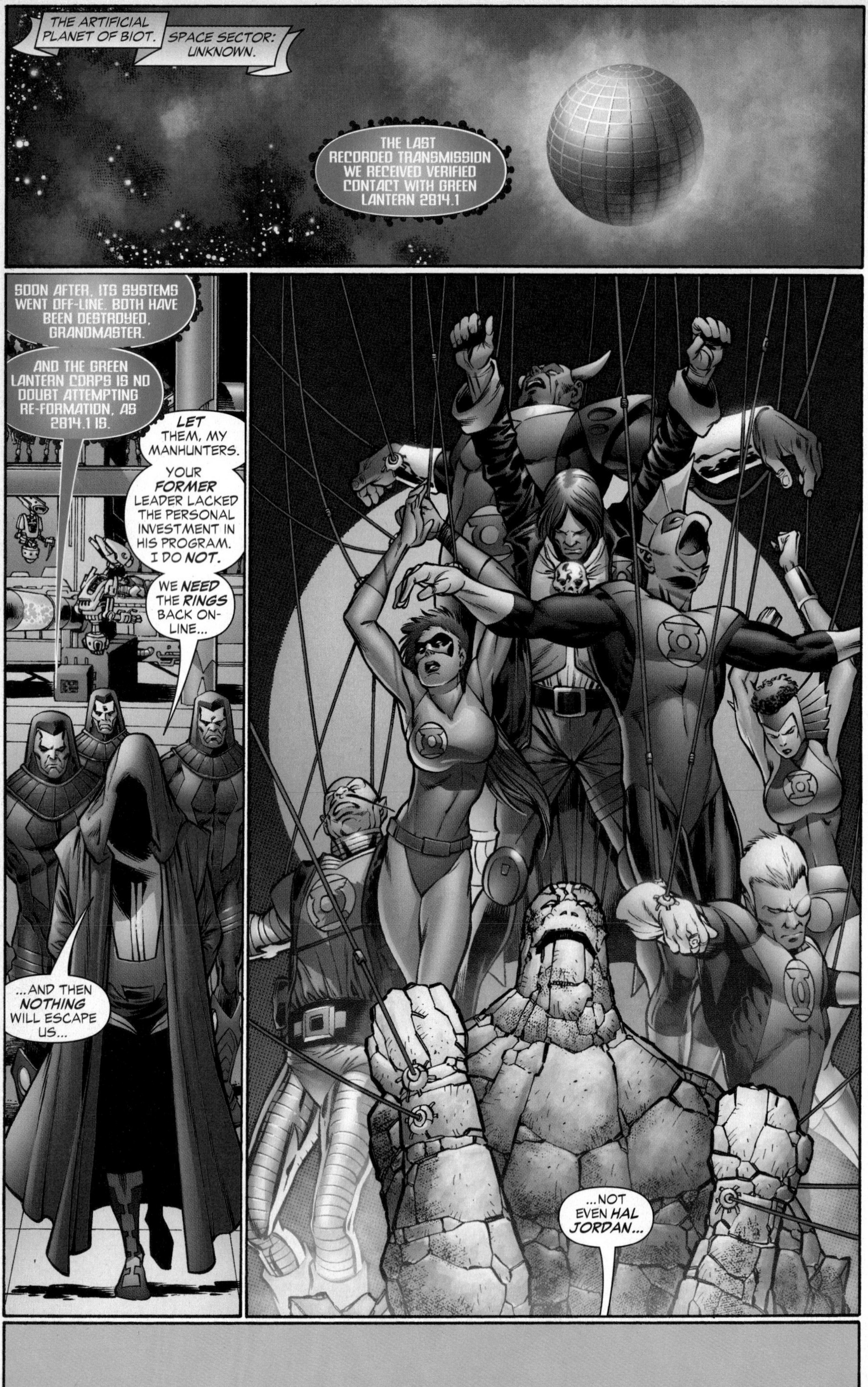
THE ARTIFICIAL PLANET OF BIOT.
SPACE SECTOR: UNKNOWN.
THE LAST RECORDED TRANSMISSION WE RECEIVED VERIFIED CONTACT WITH GREEN LANTERN 2814.1
SOON AFTER, ITS SYSTEMS WENT OFF-LINE. BOTH HAVE BEEN DESTROYED, GRANDMASTER.
AND THE GREEN LANTERN CORPS IS NO DOUBT ATTEMPTING RE-FORMATION, AS 2814.1 IS.
LET THEM, MY MANHUNTERS.
YOUR FORMER LEADER LACKED THE PERSONAL INVESTMENT IN HIS PROGRAM. I DO NOT.
WE NEED THE RINGS BACK ON-LINE...
...AND THEN NOTHING WILL ESCAPE US...
...NOT EVEN HAL JORDAN...

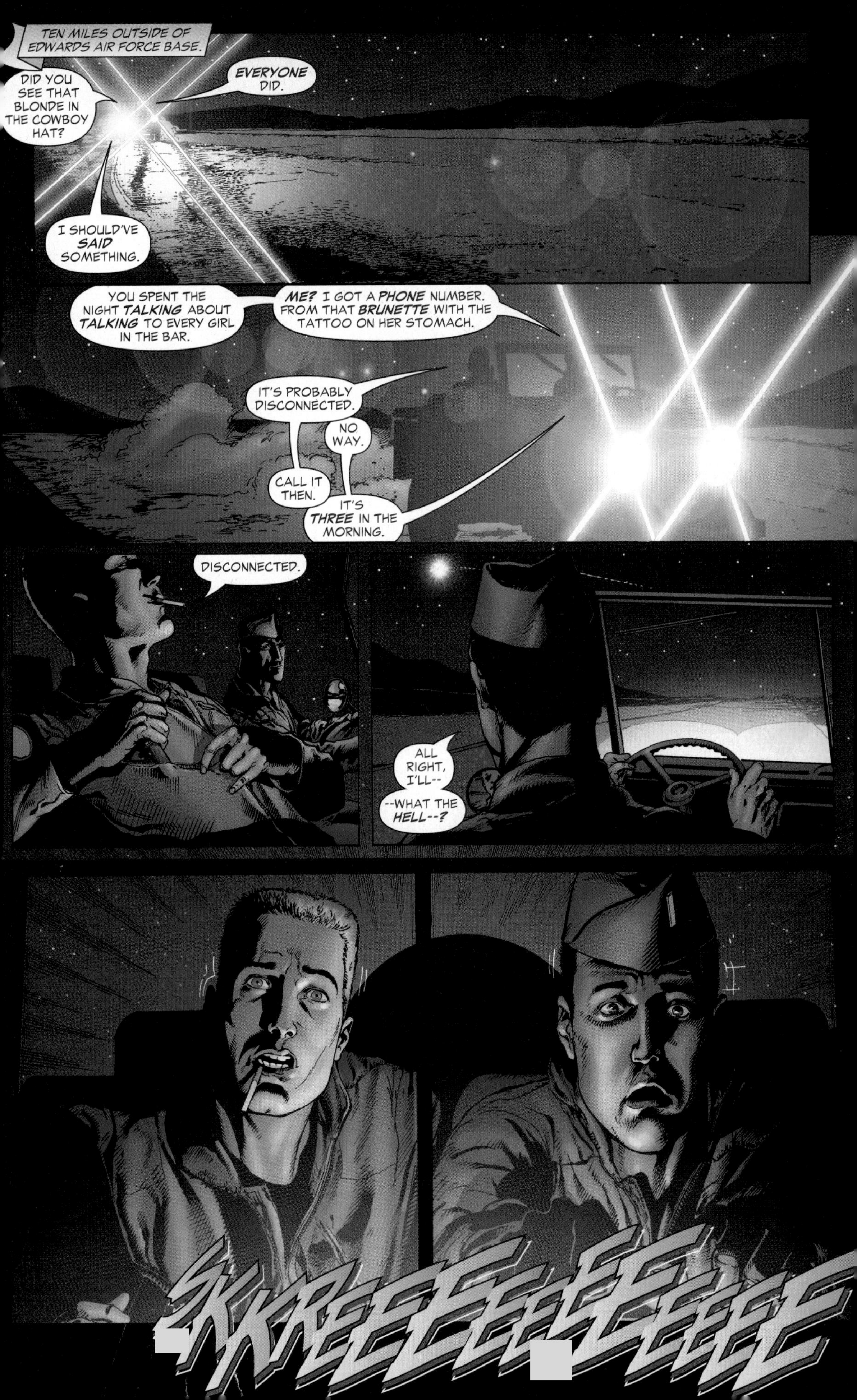

TEN MILES OUTSIDE OF EDWARDS AIR FORCE BASE.
DID YOU SEE THAT BLONDE IN THE COWBOY HAT?
EVERYONE DID.
I SHOULD'VE SAID SOMETHING.
YOU SPENT THE NIGHT TALKING ABOUT TALKING TO EVERY GIRL IN THE BAR.
ME? I GOT A PHONE NUMBER. FROM THAT BRUNETTE WITH THE TATTOO ON HER STOMACH.
IT'S PROBABLY DISCONNECTED.
NO WAY.
CALL IT THEN.
IT'S THREE IN THE MORNING.
DISCONNECTED.
ALL RIGHT, I'LL--
--WHAT THE HELL--?
SKREEEEEEEEEEEEEE

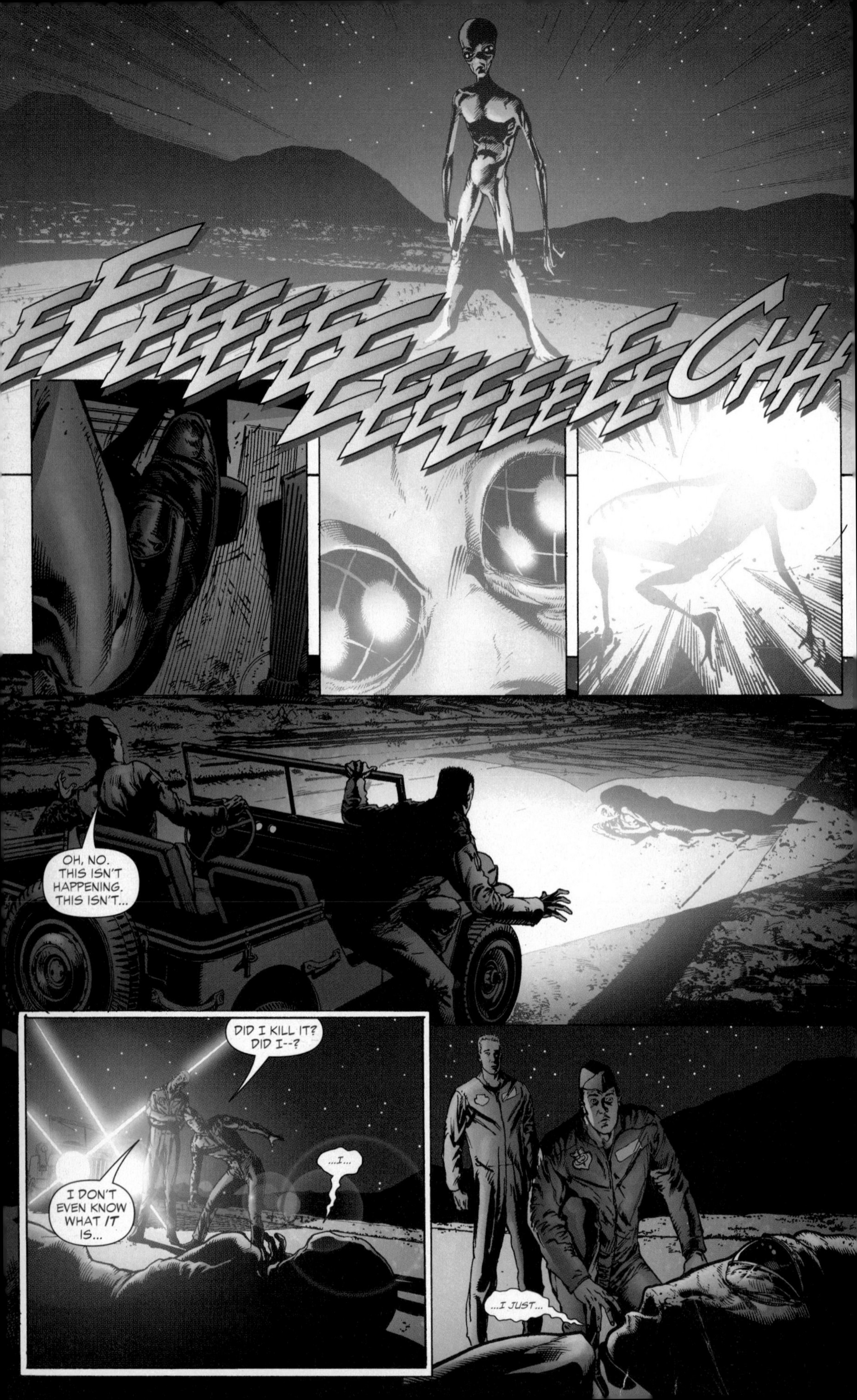
EEEEEEEEEEEEEEEEECHH
OH, NO. THIS ISN'T HAPPENING. THIS ISN'T...
DID I KILL IT? DID I--?
I DON'T EVEN KNOW WHAT *IT* IS...
...I...
...I JUST...

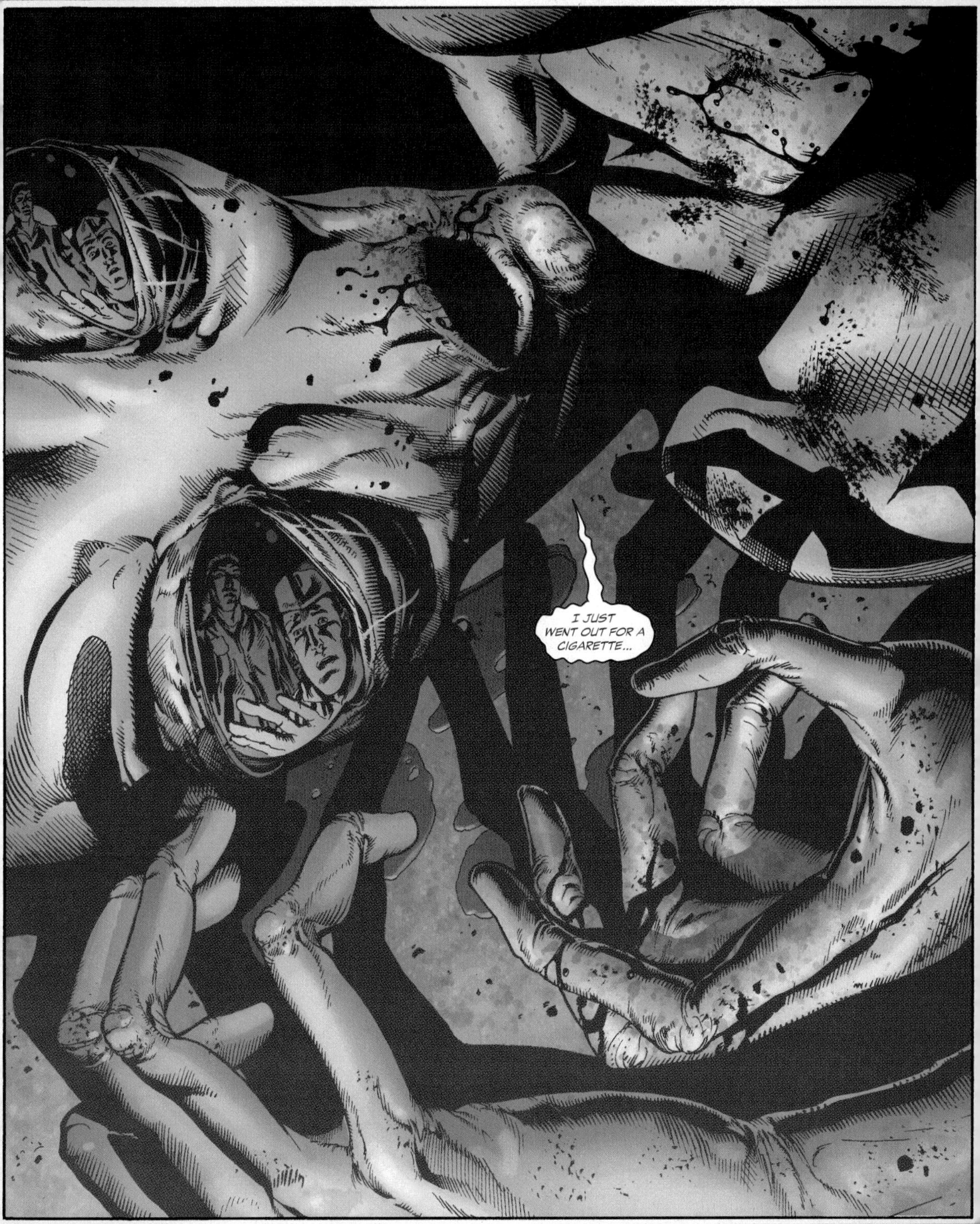
I JUST WENT OUT FOR A CIGARETTE...

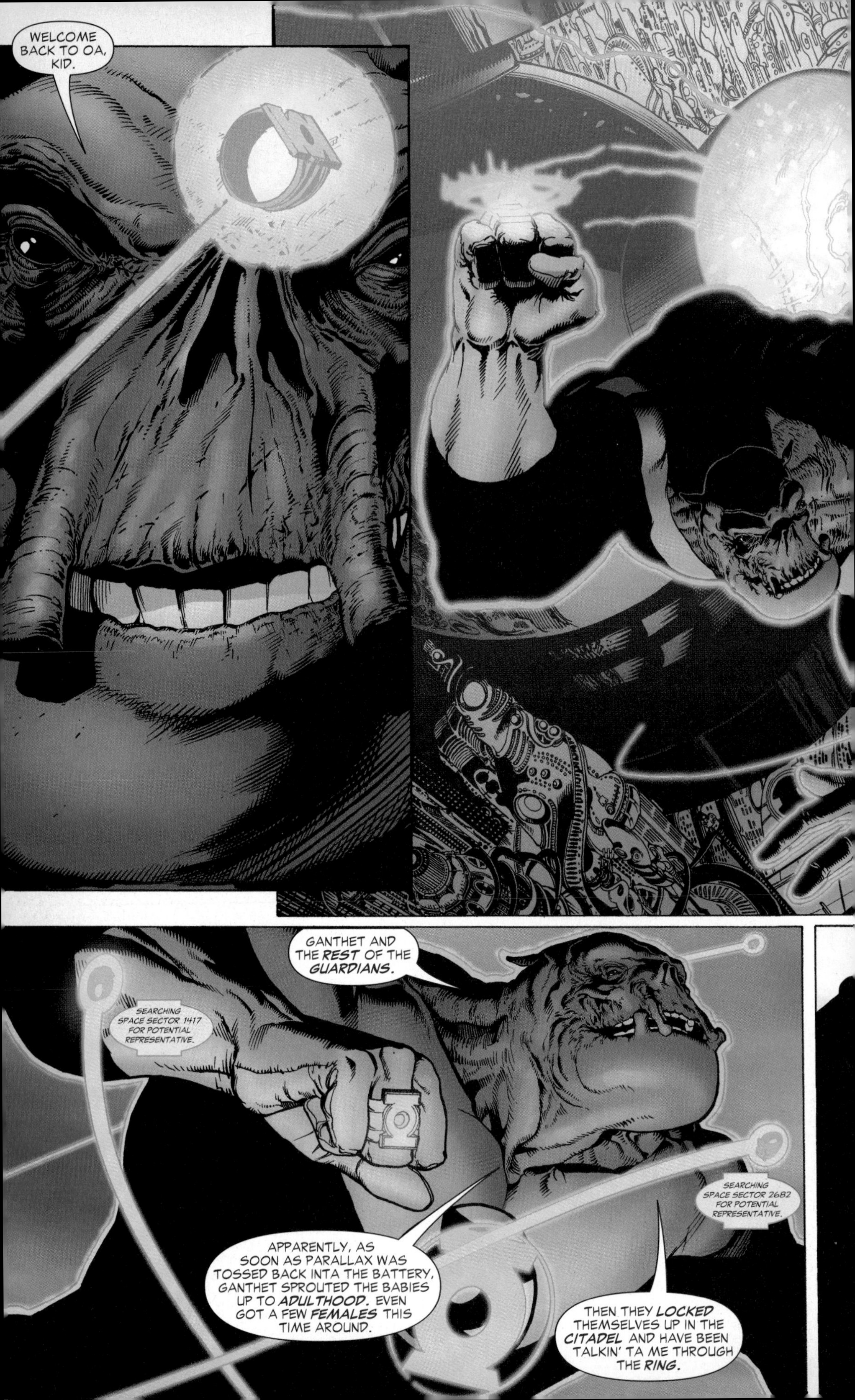
WELCOME BACK TO OA, KID.
GANTHET AND THE REST OF THE GUARDIANS.
SEARCHING SPACE SECTOR 1417 FOR POTENTIAL REPRESENTATIVE.
SEARCHING SPACE SECTOR 2682 FOR POTENTIAL REPRESENTATIVE.
APPARENTLY, AS SOON AS PARALLAX WAS TOSSED BACK INTA THE BATTERY, GANTHET SPROUTED THE BABIES UP TO ADULTHOOD. EVEN GOT A FEW FEMALES THIS TIME AROUND.
THEN THEY LOCKED THEMSELVES UP IN THE CITADEL AND HAVE BEEN TALKIN' TA ME THROUGH THE RING.

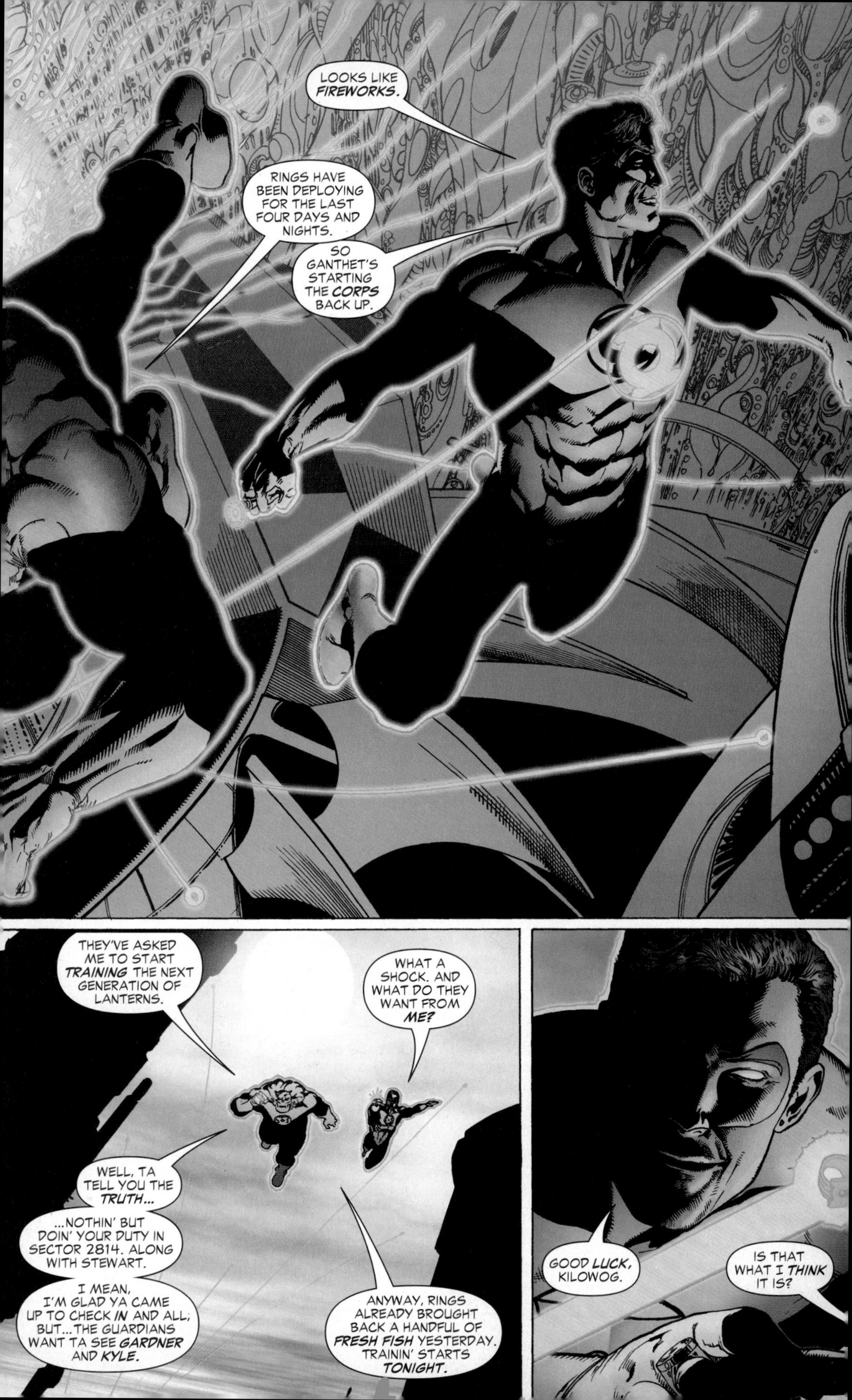
LOOKS LIKE FIREWORKS.
RINGS HAVE BEEN DEPLOYING FOR THE LAST FOUR DAYS AND NIGHTS.
SO GANTHET'S STARTING THE CORPS BACK UP.
THEY'VE ASKED ME TO START TRAINING THE NEXT GENERATION OF LANTERNS.
WHAT A SHOCK. AND WHAT DO THEY WANT FROM ME?
WELL, TA TELL YOU THE TRUTH...
...NOTHIN' BUT DOIN' YOUR DUTY IN SECTOR 2814. ALONG WITH STEWART.
I MEAN, I'M GLAD YA CAME UP TO CHECK IN AND ALL; BUT... THE GUARDIANS WANT TA SEE GARDNER AND KYLE.
ANYWAY, RINGS ALREADY BROUGHT BACK A HANDFUL OF FRESH FISH YESTERDAY. TRAININ' STARTS TONIGHT.
GOOD LUCK, KILOWOG.
IS THAT WHAT I THINK IT IS?

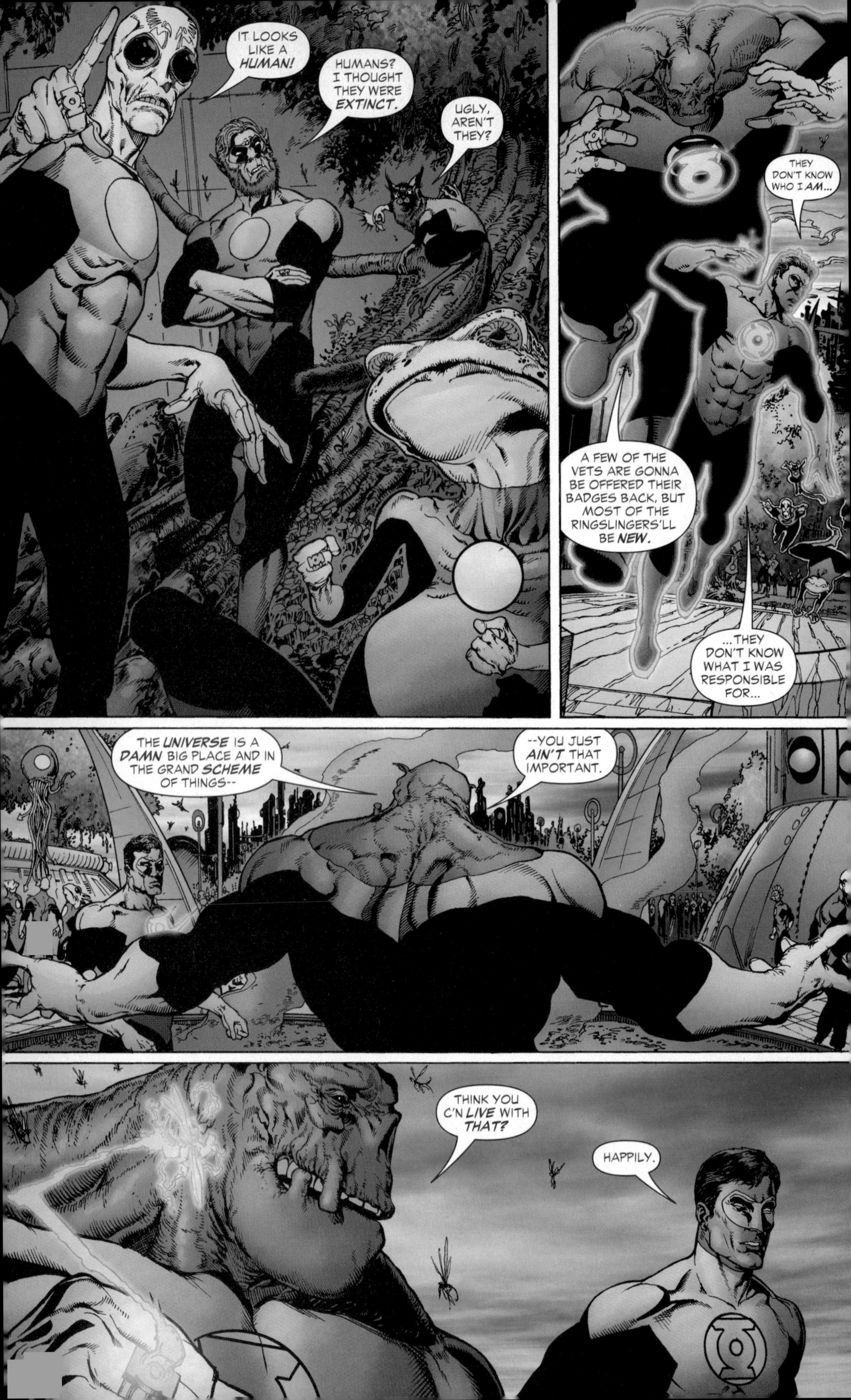
IT LOOKS LIKE A HUMAN!
HUMANS? I THOUGHT THEY WERE EXTINCT.
UGLY, AREN'T THEY?
THEY DON'T KNOW WHO I AM...
A FEW OF THE VETS ARE GONNA BE OFFERED THEIR BADGES BACK, BUT MOST OF THE RINGSLINGERS'LL BE NEW.
...THEY DON'T KNOW WHAT I WAS RESPONSIBLE FOR...
THE UNIVERSE IS A DAMN BIG PLACE AND IN THE GRAND SCHEME OF THINGS--
--YOU JUST AIN'T THAT IMPORTANT.
THINK YOU C'N LIVE WITH THAT?
HAPPILY.

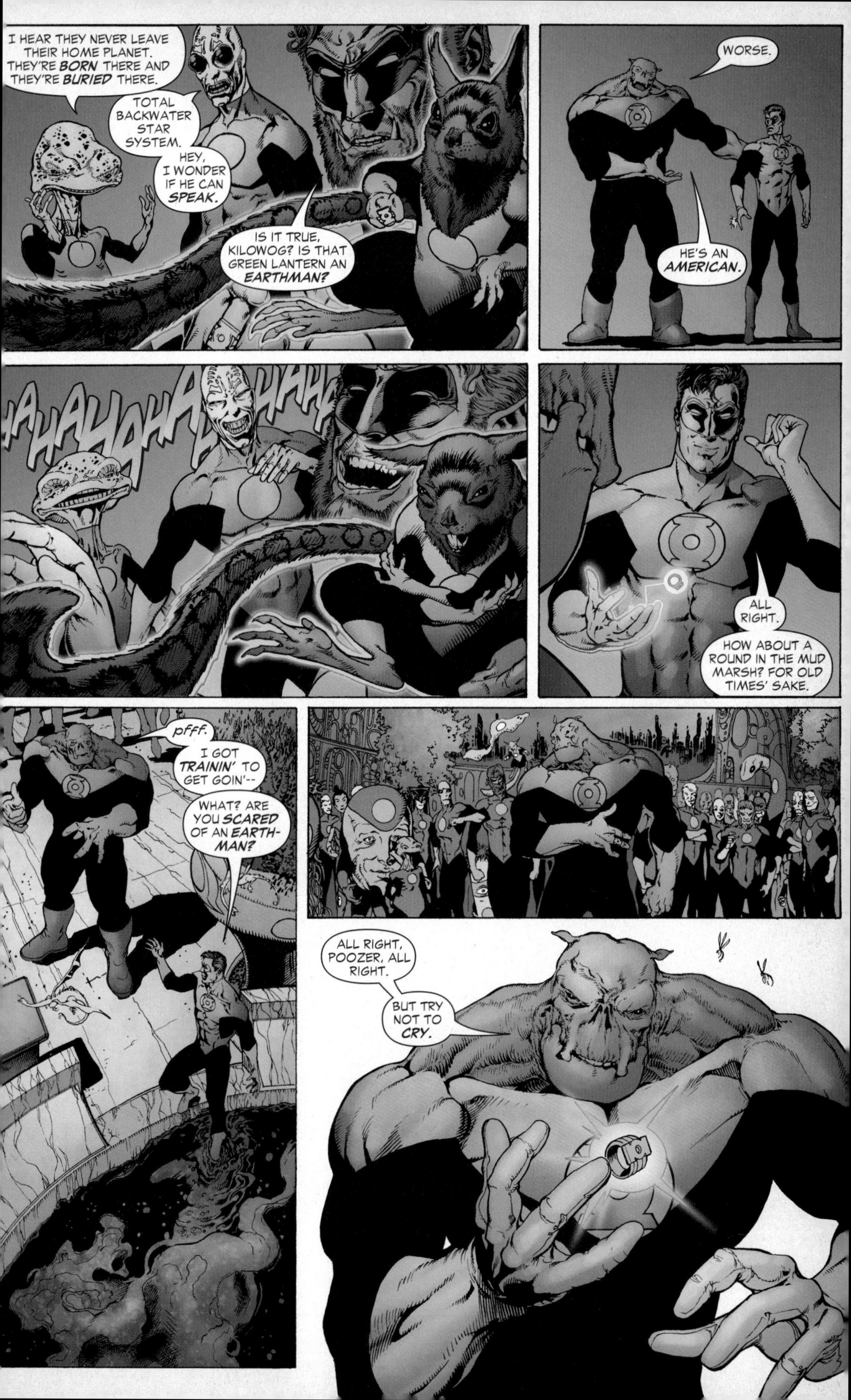
I HEAR THEY NEVER LEAVE THEIR HOME PLANET. THEY'RE BORN THERE AND THEY'RE BURIED THERE.
TOTAL BACKWATER STAR SYSTEM.
HEY, I WONDER IF HE CAN SPEAK.
IS IT TRUE, KILOWOG? IS THAT GREEN LANTERN AN EARTHMAN?
WORSE.
HE'S AN AMERICAN.
HAHAHAHAHAHAHAHA
ALL RIGHT.
HOW ABOUT A ROUND IN THE MUD MARSH? FOR OLD TIMES' SAKE.
pfff.
I GOT TRAININ' TO GET GOIN'--
WHAT? ARE YOU SCARED OF AN EARTH-MAN?
ALL RIGHT, POOZER, ALL RIGHT.
BUT TRY NOT TO CRY.

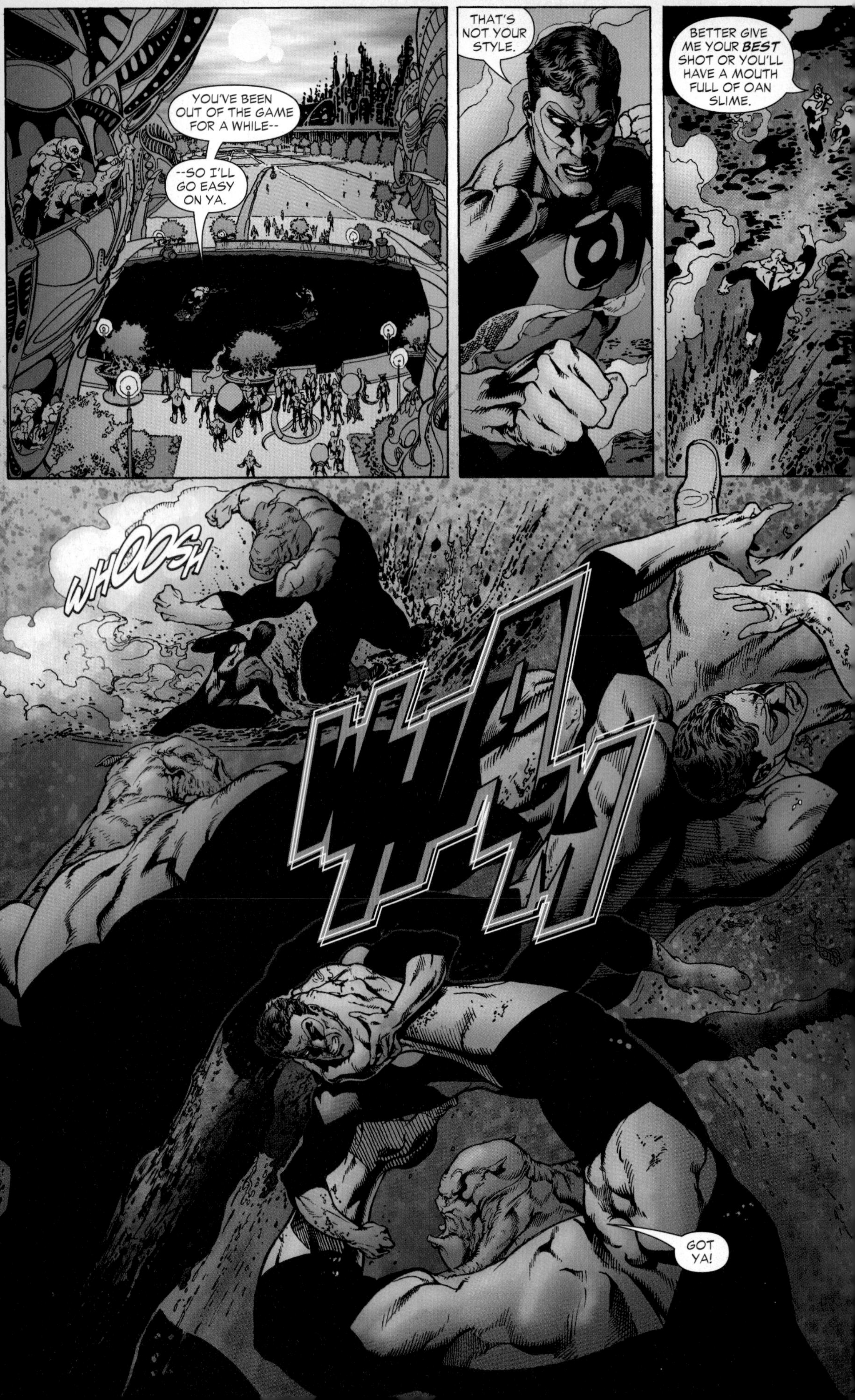
YOU'VE BEEN OUT OF THE GAME FOR A WHILE--
--SO I'LL GO EASY ON YA.
THAT'S NOT YOUR STYLE.
BETTER GIVE ME YOUR BEST SHOT OR YOU'LL HAVE A MOUTH FULL OF OAN SLIME.
WHOOSH
WHAM
GOT YA!

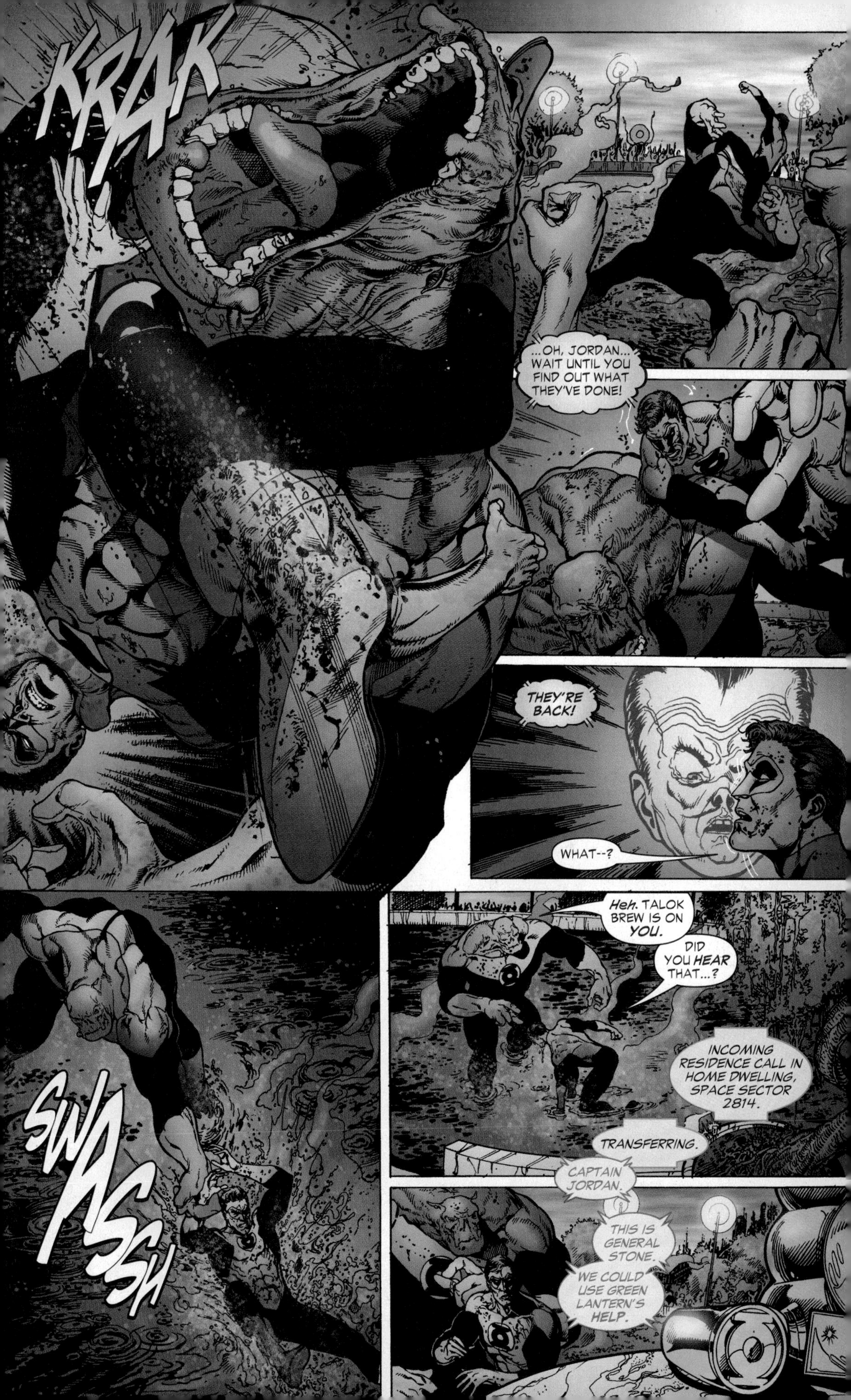
KRAK
...OH, JORDAN... WAIT UNTIL YOU FIND OUT WHAT THEY'VE DONE!
THEY'RE BACK!
WHAT--?
SWASSH
Heh. TALOK BREW IS ON YOU.
DID YOU HEAR THAT...?
INCOMING RESIDENCE CALL IN HOME DWELLING, SPACE SECTOR 2814.
TRANSFERRING.
CAPTAIN JORDAN.
THIS IS GENERAL STONE.
WE COULD USE GREEN LANTERN'S HELP.

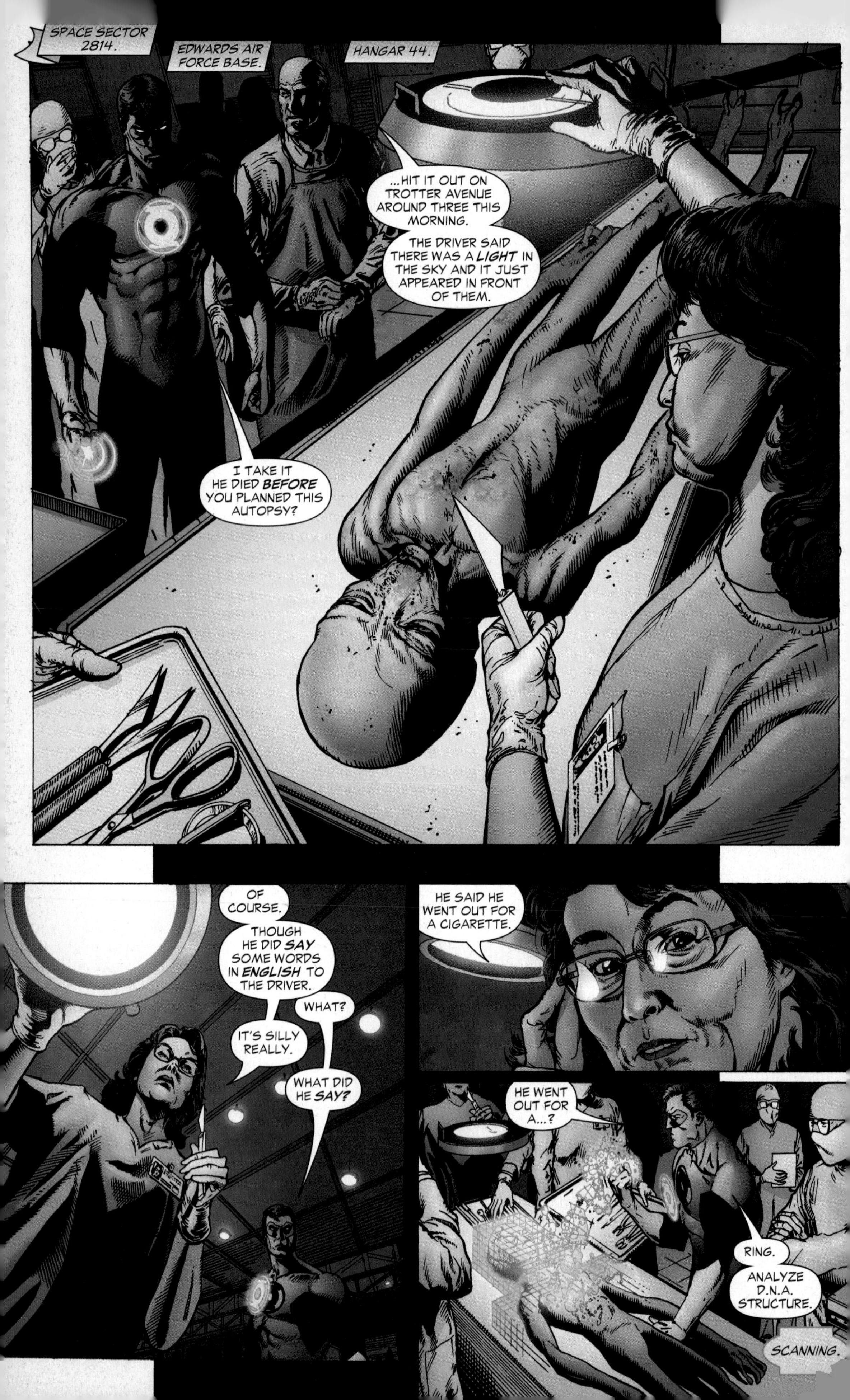
SPACE SECTOR 2814.
EDWARDS AIR FORCE BASE.
HANGAR 44.
...HIT IT OUT ON TROTTER AVENUE AROUND THREE THIS MORNING.
THE DRIVER SAID THERE WAS A LIGHT IN THE SKY AND IT JUST APPEARED IN FRONT OF THEM.
I TAKE IT HE DIED BEFORE YOU PLANNED THIS AUTOPSY?
OF COURSE.
THOUGH HE DID SAY SOME WORDS IN ENGLISH TO THE DRIVER.
WHAT?
IT'S SILLY REALLY.
WHAT DID HE SAY?
HE SAID HE WENT OUT FOR A CIGARETTE.
HE WENT OUT FOR A...?
RING.
ANALYZE D.N.A. STRUCTURE.
SCANNING.

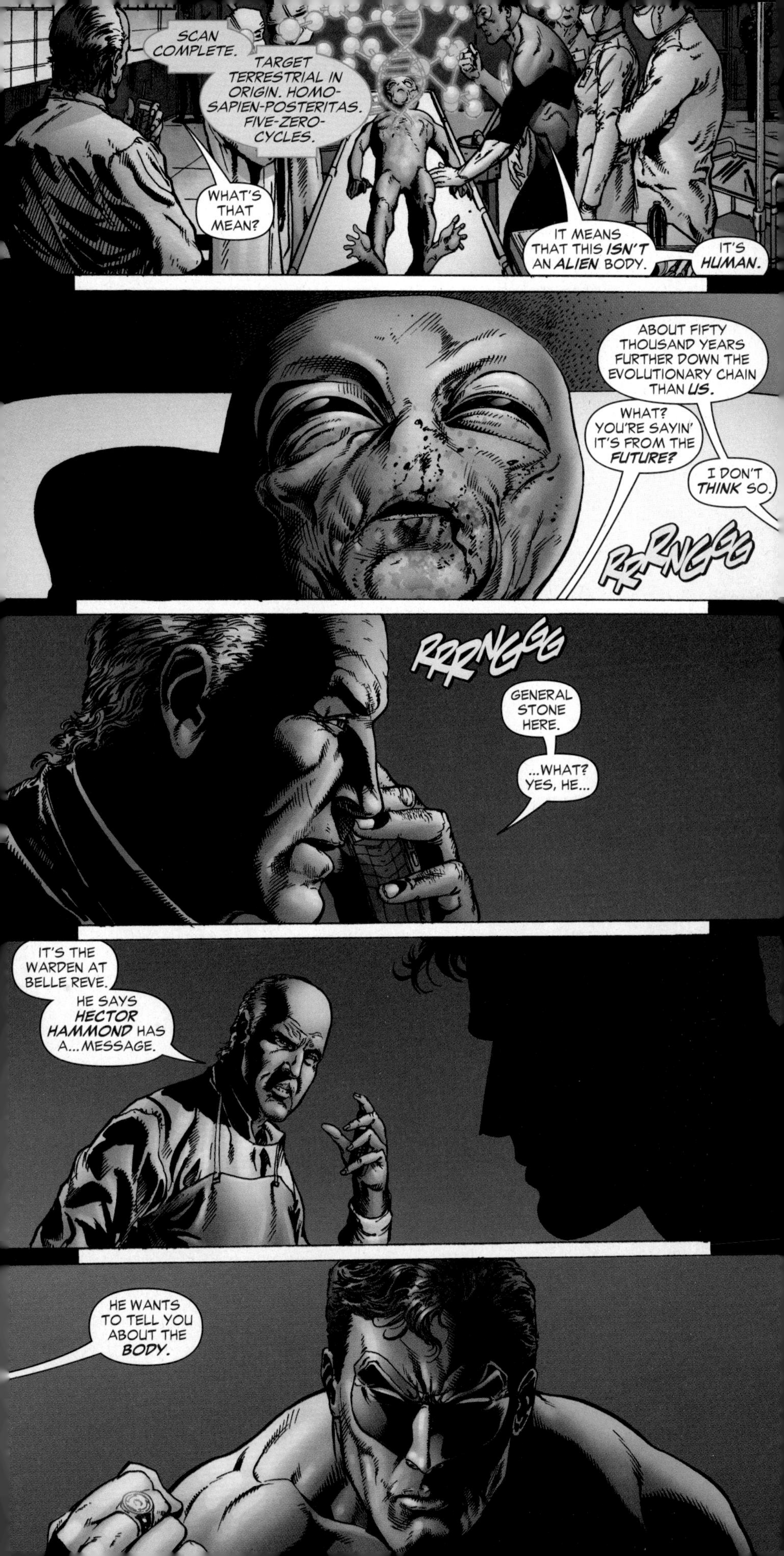
SCAN COMPLETE.
TARGET TERRESTRIAL IN ORIGIN. HOMO-SAPIEN-POSTERITAS. FIVE-ZERO-CYCLES.
WHAT'S THAT MEAN?
IT MEANS THAT THIS ISN'T AN ALIEN BODY.
IT'S HUMAN.
ABOUT FIFTY THOUSAND YEARS FURTHER DOWN THE EVOLUTIONARY CHAIN THAN US.
WHAT? YOU'RE SAYIN' IT'S FROM THE FUTURE?
I DON'T THINK SO.
RRRNGGG
RRRNGGG
GENERAL STONE HERE.
...WHAT? YES, HE...
IT'S THE WARDEN AT BELLE REVE.
HE SAYS HECTOR HAMMOND HAS A...MESSAGE.
HE WANTS TO TELL YOU ABOUT THE BODY.

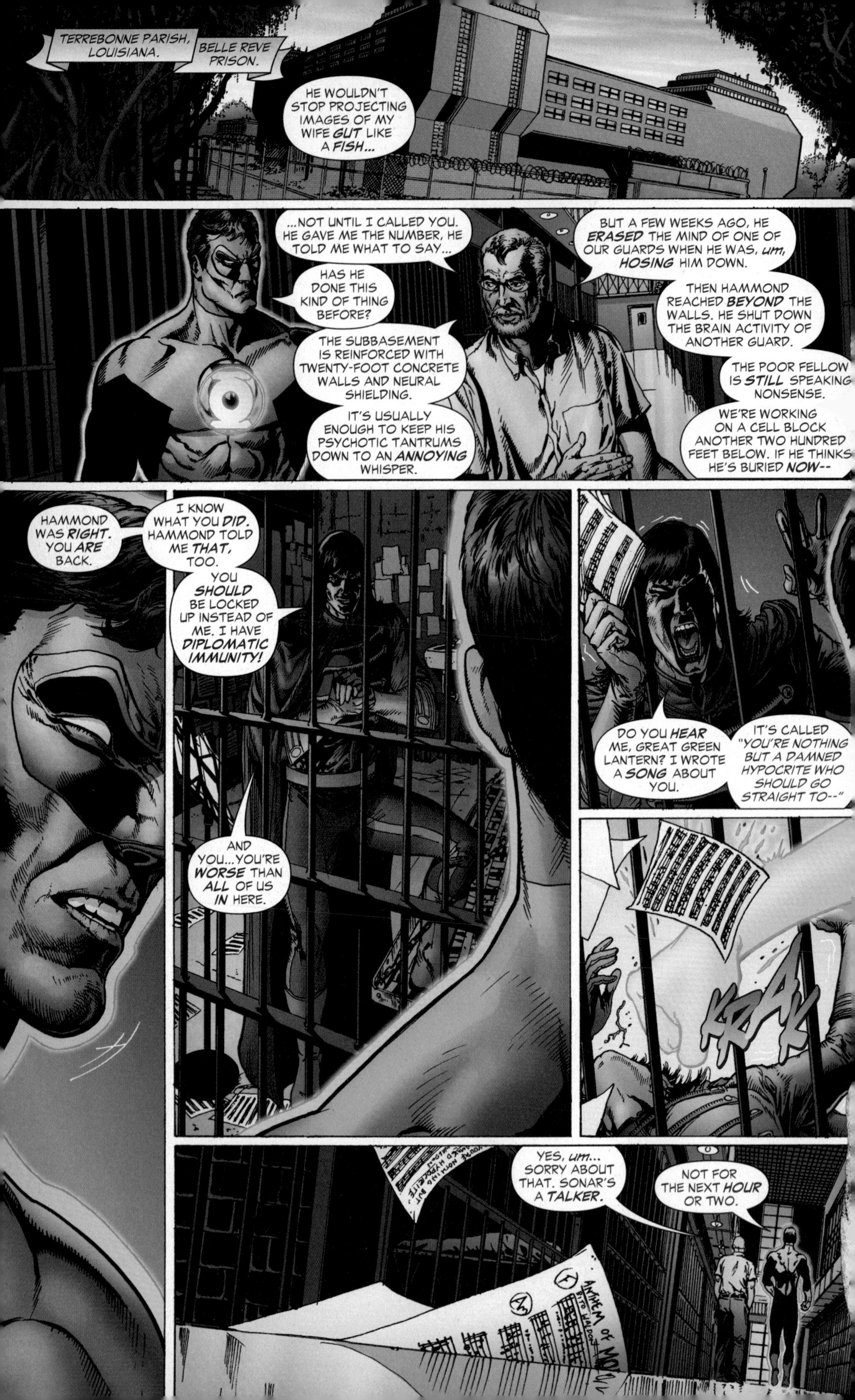
TERREBONNE PARISH, LOUISIANA.
BELLE REVE PRISON.
HE WOULDN'T STOP PROJECTING IMAGES OF MY WIFE GUT LIKE A FISH...
...NOT UNTIL I CALLED YOU. HE GAVE ME THE NUMBER, HE TOLD ME WHAT TO SAY...
HAS HE DONE THIS KIND OF THING BEFORE?
THE SUBBASEMENT IS REINFORCED WITH TWENTY-FOOT CONCRETE WALLS AND NEURAL SHIELDING.
IT'S USUALLY ENOUGH TO KEEP HIS PSYCHOTIC TANTRUMS DOWN TO AN ANNOYING WHISPER.
BUT A FEW WEEKS AGO, HE ERASED THE MIND OF ONE OF OUR GUARDS WHEN HE WAS, um, HOSING HIM DOWN.
THEN HAMMOND REACHED BEYOND THE WALLS. HE SHUT DOWN THE BRAIN ACTIVITY OF ANOTHER GUARD.
THE POOR FELLOW IS STILL SPEAKING NONSENSE.
WE'RE WORKING ON A CELL BLOCK ANOTHER TWO HUNDRED FEET BELOW. IF HE THINKS HE'S BURIED NOW--
HAMMOND WAS RIGHT. YOU ARE BACK.
I KNOW WHAT YOU DID. HAMMOND TOLD ME THAT, TOO.
YOU SHOULD BE LOCKED UP INSTEAD OF ME. I HAVE DIPLOMATIC IMMUNITY!
AND YOU...YOU'RE WORSE THAN ALL OF US IN HERE.
DO YOU HEAR ME, GREAT GREEN LANTERN? I WROTE A SONG ABOUT YOU.
IT'S CALLED "YOU'RE NOTHING BUT A DAMNED HYPOCRITE WHO SHOULD GO STRAIGHT TO--"
KRAK
YES, um... SORRY ABOUT THAT. SONAR'S A TALKER.
NOT FOR THE NEXT HOUR OR TWO.

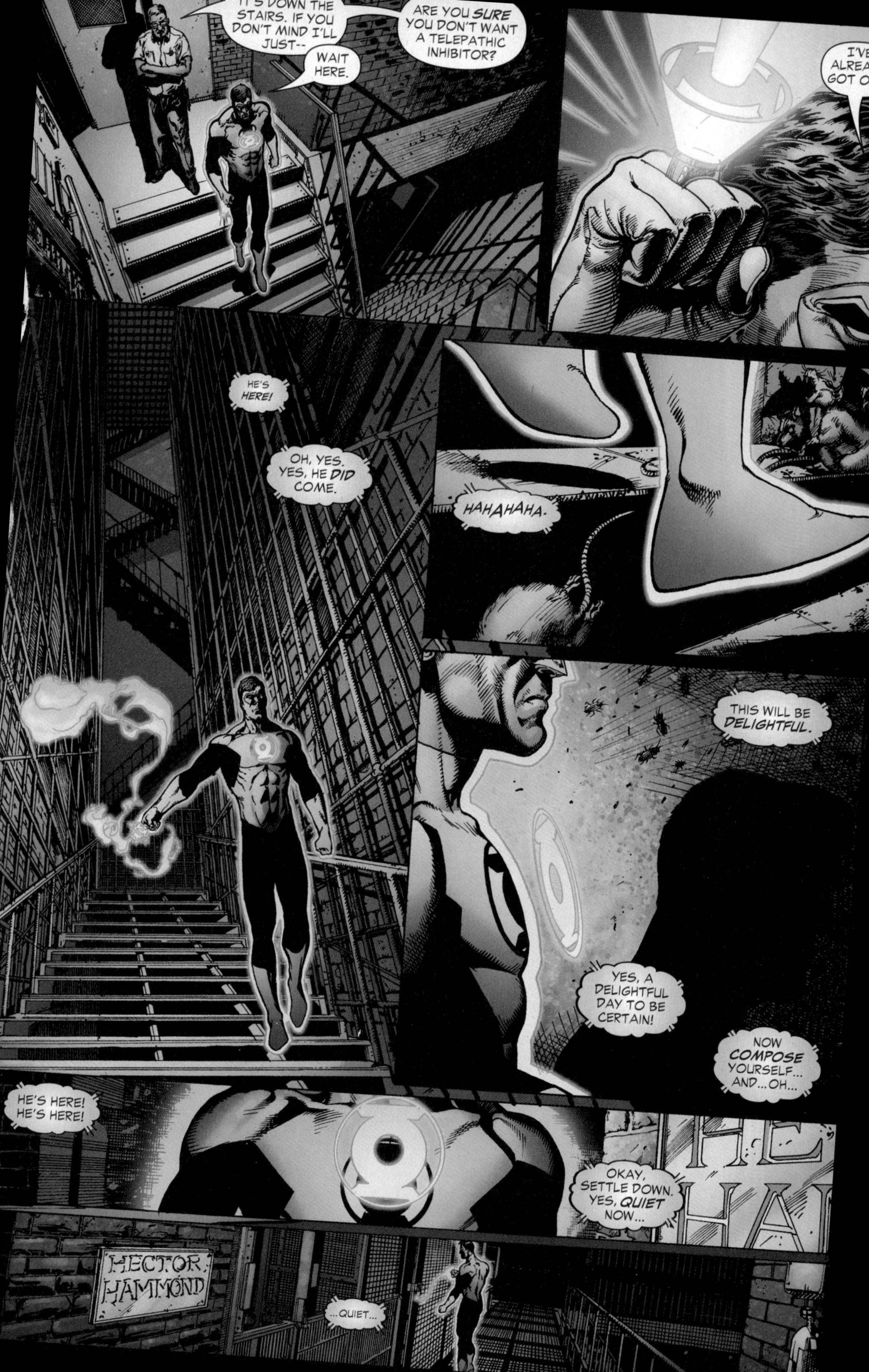
IT'S DOWN THE STAIRS. IF YOU DON'T MIND I'LL JUST--
WAIT HERE.
ARE YOU SURE YOU DON'T WANT A TELEPATHIC INHIBITOR?
HE'S HERE!
OH, YES. YES, HE DID COME.
HAHAHAHA.
THIS WILL BE DELIGHTFUL.
YES, A DELIGHTFUL DAY TO BE CERTAIN!
NOW COMPOSE YOURSELF... AND...OH...
HE'S HERE! HE'S HERE!
OKAY, SETTLE DOWN. YES, QUIET NOW...
HECTOR HAMMOND
...QUIET...

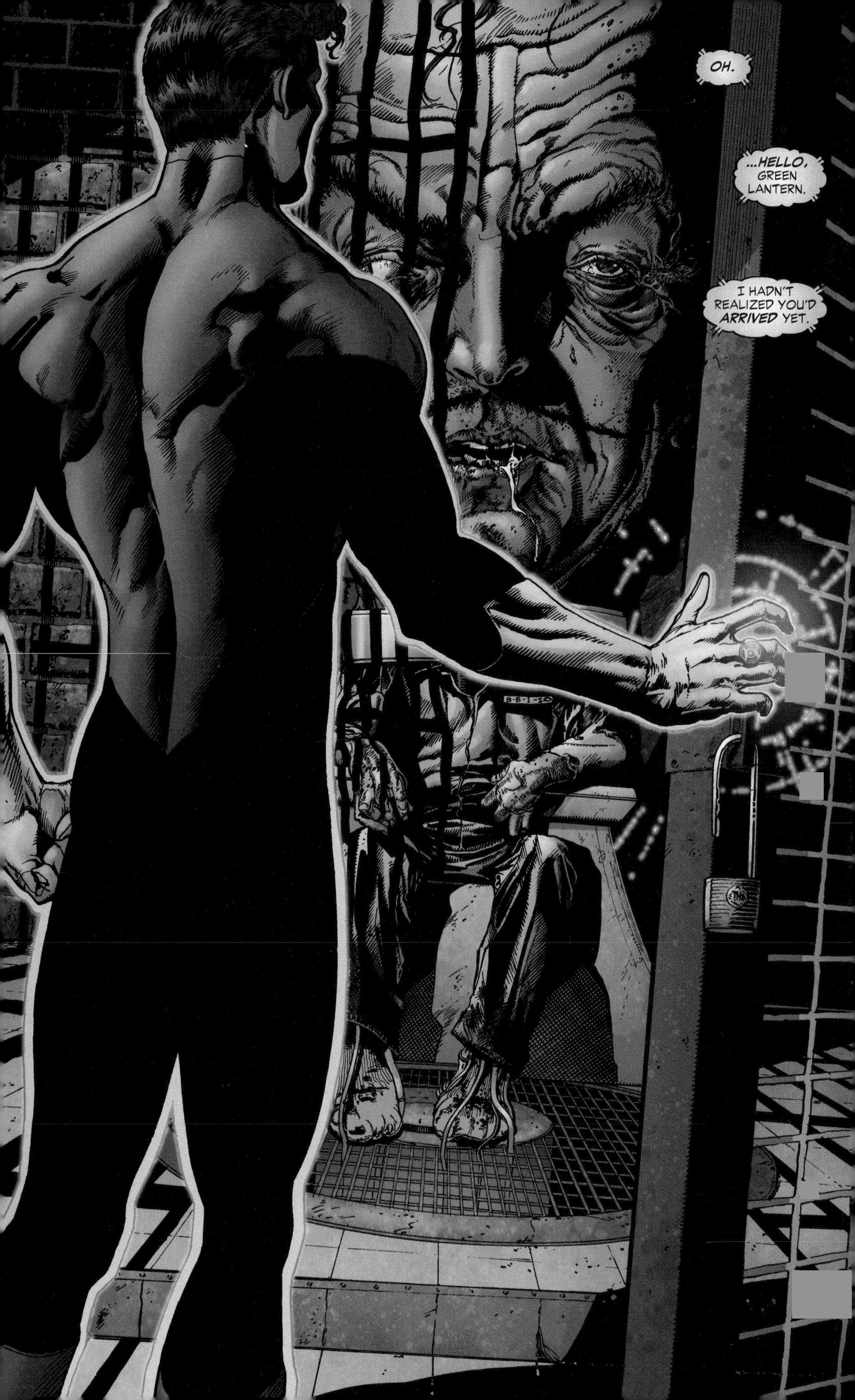
OH.
...HELLO, GREEN LANTERN.
I HADN'T REALIZED YOU'D ARRIVED YET.

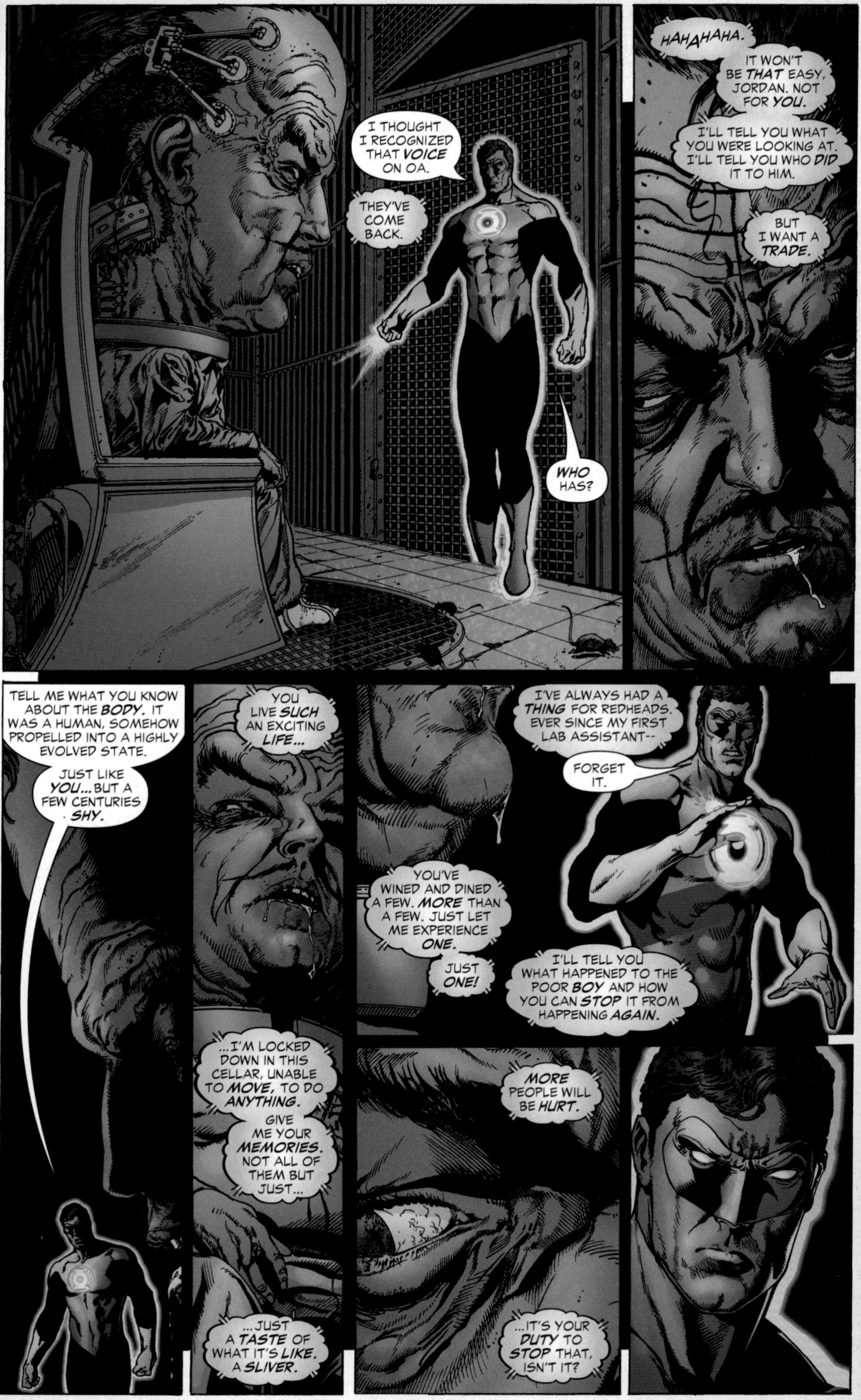
I THOUGHT I RECOGNIZED THAT VOICE ON OA.
THEY'VE COME BACK.
WHO HAS?
HAHAHAHA.
IT WON'T BE THAT EASY, JORDAN. NOT FOR YOU.
I'LL TELL YOU WHAT YOU WERE LOOKING AT. I'LL TELL YOU WHO DID IT TO HIM.
BUT I WANT A TRADE.
TELL ME WHAT YOU KNOW ABOUT THE BODY. IT WAS A HUMAN, SOMEHOW PROPELLED INTO A HIGHLY EVOLVED STATE.
JUST LIKE YOU... BUT A FEW CENTURIES SHY.
YOU LIVE SUCH AN EXCITING LIFE...
...I'M LOCKED DOWN IN THIS CELLAR, UNABLE TO MOVE, TO DO ANYTHING.
GIVE ME YOUR MEMORIES. NOT ALL OF THEM BUT JUST...
...JUST A TASTE OF WHAT IT'S LIKE. A SLIVER.
YOU'VE WINED AND DINED A FEW. MORE THAN A FEW. JUST LET ME EXPERIENCE ONE.
JUST ONE!
I'VE ALWAYS HAD A THING FOR REDHEADS. EVER SINCE MY FIRST LAB ASSISTANT--
FORGET IT.
I'LL TELL YOU WHAT HAPPENED TO THE POOR BOY AND HOW YOU CAN STOP IT FROM HAPPENING AGAIN.
MORE PEOPLE WILL BE HURT.
...IT'S YOUR DUTY TO STOP THAT, ISN'T IT?

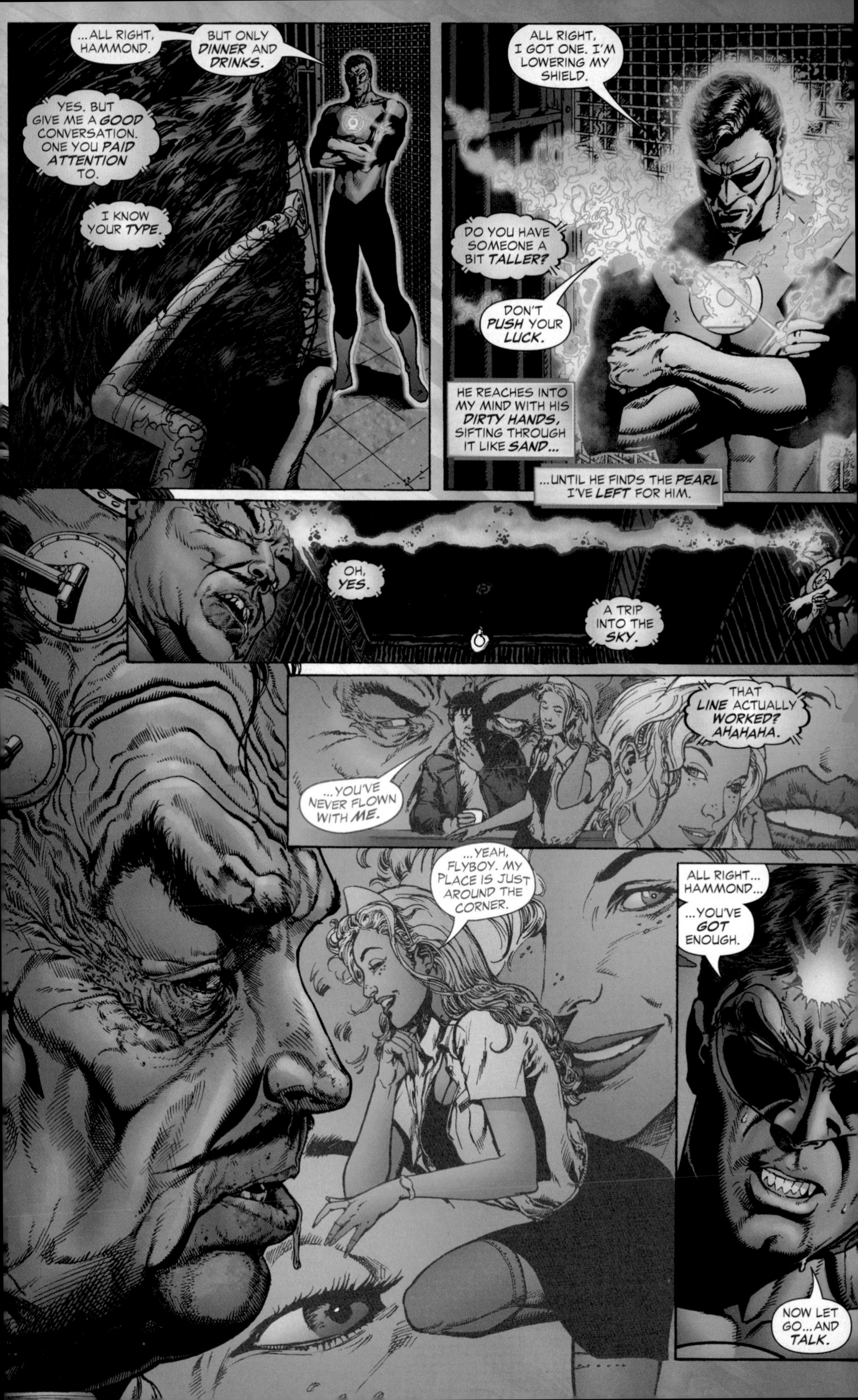
...ALL RIGHT, HAMMOND.
BUT ONLY DINNER AND DRINKS.
YES. BUT GIVE ME A GOOD CONVERSATION. ONE YOU PAID ATTENTION TO.
I KNOW YOUR TYPE.
ALL RIGHT, I GOT ONE. I'M LOWERING MY SHIELD.
DO YOU HAVE SOMEONE A BIT TALLER?
DON'T PUSH YOUR LUCK.
HE REACHES INTO MY MIND WITH HIS DIRTY HANDS, SIFTING THROUGH IT LIKE SAND...
...UNTIL HE FINDS THE PEARL I'VE LEFT FOR HIM.
OH, YES.
A TRIP INTO THE SKY.
THAT LINE ACTUALLY WORKED? AHAHAHA.
...YOU'VE NEVER FLOWN WITH ME.
...YEAH, FLYBOY. MY PLACE IS JUST AROUND THE CORNER.
ALL RIGHT... HAMMOND...
...YOU'VE GOT ENOUGH.
NOW LET GO... AND TALK.

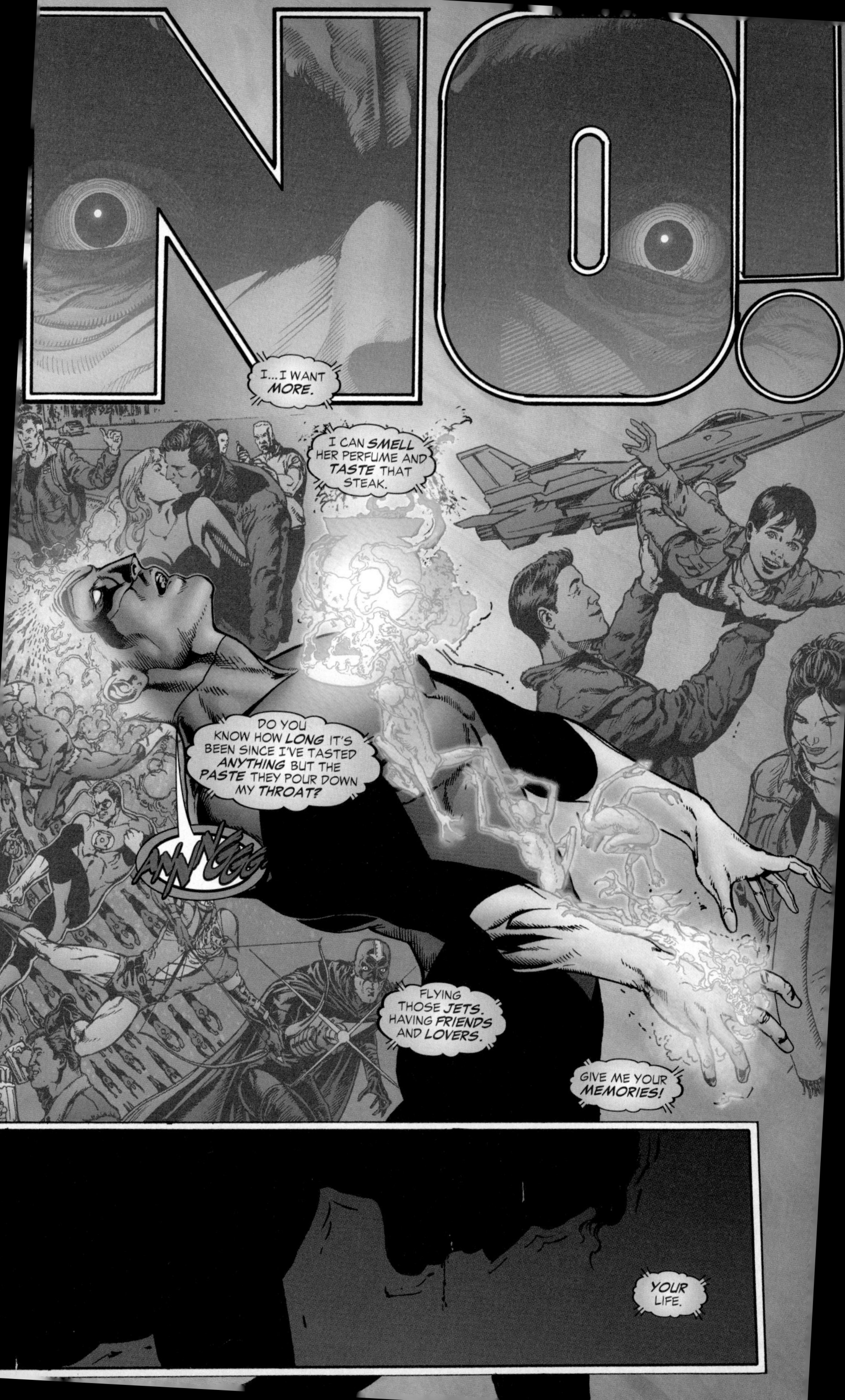
NO!
I...I WANT MORE.
I CAN SMELL HER PERFUME AND TASTE THAT STEAK.
DO YOU KNOW HOW LONG IT'S BEEN SINCE I'VE TASTED ANYTHING BUT THE PASTE THEY POUR DOWN MY THROAT?
FLYING THOSE JETS. HAVING FRIENDS AND LOVERS.
GIVE ME YOUR MEMORIES!
YOUR LIFE.

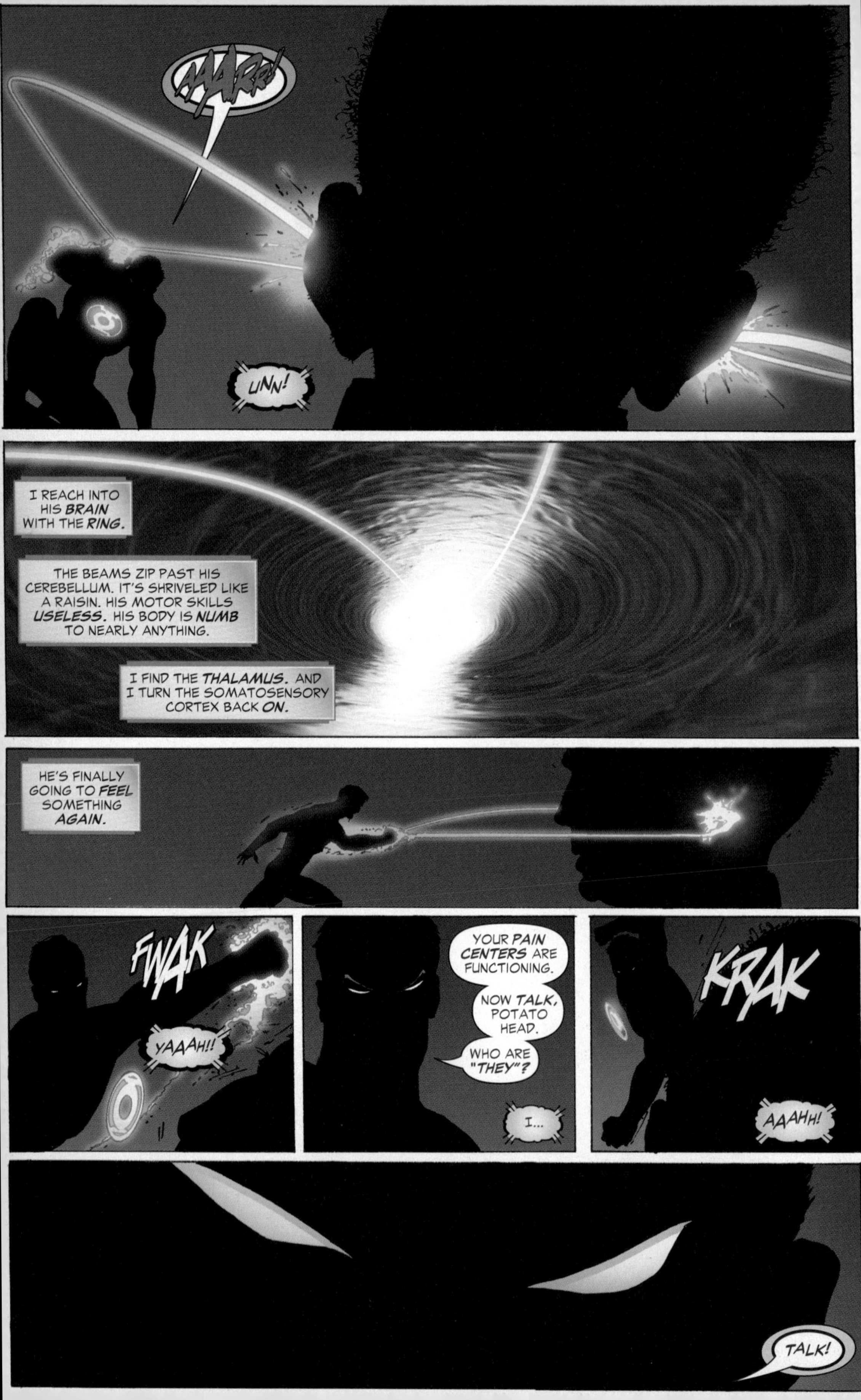
AAARR!
UNN!
I REACH INTO HIS BRAIN WITH THE RING.
THE BEAMS ZIP PAST HIS CEREBELLUM. IT'S SHRIVELED LIKE A RAISIN. HIS MOTOR SKILLS USELESS. HIS BODY IS NUMB TO NEARLY ANYTHING.
I FIND THE THALAMUS. AND I TURN THE SOMATOSENSORY CORTEX BACK ON.
HE'S FINALLY GOING TO FEEL SOMETHING AGAIN.
FWAK
YAAAH!!
YOUR PAIN CENTERS ARE FUNCTIONING.
NOW TALK, POTATO HEAD.
WHO ARE "THEY"?
I...
KRAK
AAAHH!
TALK!

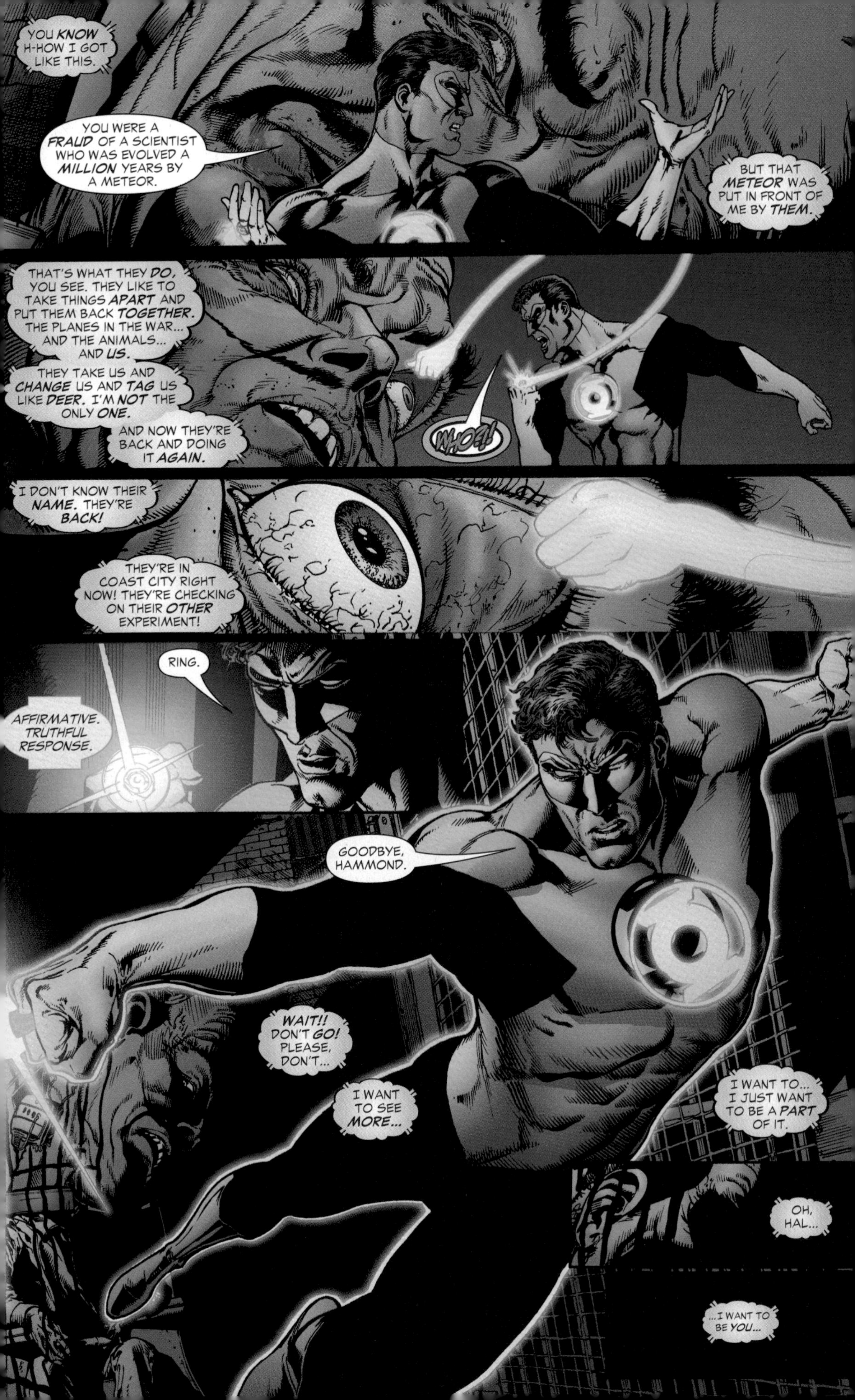

YOU KNOW H-HOW I GOT LIKE THIS.
YOU WERE A FRAUD OF A SCIENTIST WHO WAS EVOLVED A MILLION YEARS BY A METEOR.
BUT THAT METEOR WAS PUT IN FRONT OF ME BY THEM.
THAT'S WHAT THEY DO, YOU SEE. THEY LIKE TO TAKE THINGS APART AND PUT THEM BACK TOGETHER. THE PLANES IN THE WAR... AND THE ANIMALS... AND US.
THEY TAKE US AND CHANGE US AND TAG US LIKE DEER. I'M NOT THE ONLY ONE.
AND NOW THEY'RE BACK AND DOING IT AGAIN.
WHOA!
I DON'T KNOW THEIR NAME. THEY'RE BACK!
THEY'RE IN COAST CITY RIGHT NOW! THEY'RE CHECKING ON THEIR OTHER EXPERIMENT!
RING.
AFFIRMATIVE. TRUTHFUL RESPONSE.
GOODBYE, HAMMOND.
WAIT!! DON'T GO! PLEASE, DON'T...
I WANT TO SEE MORE...
I WANT TO... I JUST WANT TO BE A PART OF IT.
OH, HAL...
...I WANT TO BE YOU...

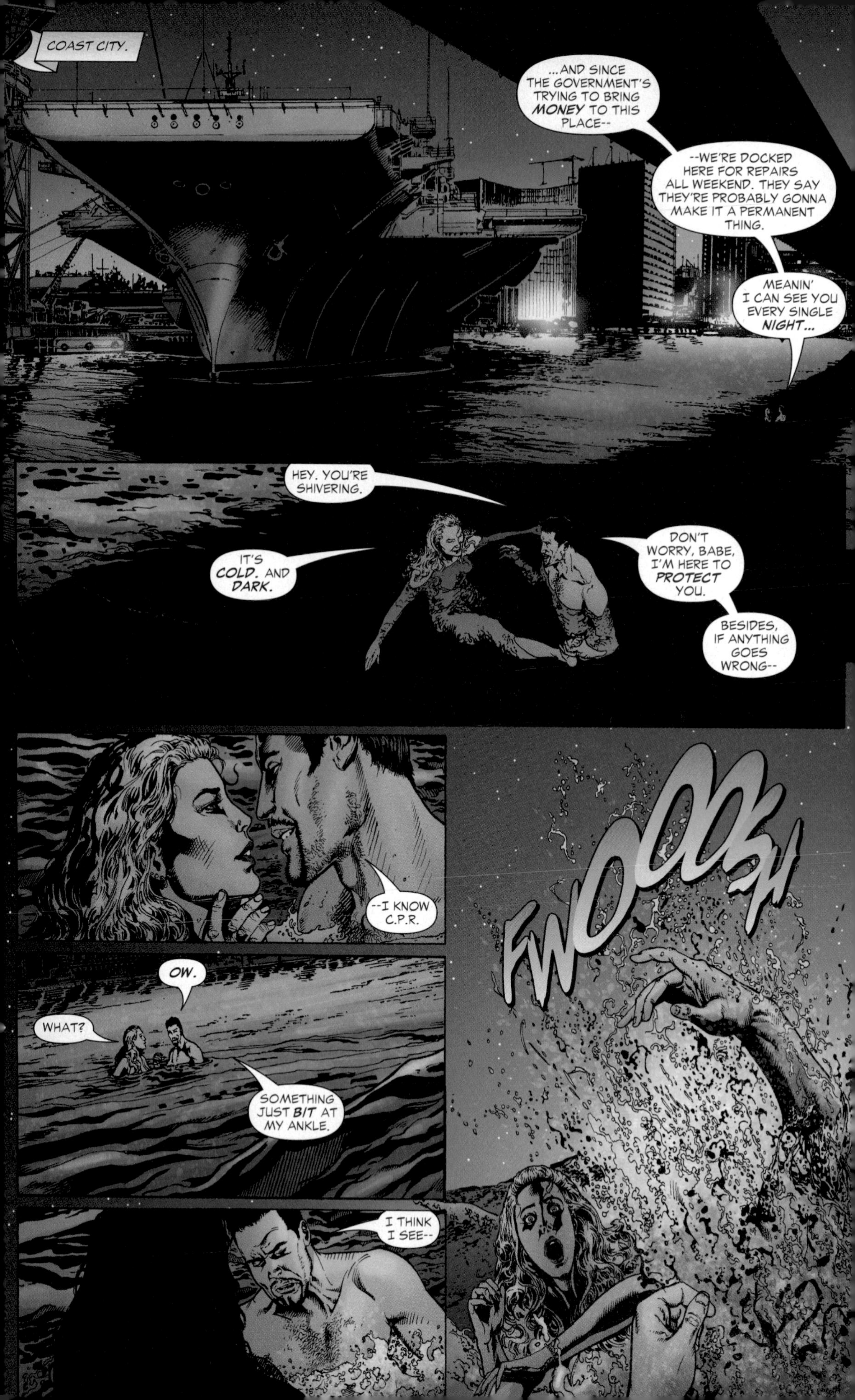
COAST CITY.
...AND SINCE THE GOVERNMENT'S TRYING TO BRING MONEY TO THIS PLACE--
--WE'RE DOCKED HERE FOR REPAIRS ALL WEEKEND. THEY SAY THEY'RE PROBABLY GONNA MAKE IT A PERMANENT THING.
MEANIN' I CAN SEE YOU EVERY SINGLE NIGHT...
HEY. YOU'RE SHIVERING.
IT'S COLD. AND DARK.
DON'T WORRY, BABE, I'M HERE TO PROTECT YOU.
BESIDES, IF ANYTHING GOES WRONG--
--I KNOW C.P.R.
OW.
WHAT?
SOMETHING JUST BIT AT MY ANKLE.
I THINK I SEE--
FWOOOSH

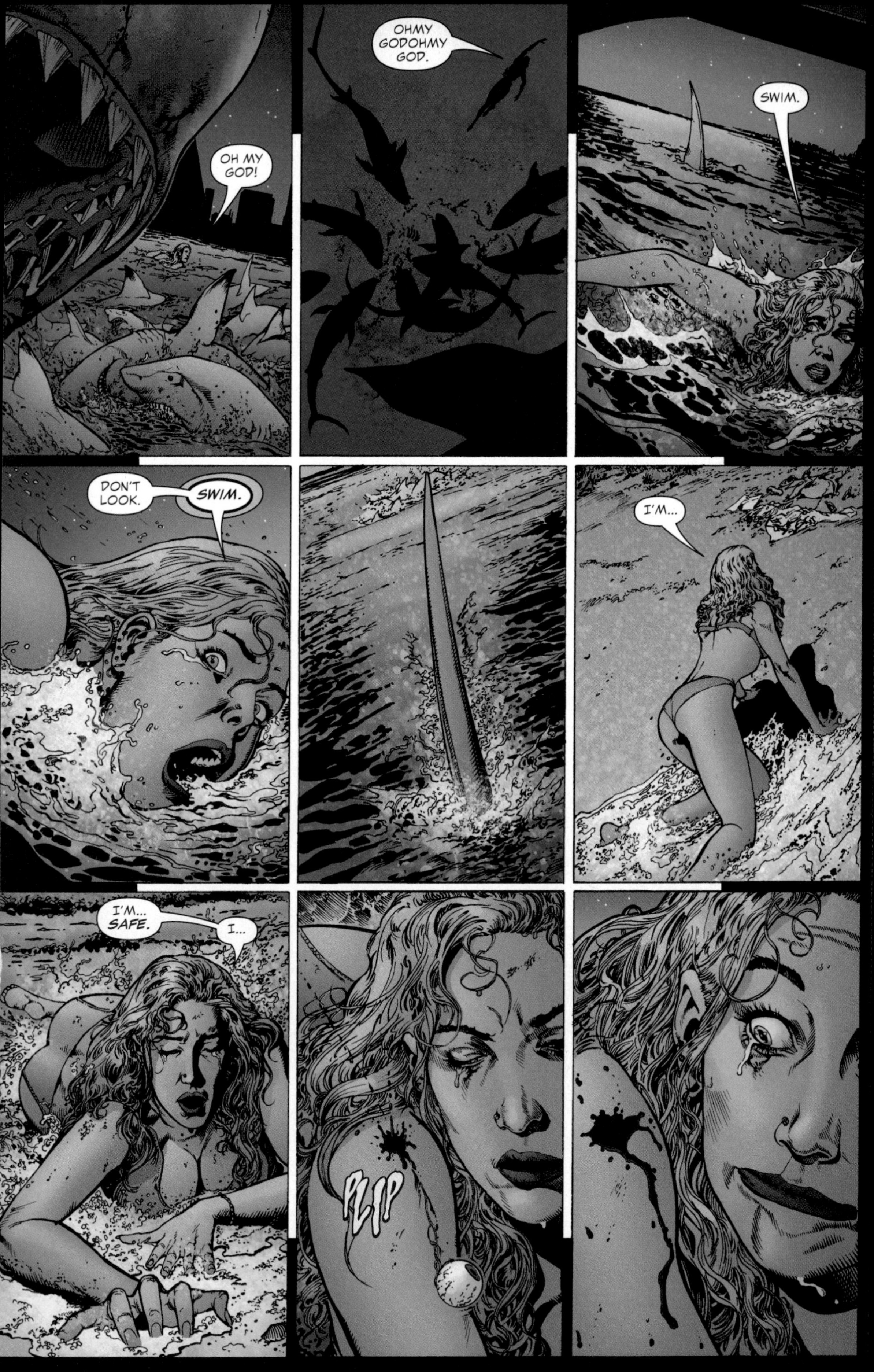
OH MY GOD!
OHMY GODOHMY GOD.
SWIM.
DON'T LOOK.
SWIM.
I'M...
I'M... SAFE.
I...
PLIP

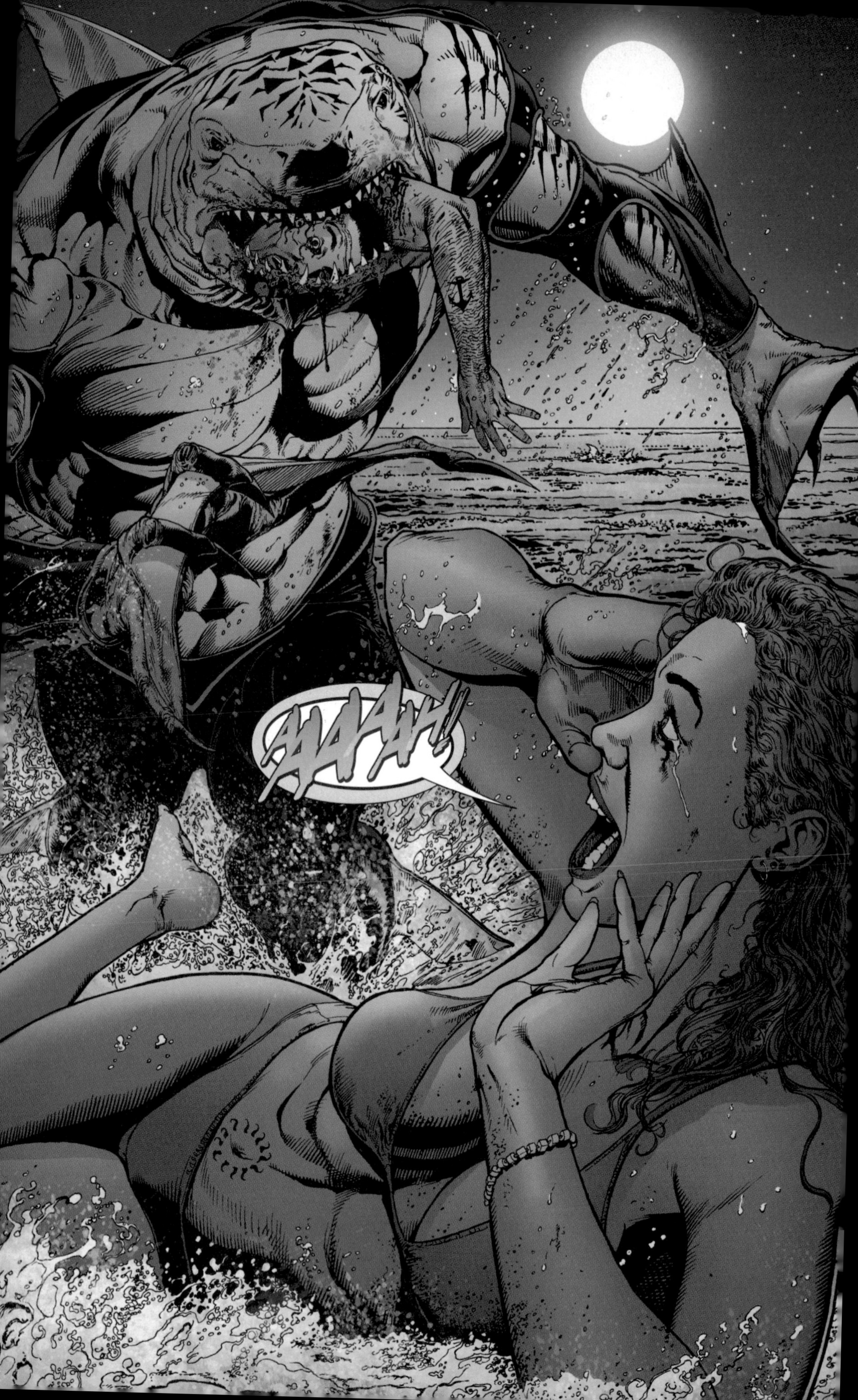
AAAAH!

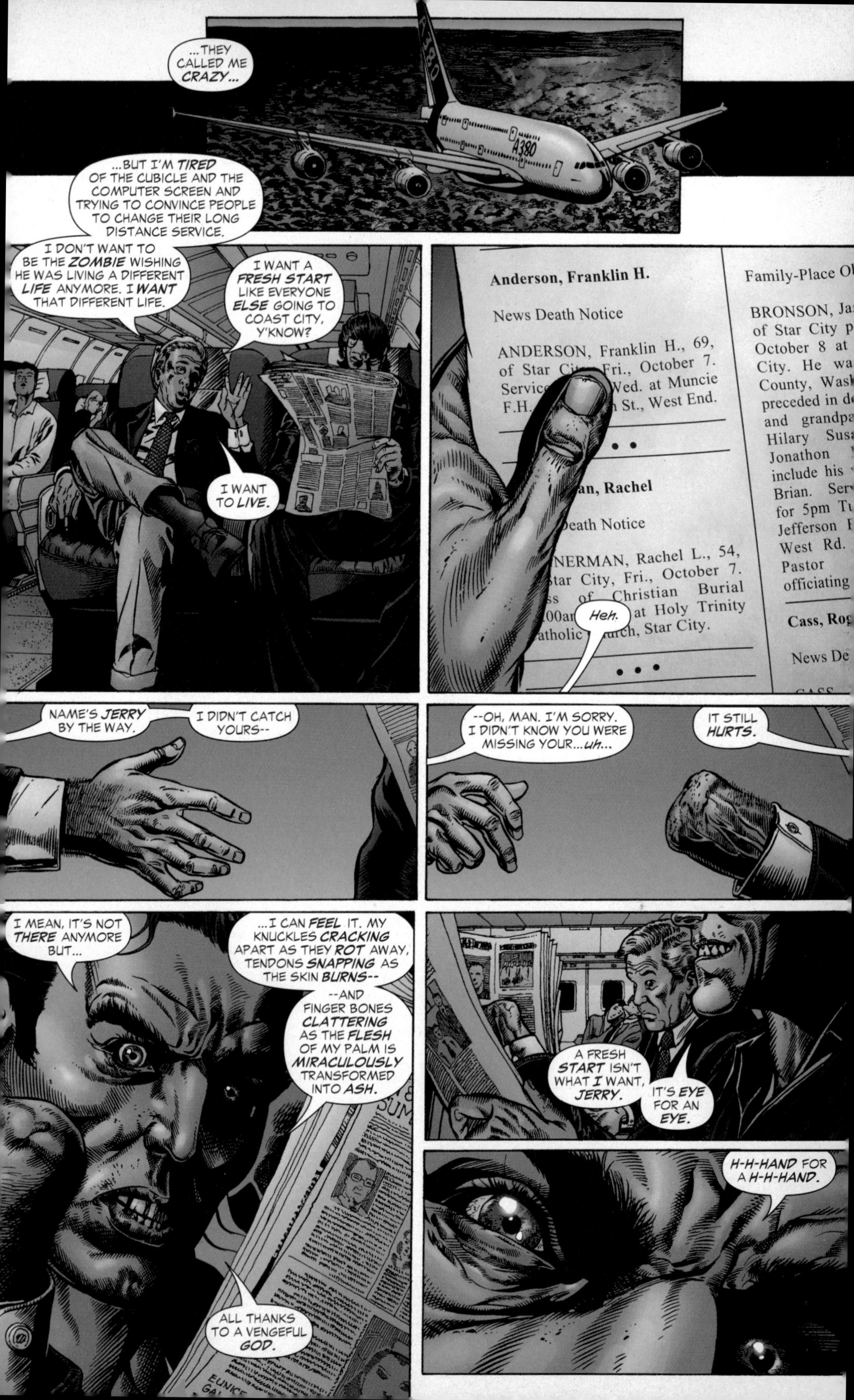

...THEY CALLED ME CRAZY...
A380
...BUT I'M TIRED OF THE CUBICLE AND THE COMPUTER SCREEN AND TRYING TO CONVINCE PEOPLE TO CHANGE THEIR LONG DISTANCE SERVICE.
I DON'T WANT TO BE THE ZOMBIE WISHING HE WAS LIVING A DIFFERENT LIFE ANYMORE. I WANT THAT DIFFERENT LIFE.
I WANT A FRESH START LIKE EVERYONE ELSE GOING TO COAST CITY, Y'KNOW?
I WANT TO LIVE.
Anderson, Franklin H.
News Death Notice
ANDERSON, Franklin H., 69,
Family-Place
Cass,
Heh.
NAME'S JERRY BY THE WAY.
I DIDN'T CATCH YOURS--
--OH, MAN. I'M SORRY. I DIDN'T KNOW YOU WERE MISSING YOUR...uh...
IT STILL HURTS.
I MEAN, IT'S NOT THERE ANYMORE BUT...
...I CAN FEEL IT. MY KNUCKLES CRACKING APART AS THEY ROT AWAY, TENDONS SNAPPING AS THE SKIN BURNS--
--AND FINGER BONES CLATTERING AS THE FLESH OF MY PALM IS MIRACULOUSLY TRANSFORMED INTO ASH.
ALL THANKS TO A VENGEFUL GOD.
A FRESH START ISN'T WHAT I WANT, JERRY.
IT'S EYE FOR AN EYE.
H-H-HAND FOR A H-H-HAND.

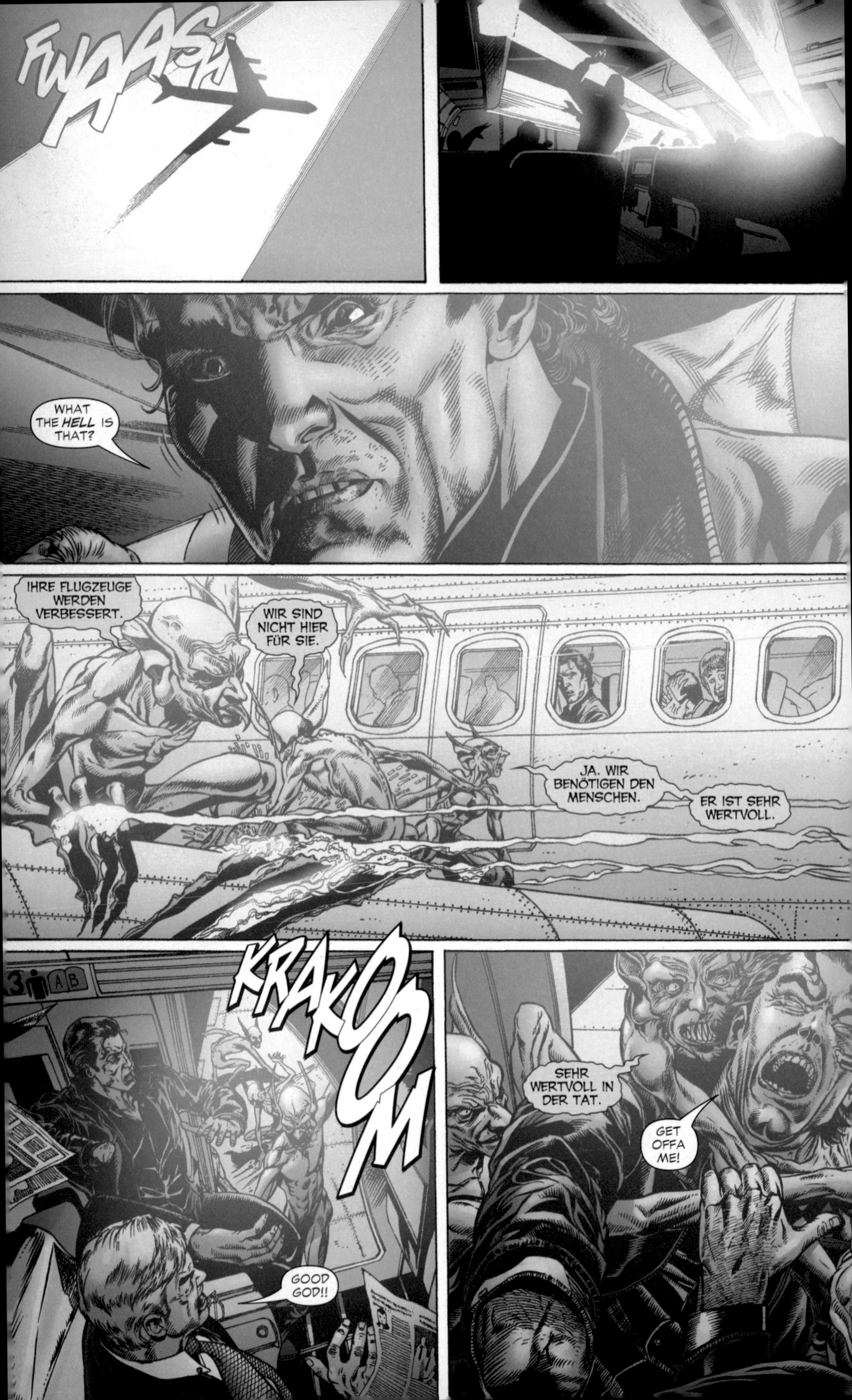
FWASH
WHAT THE HELL IS THAT?
IHRE FLUGZEUGE WERDEN VERBESSERT.
WIR SIND NICHT HIER FÜR SIE.
JA. WIR BENÖTIGEN DEN MENSCHEN.
ER IST SEHR WERTVOLL.
KRAKOOM
GOOD GOD!!
SEHR WERTVOLL IN DER TAT.
GET OFFA ME!

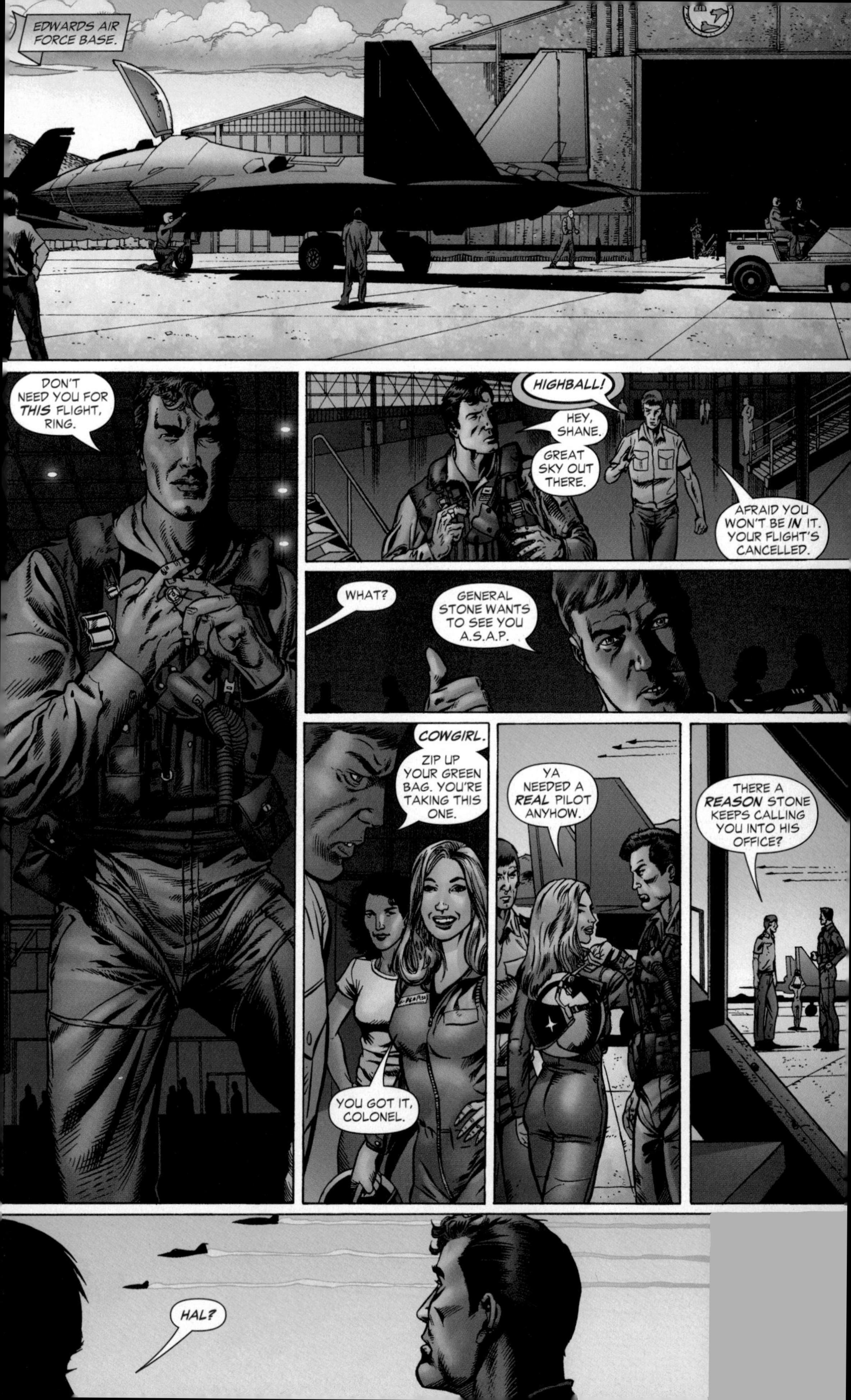
EDWARDS AIR FORCE BASE.
DON'T NEED YOU FOR THIS FLIGHT, RING.
HIGHBALL!
HEY, SHANE.
GREAT SKY OUT THERE.
AFRAID YOU WON'T BE IN IT. YOUR FLIGHT'S CANCELLED.
WHAT?
GENERAL STONE WANTS TO SEE YOU A.S.A.P.
COWGIRL.
ZIP UP YOUR GREEN BAG. YOU'RE TAKING THIS ONE.
YOU GOT IT, COLONEL.
YA NEEDED A REAL PILOT ANYHOW.
THERE A REASON STONE KEEPS CALLING YOU INTO HIS OFFICE?
HAL?

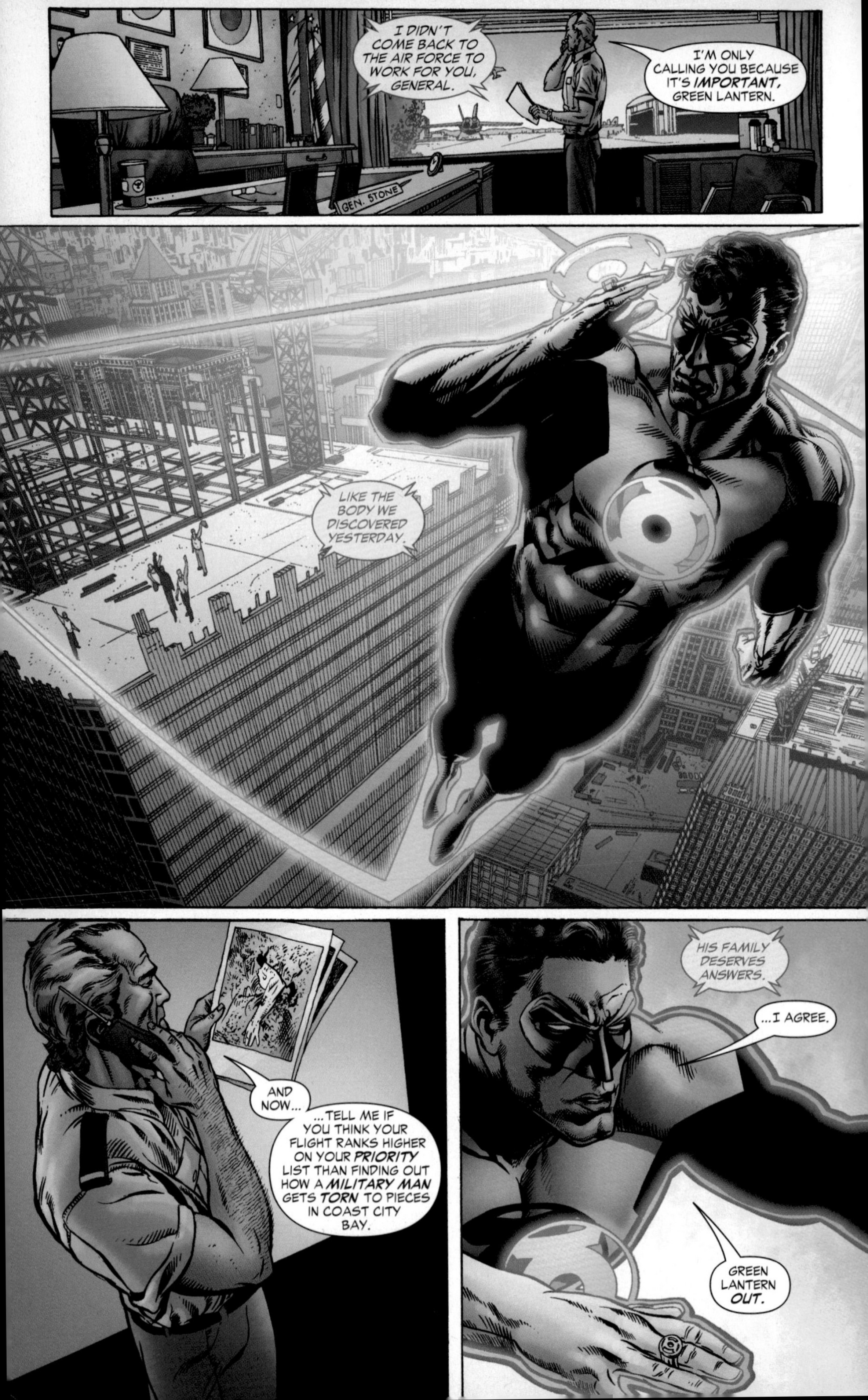
I DIDN'T COME BACK TO THE AIR FORCE TO WORK FOR YOU, GENERAL.
I'M ONLY CALLING YOU BECAUSE IT'S IMPORTANT, GREEN LANTERN.
GEN. STONE
LIKE THE BODY WE DISCOVERED YESTERDAY.
AND NOW...
...TELL ME IF YOU THINK YOUR FLIGHT RANKS HIGHER ON YOUR PRIORITY LIST THAN FINDING OUT HOW A MILITARY MAN GETS TORN TO PIECES IN COAST CITY BAY.
HIS FAMILY DESERVES ANSWERS.
...I AGREE.
GREEN LANTERN OUT.

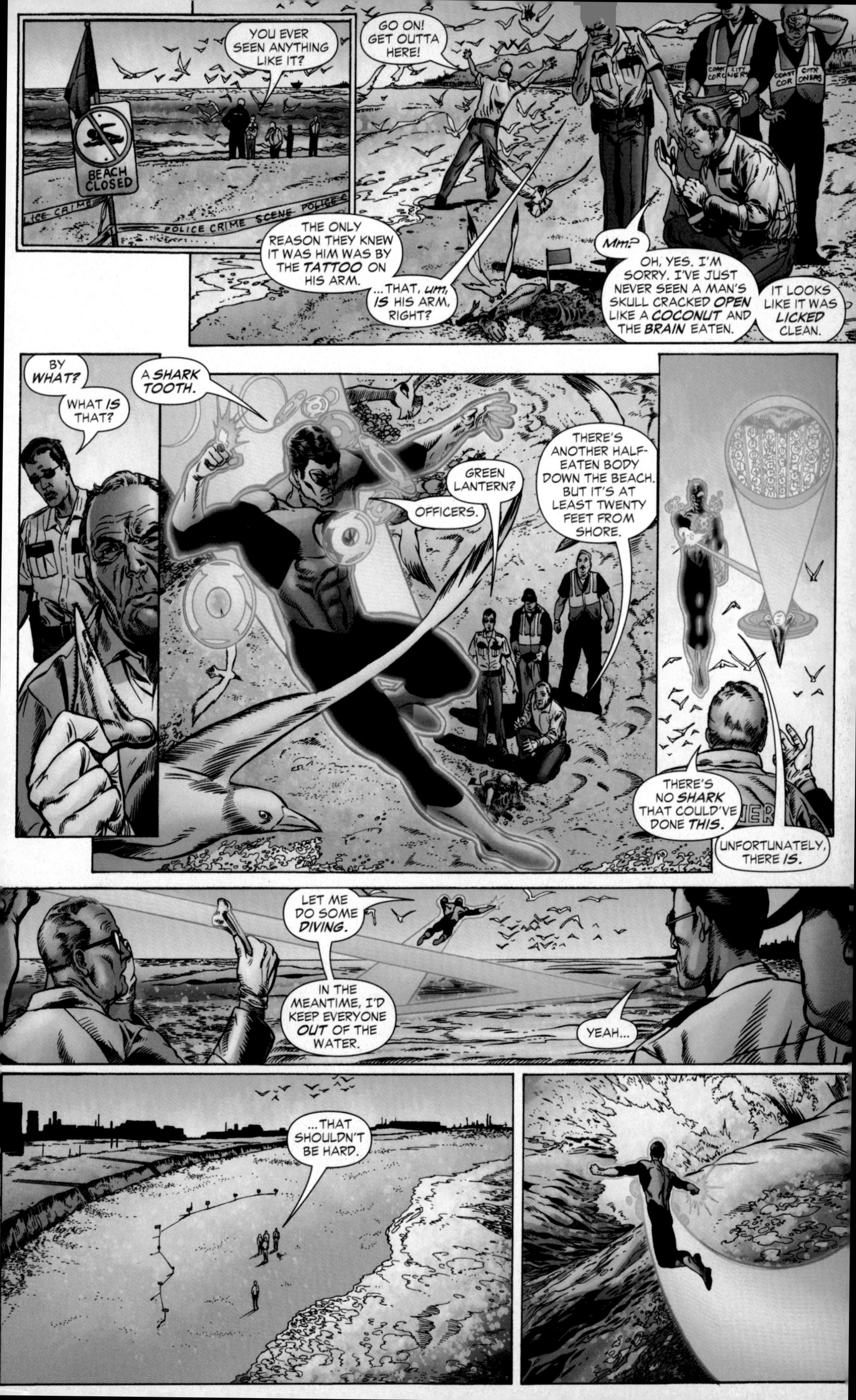
YOU EVER SEEN ANYTHING LIKE IT?
BEACH CLOSED
POLICE CRIME SCENE
GO ON! GET OUTTA HERE!
COAST CITY CORONER
THE ONLY REASON THEY KNEW IT WAS HIM WAS BY THE TATTOO ON HIS ARM.
...THAT, UM, IS HIS ARM, RIGHT?
Mm?
OH, YES. I'M SORRY. I'VE JUST NEVER SEEN A MAN'S SKULL CRACKED OPEN LIKE A COCONUT AND THE BRAIN EATEN.
IT LOOKS LIKE IT WAS LICKED CLEAN.
BY WHAT?
WHAT IS THAT?
A SHARK TOOTH.
GREEN LANTERN?
OFFICERS.
THERE'S ANOTHER HALF-EATEN BODY DOWN THE BEACH. BUT IT'S AT LEAST TWENTY FEET FROM SHORE.
THERE'S NO SHARK THAT COULD'VE DONE THIS.
UNFORTUNATELY, THERE IS.
LET ME DO SOME DIVING.
IN THE MEANTIME, I'D KEEP EVERYONE OUT OF THE WATER.
YEAH...
...THAT SHOULDN'T BE HARD.

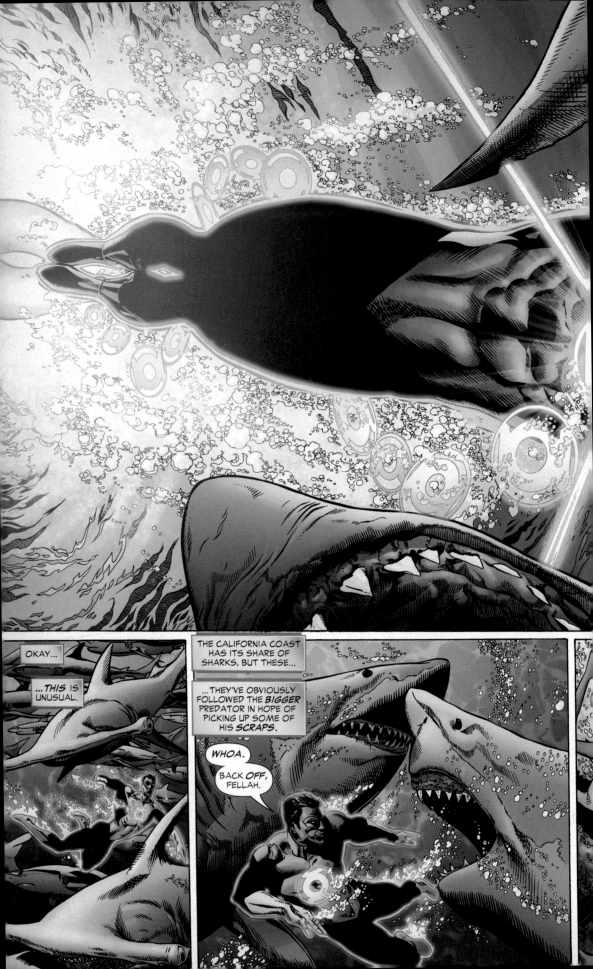

OKAY...

...THIS IS UNUSUAL.

THE CALIFORNIA COAST HAS ITS SHARE OF SHARKS, BUT THESE...

...THEY'VE OBVIOUSLY FOLLOWED THE BIGGER PREDATOR IN HOPE OF PICKING UP SOME OF HIS SCRAPS.

WHOA.

BACK OFF, FELLAH.

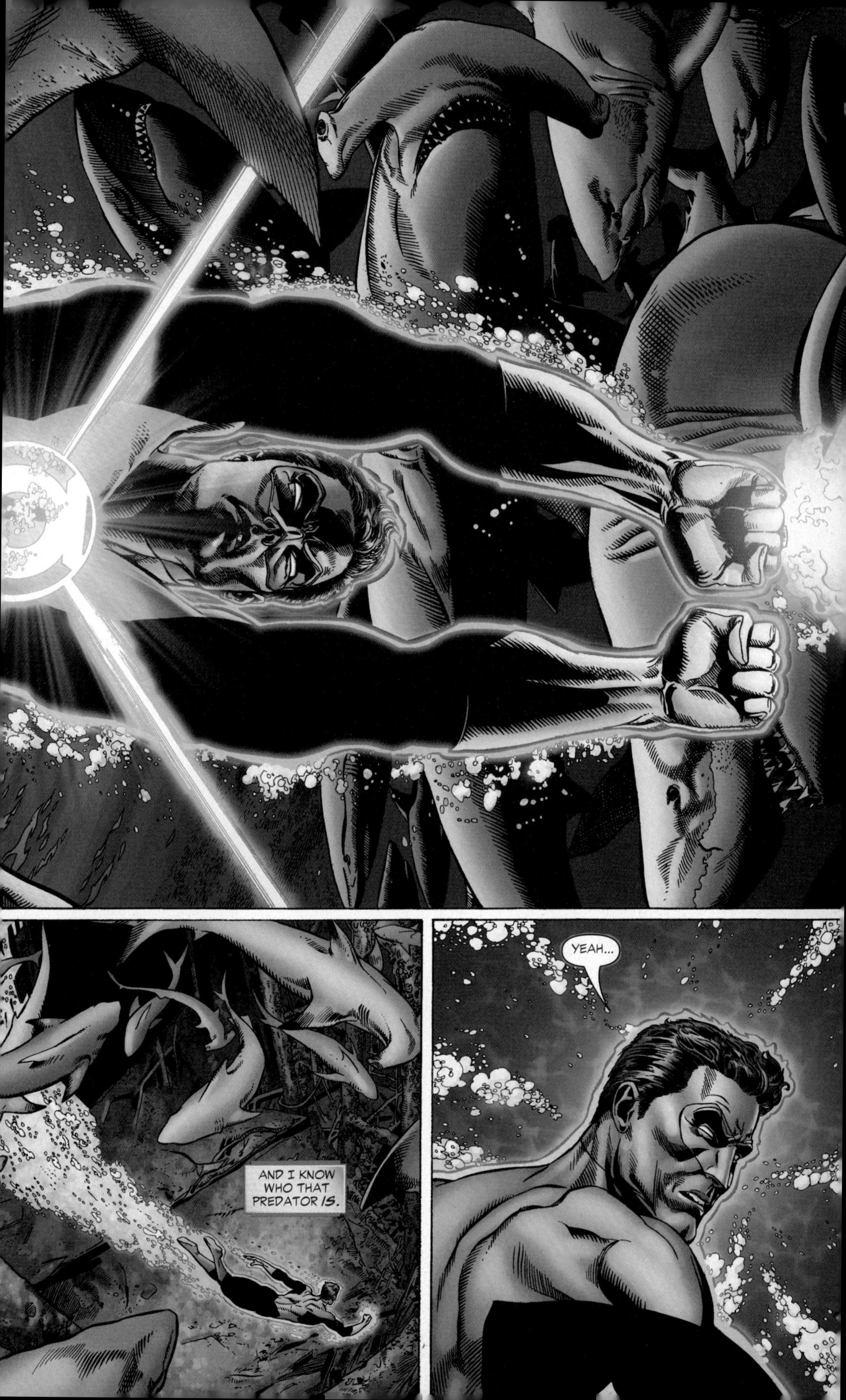
AND I KNOW
WHO THAT
PREDATOR IS.
YEAH...

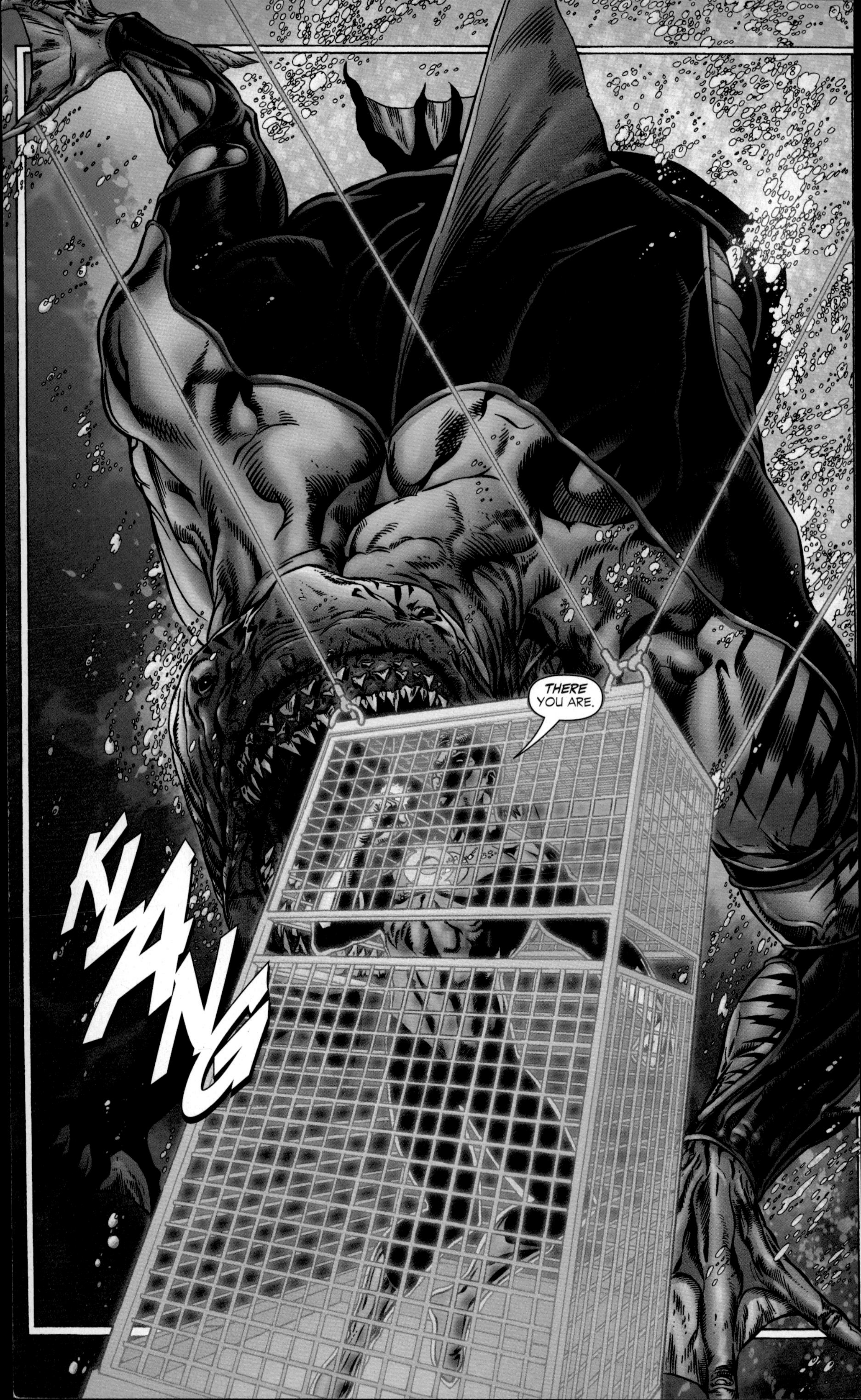
THERE YOU ARE.
KLANG

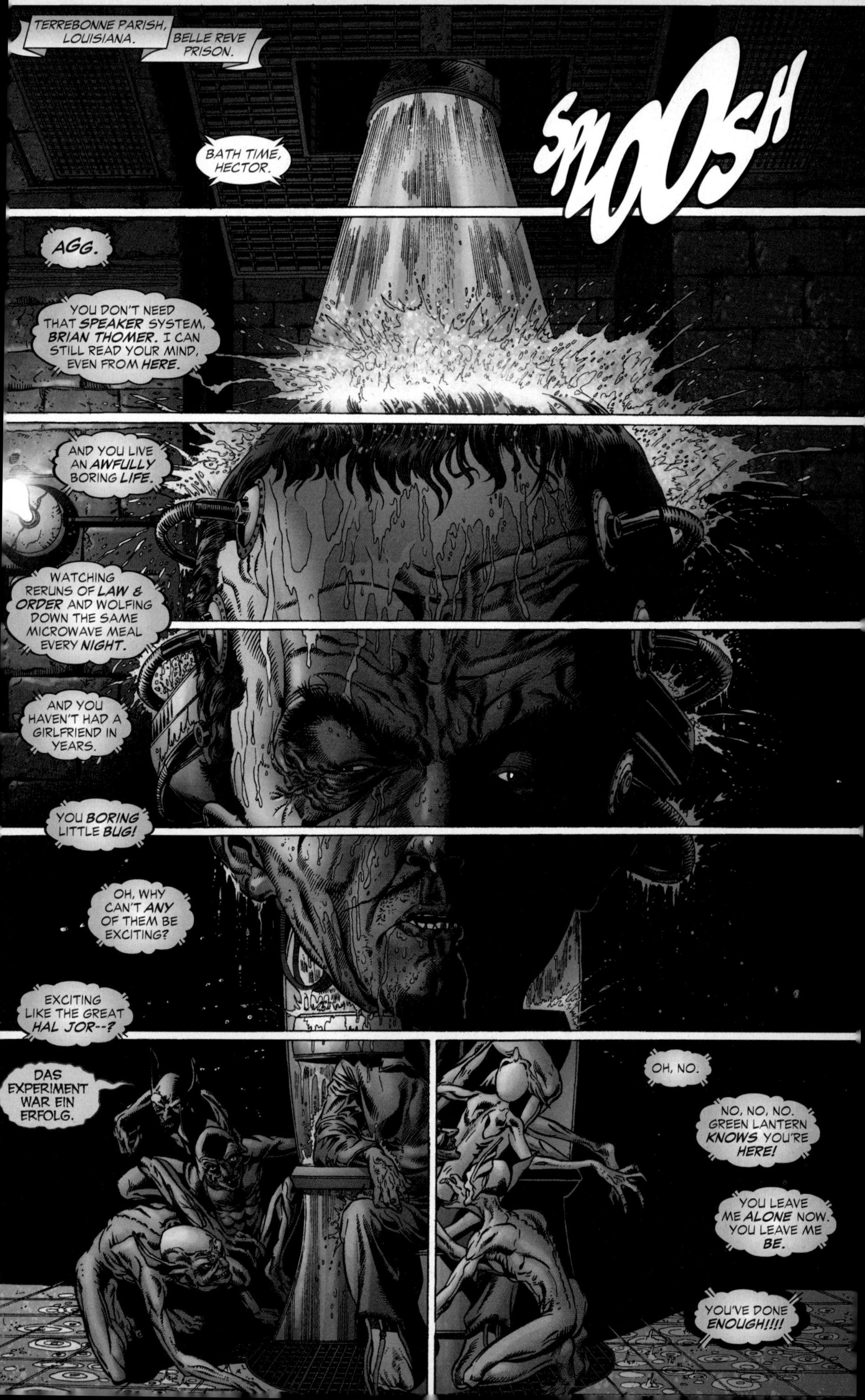
TERREBONNE PARISH, LOUISIANA.
BELLE REVE PRISON.
BATH TIME, HECTOR.
SPLOOSH
AGG.
YOU DON'T NEED THAT SPEAKER SYSTEM, BRIAN THOMER. I CAN STILL READ YOUR MIND, EVEN FROM HERE.
AND YOU LIVE AN AWFULLY BORING LIFE.
WATCHING RERUNS OF LAW & ORDER AND WOLFING DOWN THE SAME MICROWAVE MEAL EVERY NIGHT.
AND YOU HAVEN'T HAD A GIRLFRIEND IN YEARS.
YOU BORING LITTLE BUG!
OH, WHY CAN'T ANY OF THEM BE EXCITING?
EXCITING LIKE THE GREAT HAL JOR--?
DAS EXPERIMENT WAR EIN ERFOLG.
OH, NO.
NO, NO, NO. GREEN LANTERN KNOWS YOU'RE HERE!
YOU LEAVE ME ALONE NOW. YOU LEAVE ME BE.
YOU'VE DONE ENOUGH!!!!

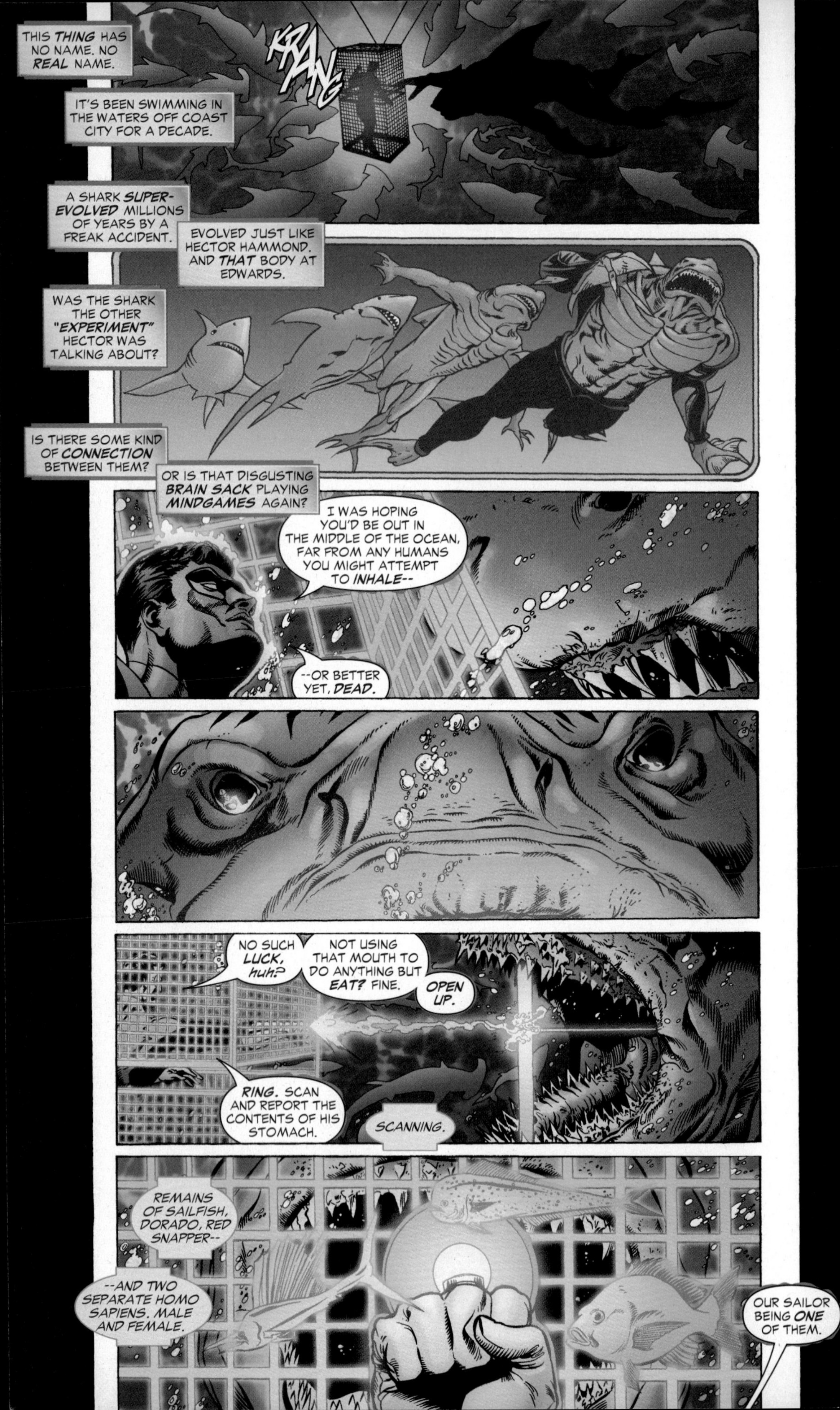
THIS THING HAS NO NAME. NO REAL NAME.
KRANG
IT'S BEEN SWIMMING IN THE WATERS OFF COAST CITY FOR A DECADE.
A SHARK SUPER-EVOLVED MILLIONS OF YEARS BY A FREAK ACCIDENT.
EVOLVED JUST LIKE HECTOR HAMMOND. AND THAT BODY AT EDWARDS.
WAS THE SHARK THE OTHER "EXPERIMENT" HECTOR WAS TALKING ABOUT?
IS THERE SOME KIND OF CONNECTION BETWEEN THEM?
OR IS THAT DISGUSTING BRAIN SACK PLAYING MINDGAMES AGAIN?
I WAS HOPING YOU'D BE OUT IN THE MIDDLE OF THE OCEAN, FAR FROM ANY HUMANS YOU MIGHT ATTEMPT TO INHALE--
--OR BETTER YET, DEAD.
NO SUCH LUCK, huh?
NOT USING THAT MOUTH TO DO ANYTHING BUT EAT? FINE.
OPEN UP.
RING. SCAN AND REPORT THE CONTENTS OF HIS STOMACH.
SCANNING.
REMAINS OF SAILFISH, DORADO, RED SNAPPER--
--AND TWO SEPARATE HOMO SAPIENS. MALE AND FEMALE.
OUR SAILOR BEING ONE OF THEM.

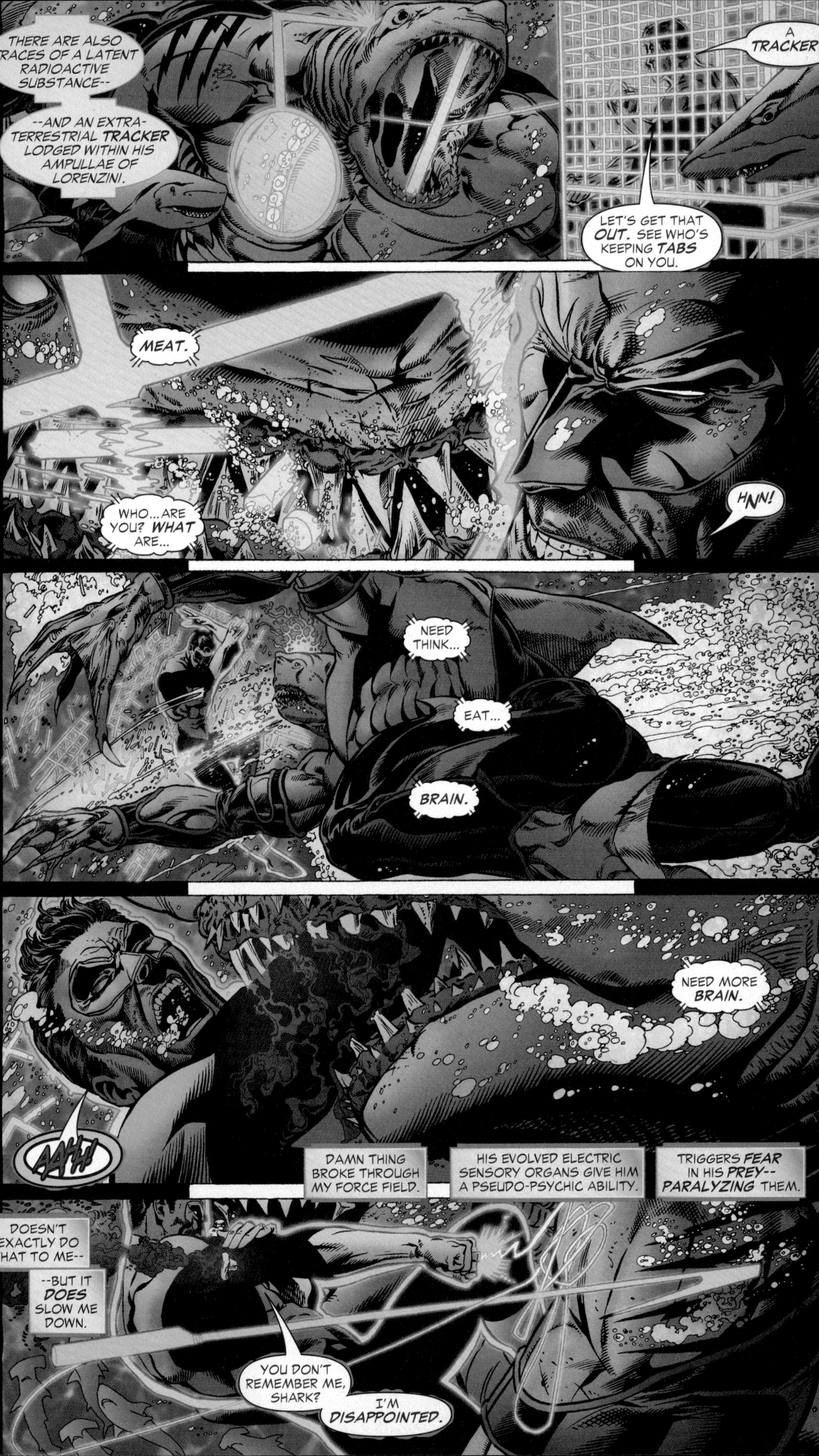
THERE ARE ALSO TRACES OF A LATENT RADIOACTIVE SUBSTANCE--
--AND AN EXTRA-TERRESTRIAL TRACKER LODGED WITHIN HIS AMPULLAE OF LORENZINI.
A TRACKER?
LET'S GET THAT OUT. SEE WHO'S KEEPING TABS ON YOU.
MEAT.
WHO...ARE YOU? WHAT ARE...
HNN!
NEED THINK...
EAT...
BRAIN.
NEED MORE BRAIN.
AAHH
DAMN THING BROKE THROUGH MY FORCE FIELD.
HIS EVOLVED ELECTRIC SENSORY ORGANS GIVE HIM A PSEUDO-PSYCHIC ABILITY.
TRIGGERS FEAR IN HIS PREY--PARALYZING THEM.
DOESN'T EXACTLY DO THAT TO ME--
--BUT IT DOES SLOW ME DOWN.
YOU DON'T REMEMBER ME, SHARK?
I'M DISAPPOINTED.

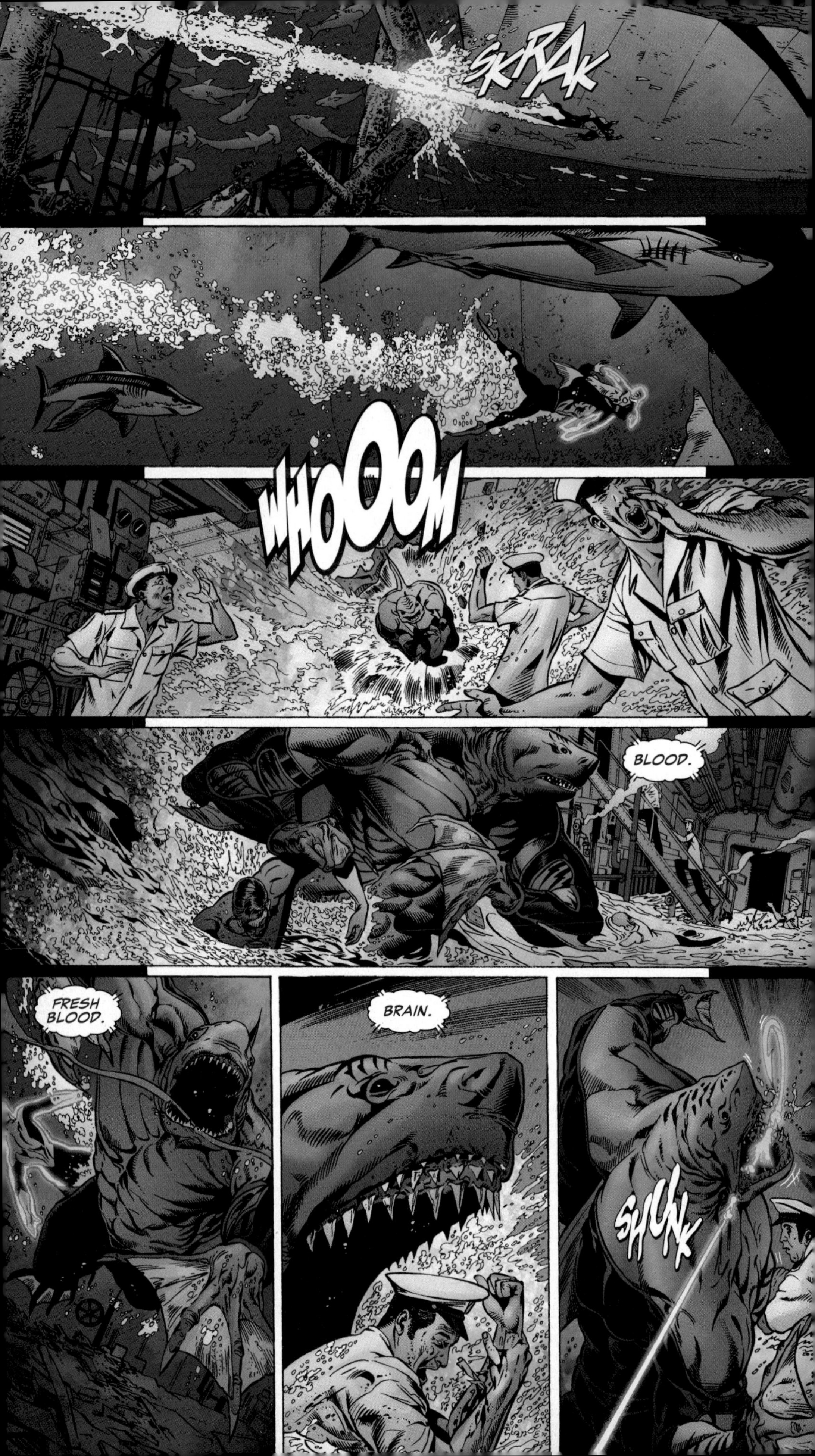
SKRAK
WHOOOM
BLOOD.
FRESH BLOOD.
BRAIN.
SHUNK

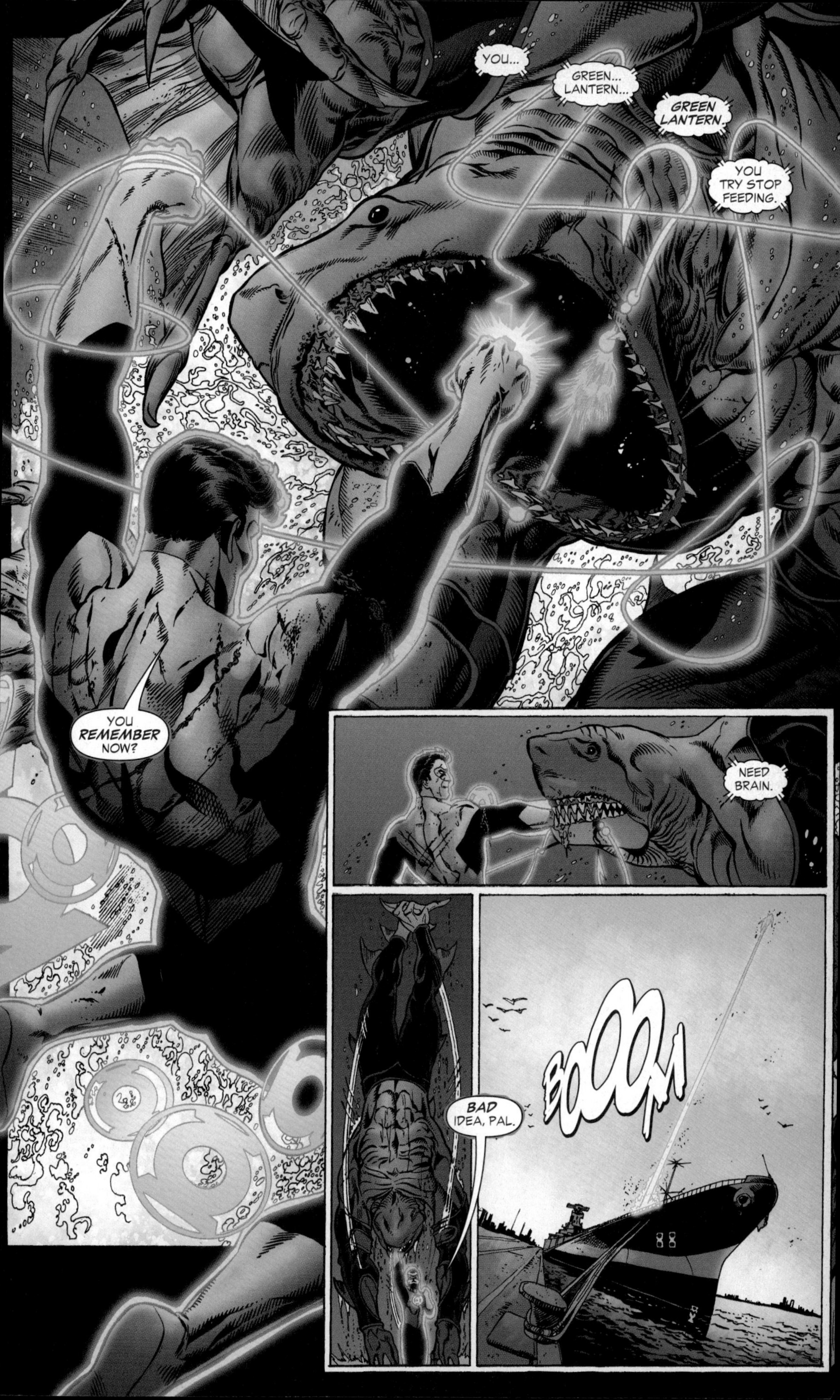
YOU...
GREEN... LANTERN...
GREEN LANTERN.
YOU TRY STOP FEEDING.
YOU REMEMBER NOW?
NEED BRAIN.
BAD IDEA, PAL.
BOOOM

PALMDALE. HILLSIDE PARK.

UMM.

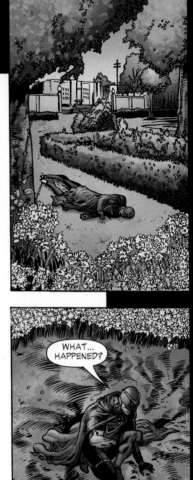

WHAT... HAPPENED?

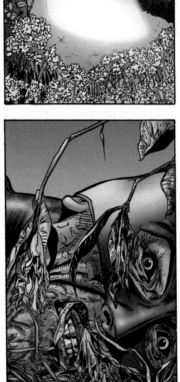

NEED A DRINK. I NEED...

MY H-H-H...

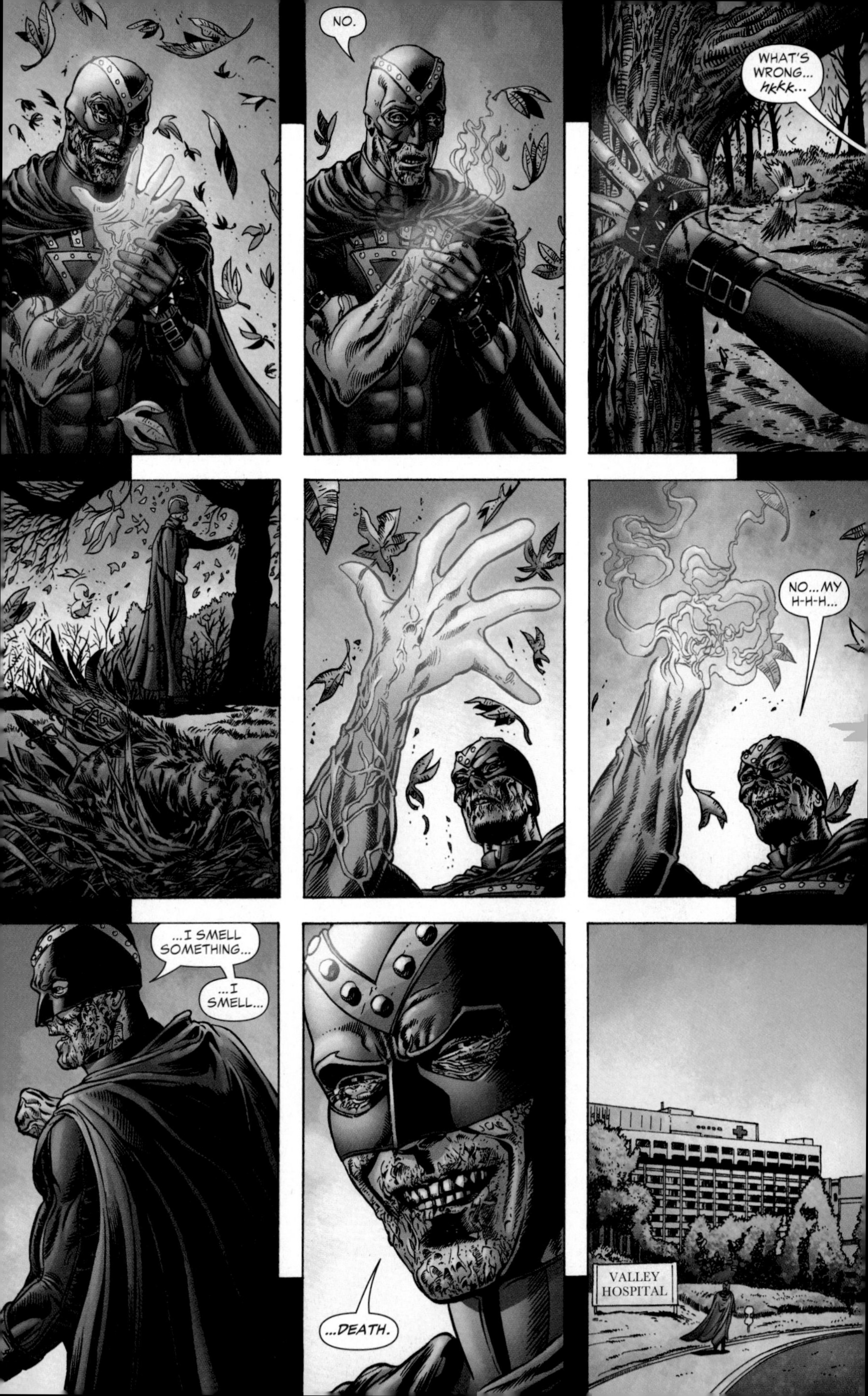
NO.
WHAT'S WRONG... HKKK...
NO... MY H-H-H...
...I SMELL SOMETHING...
...I SMELL...
...DEATH.
VALLEY HOSPITAL

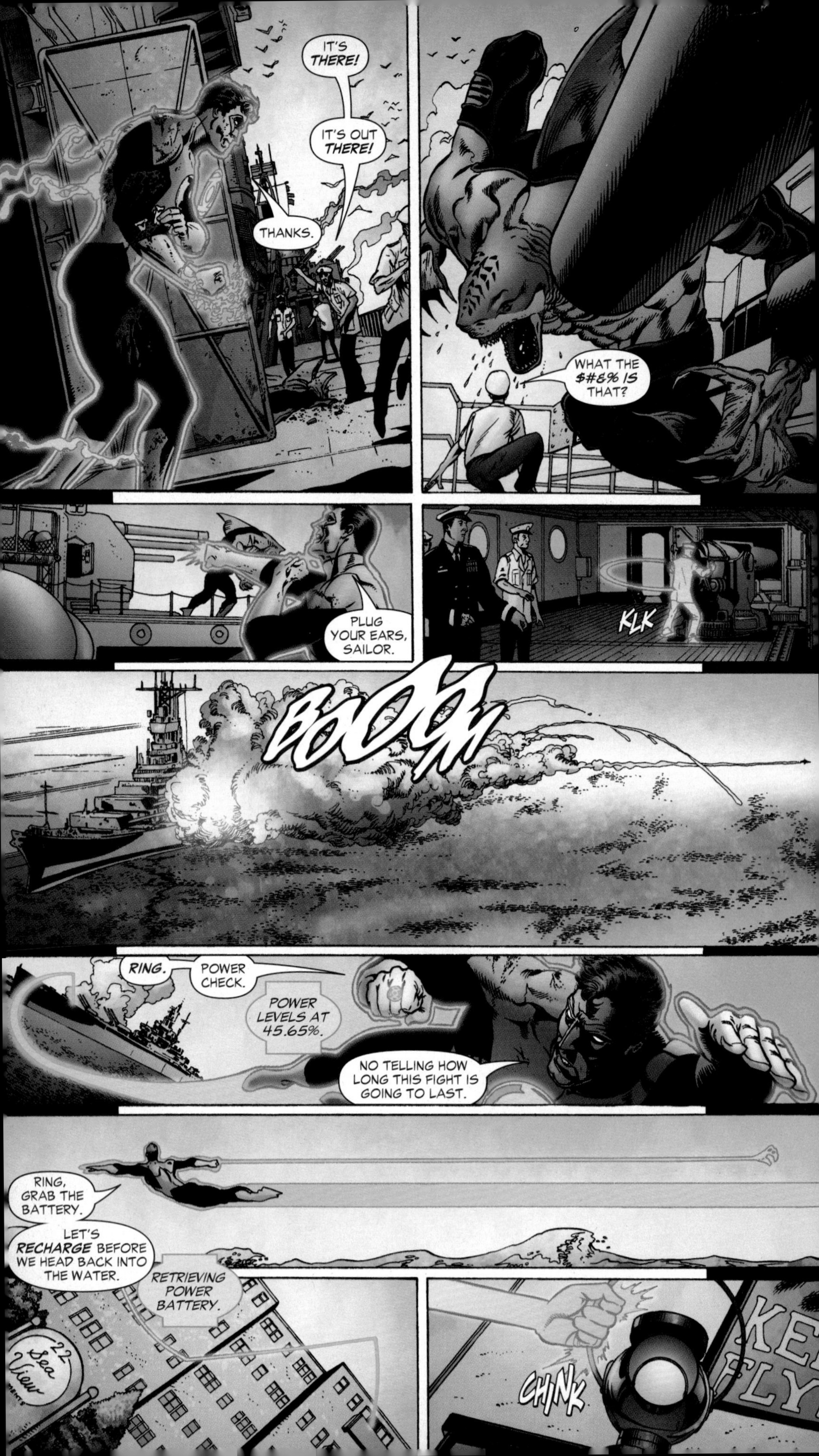

IT'S THERE!
IT'S OUT THERE!
THANKS.
WHAT THE $#&% IS THAT?
PLUG YOUR EARS, SAILOR.
KLK
BOOOM
RING.
POWER CHECK.
POWER LEVELS AT 45.65%.
NO TELLING HOW LONG THIS FIGHT IS GOING TO LAST.
RING, GRAB THE BATTERY.
LET'S RECHARGE BEFORE WE HEAD BACK INTO THE WATER.
RETRIEVING POWER BATTERY.
22 Sea View
CHINK

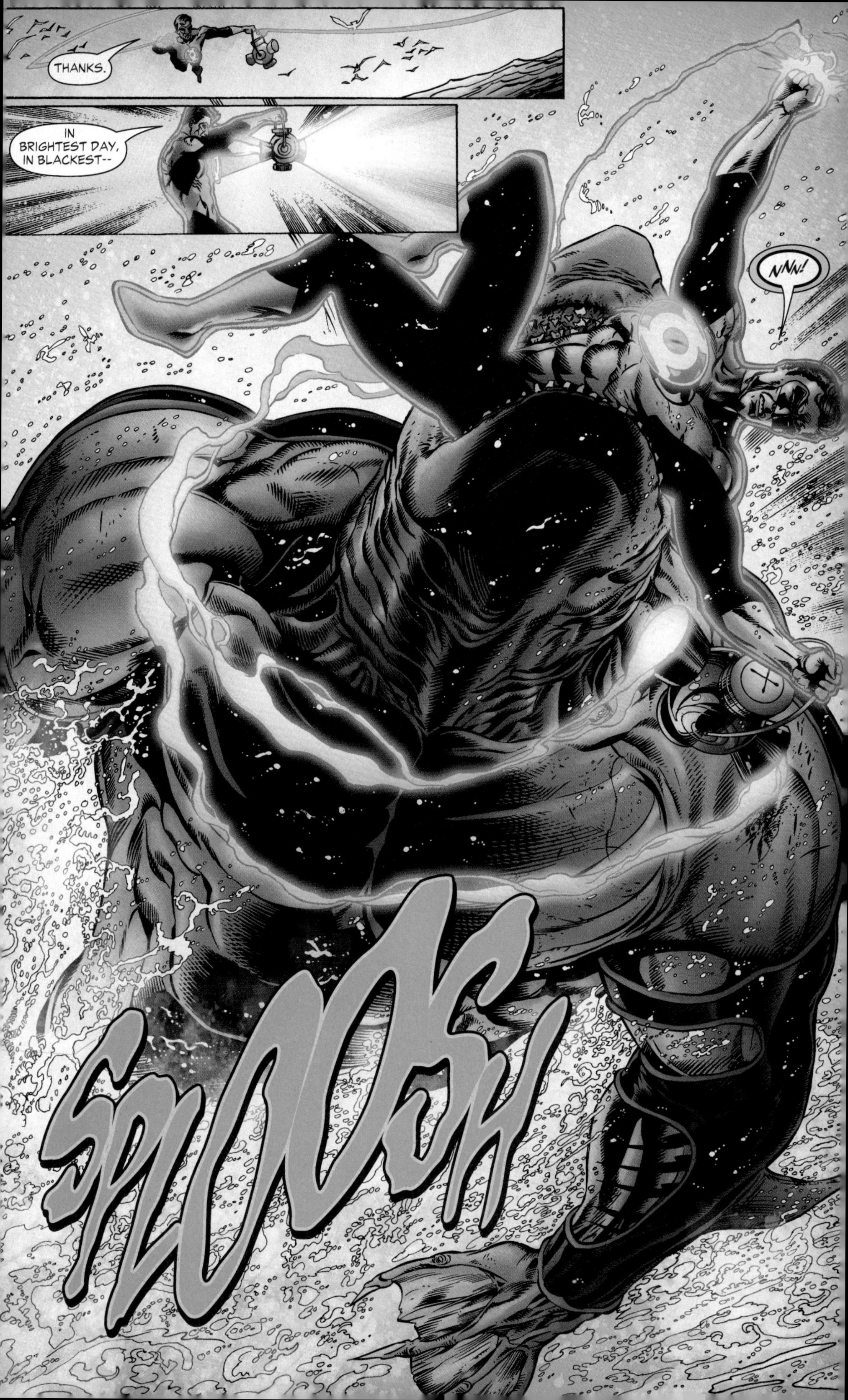
THANKS.
IN BRIGHTEST DAY, IN BLACKEST--
NNN!
SPLOOSH

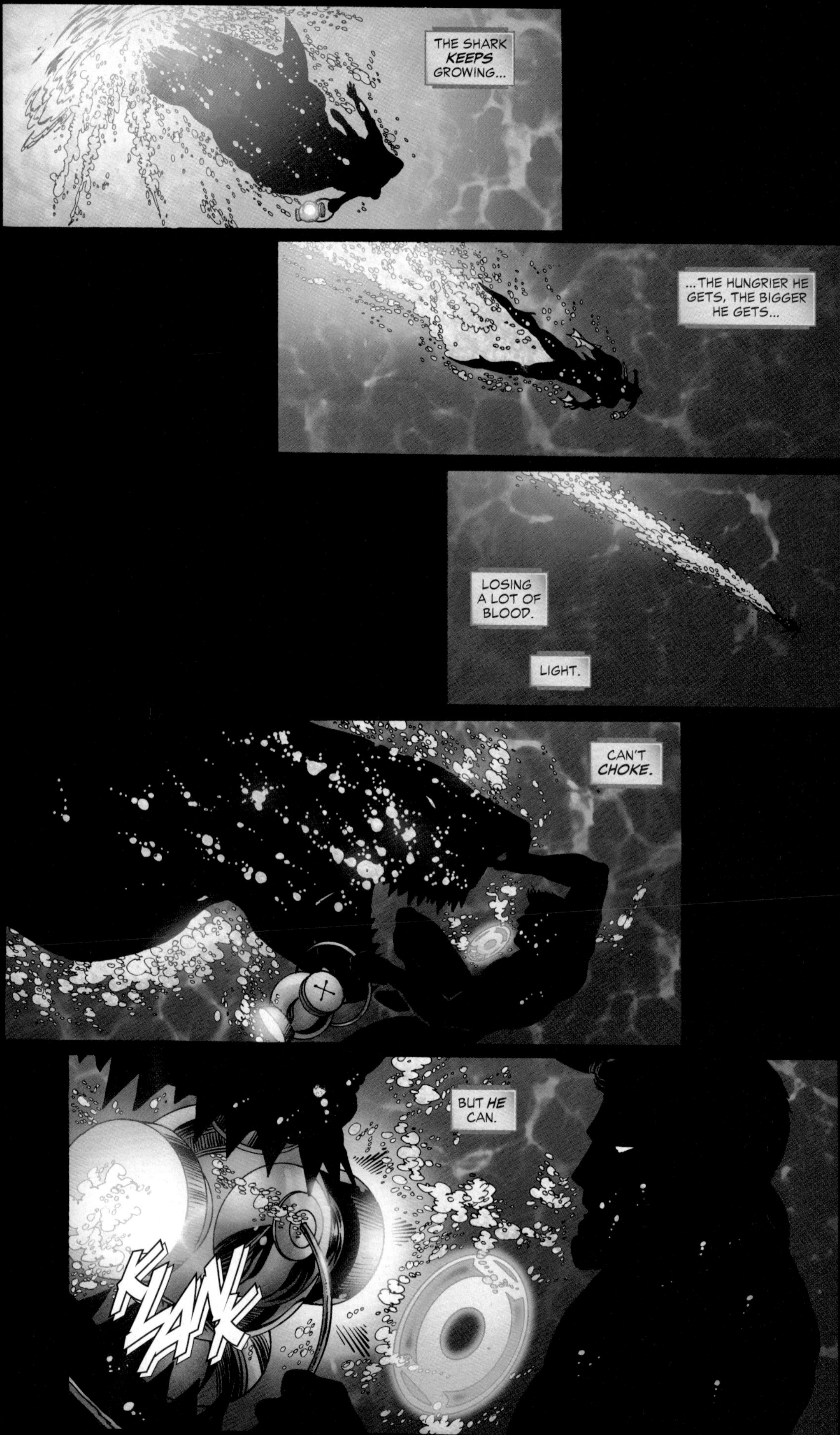
THE SHARK KEEPS GROWING...
...THE HUNGRIER HE GETS, THE BIGGER HE GETS...
LOSING A LOT OF BLOOD.
LIGHT.
CAN'T CHOKE.
BUT HE CAN.
KLANK

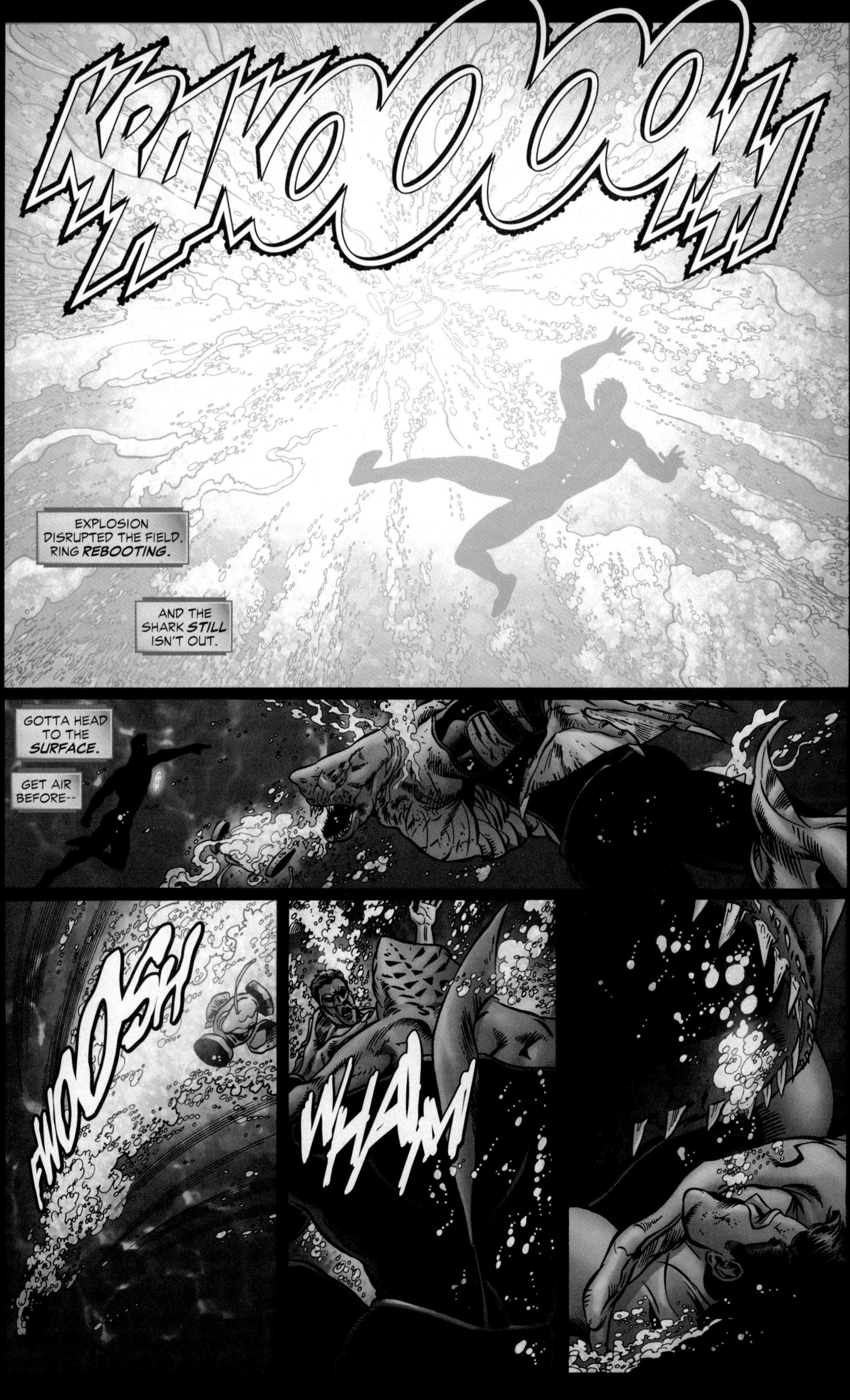
EXPLOSION DISRUPTED THE FIELD. RING *REBOOTING*.
AND THE SHARK *STILL* ISN'T OUT.
GOTTA HEAD TO THE *SURFACE*.
GET AIR BEFORE--
WHAM

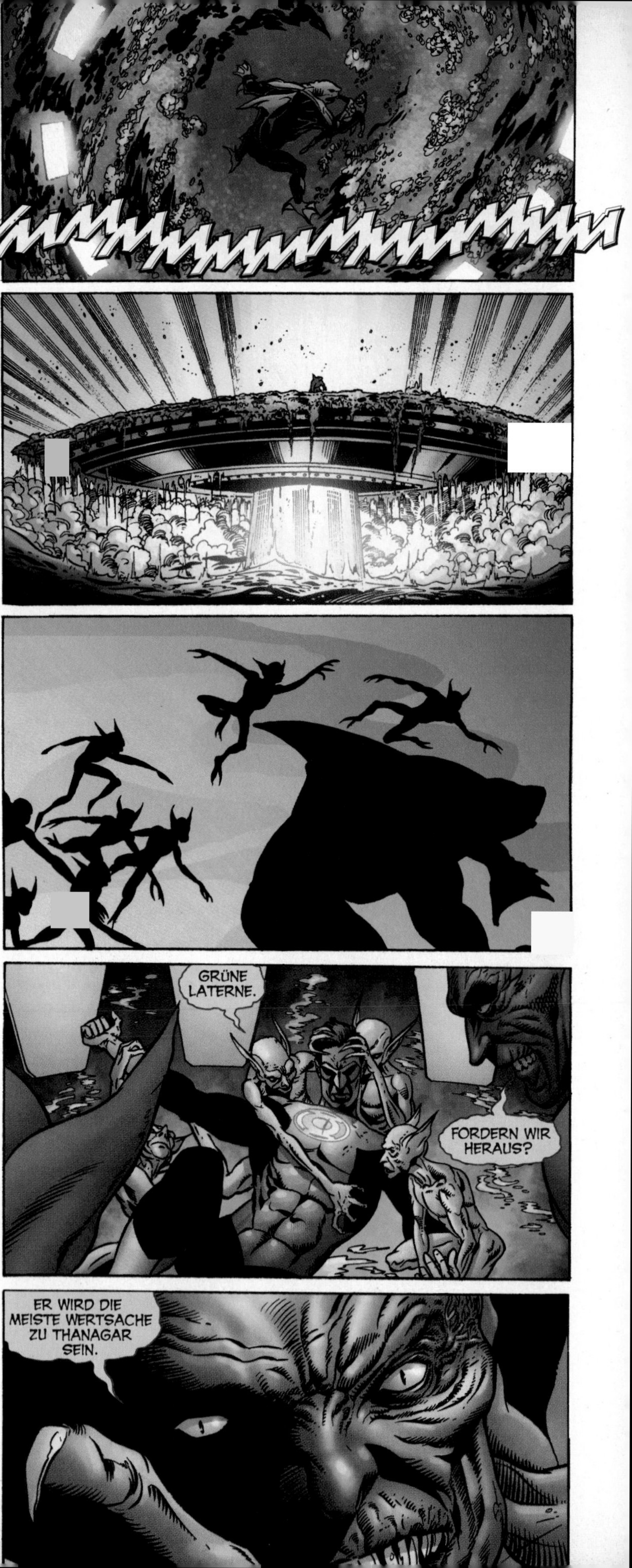
VMMMMMMMMMMMMMMM
GRÜNE LATERNE.
FORDERN WIR HERAUS?
ER WIRD DIE MEISTE WERTSACHE ZU THANAGAR SEIN.

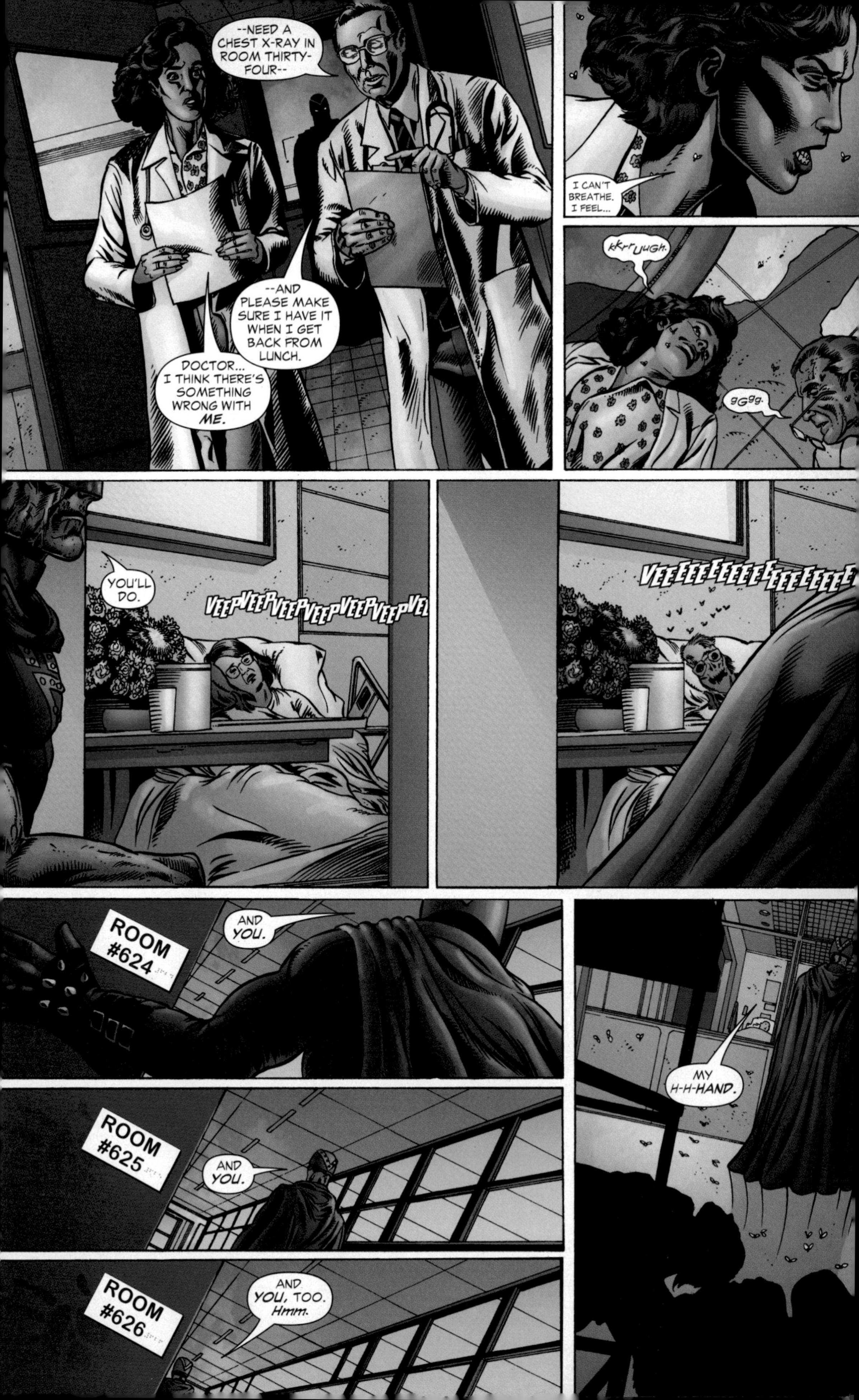
--NEED A CHEST X-RAY IN ROOM THIRTY-FOUR--
--AND PLEASE MAKE SURE I HAVE IT WHEN I GET BACK FROM LUNCH.
DOCTOR... I THINK THERE'S SOMETHING WRONG WITH *ME.*
I CAN'T BREATHE. I FEEL...
kkrruugh.
gGgg.
YOU'LL DO.
VEEPVEEPVEEPVEEPVEEPVEEPVEEPVEI
VEEEEEEEEEEEEEEEEEEEEEE
ROOM #624
AND *YOU.*
MY *H-H-HAND.*
ROOM #625
AND *YOU.*
ROOM #626
AND *YOU,* TOO. *Hmm.*

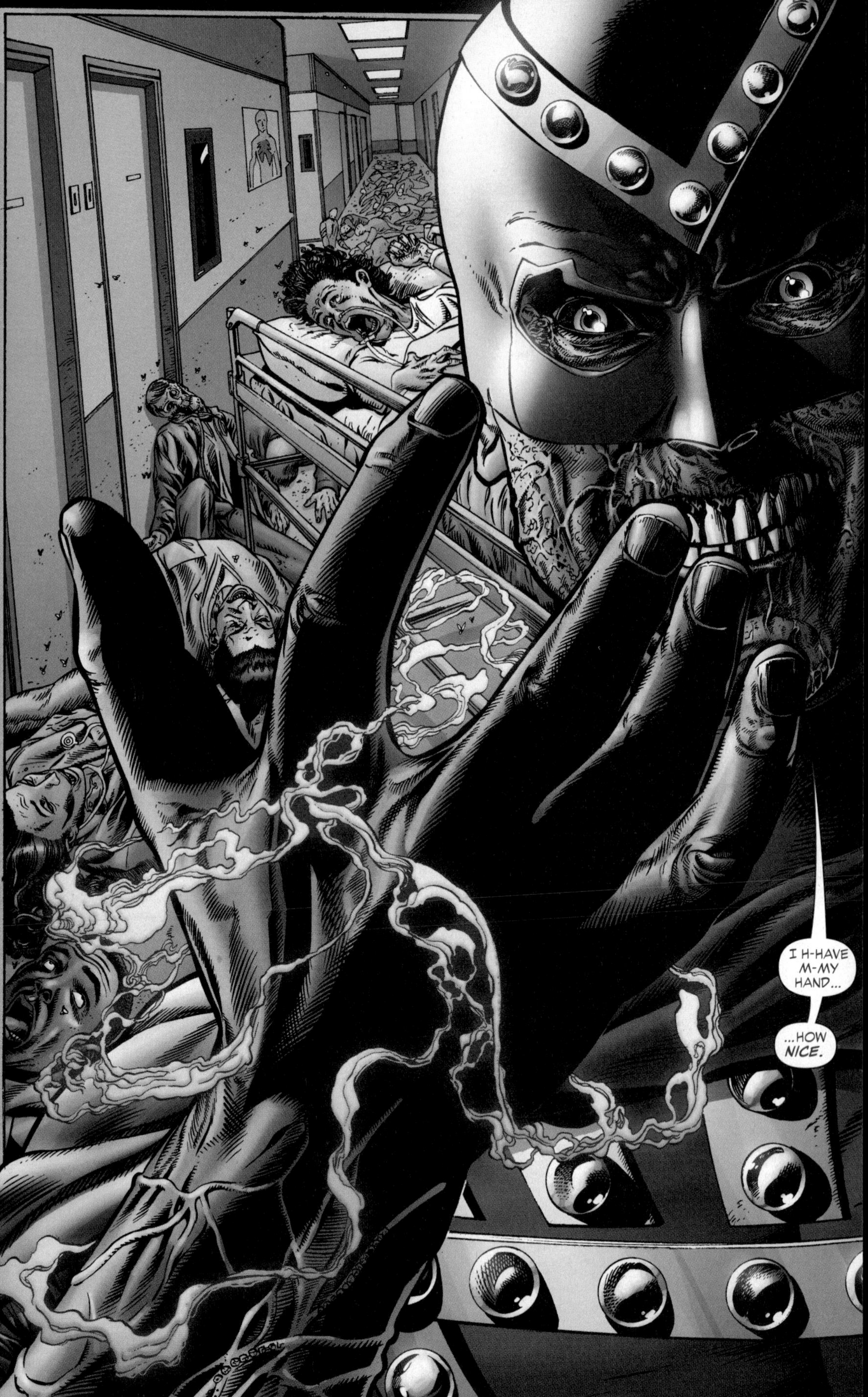

I H-HAVE M-MY HAND...
...HOW NICE.

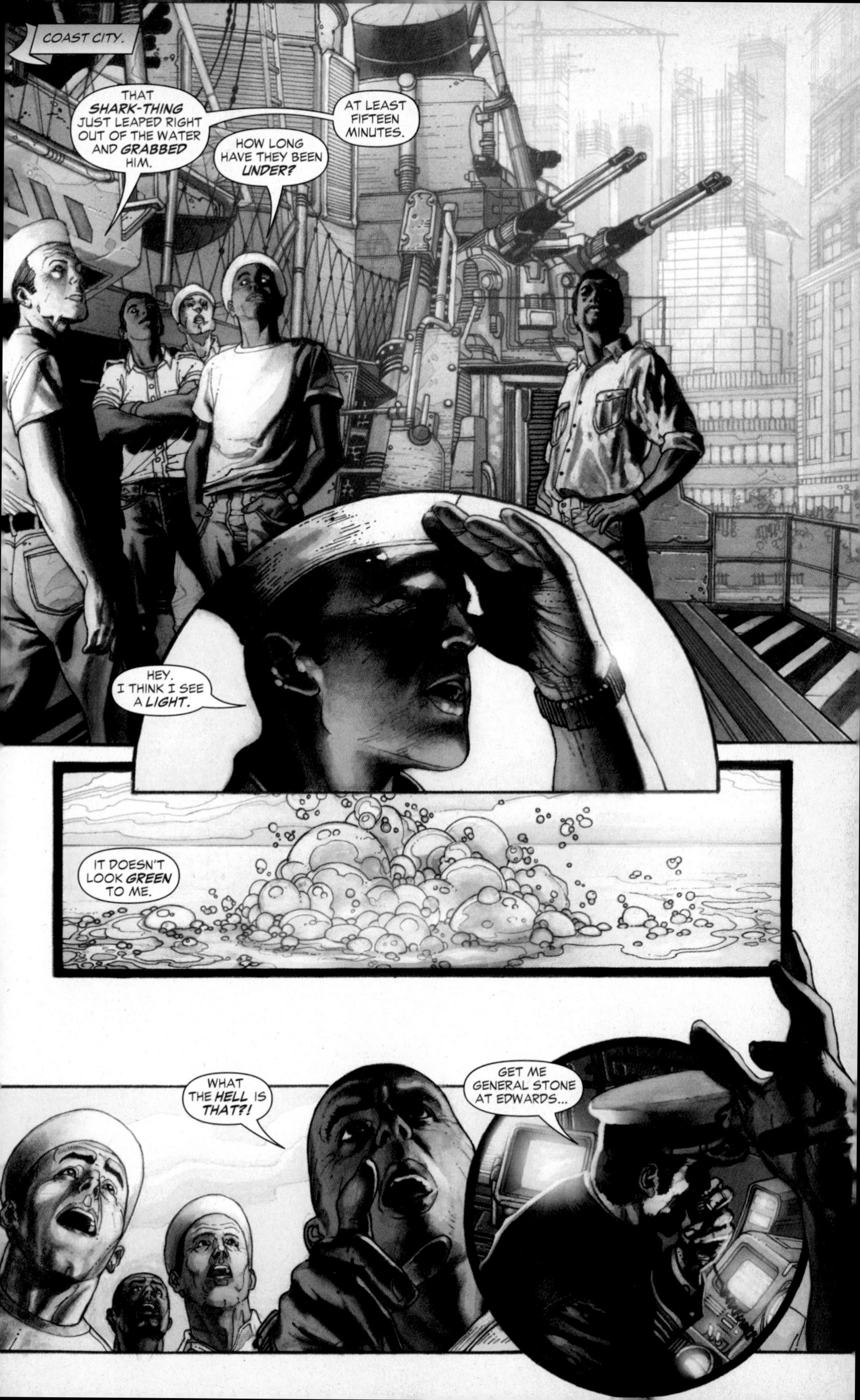

COAST CITY.
THAT SHARK-THING JUST LEAPED RIGHT OUT OF THE WATER AND GRABBED HIM.
HOW LONG HAVE THEY BEEN UNDER?
AT LEAST FIFTEEN MINUTES.
HEY. I THINK I SEE A LIGHT.
IT DOESN'T LOOK GREEN TO ME.
WHAT THE HELL IS THAT?!
GET ME GENERAL STONE AT EDWARDS...

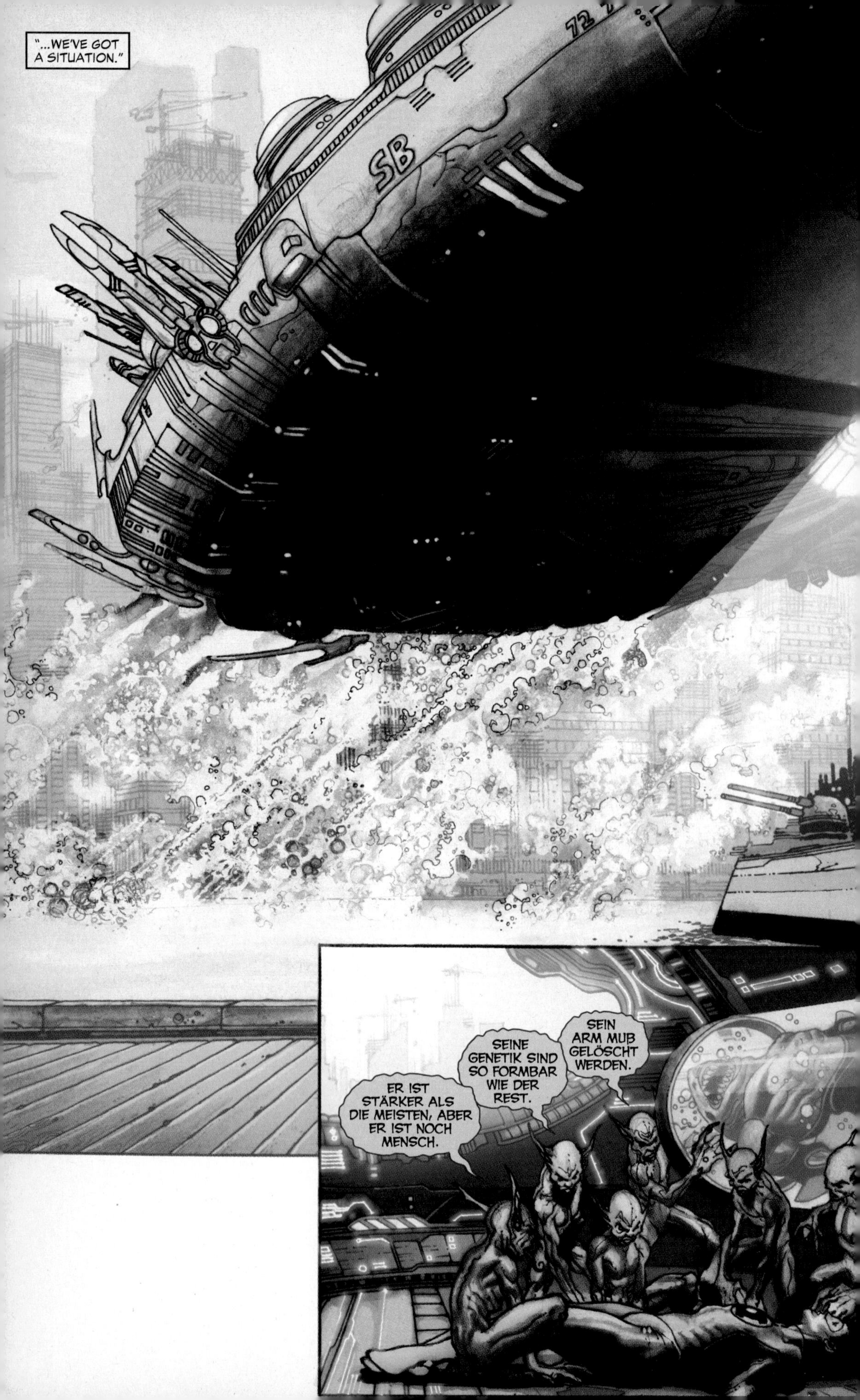
"...WE'VE GOT A SITUATION."
SB
ER IST STÄRKER ALS DIE MEISTEN, ABER ER IST NOCH MENSCH.
SEINE GENETIK SIND SO FORMBAR WIE DER REST.
SEIN ARM MUß GELÖSCHT WERDEN.

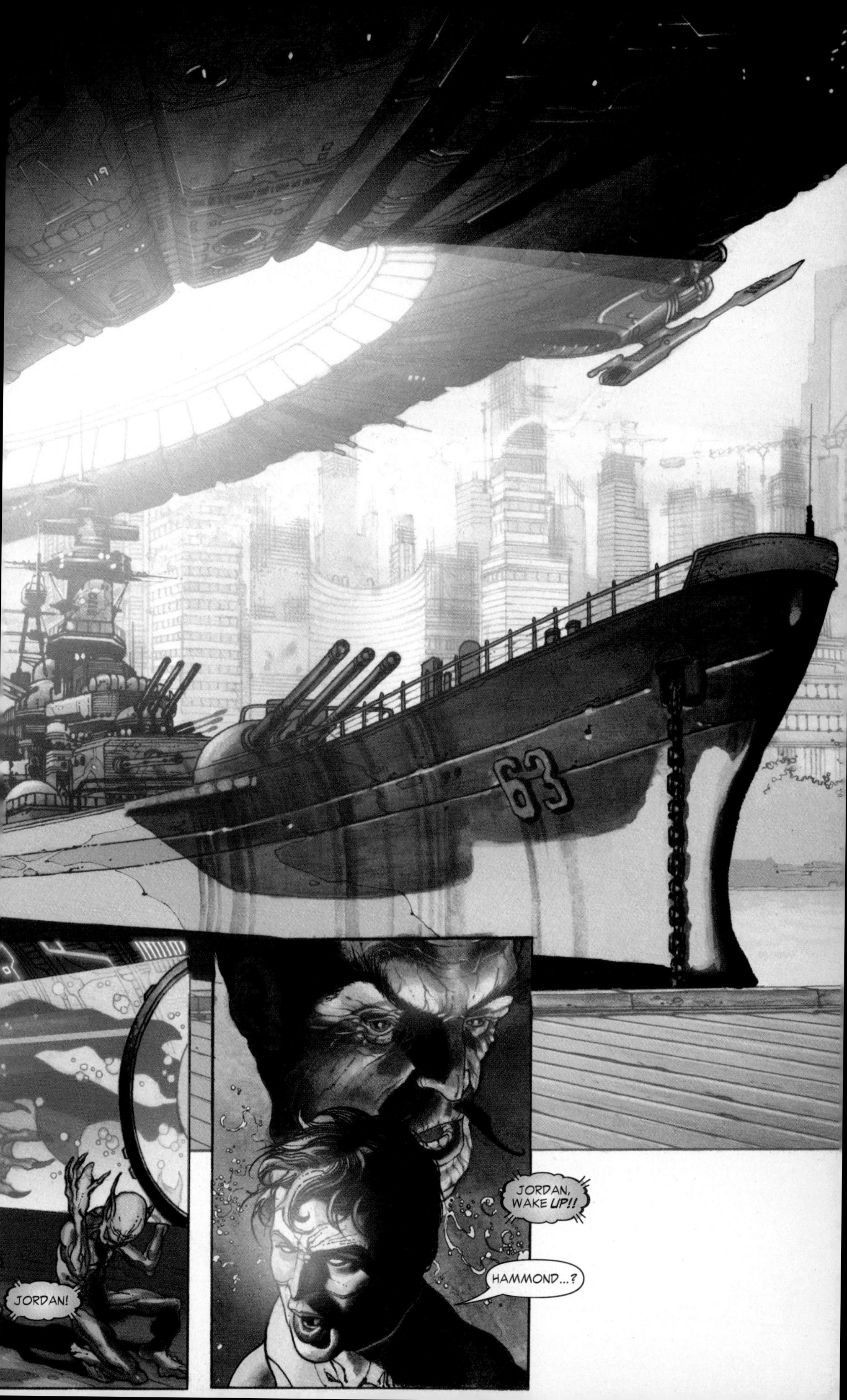
JORDAN!
JORDAN,
WAKE UP!!
HAMMOND...?

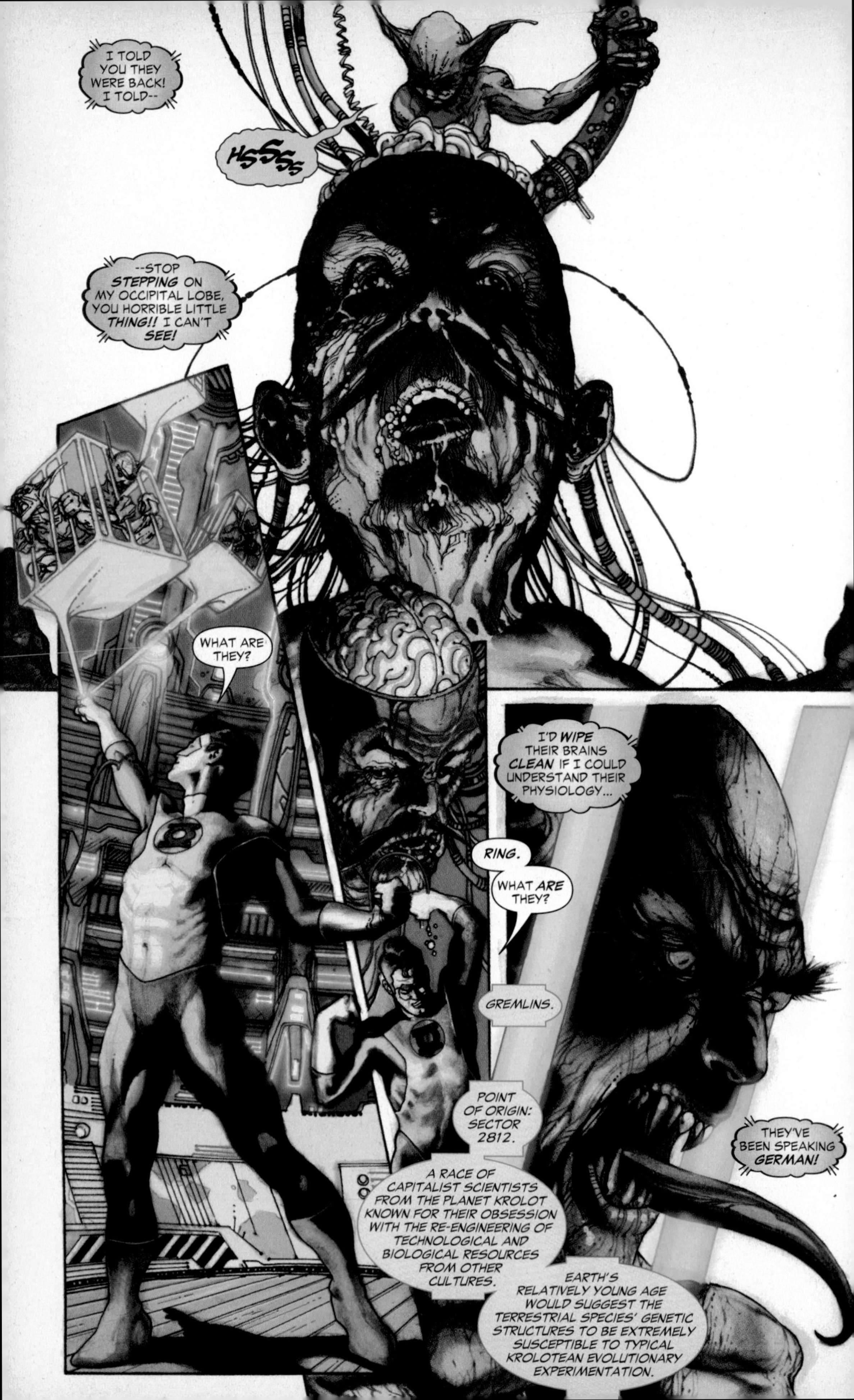
I TOLD YOU THEY WERE BACK! I TOLD--
HSSSS
--STOP STEPPING ON MY OCCIPITAL LOBE, YOU HORRIBLE LITTLE THING!! I CAN'T SEE!
WHAT ARE THEY?
I'D WIPE THEIR BRAINS CLEAN IF I COULD UNDERSTAND THEIR PHYSIOLOGY...
RING.
WHAT ARE THEY?
GREMLINS.
POINT OF ORIGIN: SECTOR 2812.
A RACE OF CAPITALIST SCIENTISTS FROM THE PLANET KROLOT KNOWN FOR THEIR OBSESSION WITH THE RE-ENGINEERING OF TECHNOLOGICAL AND BIOLOGICAL RESOURCES FROM OTHER CULTURES.
THEY'VE BEEN SPEAKING GERMAN!
EARTH'S RELATIVELY YOUNG AGE WOULD SUGGEST THE TERRESTRIAL SPECIES' GENETIC STRUCTURES TO BE EXTREMELY SUSCEPTIBLE TO TYPICAL KROLOTEAN EVOLUTIONARY EXPERIMENTATION.

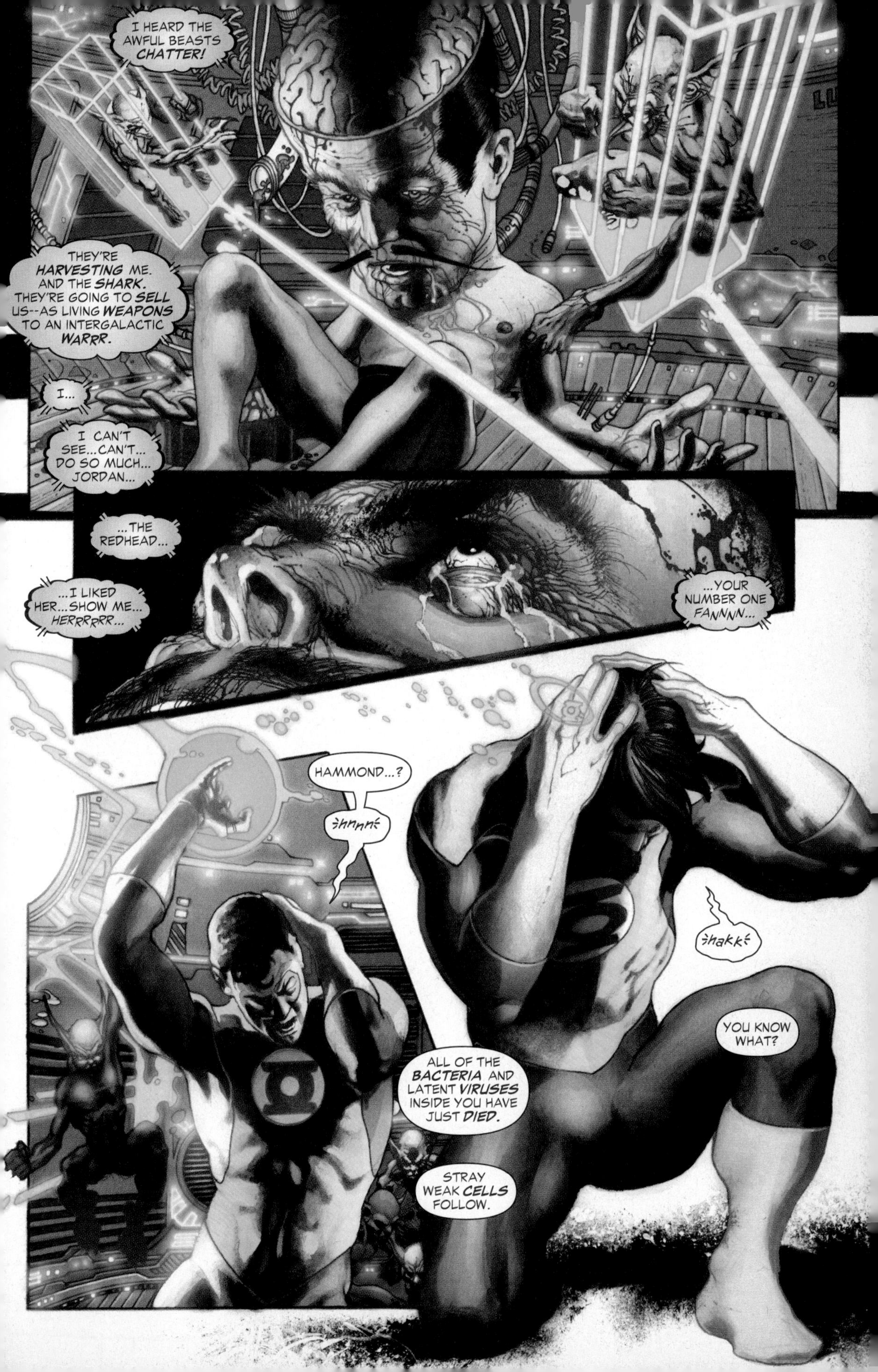
I HEARD THE AWFUL BEASTS CHATTER!
THEY'RE HARVESTING ME. AND THE SHARK. THEY'RE GOING TO SELL US--AS LIVING WEAPONS TO AN INTERGALACTIC WARRR.
I...
I CAN'T SEE...CAN'T... DO SO MUCH... JORDAN...
...THE REDHEAD...
...I LIKED HER...SHOW ME... HERRRRRR...
...YOUR NUMBER ONE FANNNNN...
HAMMOND...?
hnnn
hakk
YOU KNOW WHAT?
ALL OF THE BACTERIA AND LATENT VIRUSES INSIDE YOU HAVE JUST DIED.
STRAY WEAK CELLS FOLLOW.

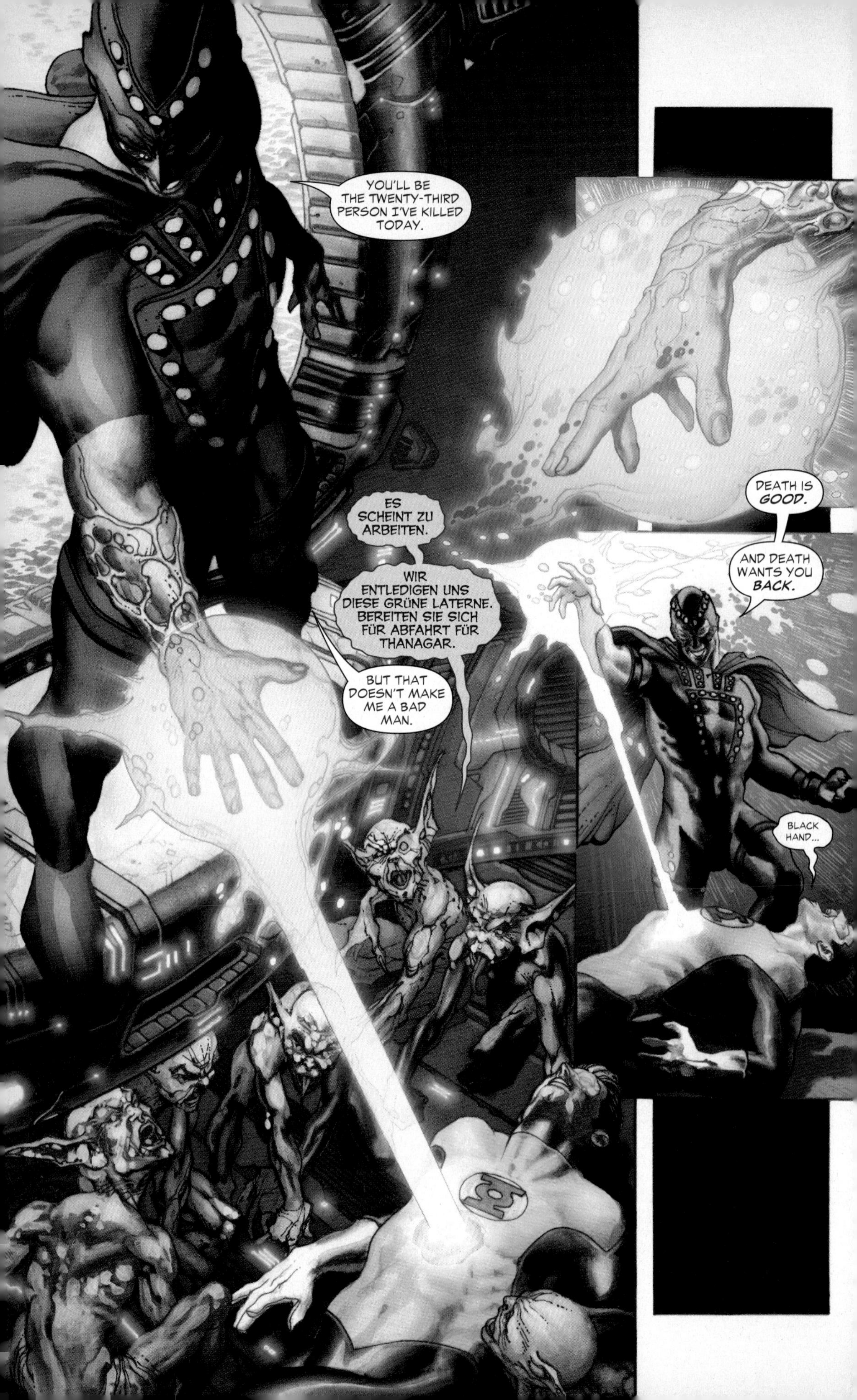

YOU'LL BE THE TWENTY-THIRD PERSON I'VE KILLED TODAY.
ES SCHEINT ZU ARBEITEN.
WIR ENTLEDIGEN UNS DIESE GRÜNE LATERNE. BEREITEN SIE SICH FÜR ABFAHRT FÜR THANAGAR.
BUT THAT DOESN'T MAKE ME A BAD MAN.
DEATH IS *GOOD*.
AND DEATH WANTS YOU *BACK*.
BLACK HAND...

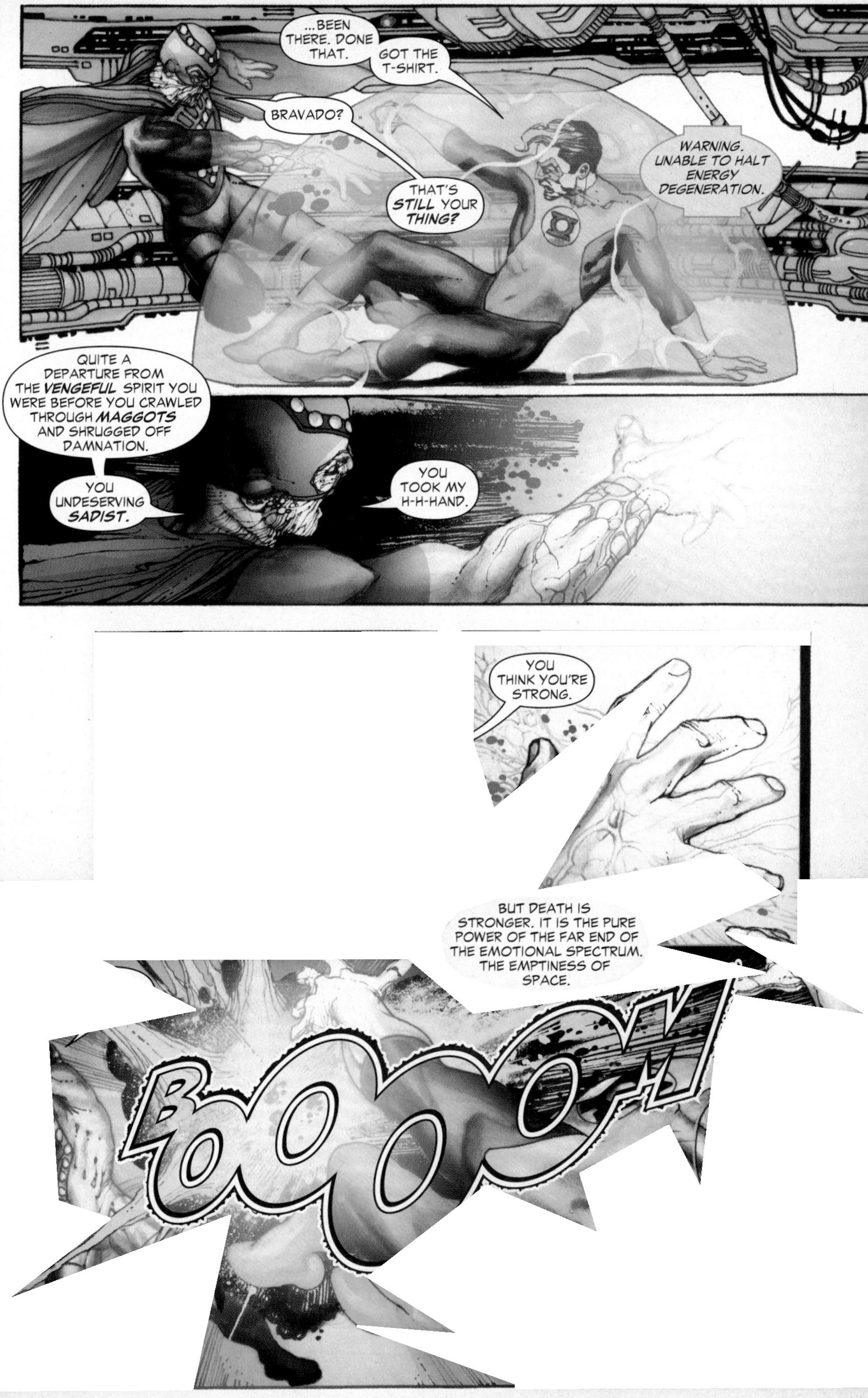
...BEEN THERE. DONE THAT.
GOT THE T-SHIRT.
BRAVADO?
THAT'S STILL YOUR THING?
WARNING. UNABLE TO HALT ENERGY DEGENERATION.
QUITE A DEPARTURE FROM THE VENGEFUL SPIRIT YOU WERE BEFORE YOU CRAWLED THROUGH MAGGOTS AND SHRUGGED OFF DAMNATION.
YOU UNDESERVING SADIST.
YOU TOOK MY H-H-HAND.
YOU THINK YOU'RE STRONG.
BUT DEATH IS STRONGER. IT IS THE PURE POWER OF THE FAR END OF THE EMOTIONAL SPECTRUM. THE EMPTINESS OF SPACE.
BOOOOM

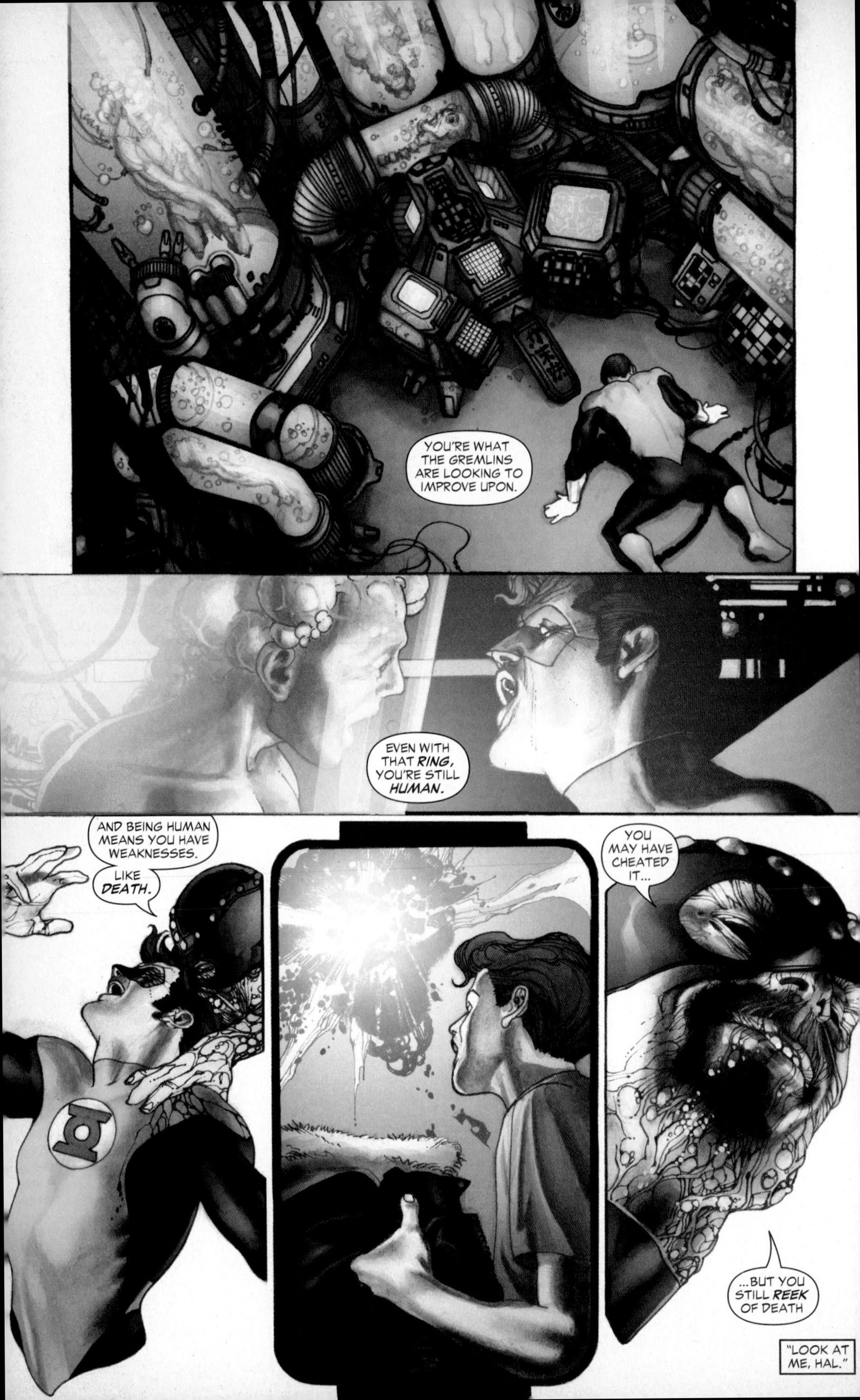

YOU'RE WHAT THE GREMLINS ARE LOOKING TO IMPROVE UPON.
EVEN WITH THAT RING, YOU'RE STILL HUMAN.
AND BEING HUMAN MEANS YOU HAVE WEAKNESSES.
LIKE DEATH.
YOU MAY HAVE CHEATED IT...
...BUT YOU STILL REEK OF DEATH
"LOOK AT ME, HAL."

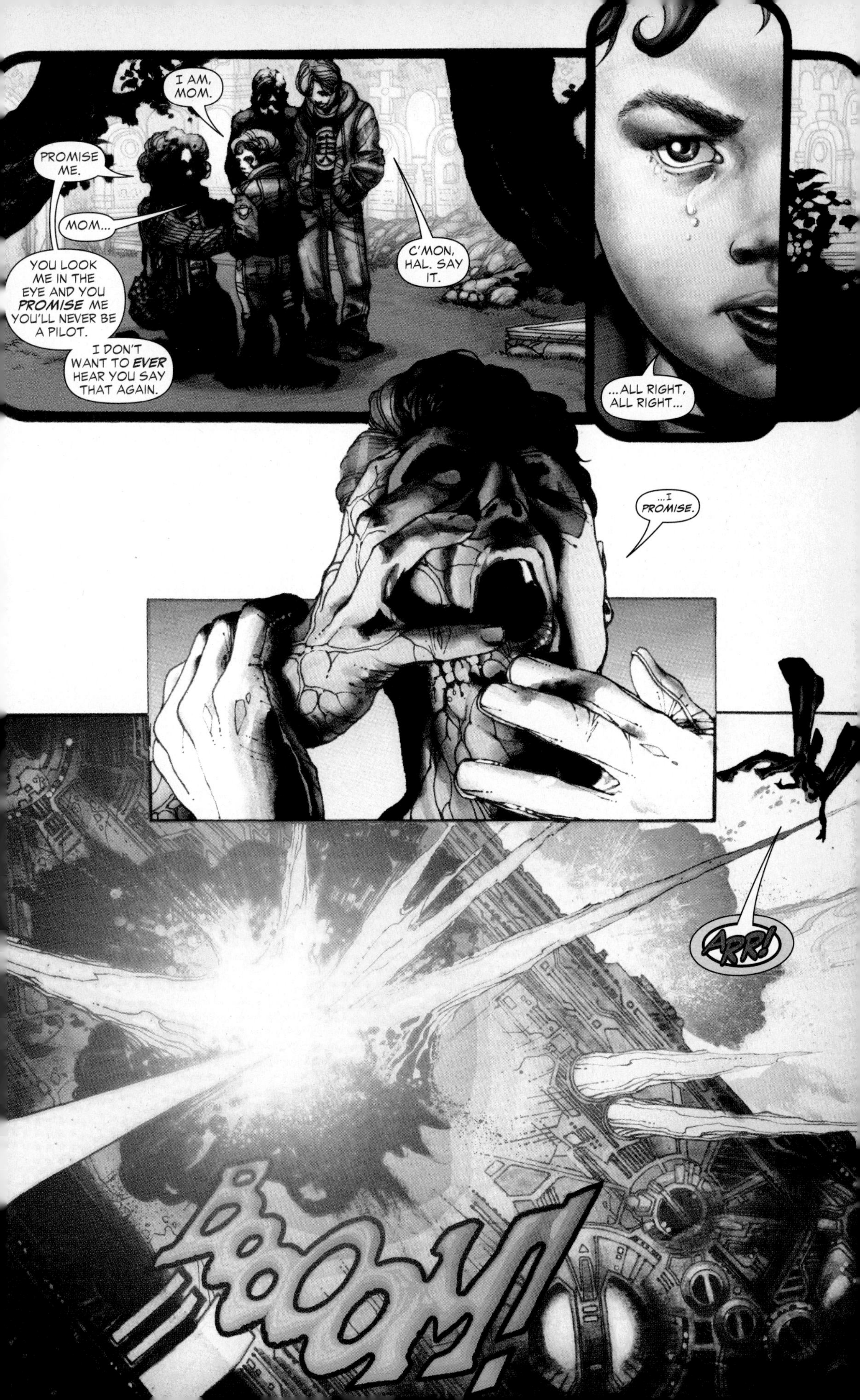
PROMISE ME.
I AM, MOM.
MOM...
YOU LOOK ME IN THE EYE AND YOU PROMISE ME YOU'LL NEVER BE A PILOT.
I DON'T WANT TO EVER HEAR YOU SAY THAT AGAIN.
C'MON, HAL. SAY IT.
...ALL RIGHT, ALL RIGHT...
...I PROMISE.
ARR!
KOOM!

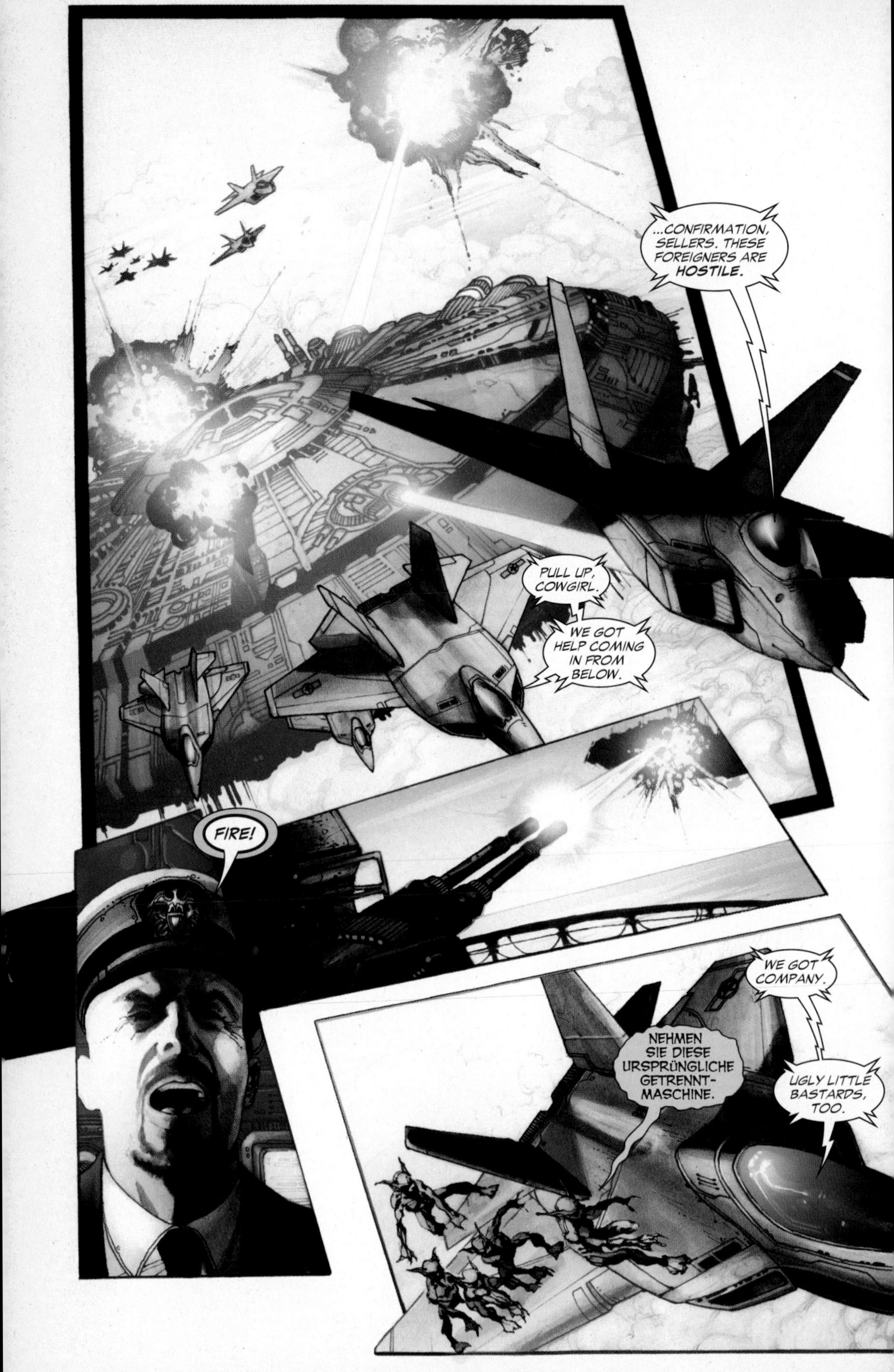
...CONFIRMATION, SELLERS. THESE FOREIGNERS ARE HOSTILE.
PULL UP, COWGIRL.
WE GOT HELP COMING IN FROM BELOW.
FIRE!
WE GOT COMPANY.
NEHMEN SIE DIESE URSPRÜNGLICHE GETRENNT-MASCHINE.
UGLY LITTLE BASTARDS, TOO.

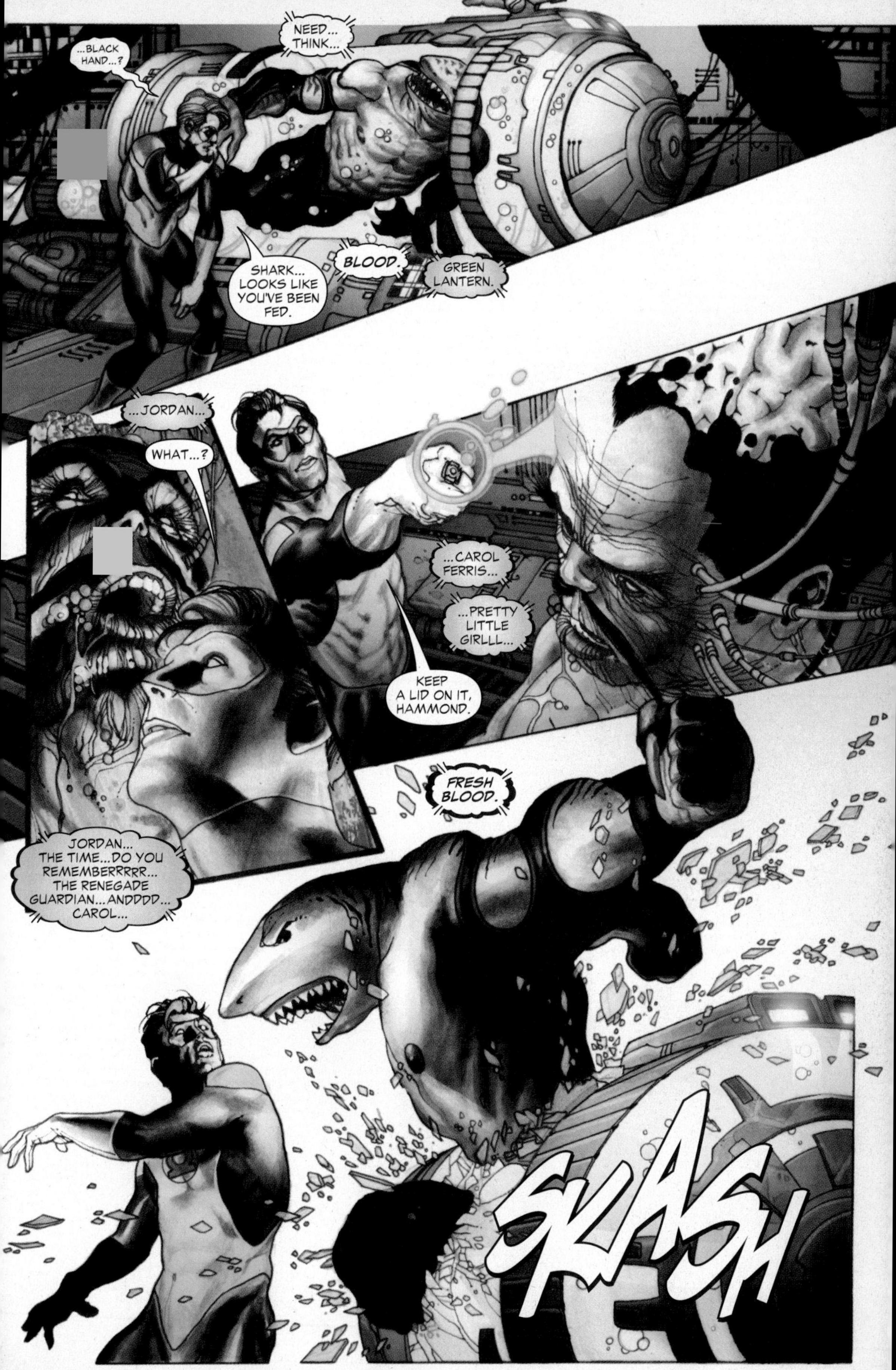
...BLACK HAND...?
NEED... THINK...
SHARK... LOOKS LIKE YOU'VE BEEN FED.
BLOOD.
GREEN LANTERN.
...JORDAN...
WHAT...?
...CAROL FERRIS...
...PRETTY LITTLE GIRLLL...
KEEP A LID ON IT, HAMMOND.
JORDAN... THE TIME...DO YOU REMEMBERRRR... THE RENEGADE GUARDIAN...ANDDDD... CAROL...
FRESH BLOOD.
SKASH

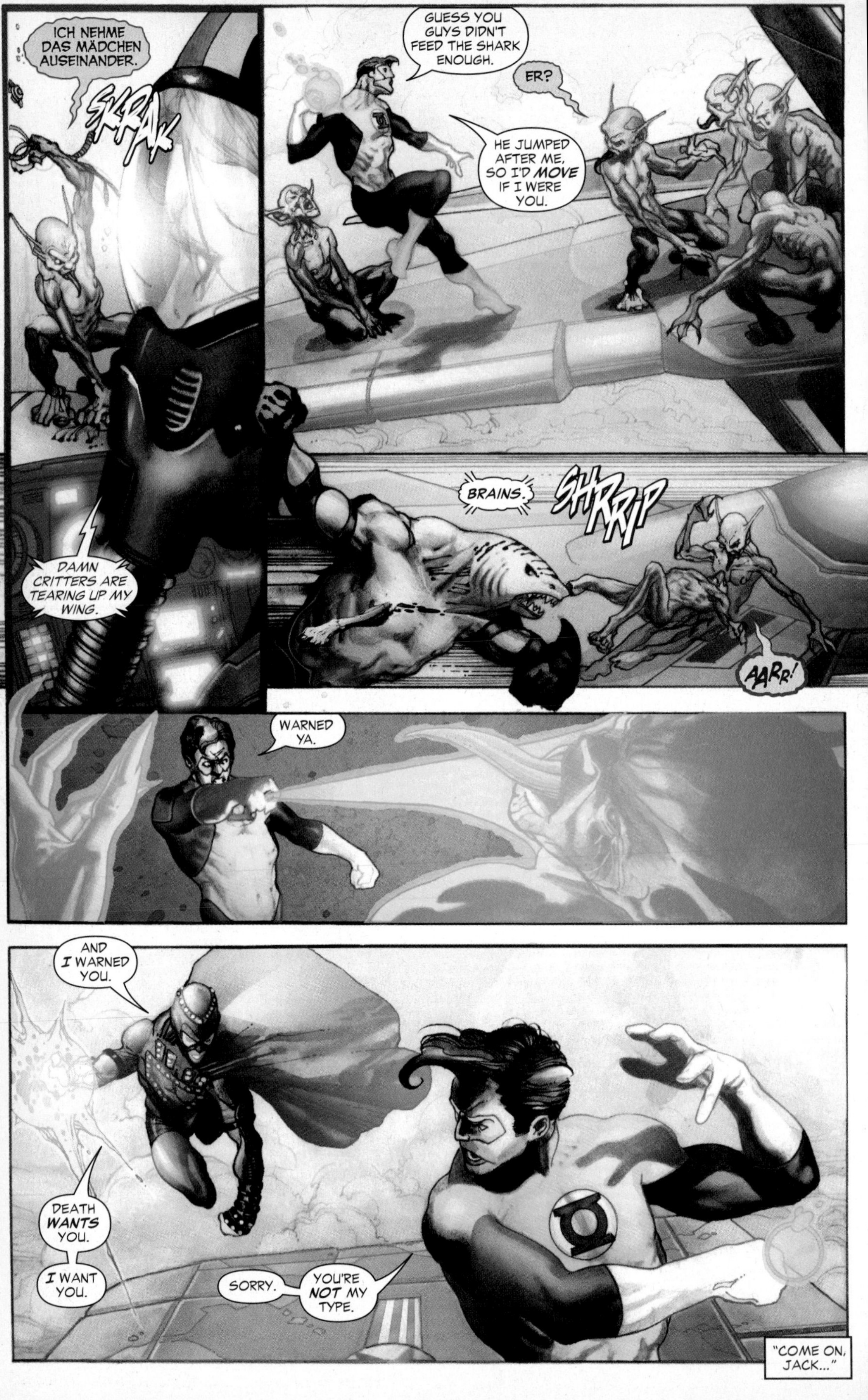
ICH NEHME DAS MÄDCHEN AUSEINANDER.
SKRAK
GUESS YOU GUYS DIDN'T FEED THE SHARK ENOUGH.
ER?
HE JUMPED AFTER ME, SO I'D MOVE IF I WERE YOU.
DAMN CRITTERS ARE TEARING UP MY WING.
BRAINS.
SHRRIP
AARR!
WARNED YA.
AND I WARNED YOU.
DEATH WANTS YOU.
I WANT YOU.
SORRY.
YOU'RE NOT MY TYPE.
"COME ON, JACK..."

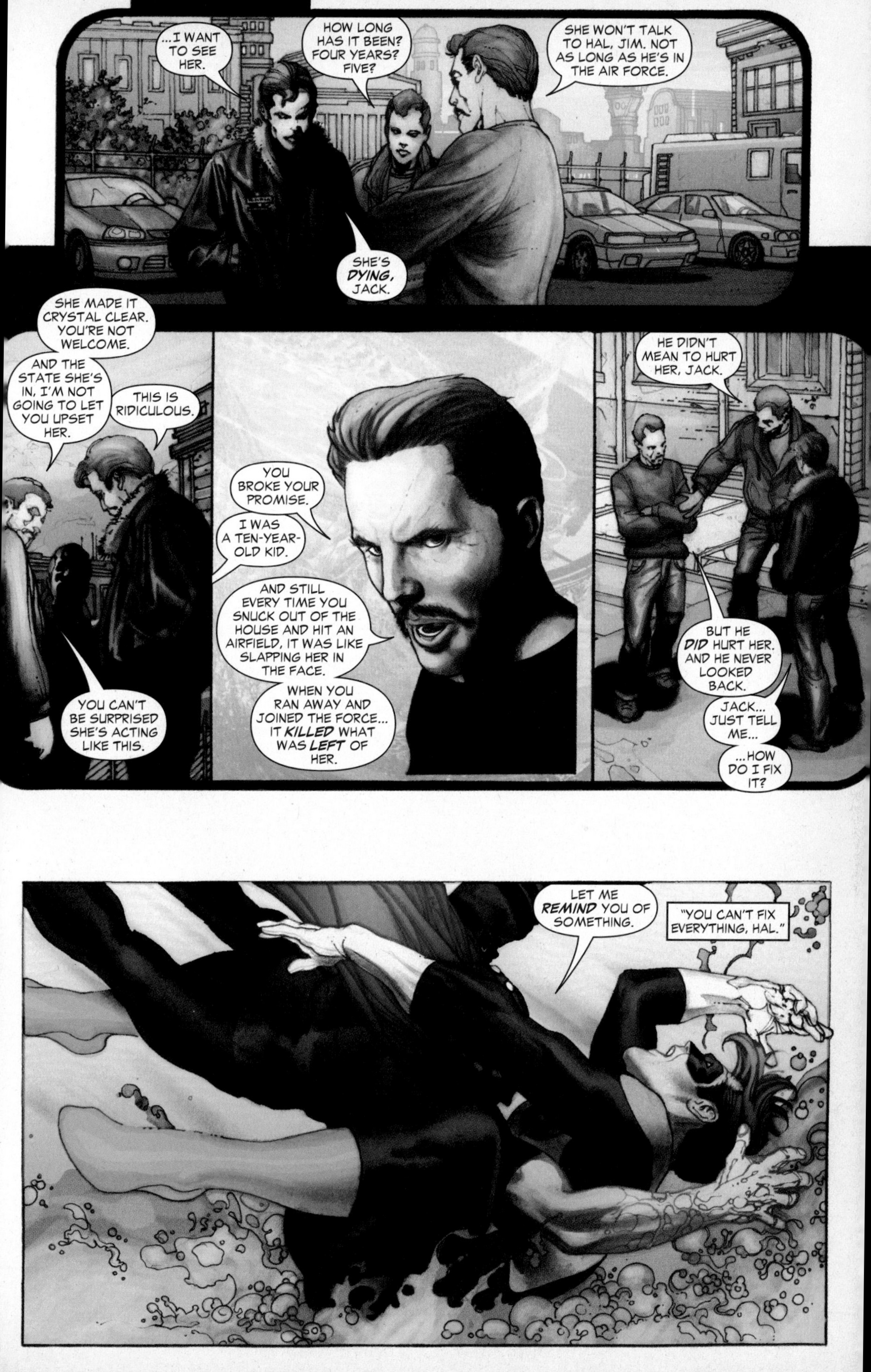
...I WANT TO SEE HER.
HOW LONG HAS IT BEEN? FOUR YEARS? FIVE?
SHE WON'T TALK TO HAL, JIM. NOT AS LONG AS HE'S IN THE AIR FORCE.
SHE'S DYING, JACK.
SHE MADE IT CRYSTAL CLEAR. YOU'RE NOT WELCOME.
AND THE STATE SHE'S IN, I'M NOT GOING TO LET YOU UPSET HER.
THIS IS RIDICULOUS.
YOU CAN'T BE SURPRISED SHE'S ACTING LIKE THIS.
YOU BROKE YOUR PROMISE.
I WAS A TEN-YEAR-OLD KID.
AND STILL EVERY TIME YOU SNUCK OUT OF THE HOUSE AND HIT AN AIRFIELD, IT WAS LIKE SLAPPING HER IN THE FACE.
WHEN YOU RAN AWAY AND JOINED THE FORCE... IT KILLED WHAT WAS LEFT OF HER.
HE DIDN'T MEAN TO HURT HER, JACK.
BUT HE DID HURT HER. AND HE NEVER LOOKED BACK.
JACK... JUST TELL ME...
...HOW DO I FIX IT?
LET ME REMIND YOU OF SOMETHING.
"YOU CAN'T FIX EVERYTHING, HAL."

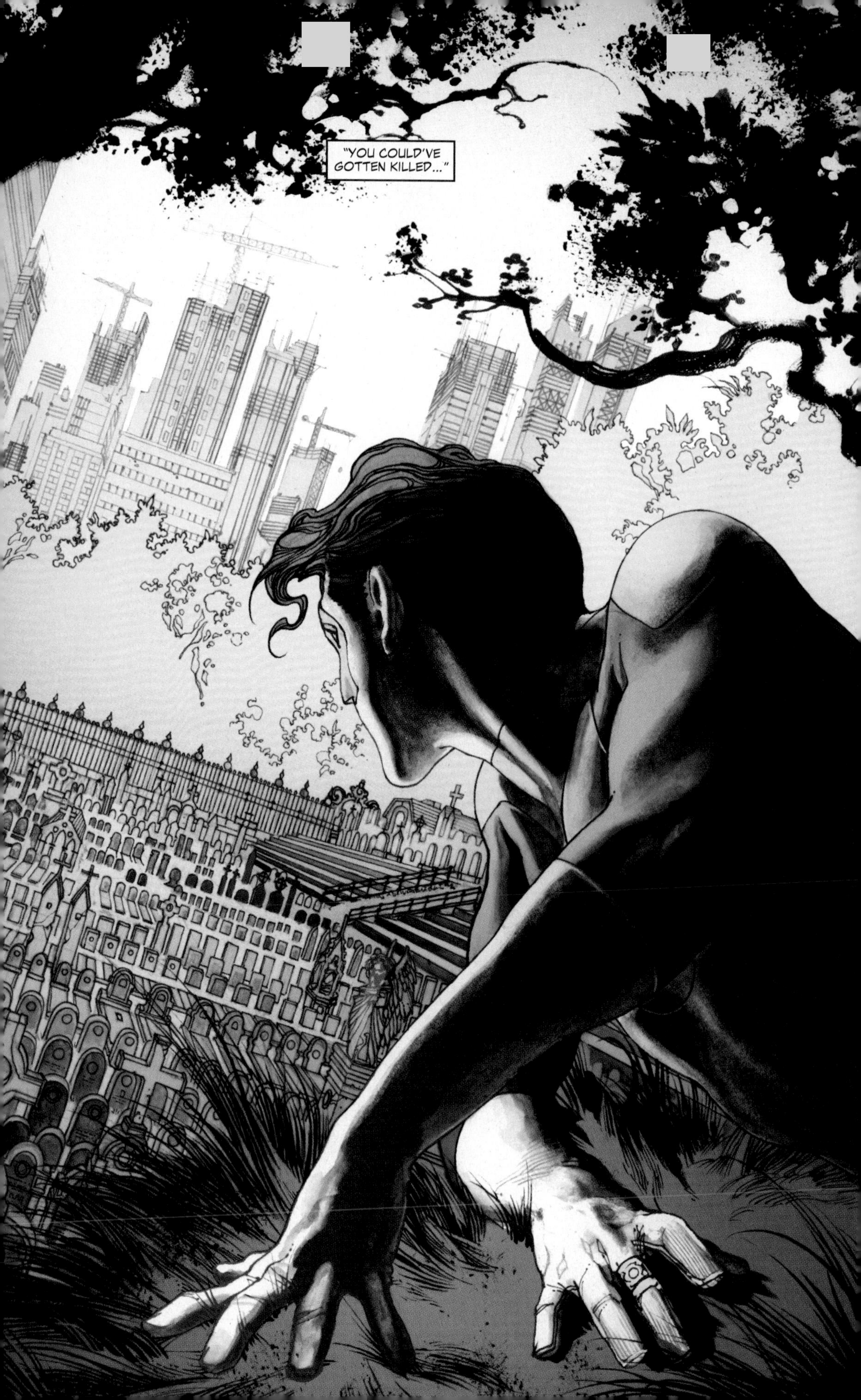
"YOU COULD'VE GOTTEN KILLED..."

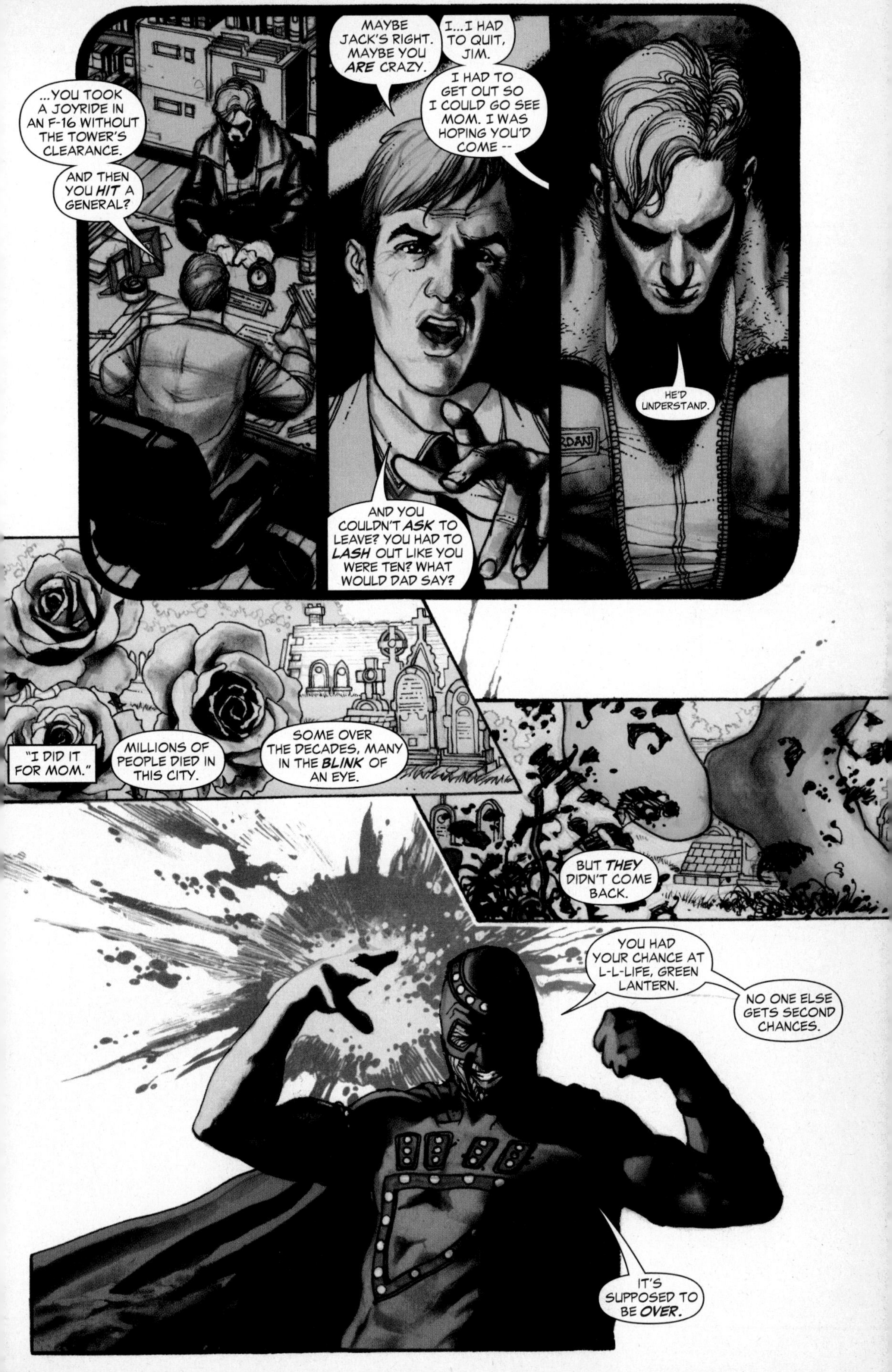
...YOU TOOK A JOYRIDE IN AN F-16 WITHOUT THE TOWER'S CLEARANCE.
AND THEN YOU HIT A GENERAL?
MAYBE JACK'S RIGHT. MAYBE YOU ARE CRAZY.
AND YOU COULDN'T ASK TO LEAVE? YOU HAD TO LASH OUT LIKE YOU WERE TEN? WHAT WOULD DAD SAY?
I...I HAD TO QUIT, JIM.
I HAD TO GET OUT SO I COULD GO SEE MOM. I WAS HOPING YOU'D COME --
HE'D UNDERSTAND.
"I DID IT FOR MOM."
MILLIONS OF PEOPLE DIED IN THIS CITY.
SOME OVER THE DECADES, MANY IN THE BLINK OF AN EYE.
BUT THEY DIDN'T COME BACK.
YOU HAD YOUR CHANCE AT L-L-LIFE, GREEN LANTERN.
NO ONE ELSE GETS SECOND CHANCES.
IT'S SUPPOSED TO BE OVER.

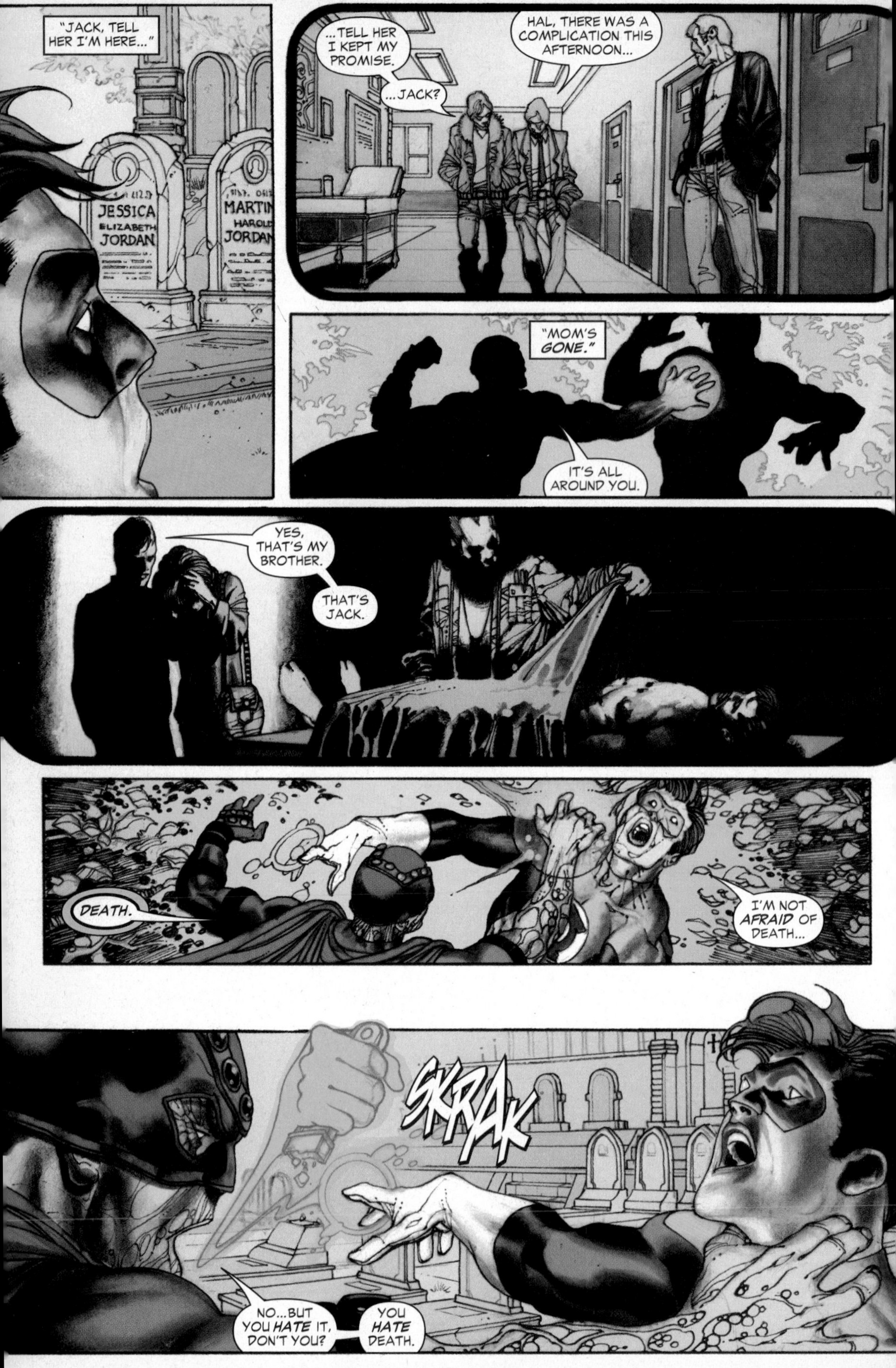
"JACK, TELL HER I'M HERE..."
JESSICA ELIZABETH JORDAN
MARTIN HAROLD JORDAN
...TELL HER I KEPT MY PROMISE.
...JACK?
HAL, THERE WAS A COMPLICATION THIS AFTERNOON...
"MOM'S GONE."
IT'S ALL AROUND YOU.
YES, THAT'S MY BROTHER.
THAT'S JACK.
DEATH.
I'M NOT AFRAID OF DEATH...
SKRAK
NO...BUT YOU HATE IT, DON'T YOU?
YOU HATE DEATH.

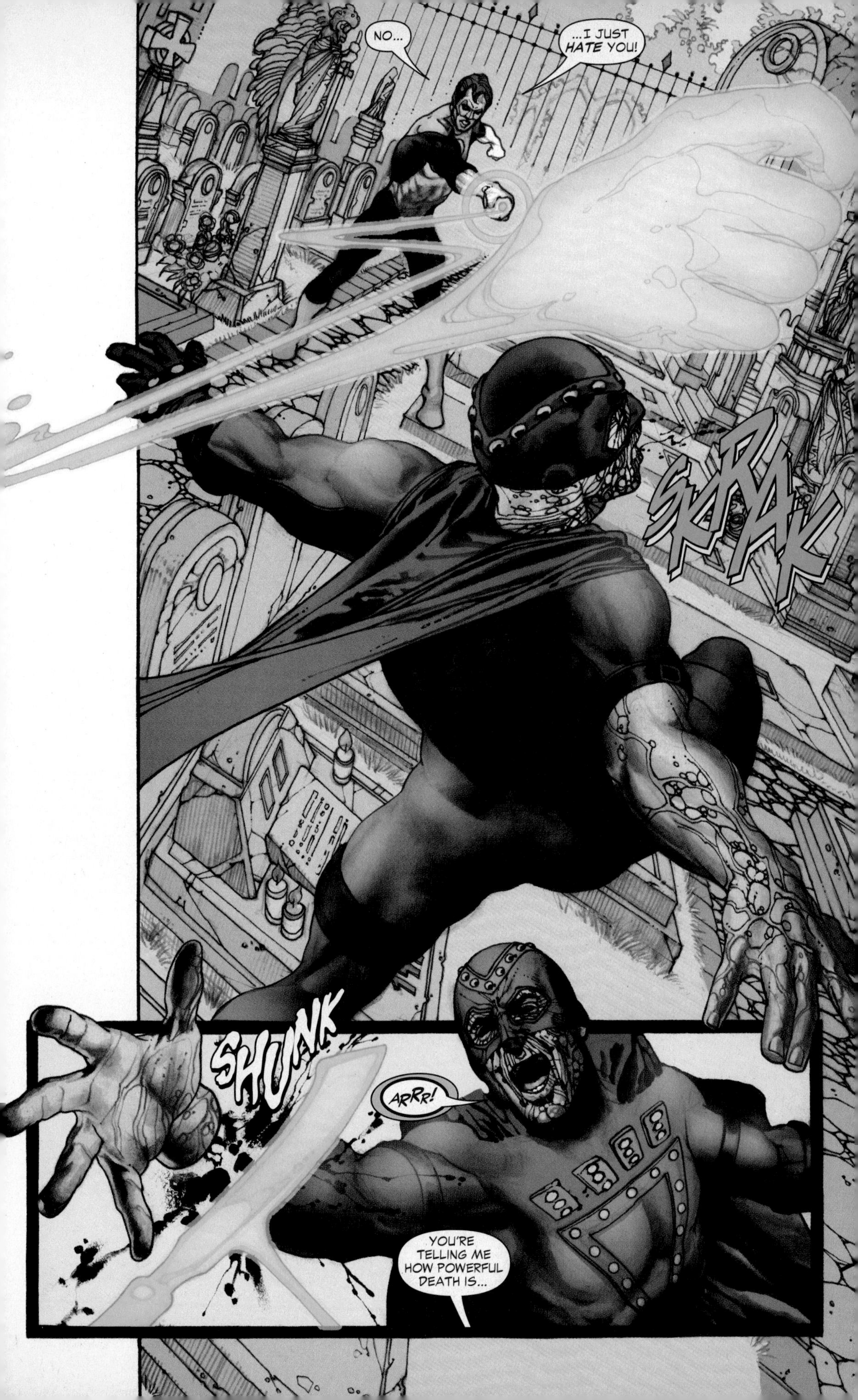
NO...
...I JUST HATE YOU!
SKRAK
SHUNK
ARRR!
YOU'RE TELLING ME HOW POWERFUL DEATH IS...

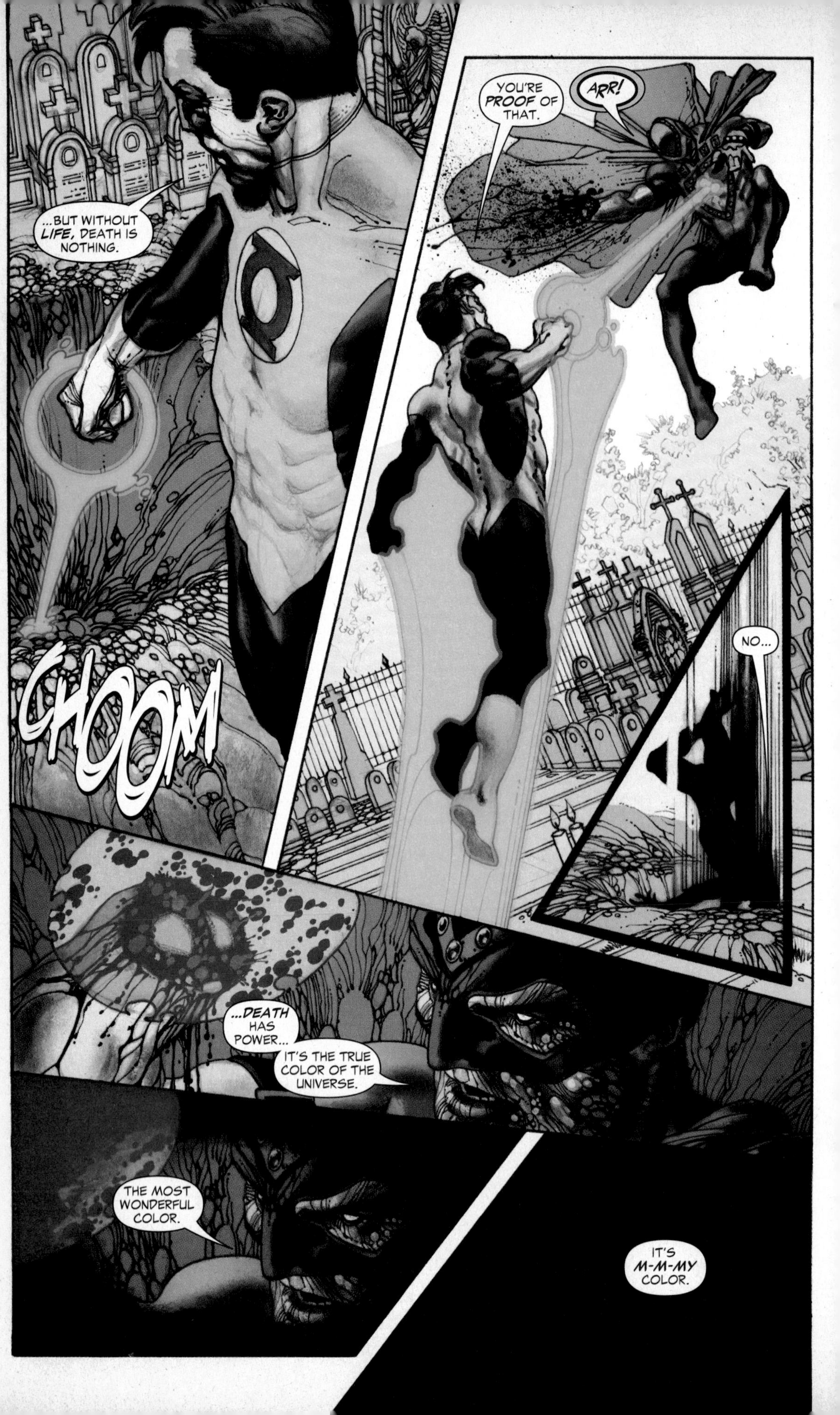
...BUT WITHOUT LIFE, DEATH IS NOTHING.
CHOOM
YOU'RE PROOF OF THAT.
ARR!
NO...
...DEATH HAS POWER...
IT'S THE TRUE COLOR OF THE UNIVERSE.
THE MOST WONDERFUL COLOR.
IT'S M-M-MY COLOR.

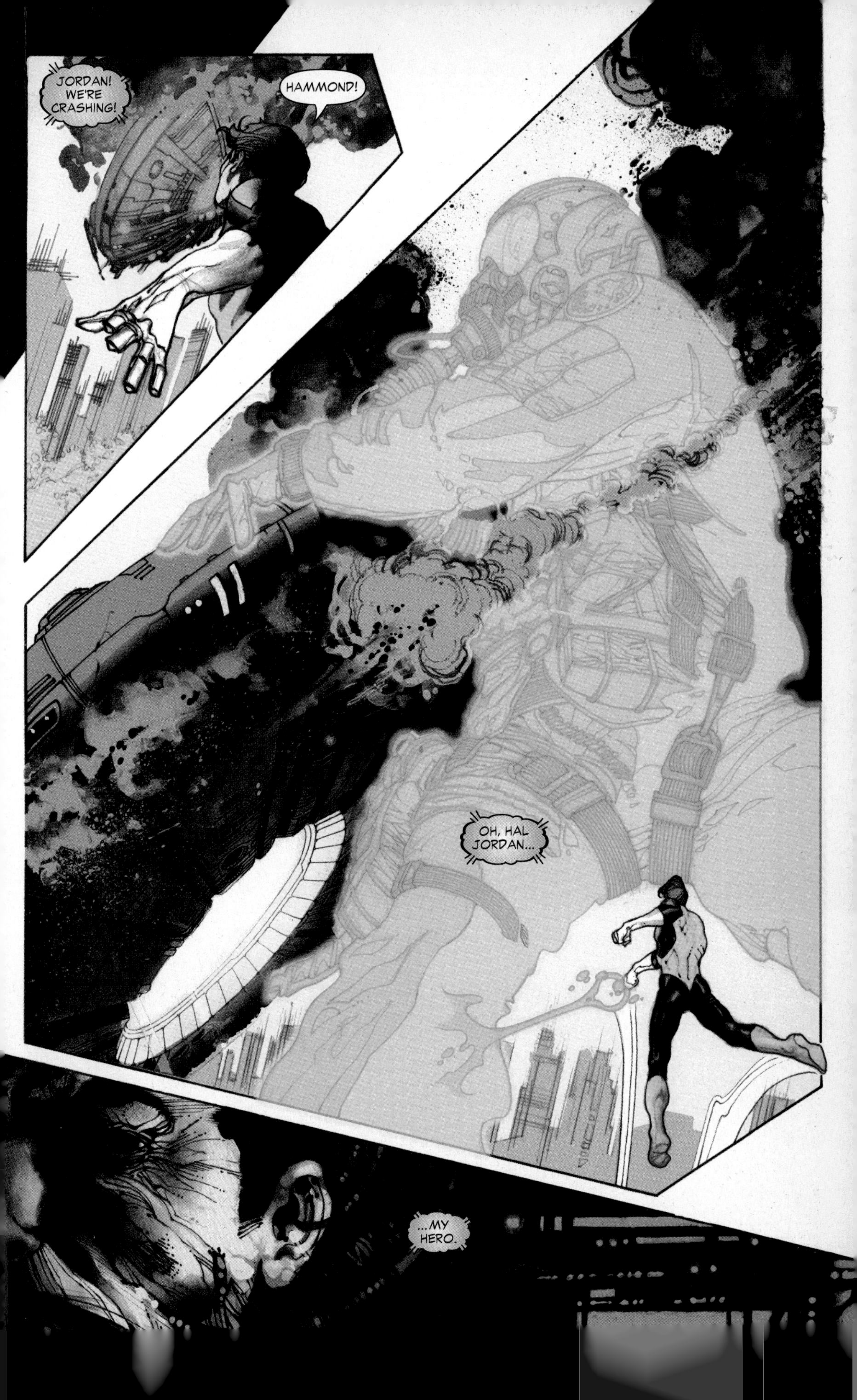
JORDAN! WE'RE CRASHING!
HAMMOND!
OH, HAL JORDAN...
...MY HERO.

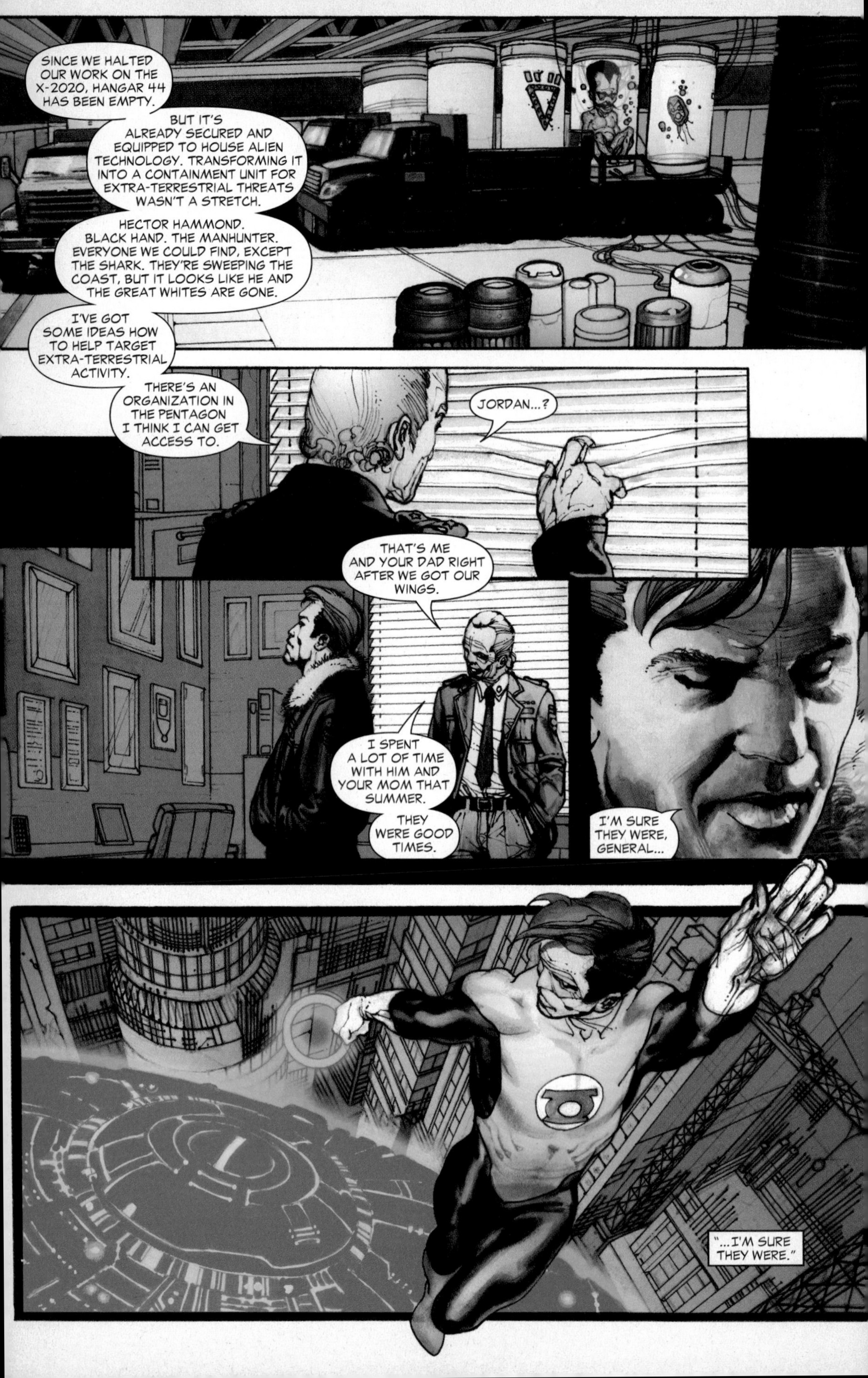
SINCE WE HALTED OUR WORK ON THE X-2020, HANGAR 44 HAS BEEN EMPTY.
BUT IT'S ALREADY SECURED AND EQUIPPED TO HOUSE ALIEN TECHNOLOGY. TRANSFORMING IT INTO A CONTAINMENT UNIT FOR EXTRA-TERRESTRIAL THREATS WASN'T A STRETCH.
HECTOR HAMMOND. BLACK HAND. THE MANHUNTER. EVERYONE WE COULD FIND, EXCEPT THE SHARK. THEY'RE SWEEPING THE COAST, BUT IT LOOKS LIKE HE AND THE GREAT WHITES ARE GONE.
I'VE GOT SOME IDEAS HOW TO HELP TARGET EXTRA-TERRESTRIAL ACTIVITY.
THERE'S AN ORGANIZATION IN THE PENTAGON I THINK I CAN GET ACCESS TO.
JORDAN...?
THAT'S ME AND YOUR DAD RIGHT AFTER WE GOT OUR WINGS.
I SPENT A LOT OF TIME WITH HIM AND YOUR MOM THAT SUMMER.
THEY WERE GOOD TIMES.
I'M SURE THEY WERE, GENERAL...
"...I'M SURE THEY WERE."

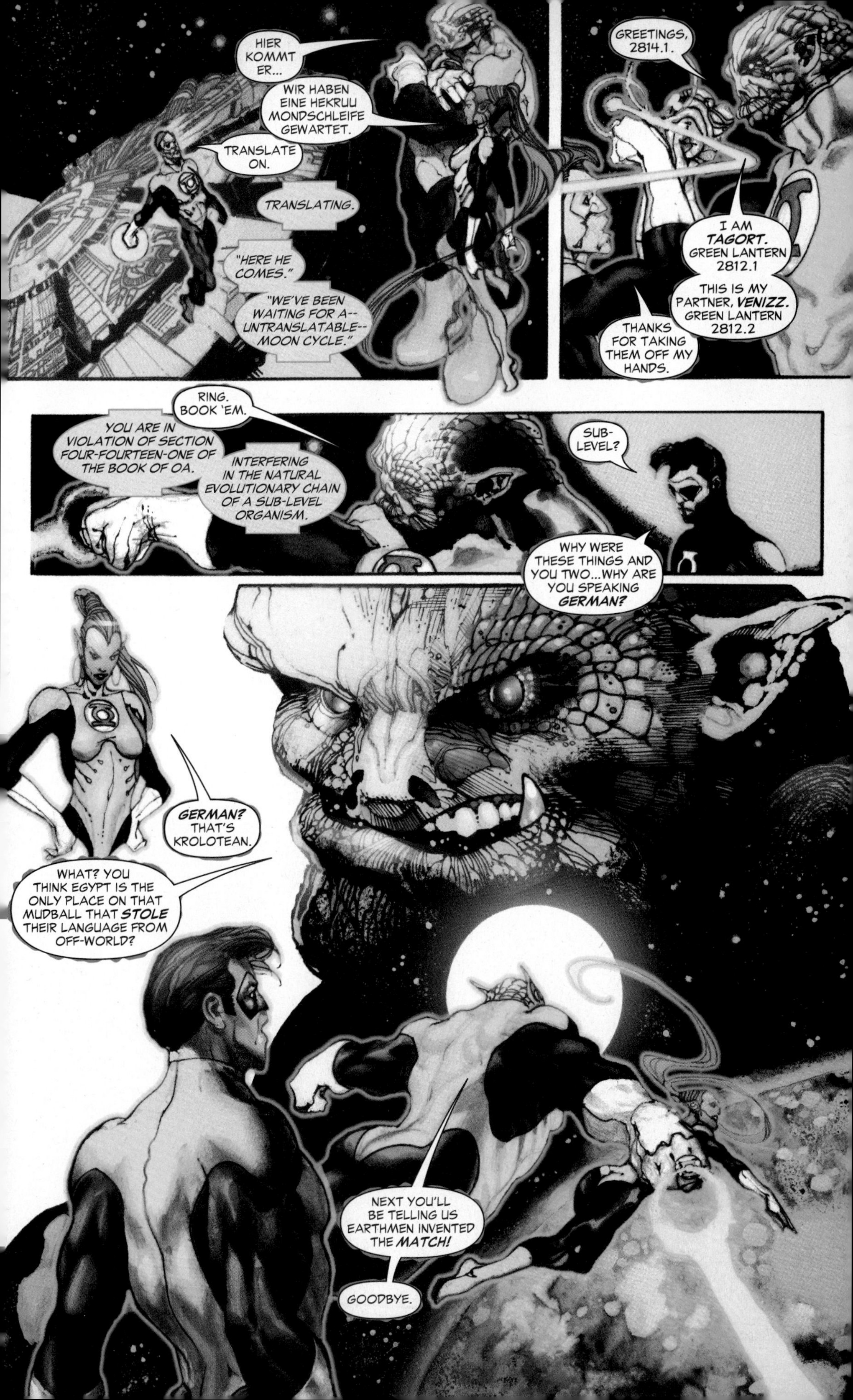

HIER KOMMT ER...
WIR HABEN EINE HEKRUU MONDSCHLEIFE GEWARTET.
TRANSLATE ON.
TRANSLATING.
"HERE HE COMES."
"WE'VE BEEN WAITING FOR A-- UNTRANSLATABLE-- MOON CYCLE."
GREETINGS, 2814.1.
I AM TAGORT. GREEN LANTERN 2812.1
THIS IS MY PARTNER, VENIZZ. GREEN LANTERN 2812.2
THANKS FOR TAKING THEM OFF MY HANDS.
RING. BOOK 'EM.
YOU ARE IN VIOLATION OF SECTION FOUR-FOURTEEN-ONE OF THE BOOK OF OA.
INTERFERING IN THE NATURAL EVOLUTIONARY CHAIN OF A SUB-LEVEL ORGANISM.
SUB-LEVEL?
WHY WERE THESE THINGS AND YOU TWO...WHY ARE YOU SPEAKING GERMAN?
GERMAN? THAT'S KROLOTEAN.
WHAT? YOU THINK EGYPT IS THE ONLY PLACE ON THAT MUDBALL THAT STOLE THEIR LANGUAGE FROM OFF-WORLD?
NEXT YOU'LL BE TELLING US EARTHMEN INVENTED THE MATCH!
GOODBYE.

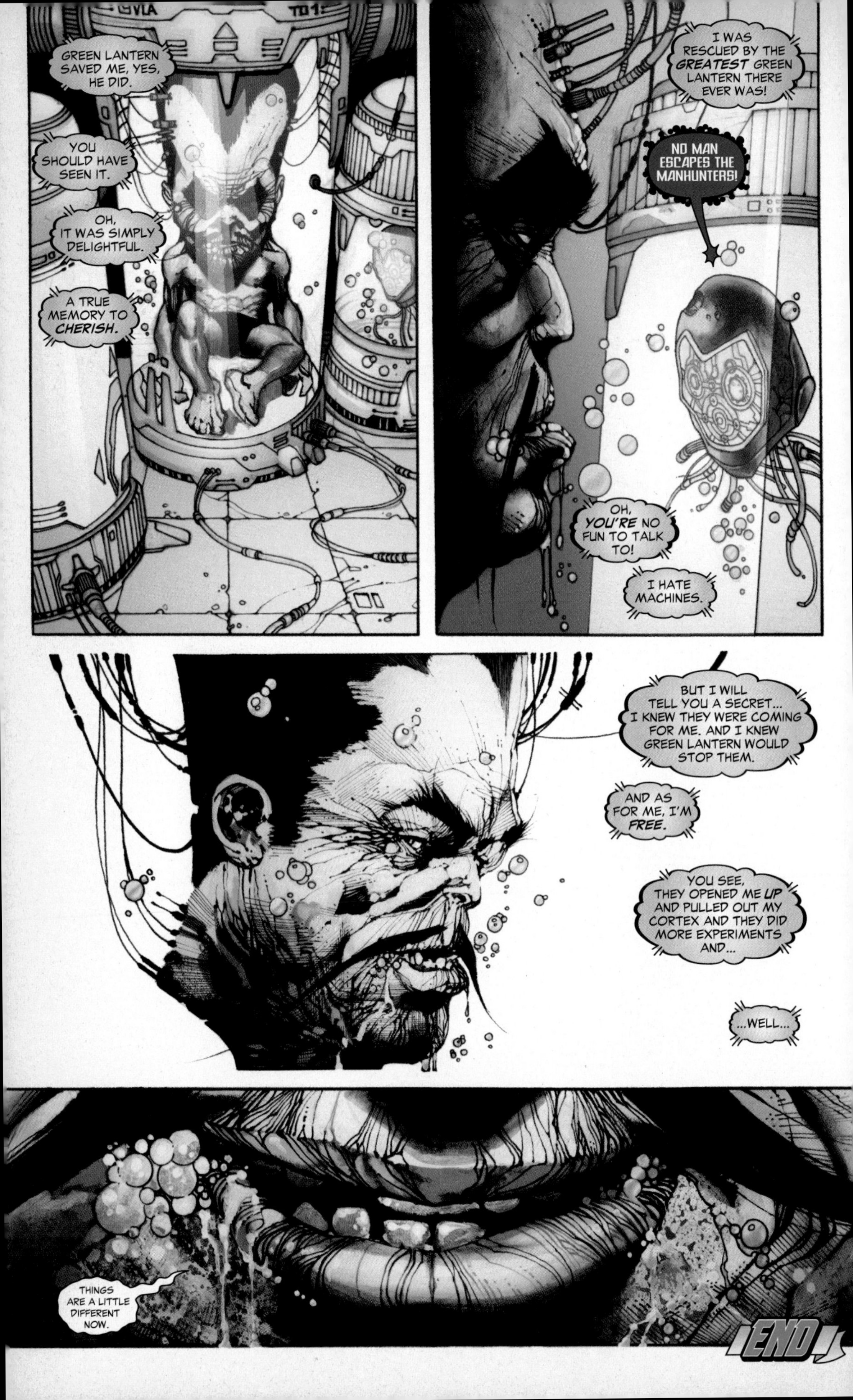
GREEN LANTERN SAVED ME, YES, HE DID.
YOU SHOULD HAVE SEEN IT.
OH, IT WAS SIMPLY DELIGHTFUL.
A TRUE MEMORY TO *CHERISH*.
I WAS RESCUED BY THE *GREATEST* GREEN LANTERN THERE EVER WAS!
NO MAN ESCAPES THE MANHUNTERS!
OH, *YOU'RE* NO FUN TO TALK TO!
I HATE MACHINES.
BUT I WILL TELL YOU A SECRET... I KNEW THEY WERE COMING FOR ME. AND I KNEW GREEN LANTERN WOULD STOP THEM.
AND AS FOR ME, I'M *FREE*.
YOU SEE, THEY OPENED ME *UP* AND PULLED OUT MY CORTEX AND THEY DID MORE EXPERIMENTS AND...
...WELL...
THINGS ARE A LITTLE DIFFERENT NOW.
END

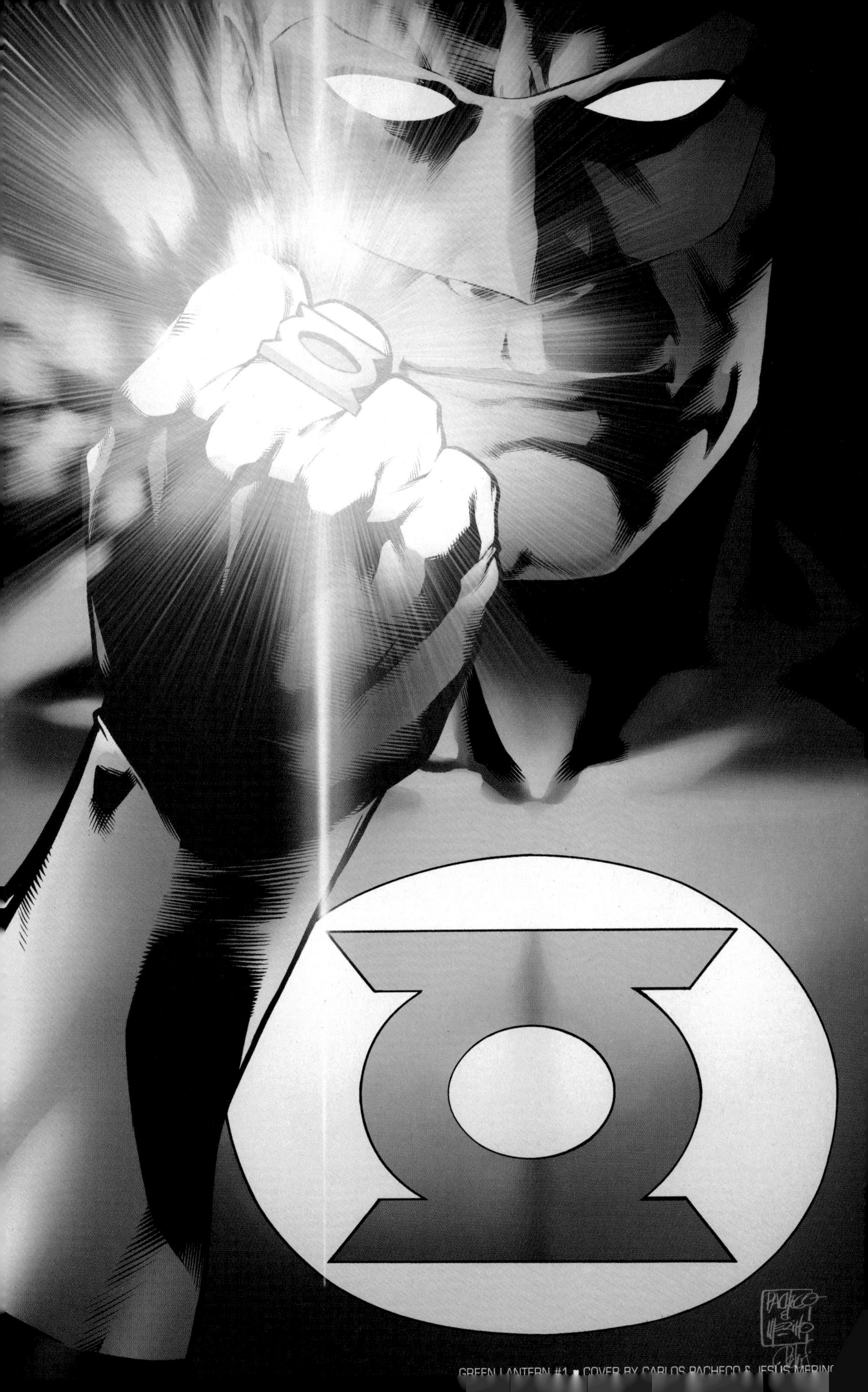

GREEN LANTERN #1 ■ COVER BY CARLOS PACHECO & JESÚS MERINO

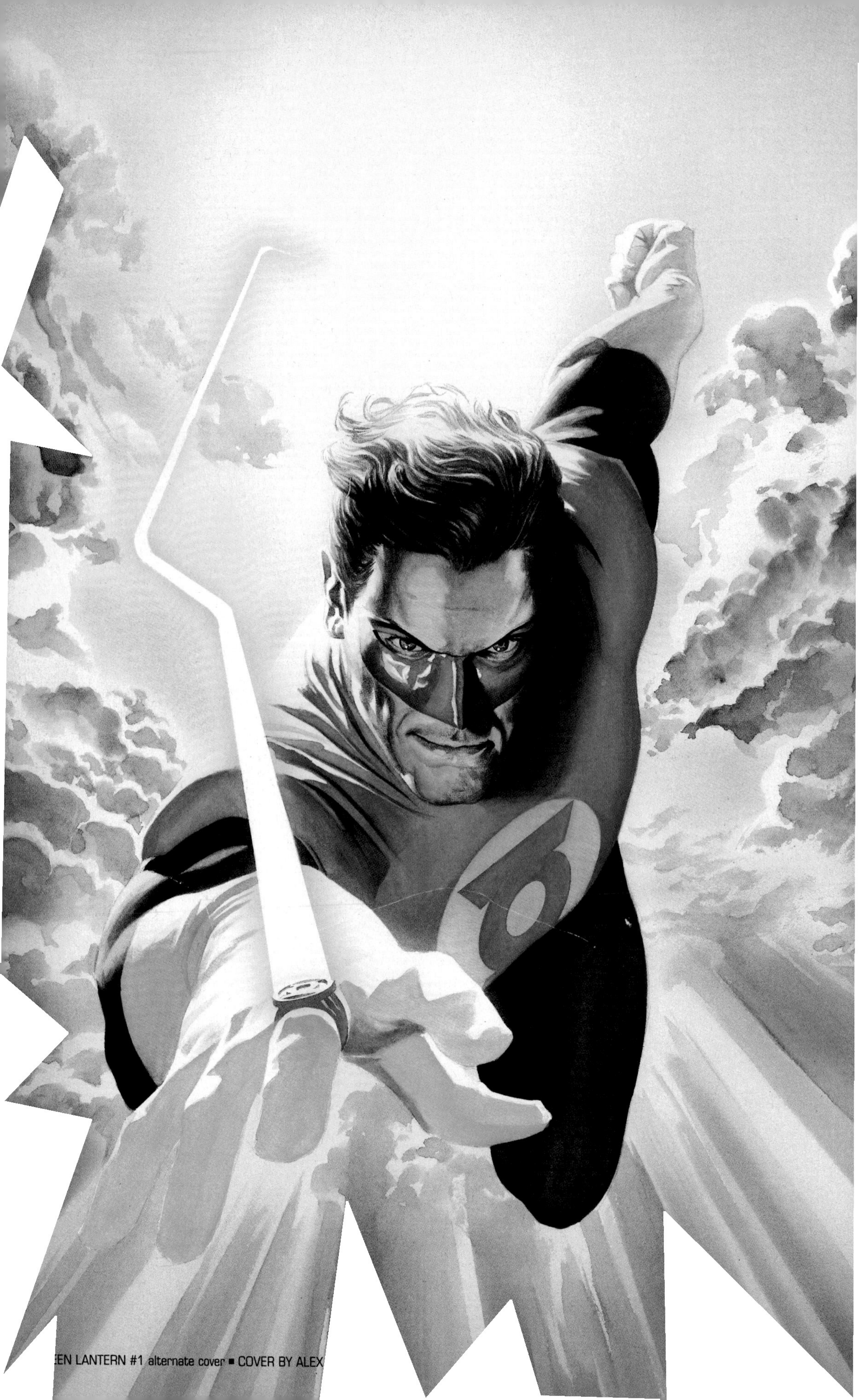

EEN LANTERN #1 alternate cover ■ COVER BY ALEX

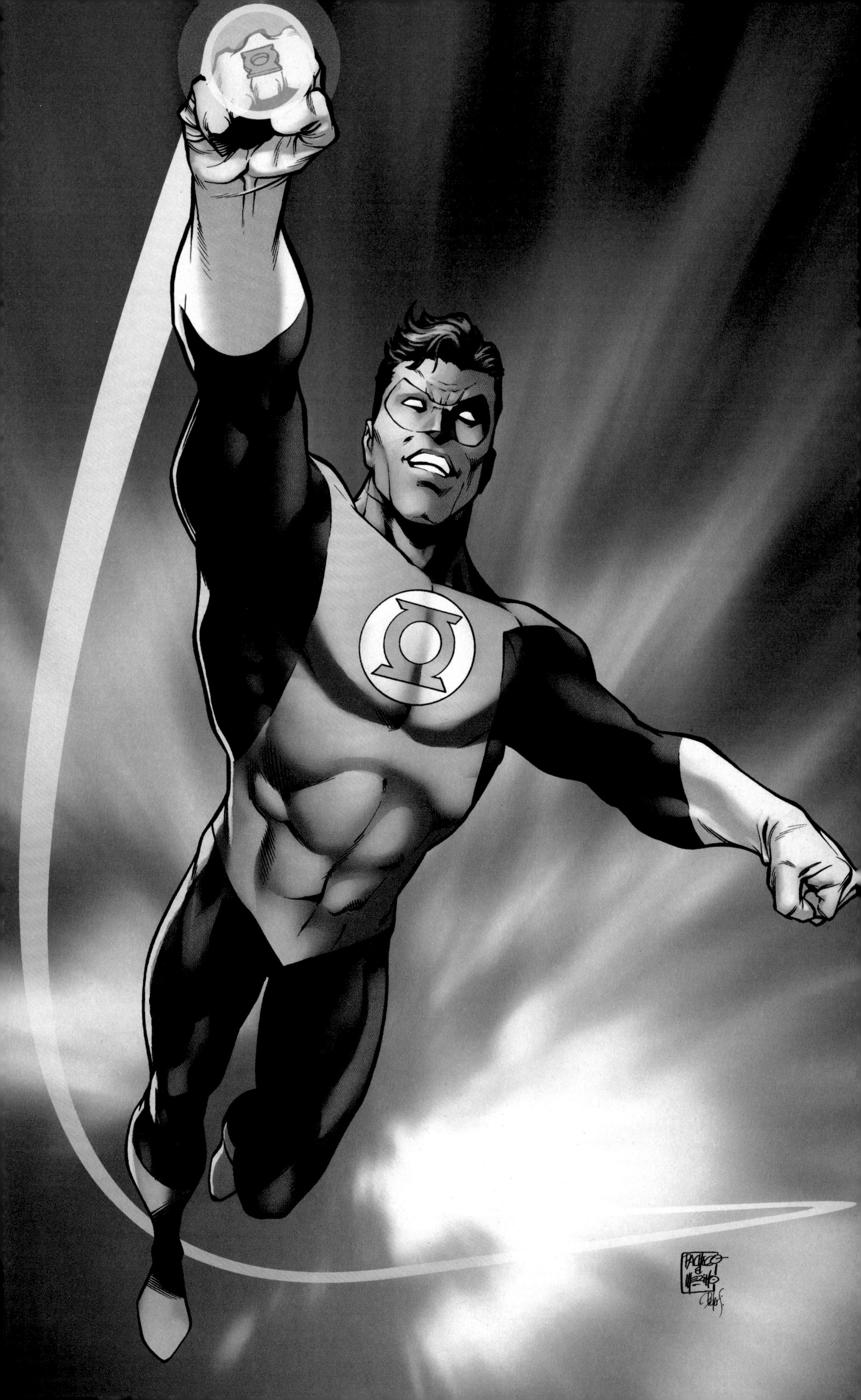

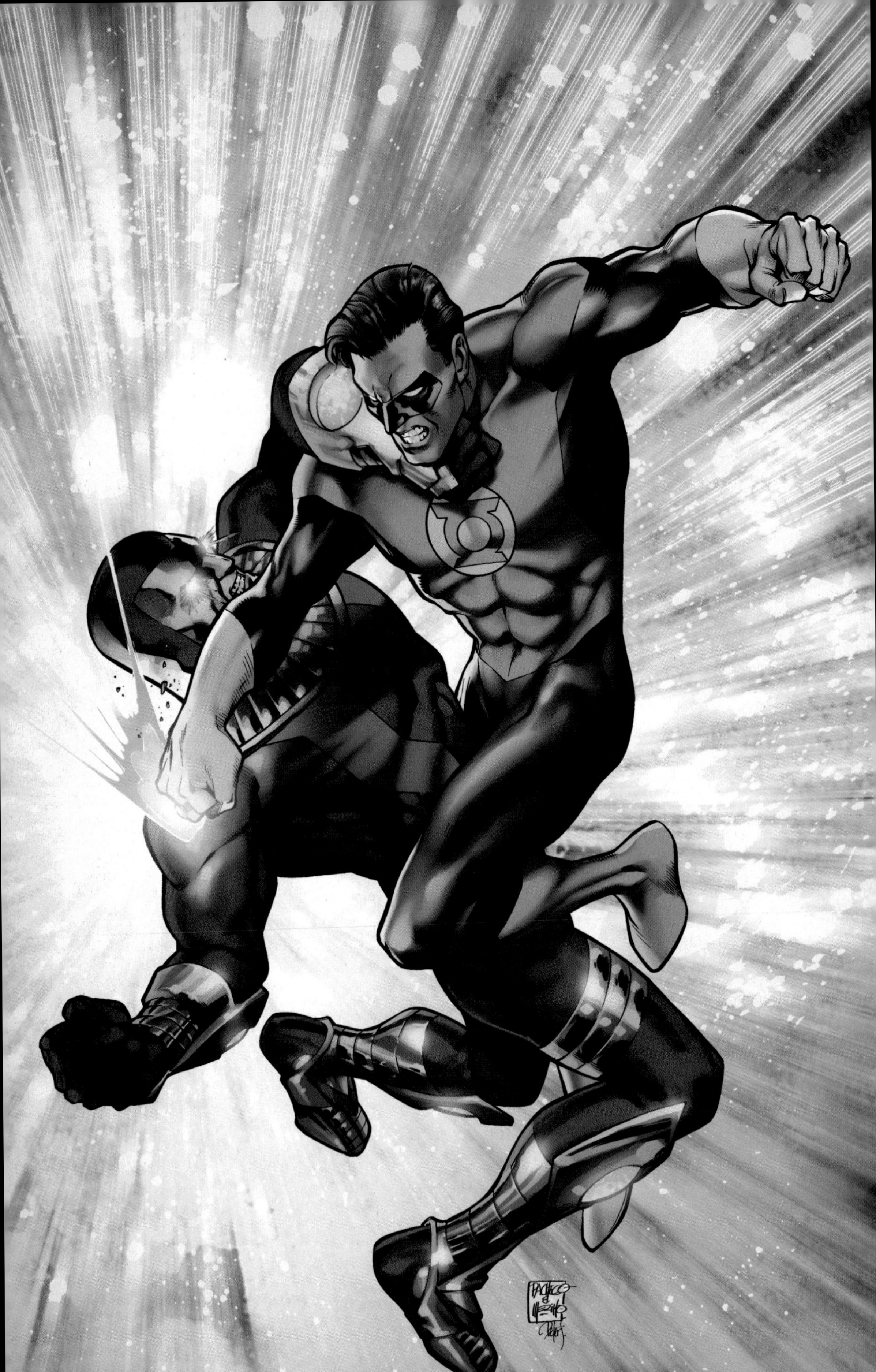

GREEN LANTERN #3 ■ COVER BY CARLOS PACHECO & JESÚS MERINO

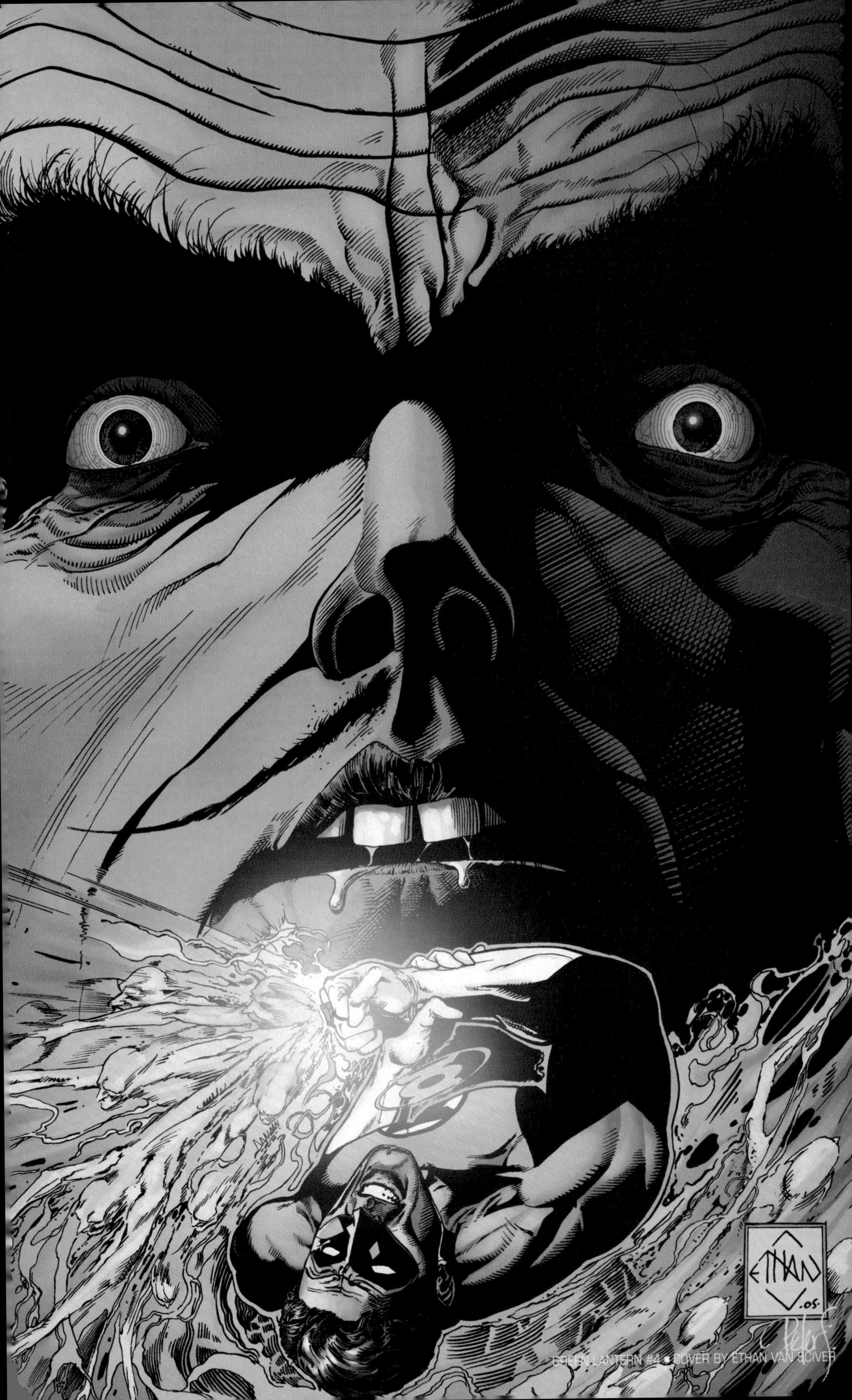

GREEN LANTERN #4 • COVER BY ETHAN VAN SCIVER

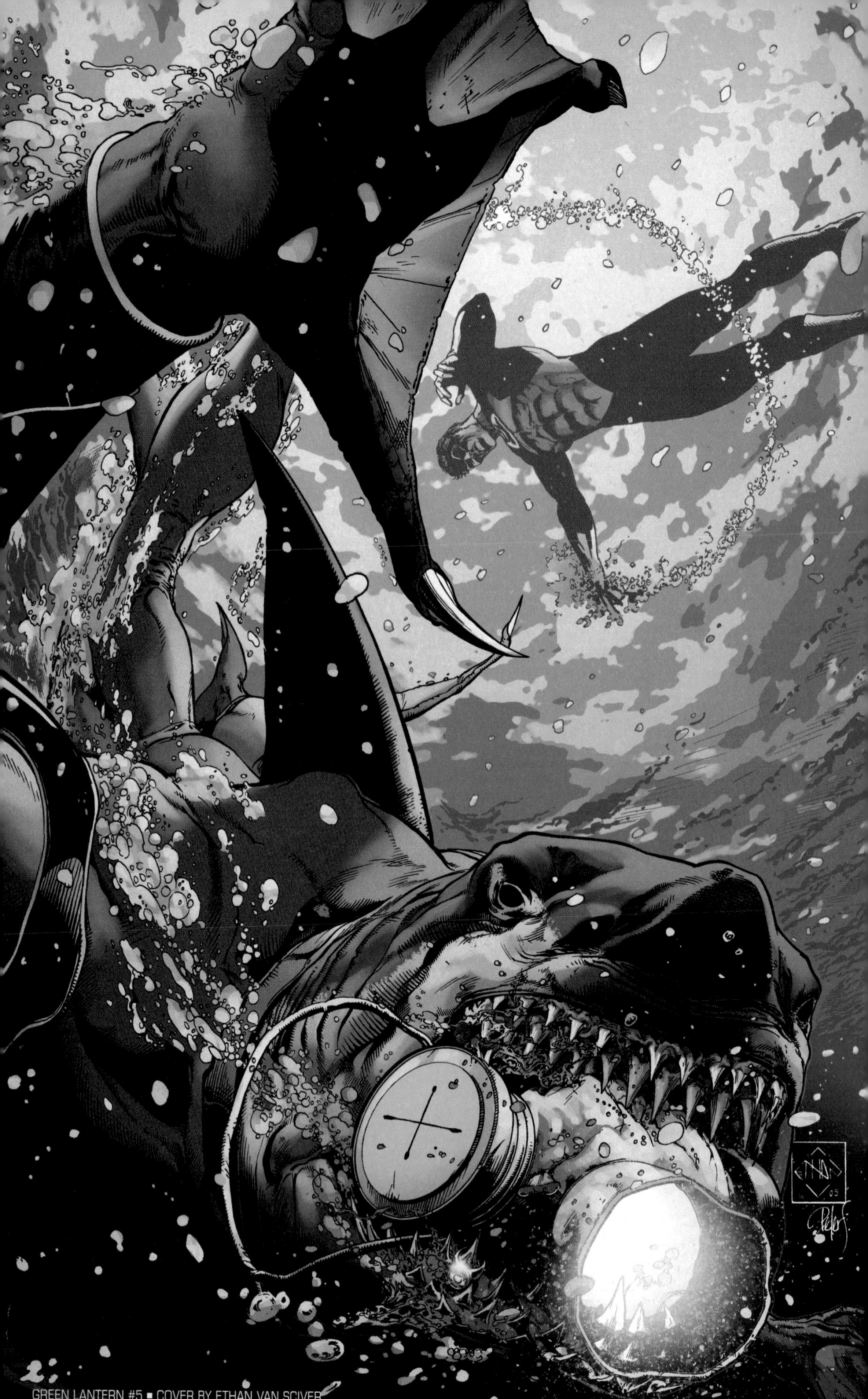

GREEN LANTERN #5 ■ COVER BY ETHAN VAN SCIVER

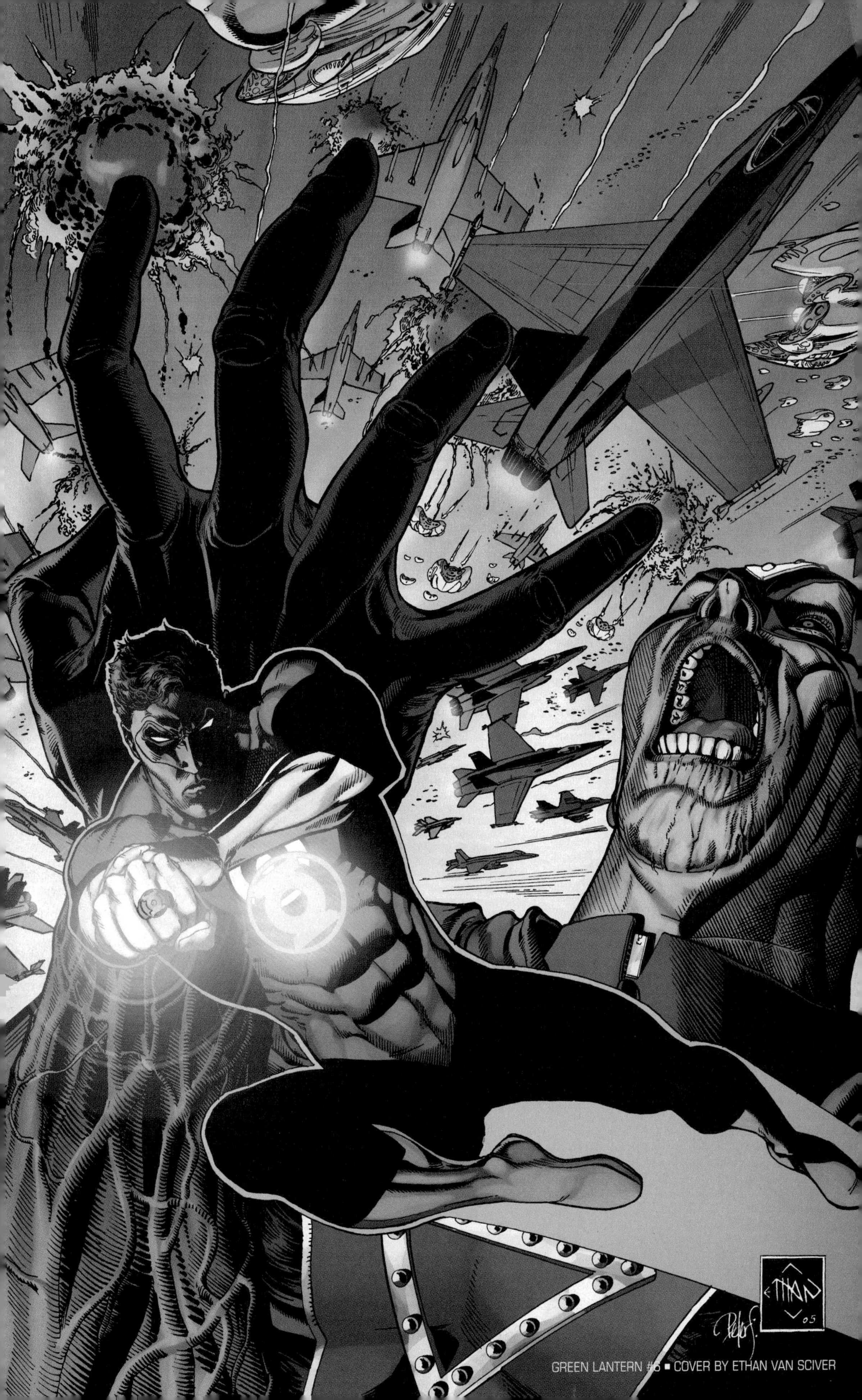

GREEN LANTERN #6 ■ COVER BY ETHAN VAN SCIVER

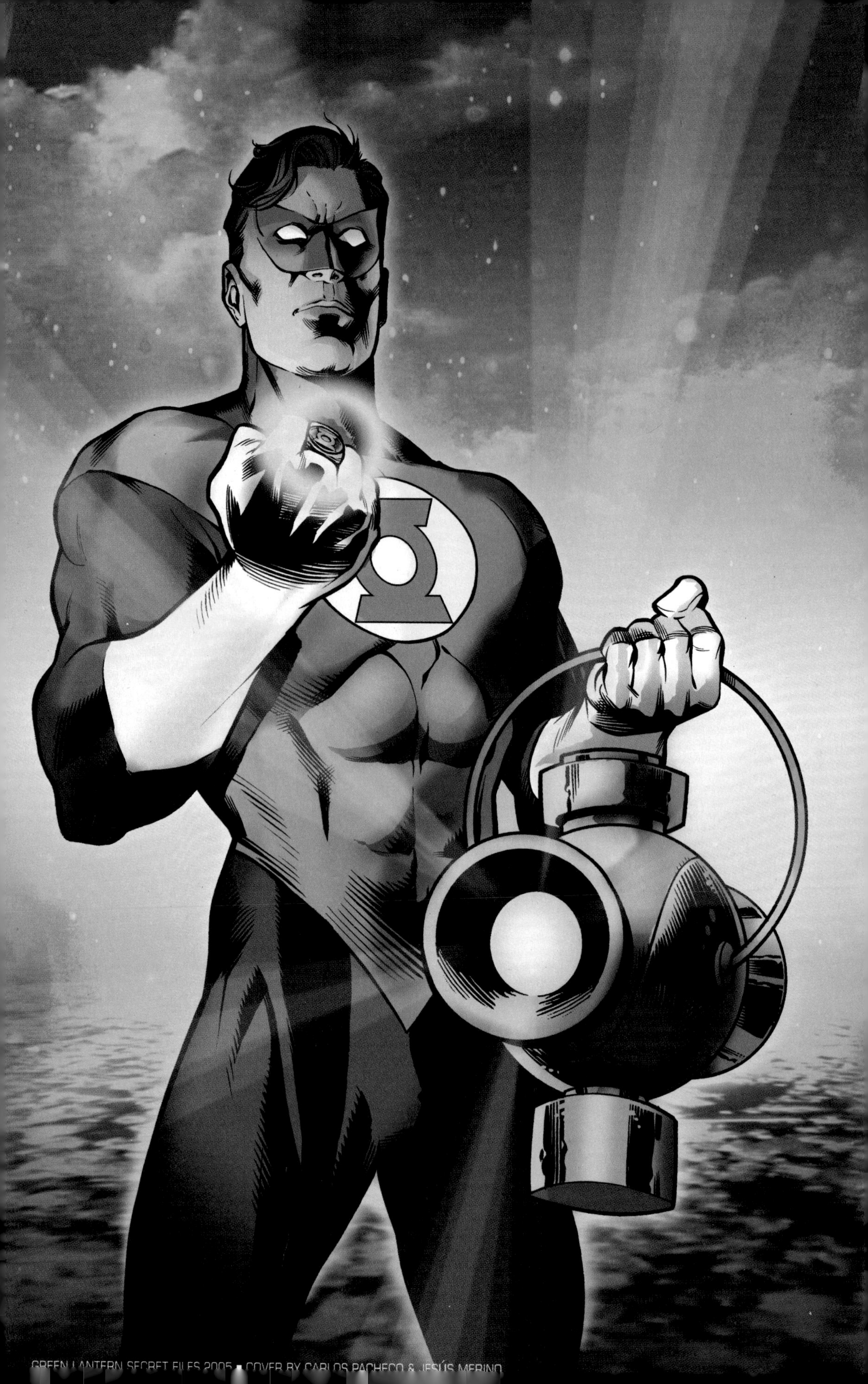

GREEN LANTERN SECRET FILES 2005 • COVER BY CARLOS PACHECO & JESÚS MERINO

THE STARS OF THE DC UNIVERSE
CAN ALSO BE FOUND IN THESE BOOKS:

ACROSS THE UNIVERSE:
THE DC UNIVERSE STORIES
OF ALAN MOORE
A. Moore/D. Gibbons/various

BATGIRL: YEAR ONE
S. Beatty/C. Dixon/M. Martin/
J. Lopez

BATMAN/SUPERMAN/
WONDER WOMAN: TRINITY
M. Wagner

BATMAN BLACK AND WHITE
Vols. 1-2
Various

BATMAN: HUSH Vols. 1-2
J. Loeb/J. Lee/S. Williams

BATMAN: YEAR ONE
F. Miller/D. Mazzucchelli

BIRDS OF PREY
C. Dixon/G. Simone/G. Land/
E. Benes/various
    BIRDS OF PREY
    OLD FRIENDS, NEW ENEMIES
    OF LIKE MINDS
    SENSEI AND STUDENT

BIZARRO COMICS
various

BIZARRO WORLD
various

CRISIS ON INFINITE EARTHS
M. Wolfman/G. Pérez/J. Ordway/
various

CRISIS ON MULTIPLE EARTHS
Vols. 1-3
G. Fox/D. O'Neil/L. Wein/
M. Sekowsky/D. Dillin/various

FALLEN ANGEL
(SUGGESTED FOR MATURE READERS)
P. David/D. Lopez/F. Blanco

THE FINAL NIGHT
K. Kesel/S. Immonen/J. Marzan/
various

THE FLASH
M. Waid/G. Johns/G. Larocque/
S. Kollins/various
    BORN TO RUN
    THE RETURN OF BARRY ALLEN
    TERMINAL VELOCITY
    DEAD HEAT
    RACE AGAINST TIME
    BLOOD WILL RUN
    ROGUES
    CROSSFIRE
    BLITZ
    IGNITION

FORMERLY KNOWN AS THE
JUSTICE LEAGUE
K. Giffen/J.M. DeMatteis/
K. Maguire/J. Rubinstein

GOTHAM CENTRAL
E. Brubaker/G. Rucka/M. Lark
Vol. 1: IN THE LINE OF DUTY

GREEN ARROW
K. Smith/B. Meltzer/J. Winick/
P. Hester/A. Parks
Vol. 1: QUIVER
Vol. 2: SOUNDS OF SILENCE
Vol. 3: ARCHER'S QUEST
Vol. 4: STRAIGHT SHOOTER
Vol. 5: CITY WALLS

GREEN LANTERN/GREEN ARROW
Vols. 1-2
D. O'Neil/N. Adams/various

GREEN LANTERN
J. Winick/G. Jones/R. Marz/
D. Banks/M.D. Bright/
D. Eaglesham/various
    EMERALD DAWN
    EMERALD DAWN II
    THE ROAD BACK
    EMERALD TWILIGHT/
      A NEW DAWN
    BAPTISM OF FIRE
    EMERALD ALLIES
    EMERALD KNIGHTS
    NEW JOURNEY, OLD PATH
    THE POWER OF ION
    BROTHER'S KEEPER
    PASSING THE TORCH

GREEN LANTERN: LEGACY —
THE LAST WILL AND TESTAMENT
OF HAL JORDAN
J. Kelly/B. Anderson/B. Sienkiewicz

GREEN LANTERN: WILLWORLD
J.M. DeMatteis/S. Fisher

HARD TIME: 50 TO LIFE
S. Gerber/B. Hurtt

HAWKMAN
G. Johns/J. Robinson/R. Morales/
M. Bair/various
Vol. 1: ENDLESS FLIGHT
Vol. 2: ALLIES AND ENEMIES

HISTORY OF THE DC UNIVERSE
M. Wolfman/G. Pérez/K. Kesel

JACK KIRBY'S FOURTH WORLD
Jack Kirby/various
    FOREVER PEOPLE
    FOURTH WORLD
    NEW GODS
    MISTER MIRACLE

JIMMY OLSEN ADVENTURES BY
JACK KIRBY Vols. 1-2
J. Kirby/V. Colletta/M. Royer

JLA
G. Morrison/M. Waid/J. Kelly/
J. Byrne/C. Claremont/H. Porter/
B. Hitch/D. Mahnke/J. Ordway/
various
Vol. 1: NEW WORLD ORDER
Vol. 2: AMERICAN DREAMS
Vol. 3: ROCK OF AGES
Vol. 4: STRENGTH IN NUMBERS
Vol. 5: JUSTICE FOR ALL
Vol. 6: WORLD WAR III
Vol. 7: TOWER OF BABEL
Vol. 8: DIVIDED WE FALL
Vol. 9: TERROR INCOGNITA
VolI. 10: GOLDEN PERFECT
Vol. 11: THE OBSIDIAN AGE
    BOOK ONE
Vol. 12: THE OBSIDIAN AGE
    BOOK TWO
Vol. 13: RULES OF ENGAGEMENT
Vol. 14: TRIAL BY FIRE
Vol. 15: THE TENTH CIRCLE
Vol. 16: PAIN OF THE GODS

JLA: EARTH 2
G. Morrison/F. Quitely

JLA/JSA: VIRTUE & VICE
D. Goyer/G. Johns/C. Pacheco/
J Meriño

JLA: ONE MILLION
G. Morrison/V. Semeiks/P. Rollins/
various

JLA/TITANS: THE TECHNIS
IMPERATIVE
D. Grayson/P. Jimenez/P. Pelletier/
various

JLA: WORLD WITHOUT
GROWN-UPS
T. Dezago/T. Nauck/H. Ramos/
M. McKone/various

JLA: YEAR ONE
M. Waid/B. Augustyn/B. Kitson/
various

JUSTICE LEAGUE:
A MIDSUMMER'S NIGHTMARE
M. Waid/F. Nicieza/J. Johnson/
D. Robertson/various

JUSTICE LEAGUE: A NEW
BEGINNING
K. Giffen/J.M. DeMatteis/
K. Maguire/various

JUSTICE LEAGUE OF AMERICA:
THE NAIL
JUSTICE LEAGUE OF AMERICA:
ANOTHER NAIL
Alan Davis/Mark Farmer

JSA
G. Johns/J. Robinson/D. Goyer/
S. Sadowski/R. Morales/L. Kirk/
various
Vol. 1: JUSTICE BE DONE
Vol. 2: DARKNESS FALLS
Vol. 3: THE RETURN OF
    HAWKMAN
Vol. 4: FAIR PLAY
Vol. 5: STEALING THUNDER
Vol. 6: SAVAGE TIMES
Vol. 7: PRINCES OF DARKNESS

JSA: ALL STARS
D. Goyer/G. Johns/S. Velluto/
various

JSA: THE GOLDEN AGE
J. Robinson/P. Smith

JSA: THE LIBERTY FILES
D. Jolley/T. Harris/various

THE JUSTICE SOCIETY RETURNS
J. Robinson/D. Goyer/various

THE KINGDOM
M. Waid/various

KINGDOM COME
M. Waid/A. Ross

LEGENDS: THE COLLECTED
EDITION
J. Ostrander/L. Wein/J. Byrne/
K. Kesel

THE LEGION: FOUNDATIONS
D. Abnett/A. Lanning/T. Harris/
T. Batista/various

MAJESTIC: STRANGE NEW
VISITOR
D. Abnett/A. Lanning/K. Kerschl

THE NEW TEEN TITANS
M. Wolfman/G. Pérez/D. Giordano/
R. Tanghal
    THE JUDAS CONTRACT
    THE TERROR OF TRIGON

OUTSIDERS
J. Winick/T. Raney/Chriscross/
various
Vol. 1: LOOKING FOR TROUBLE
Vol. 2: SUM OF ALL EVIL

PLASTIC MAN: ON THE LAM
K. Baker

THE POWER OF SHAZAM!
J. Ordway

RONIN
F. Miller

STARMAN
J. Robinson/T. Harris/P. Snejbjerg/
W. Grawbadger/various
    SINS OF THE FATHER
    NIGHT AND DAY
    INFERNAL DEVICES
    TO REACH THE STARS
    A STARRY KNIGHT
    STARS MY DESTINATION
    GRAND GUIGNOL
    SONS OF THE FATHER

SUPERGIRL: MANY HAPPY
RETURNS
P. David/E. Benes/A. Lei

SUPERMAN/BATMAN
J. Loeb/E. McGuinness/D. Vines/
M. Turner/P. Steigerwald
Vol. 1: PUBLIC ENEMIES
Vol. 2: SUPERGIRL

SUPERMAN FOR ALL SEASONS
J. Loeb/T. Sale

SUPERMAN: BIRTHRIGHT
M. Waid/L. Yu/G. Alanguilan

SUPERMAN: GODFALL
M. Turner/J. Kelly/T. Caldwell/
P. Steigerwald

SUPERMAN: RED SON
M. Millar/D. Johnson/
K. Plunkett/various

SUPERMAN: UNCONVENTIONAL
WARFARE
G. Rucka/I. Reis/various

TEEN TITANS
G. Johns/M. McKone/T. Grummett
Vol. 1: A KID'S GAME
Vol. 2: FAMILY LOST

UNDERWORLD UNLEASHED
M. Waid/H. Porter/P. Jimenez/
various

WATCHMEN
A. Moore/D. Gibbons

WONDER WOMAN (early years)
G. Pérez/L. Wein/B. Patterson
Vol. 1: GODS AND MORTALS
Vol. 2: CHALLENGE OF THE GODS

WONDER WOMAN
G. Rucka/P. Jimenez/J. Byrne/
W.M. Loebs/D. Johnson/
M. Deodato/various
    THE CONTEST
    SECOND GENESIS
    LIFELINES
    PARADISE LOST
    PARADISE FOUND
    DOWN TO EARTH
    BITTER RIVALS

WONDER WOMAN: THE HIKETEIA
G. Rucka/J.G. Jones/
W. Grawbadger

ZERO HOUR: CRISIS IN TIME
D. Jurgens/J. Ordway/various

TO FIND MORE COLLECTED EDITIONS AND MONTHLY COMIC BOOKS FROM DC COMICS,
CALL 1-888-COMIC BOOK FOR THE NEAREST COMICS SHOP OR GO TO YOUR LOCAL BOOK STORE.

DCUBLO5.1